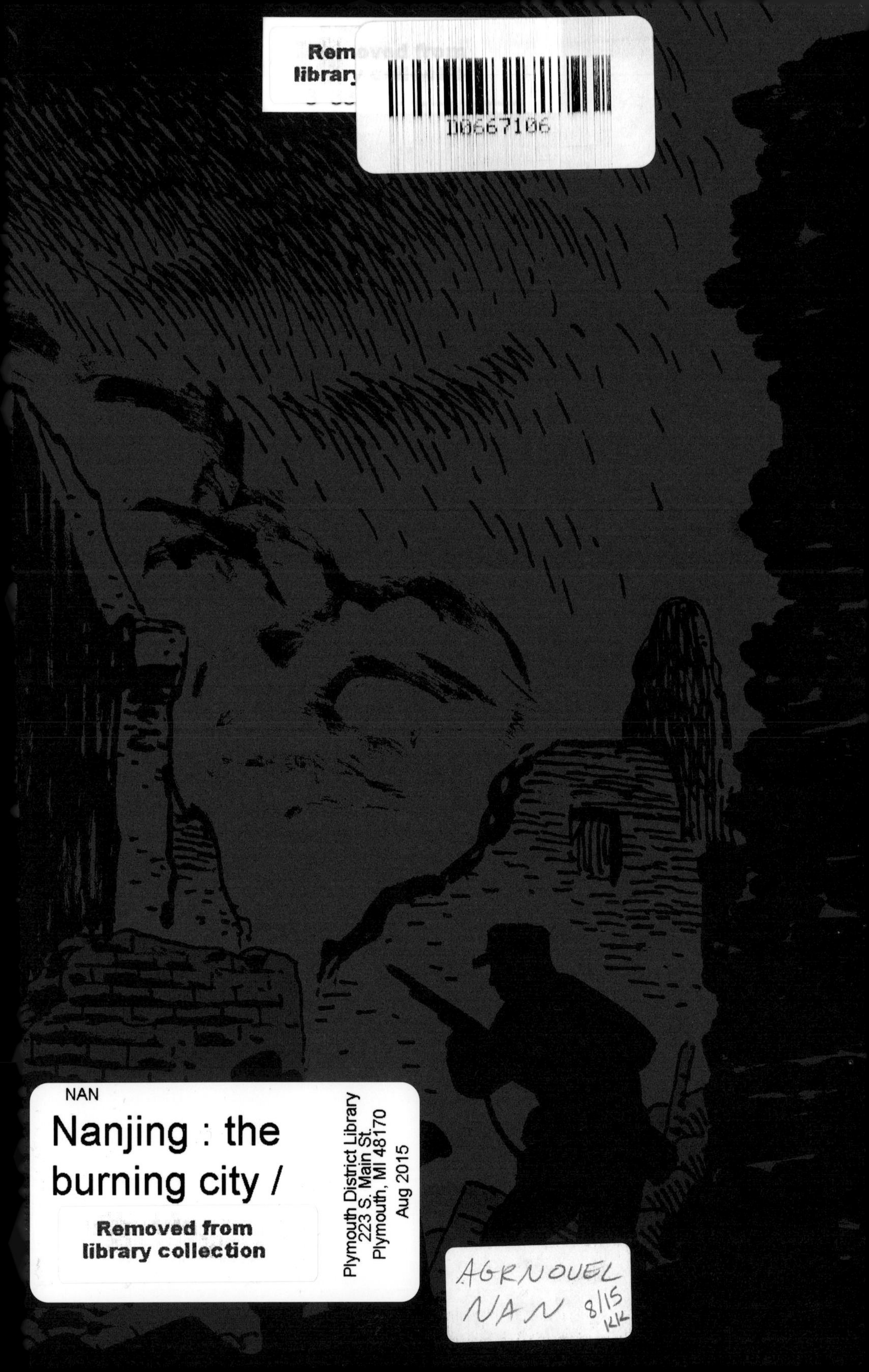

NANJING

THE BURNING CITY

"*Haunting and powerful,* Nanjing *is a moving tribute to an event which needs to be remembered, as much as we'd like to forget it.*"

—Eisner and Harvey Award–winning creator **Derek Kirk Kim** (*Same Difference, Tune*)

"*Young's expressive, thoughtful line work takes full advantage of comics' power.* Nanjing *reads effortlessly while begging the eyes to savor each page. A triumph at the very soul of the medium, a perfect marriage of Toth and Tatsumi.*"

—Eisner Award–winning writer/artist **Nate Powell** (*March, Swallow Me Whole*)

"*A rugged black and white style . . . a little Kubert, a little Tardi.*"

—The Beat

"*Impeccably researched and drawn in Young's critically acclaimed style, the original graphic novel brings new insight into one of World War II's forgotten tragedies.*"

—Graphic Policy

"*With* Nanjing: The Burning City, *Ethan Young creates a wartime narrative that evokes the likes of Sam Fuller's and Harvey Kurtzman's great works. I am the son of a war veteran and* Nanjing *reminded me very much of some of the stories my father would tell. Young presents a handful of characters trying to cling to the remains of their duty and morality in an apocalyptic setting and he does it with startling authenticity. The specifics of this particular story's time and place are important (the 2nd Sino-Japanese War, 1937), but sadly the themes and situations can be seen as recurring. Vietnam, Somalia, Iraq: novels, movies, and comics like* Nanjing *are important reminders of the horrors and subsequent burdens war inflicts on soldiers and civilians alike, down through generations.*"

—Ignatz Award nominee **John Pham** (*Deep Space, Sublife*)

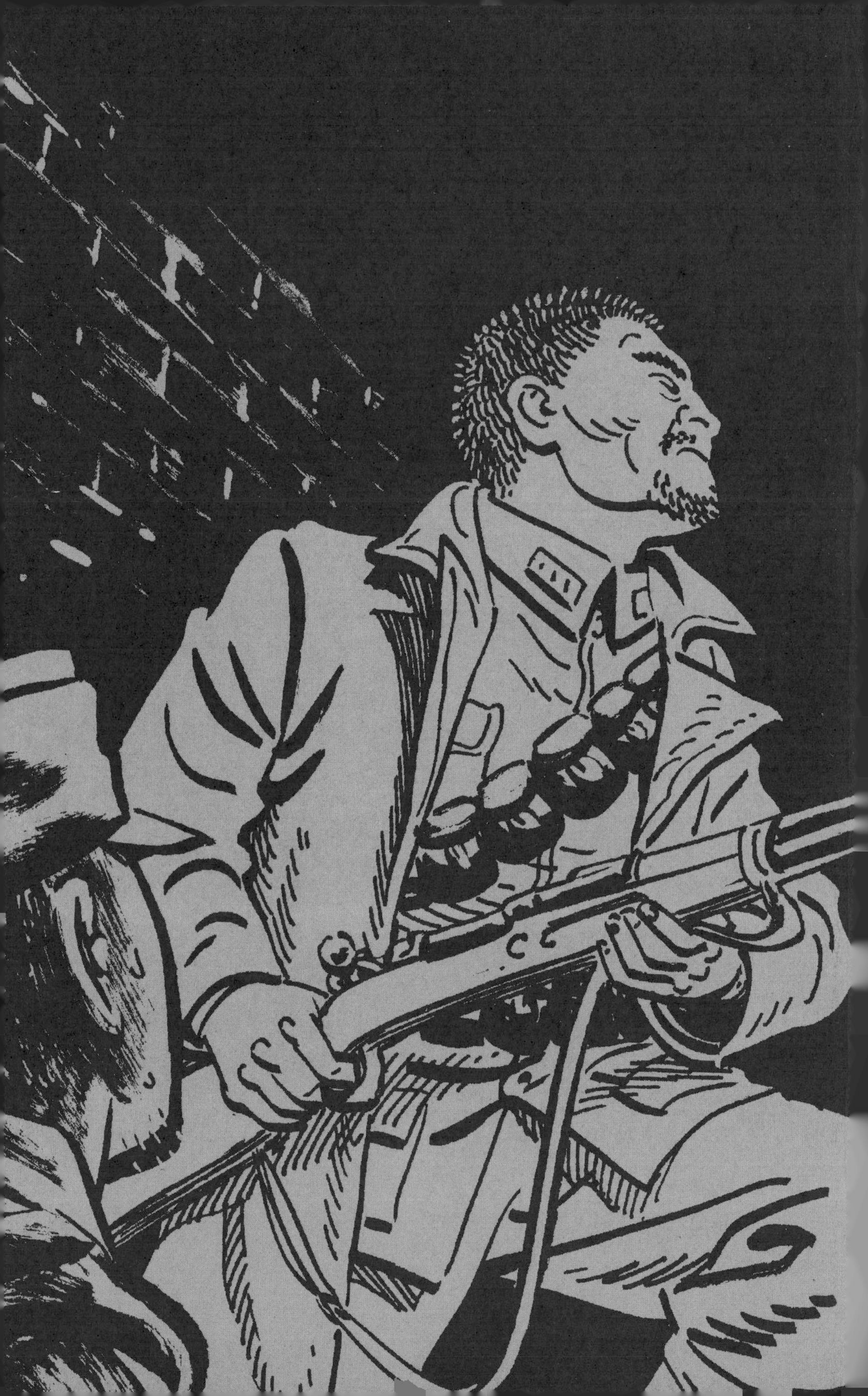

NANJING™

THE BURNING CITY

BY

ETHAN YOUNG

DARK HORSE BOOKS

PRESIDENT AND PUBLISHER
MIKE RICHARDSON

EDITOR
JIM GIBBONS

DIGITAL PRODUCTION
CHRISTINA McKENZIE

COLLECTION DESIGNER
NICK JAMES

SPECIAL THANKS

DEREK KIRK KIM, GENE LUEN YANG, KURT BUSIEK, HANNAH MEANS-SHANNON,
JOHN PHAM, RANA MITTER, NATE POWELL, CHRISTOPHER IRVING, SIERRA HAHN,
SCOTT ALLIE, STEVE SUNU, AND DIANA SCHUTZ

NEIL HANKERSON EXECUTIVE VICE PRESIDENT · **TOM WEDDLE** CHIEF FINANCIAL OFFICER · **RANDY STRADLEY**
VICE PRESIDENT OF PUBLISHING · **MICHAEL MARTENS** VICE PRESIDENT OF BOOK TRADE SALES · **SCOTT ALLIE**
EDITOR IN CHIEF · **MATT PARKINSON** VICE PRESIDENT OF MARKETING · **DAVID SCROGGY** VICE PRESIDENT
OF PRODUCT DEVELOPMENT · **DALE LaFOUNTAIN** VICE PRESIDENT OF INFORMATION TECHNOLOGY · **DARLENE
VOGEL** SENIOR DIRECTOR OF PRINT, DESIGN, AND PRODUCTION · **KEN LIZZI** GENERAL COUNSEL · **DAVEY ESTRADA**
EDITORIAL DIRECTOR · **CHRIS WARNER** SENIOR BOOKS EDITOR · **DIANA SCHUTZ** EXECUTIVE EDITOR · **CARY
GRAZZINI** DIRECTOR OF PRINT AND DEVELOPMENT · **LIA RIBACCHI** ART DIRECTOR · **CARA NIECE** DIRECTOR OF
SCHEDULING · **MARK BERNARDI** DIRECTOR OF DIGITAL PUBLISHING

PUBLISHED BY DARK HORSE BOOKS
A DIVISION OF DARK HORSE COMICS, INC.
10956 SE MAIN STREET
MILWAUKIE, OR 97222

DARKHORSE.COM

FIRST EDITION: AUGUST 2015
ISBN 978-1-61655-752-2

1 3 5 7 9 10 8 6 4 2
PRINTED IN CHINA

INTERNATIONAL LICENSING: (503) 905-2377
COMIC SHOP LOCATOR SERVICE: (888) 266-4226

NANJING: THE BURNING CITY

LIBRARY OF CONGRESS CATALOGING-IN-PUBLICATION DATA

YOUNG, ETHAN, 1983-
NANJING : THE BURNING CITY / BY ETHAN YOUNG. -- FIRST EDITION.
    PAGES CM
  ISBN 978-1-61655-752-2
1. NANJING, BATTLE OF, NANJING, JIANGSU SHENG, CHINA, 1937--COMIC BOOKS, STRIPS, ETC. 2. NANJING,
BATTLE OF, NANJING, JIANGSU SHENG, CHINA, 1937--JUVENILE LITERATURE. 3. NANKING MASSACRE,
NANJING, JIANGSU SHENG, CHINA, 1937--COMIC BOOKS, STRIPS, ETC. 4. NANKING MASSACRE, NANJING,
JIANGSU SHENG, CHINA, 1937--JUVENILE LITERATURE. 5. GRAPHIC NOVELS. I. TITLE.

DS777.5316.N36Y68 2015
951.04'2--DC23

2015008366

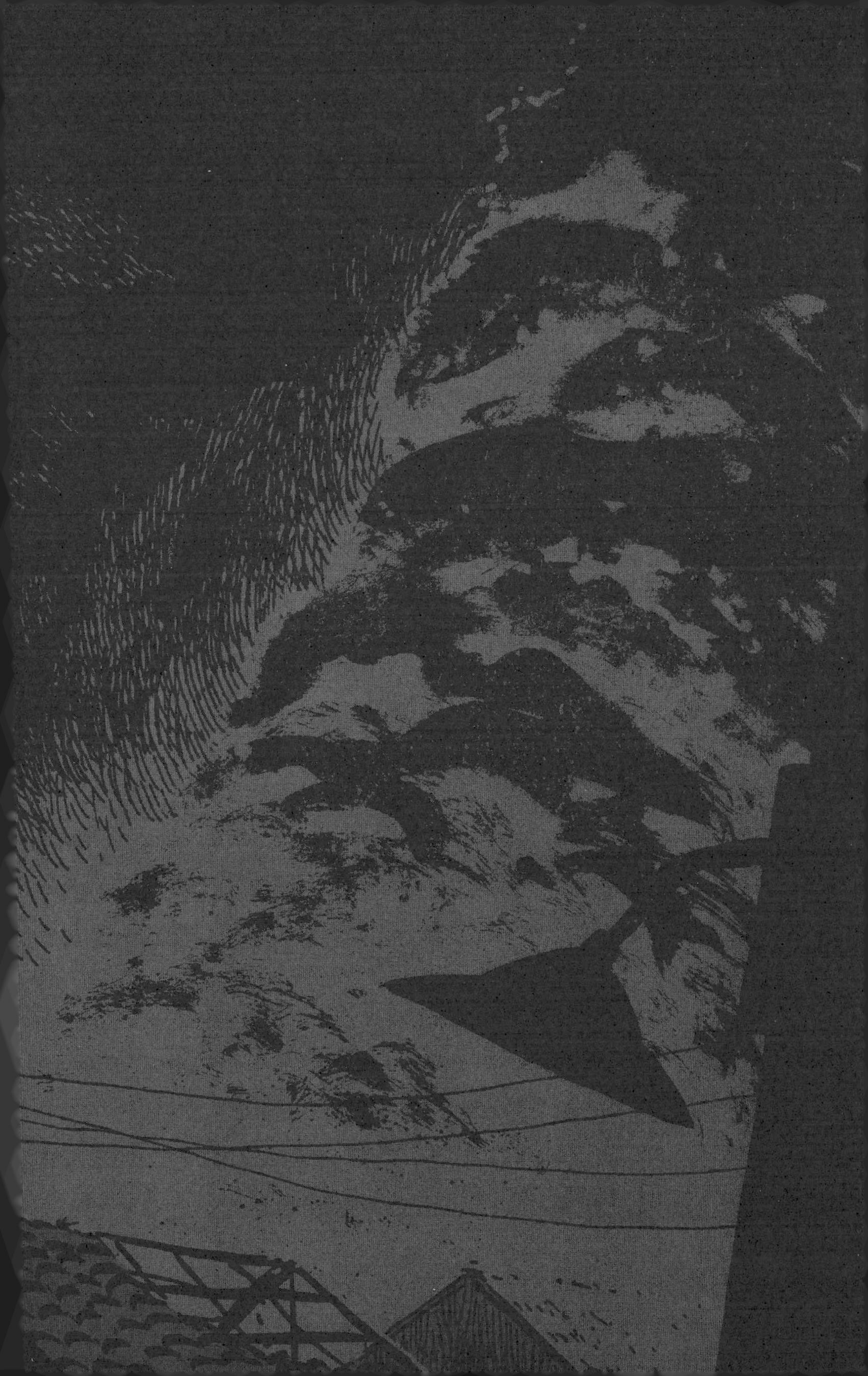

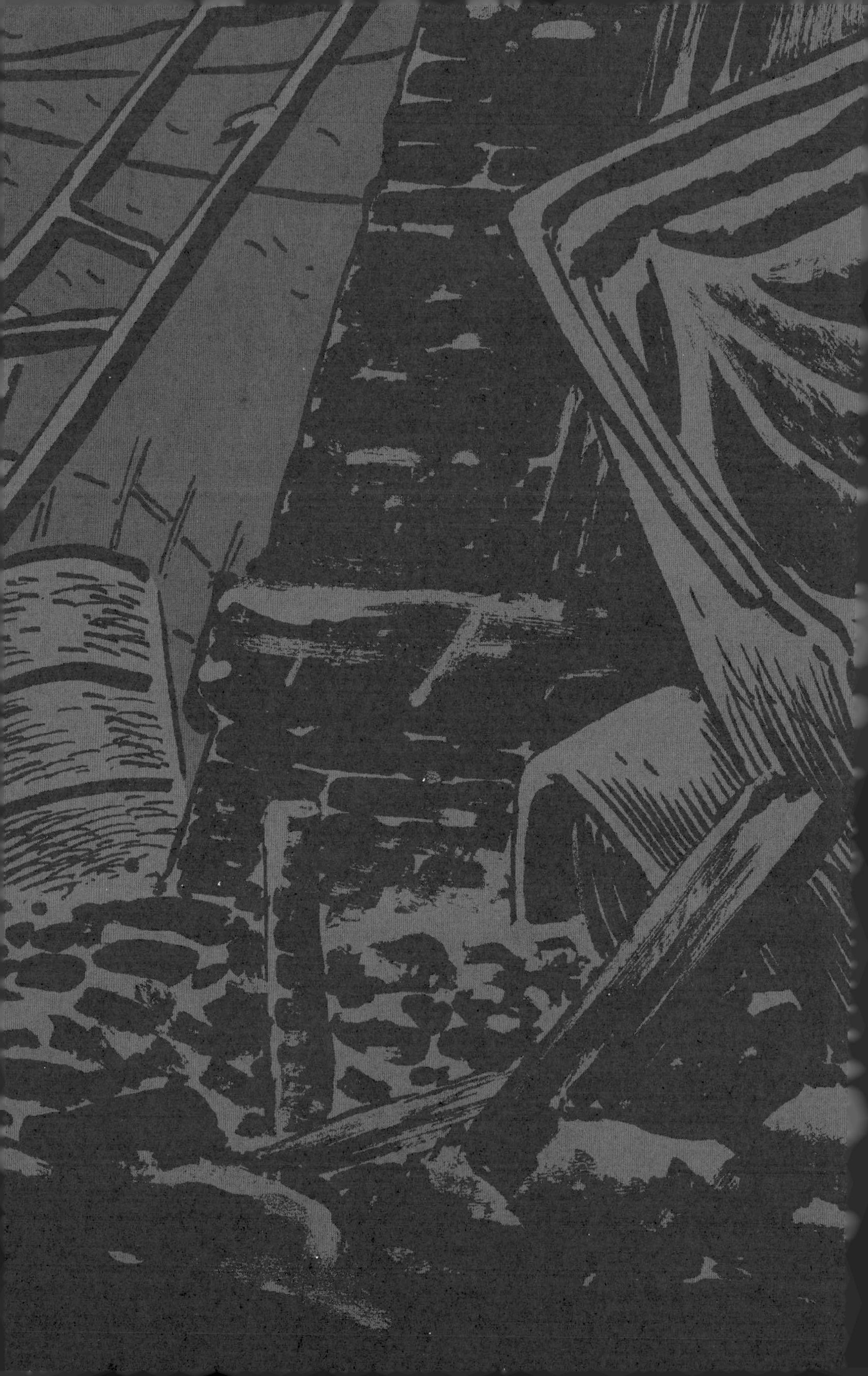

NANJING

FORMER CAPITAL OF THE REPUBLIC OF CHINA

ON JULY 7, 1937, THE 2nd SINO-JAPANESE WAR COMMENCED BETWEEN THE REPUBLIC OF CHINA AND THE EMPIRE OF JAPAN. AFTER AN INTENSE BATTLE IN SHANGHAI, THE IMPERIAL JAPANESE ARMY MADE THEIR WAY TO NANJING AND SEIZED THE CITY ON DECEMBER 13, 1937. THE DAY BEFORE THE CITY'S CAPTURE, CHINESE MILITARY OFFICIALS BEGAN FLEEING NANJING IN CHAOS. MANY COMMANDERS ABANDONED THEIR OWN TROOPS WITHOUT GIVING ANY ORDERS FOR RETREAT.

THIS IS A STORY ABOUT THE FORGOTTEN ONES.

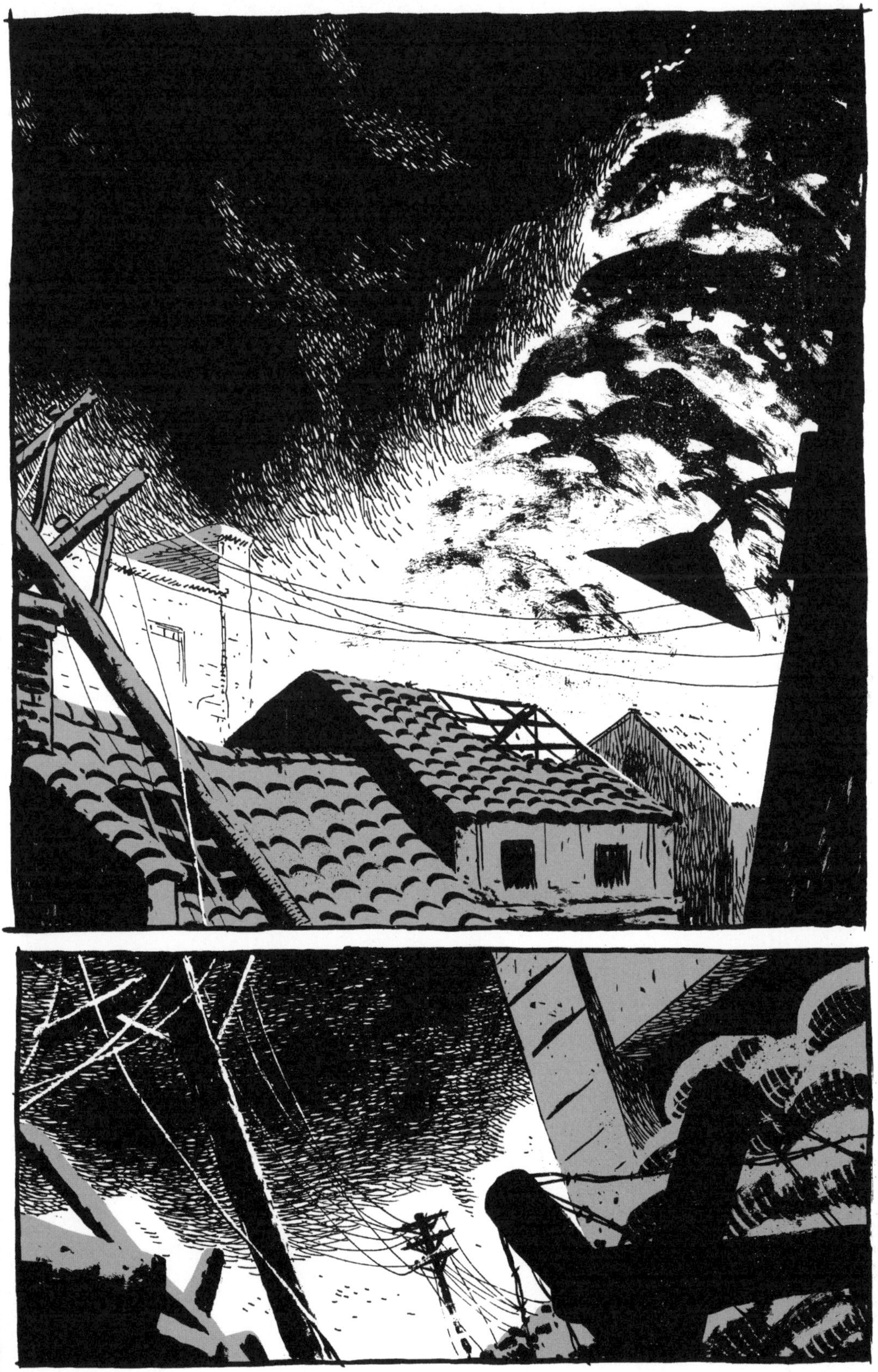

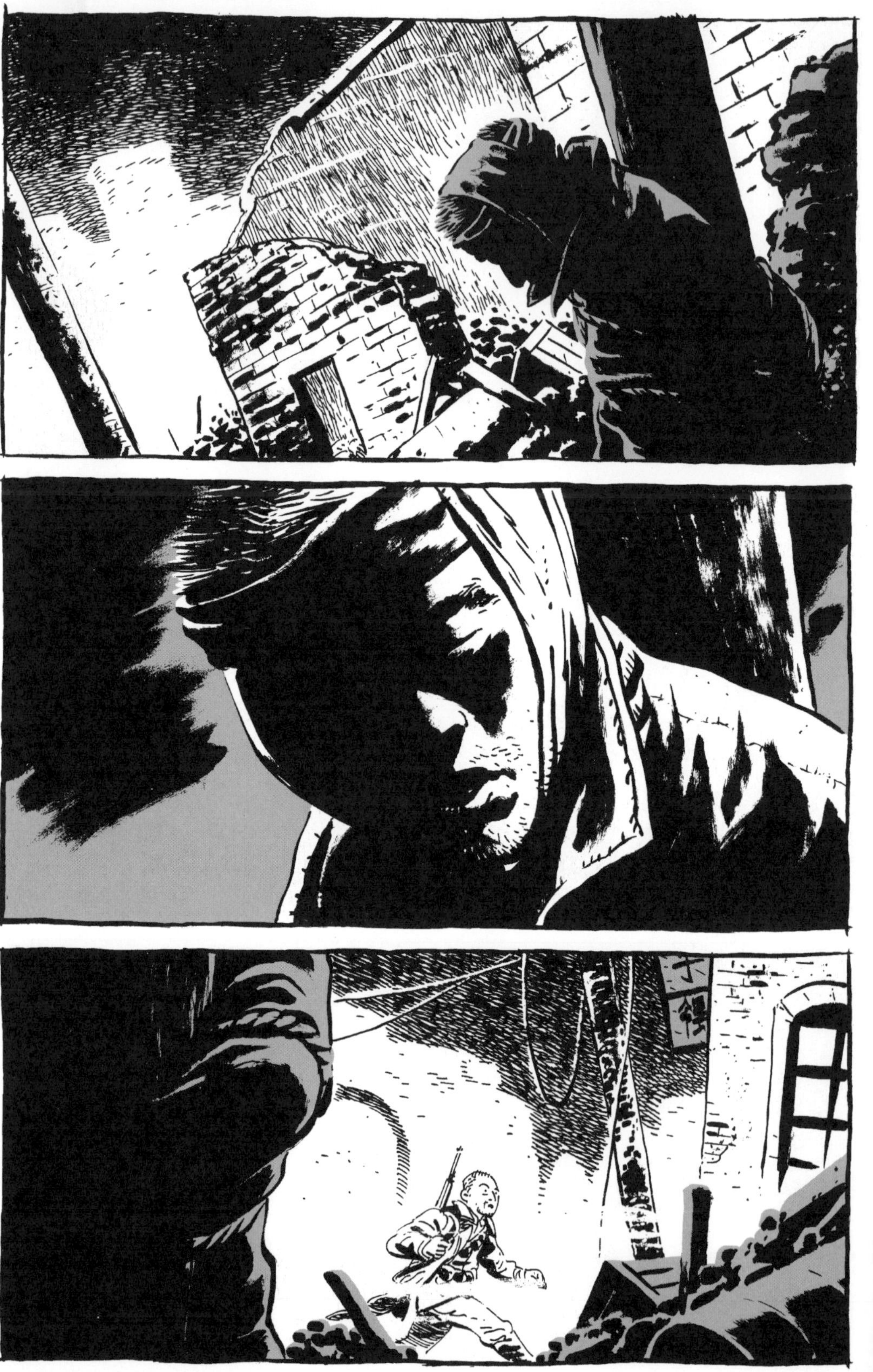

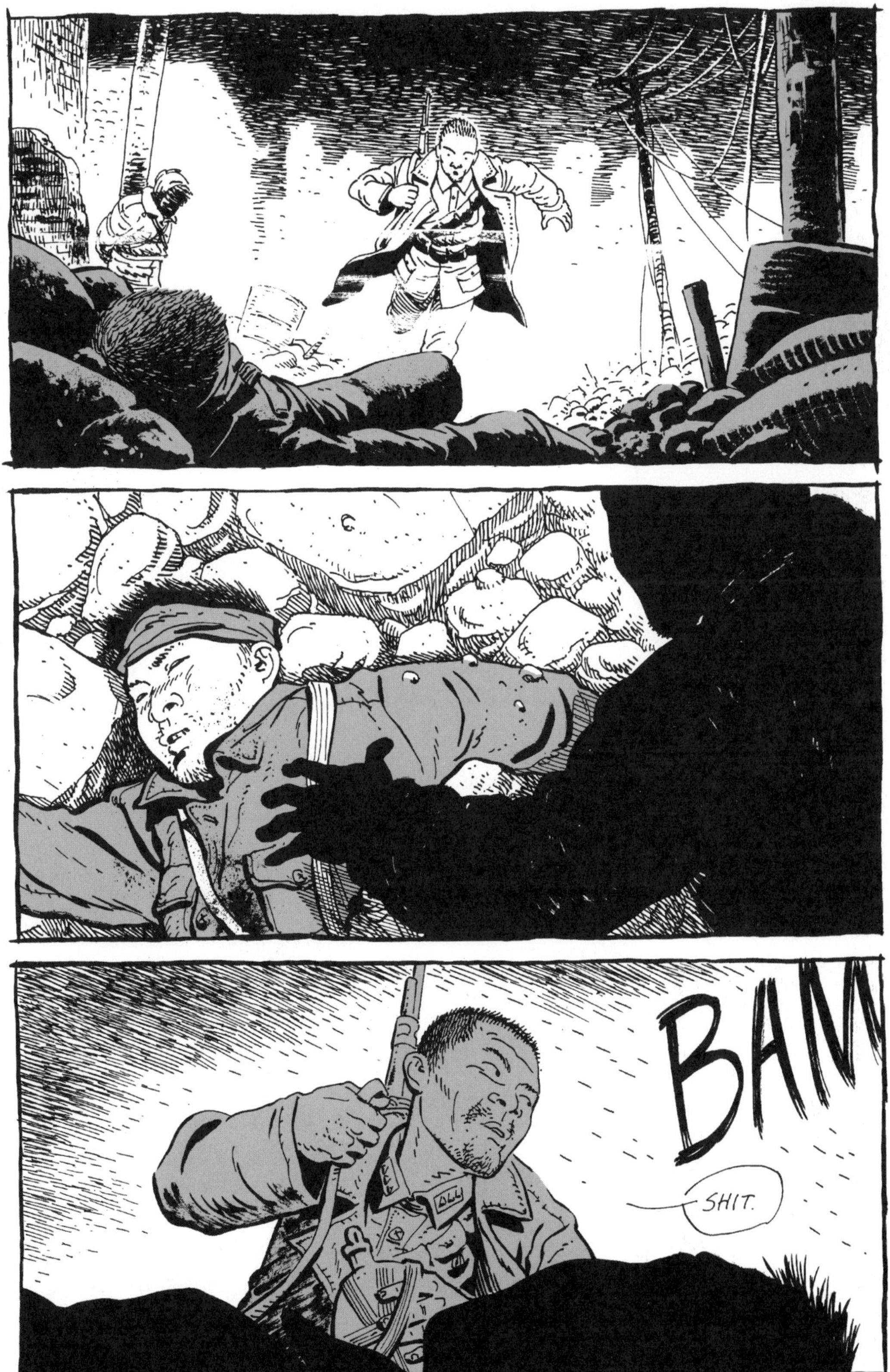
BAM
SHIT.

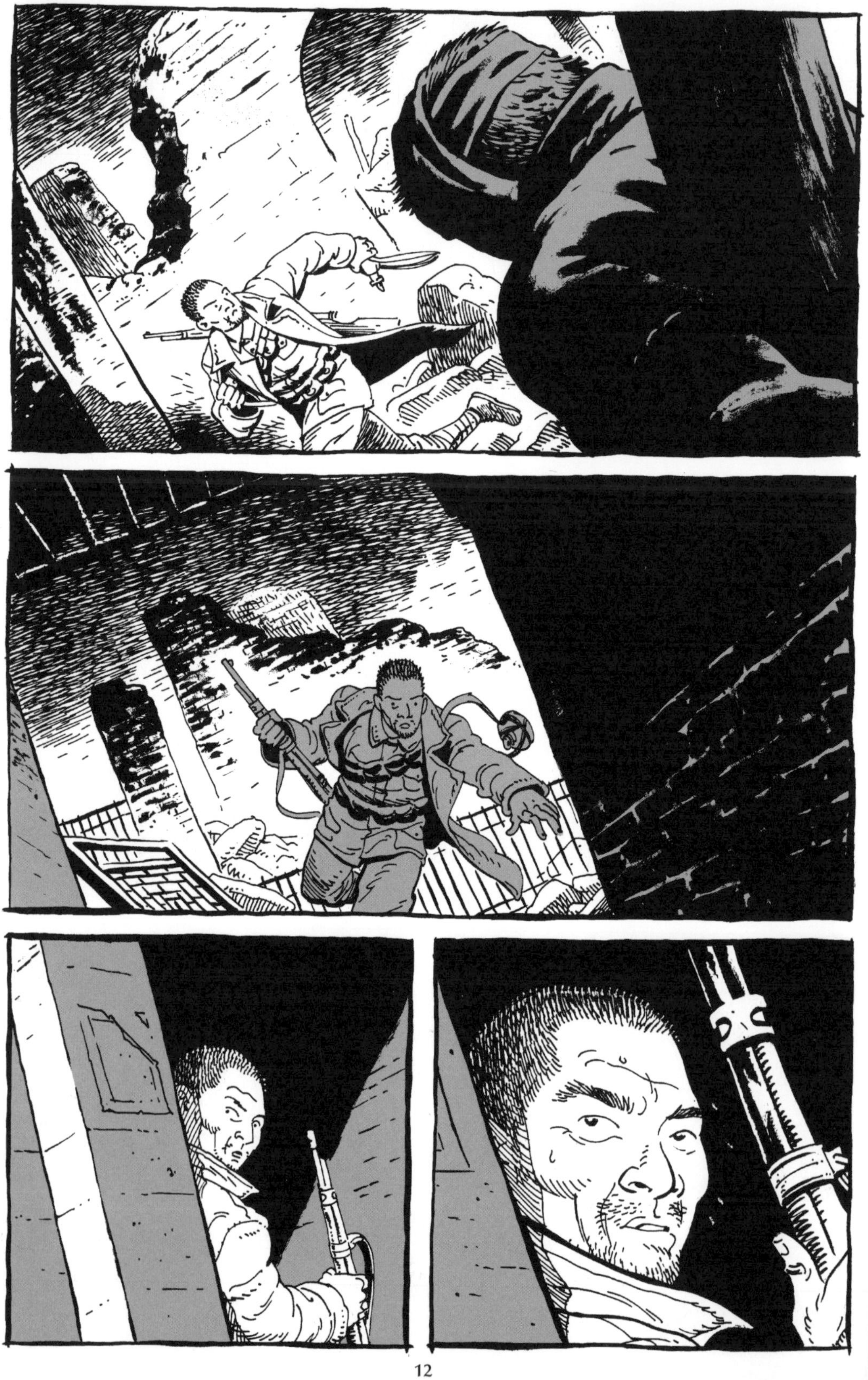

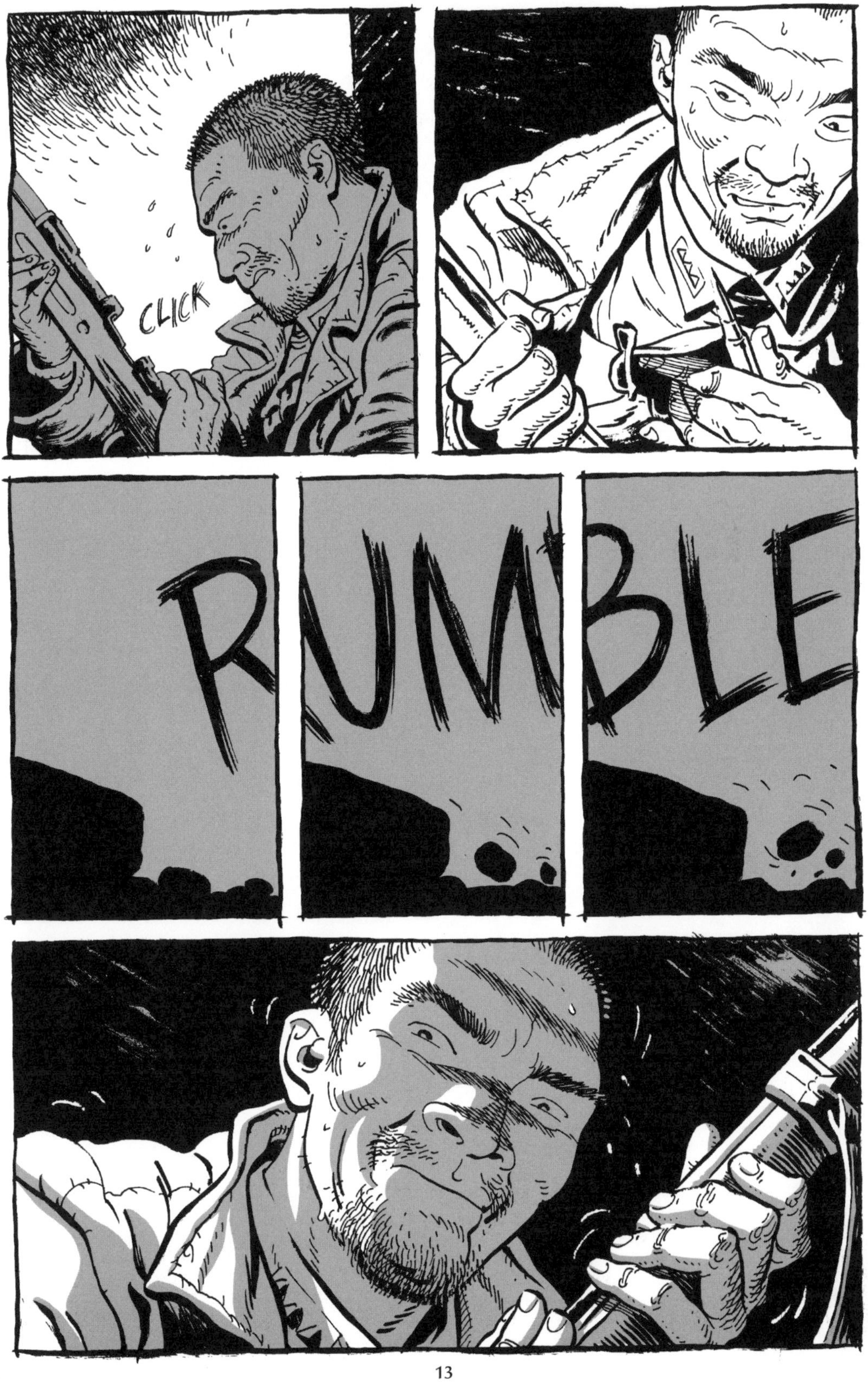
CLICK
RUMBLE

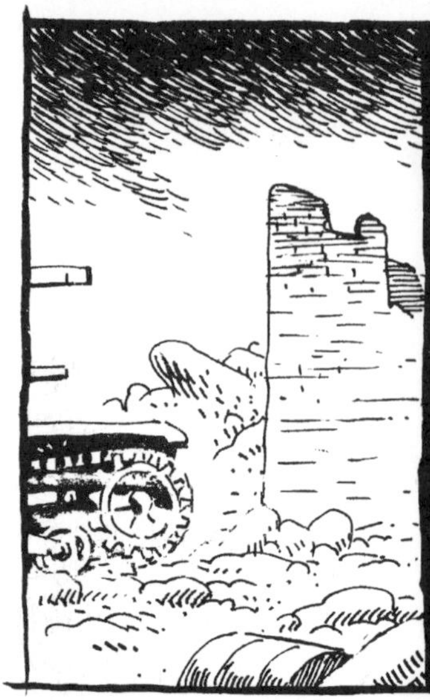

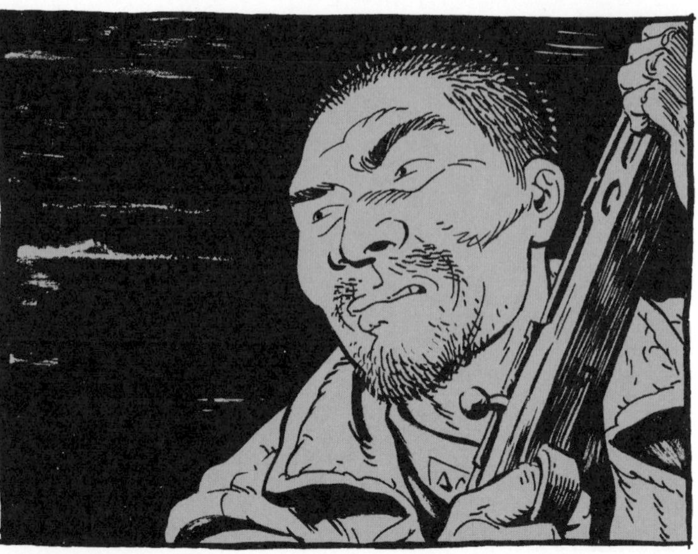

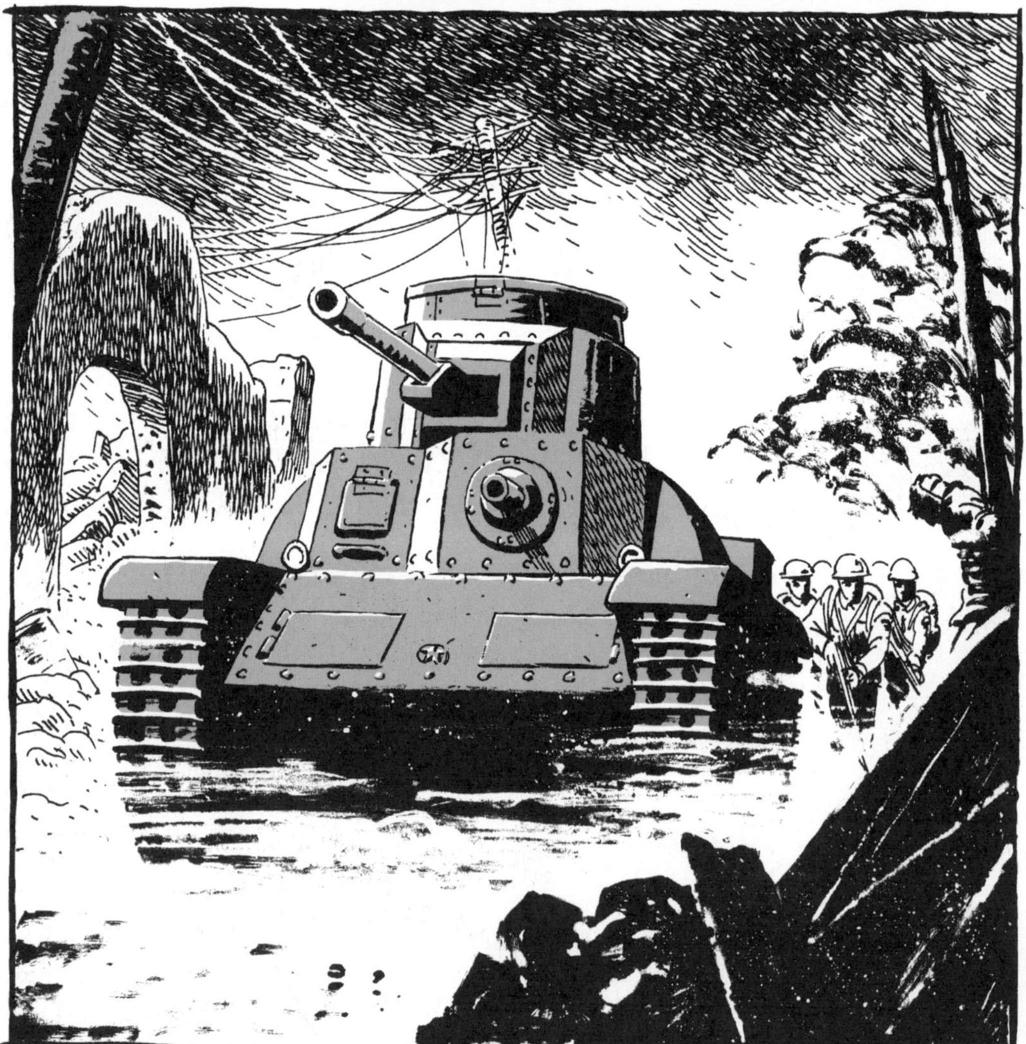

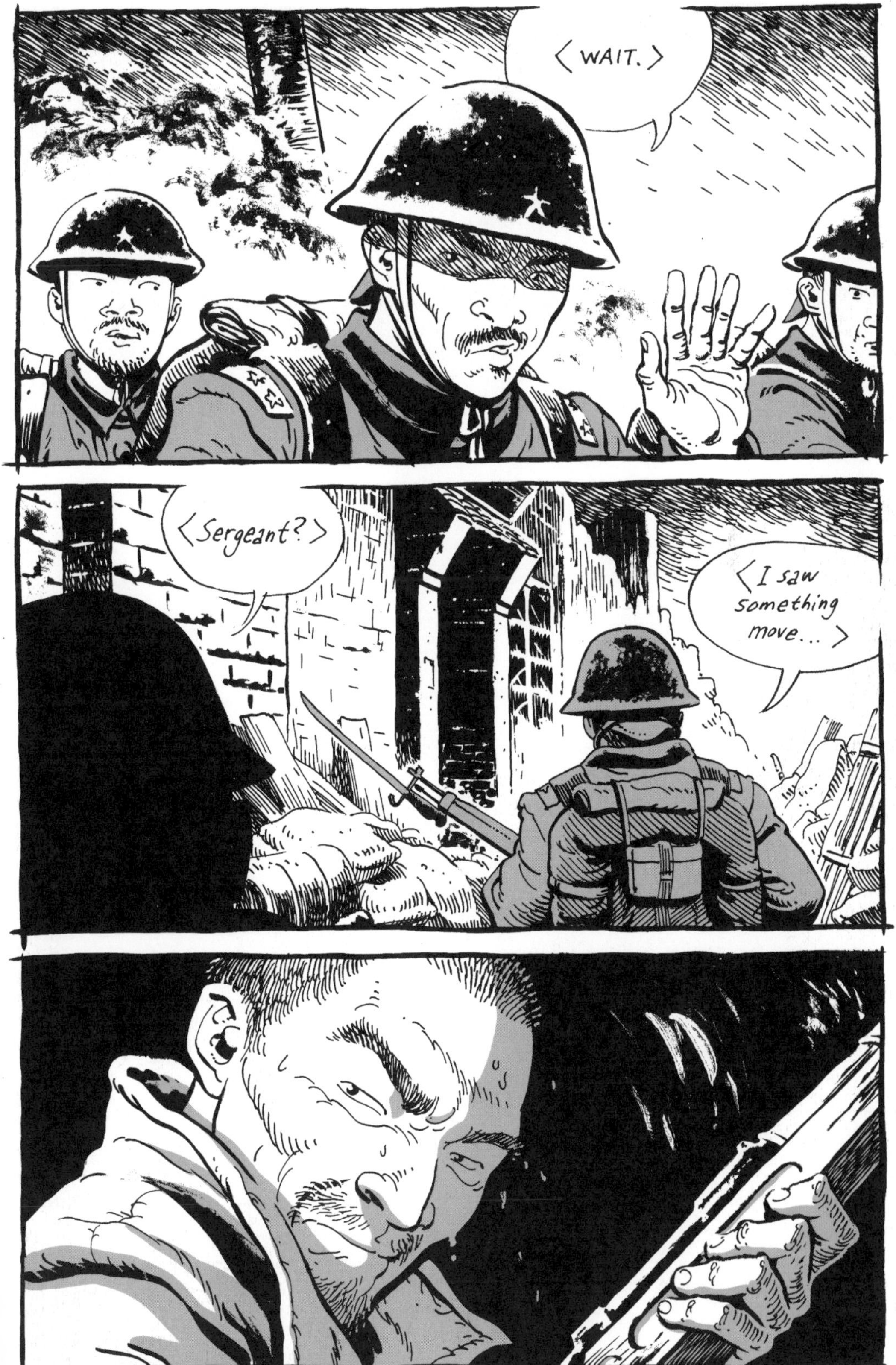
< WAIT. >
< Sergeant? >
< I saw something move... >

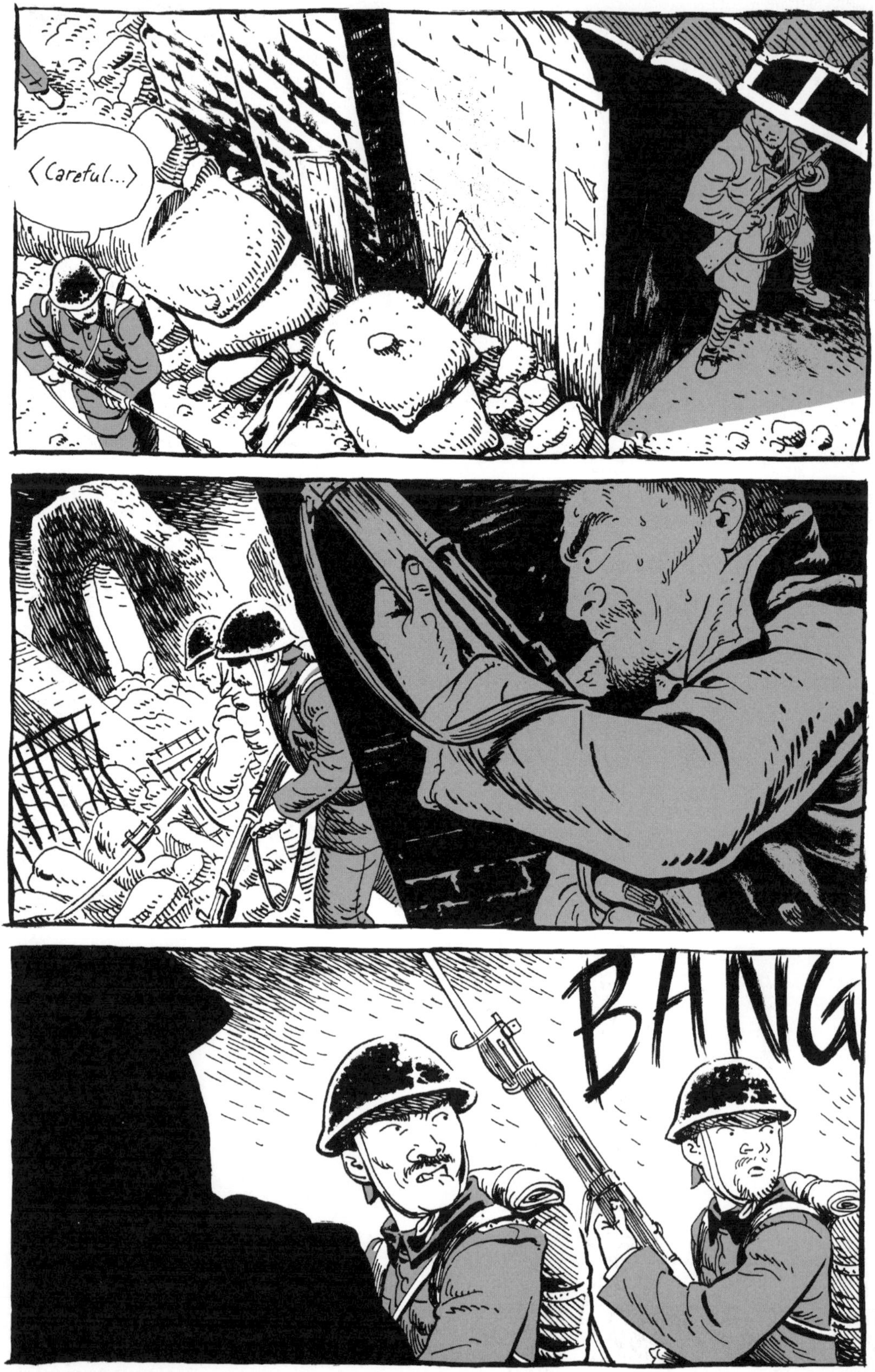
〈Careful...〉
BANG

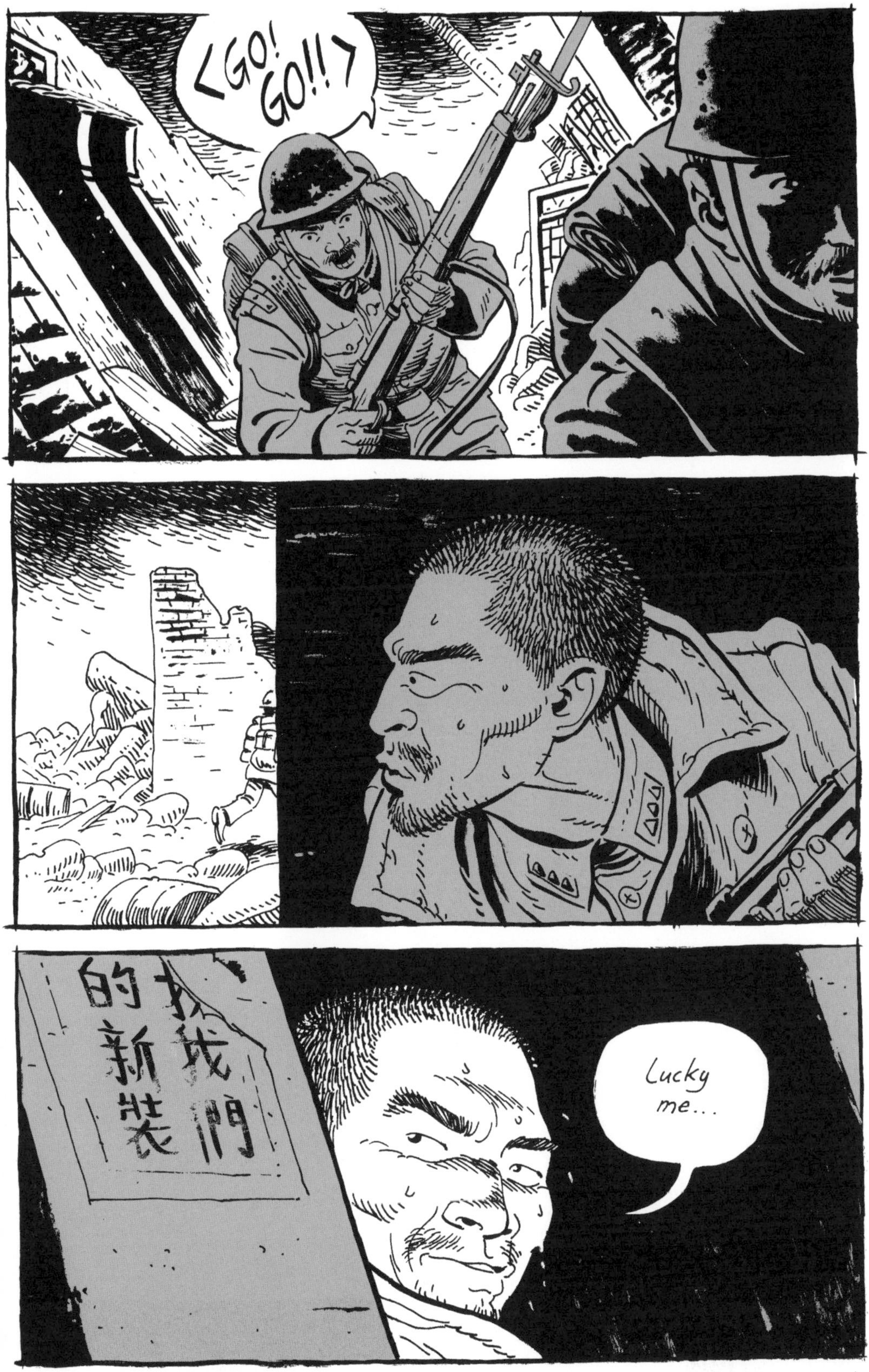
<GO! GO!!>
們
的新裝
Lucky me...

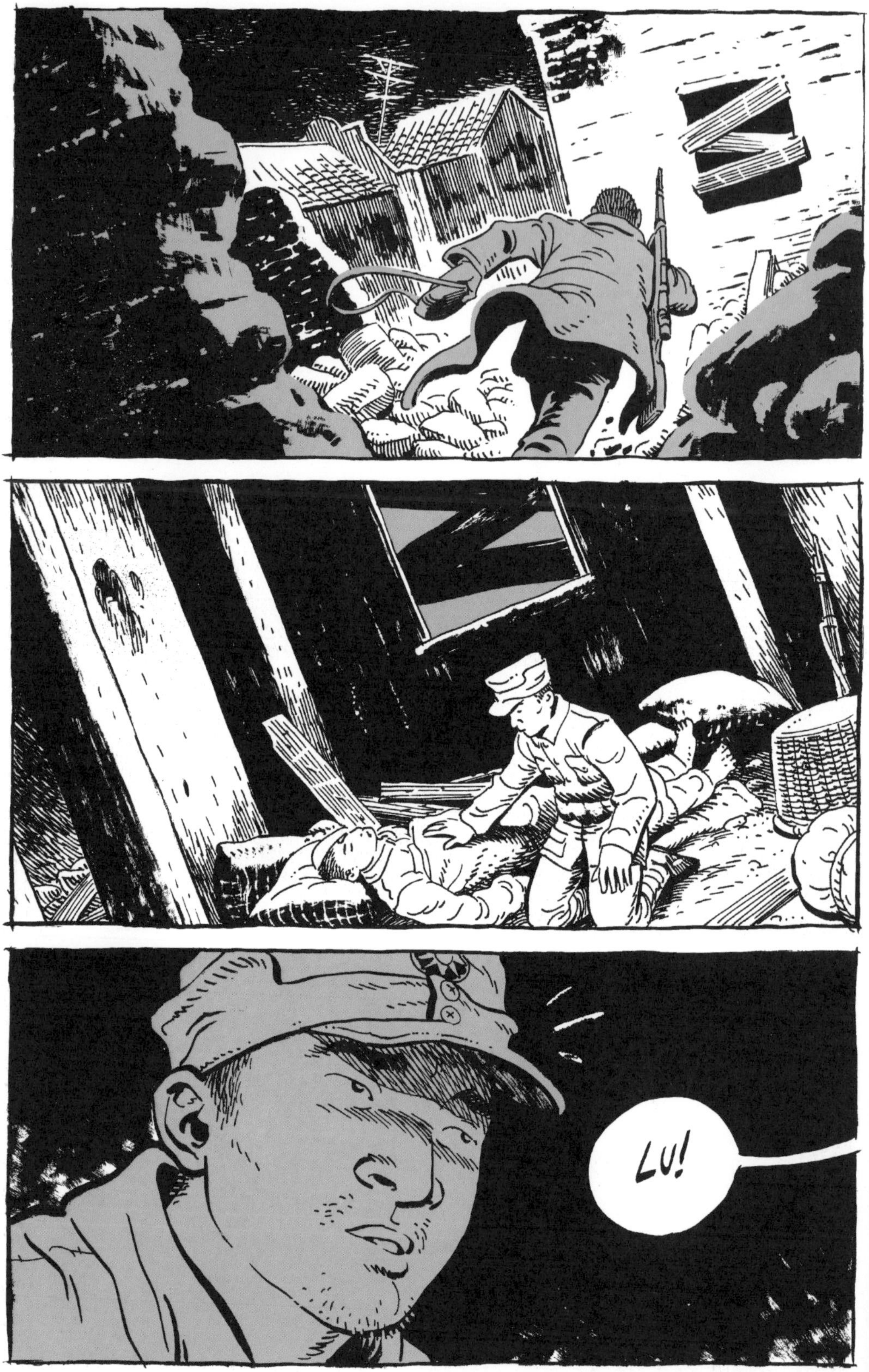
LU!

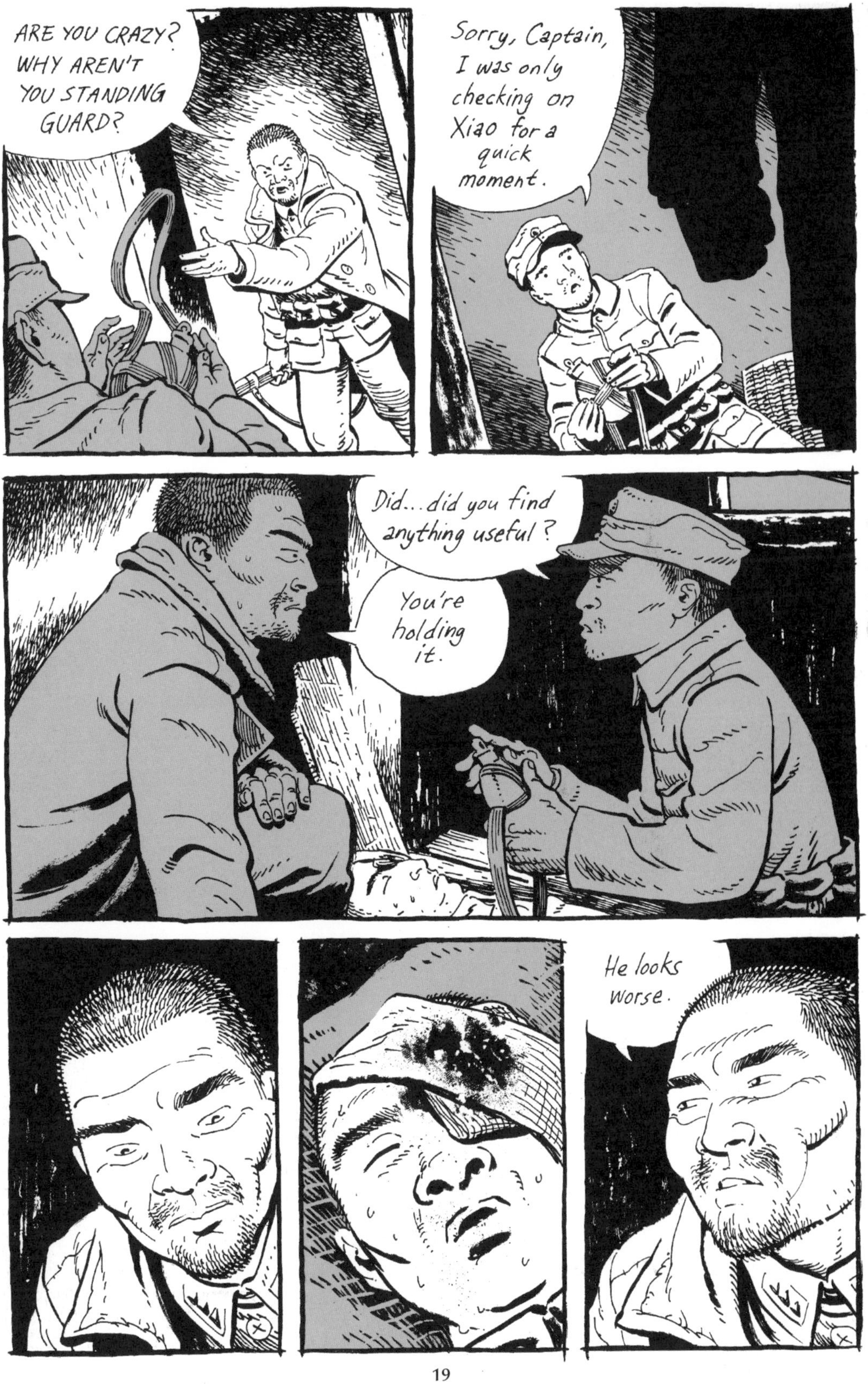
ARE YOU CRAZY? WHY AREN'T YOU STANDING GUARD?
Sorry, Captain, I was only checking on Xiao for a quick moment.
Did...did you find anything useful?
You're holding it.
He looks worse.

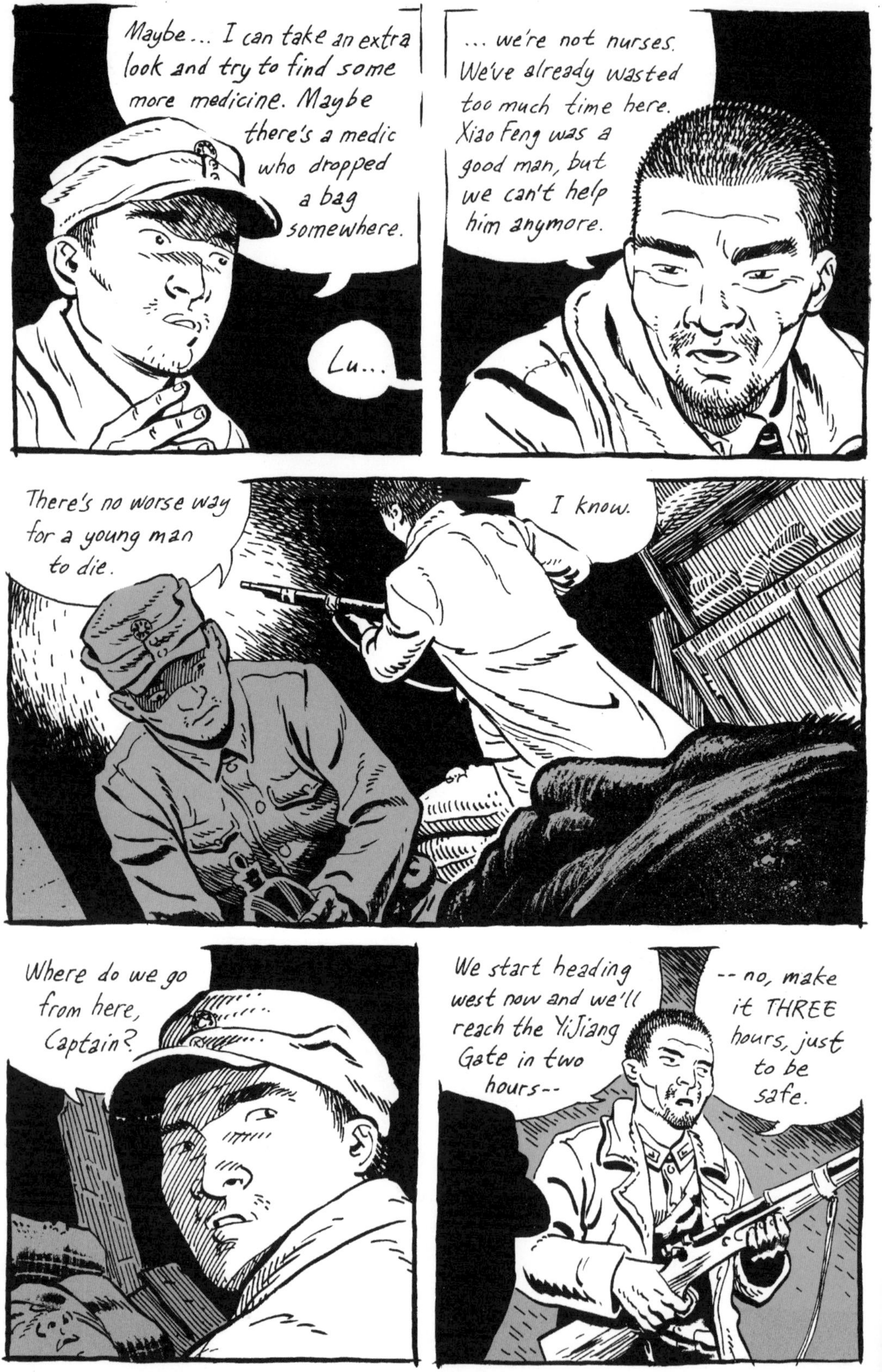
Maybe... I can take an extra look and try to find some more medicine. Maybe there's a medic who dropped a bag somewhere.
Lu...
... we're not nurses. We've already wasted too much time here. Xiao Feng was a good man, but we can't help him anymore.
There's no worse way for a young man to die.
I know.
Where do we go from here, Captain?
We start heading west now and we'll reach the YiJiang Gate in two hours--
-- no, make it THREE hours, just to be safe.

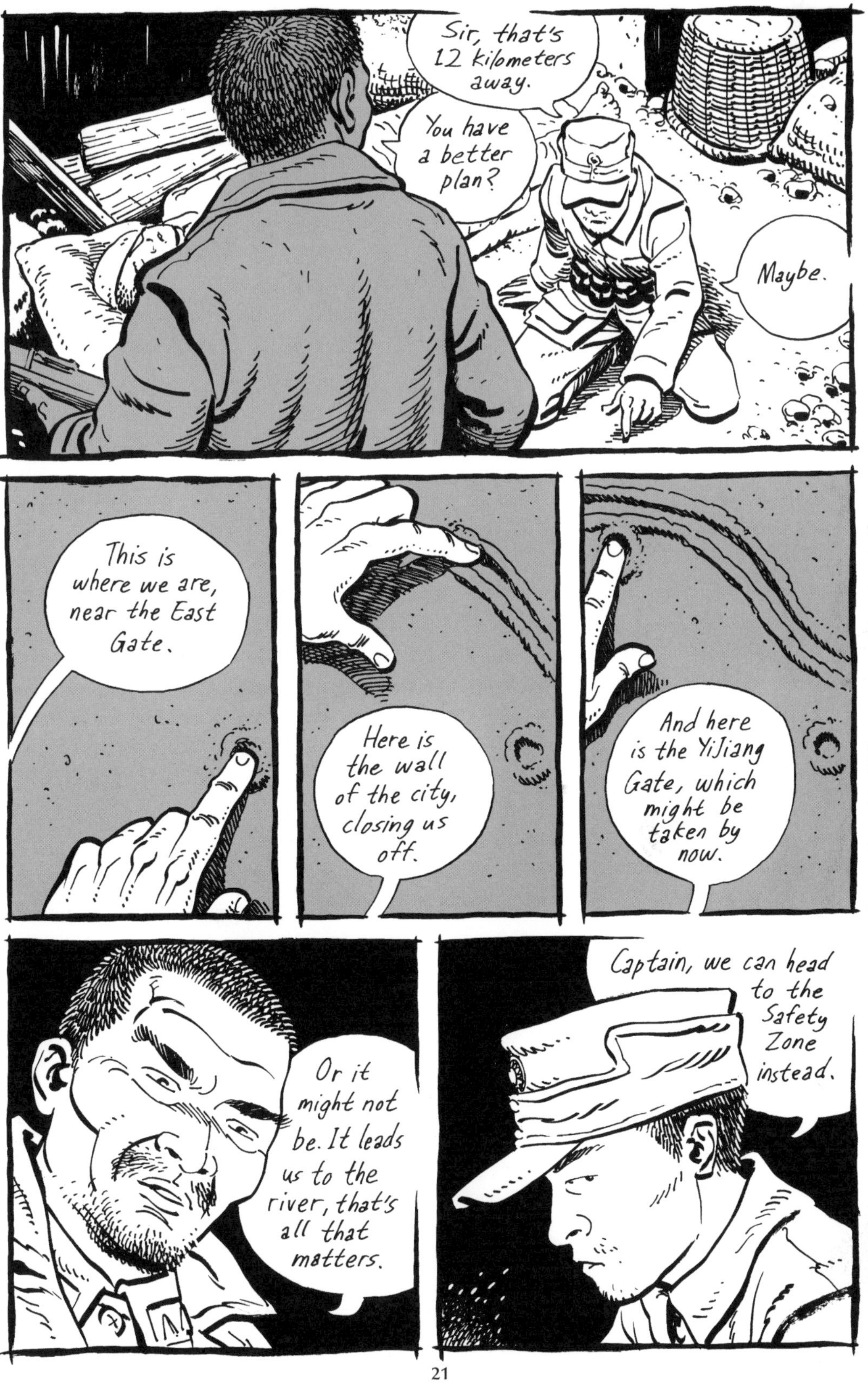
Sir, that's 12 kilometers away.
You have a better plan?
Maybe.
This is where we are, near the East Gate.
Here is the wall of the city, closing us off.
And here is the YiJiang Gate, which might be taken by now.
Or it might not be. It leads us to the river, that's all that matters.
Captain, we can head to the Safety Zone instead.

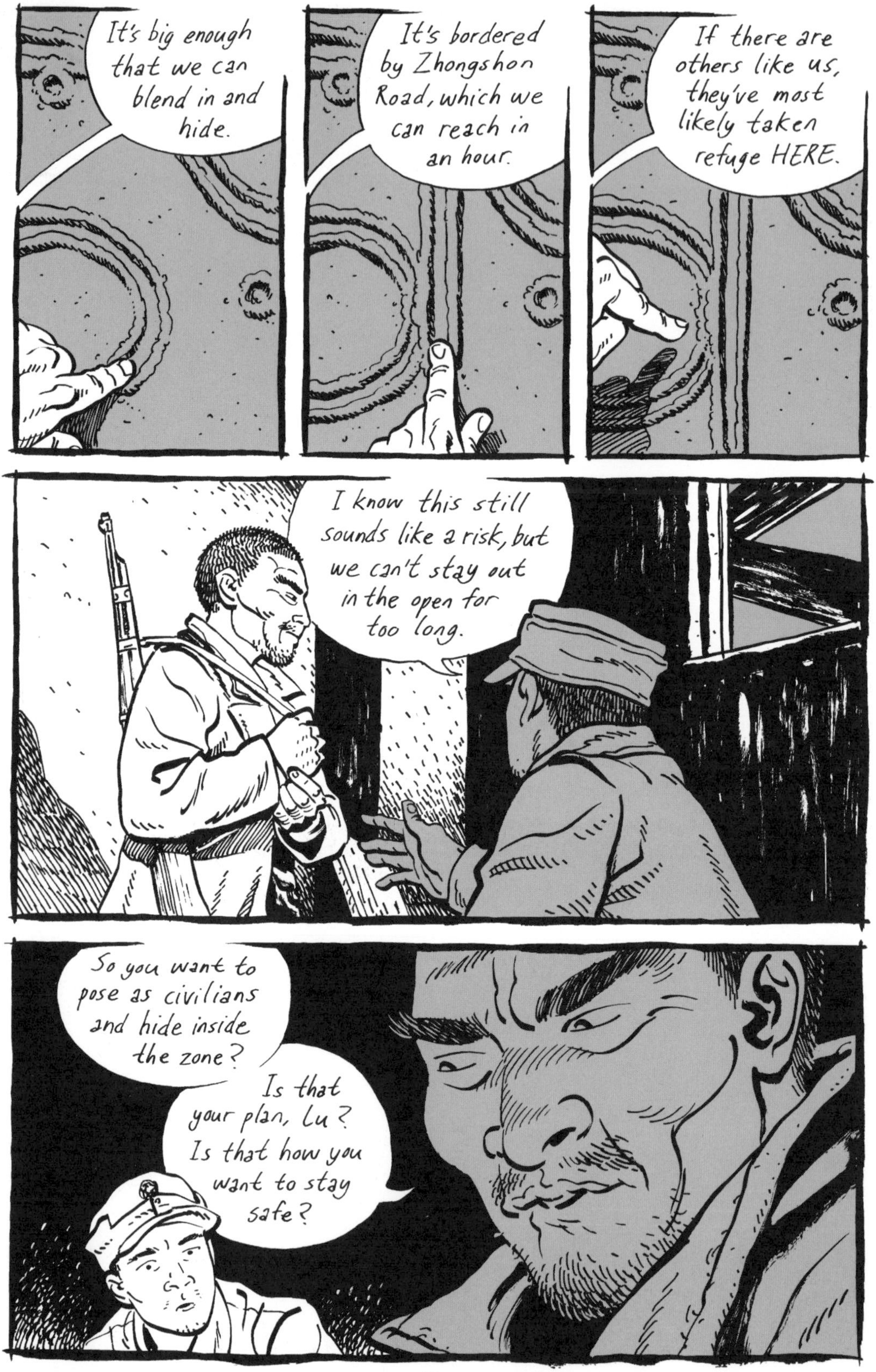
It's big enough that we can blend in and hide.
It's bordered by Zhongshon Road, which we can reach in an hour.
If there are others like us, they've most likely taken refuge HERE.
I know this still sounds like a risk, but we can't stay out in the open for too long.
So you want to pose as civilians and hide inside the zone?
Is that your plan, Lu? Is that how you want to stay safe?

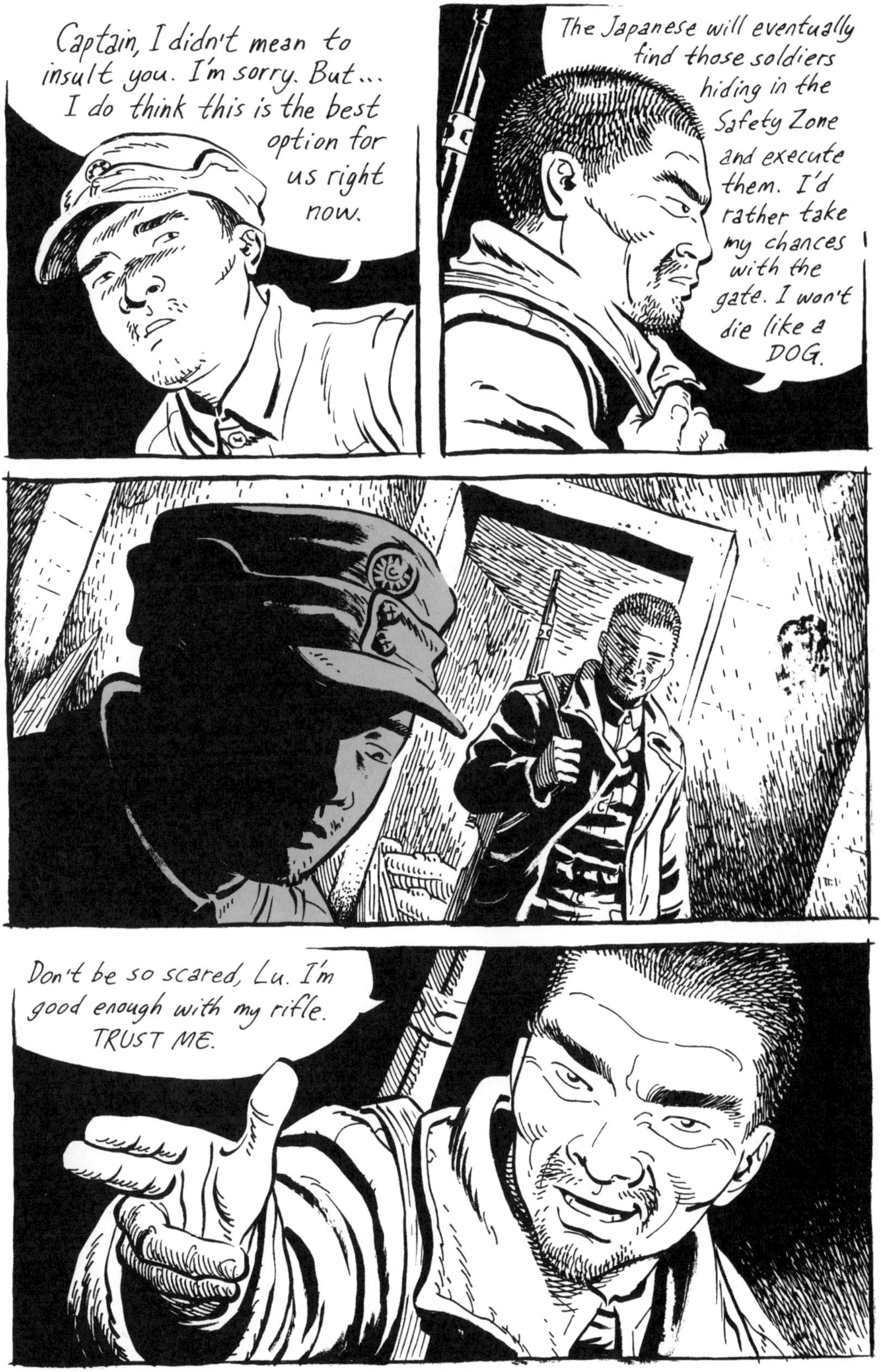
Captain, I didn't mean to insult you. I'm sorry. But... I do think this is the best option for us right now.
The Japanese will eventually find those soldiers hiding in the Safety Zone and execute them. I'd rather take my chances with the gate. I won't die like a DOG.
Don't be so scared, Lu. I'm good enough with my rifle. TRUST ME.

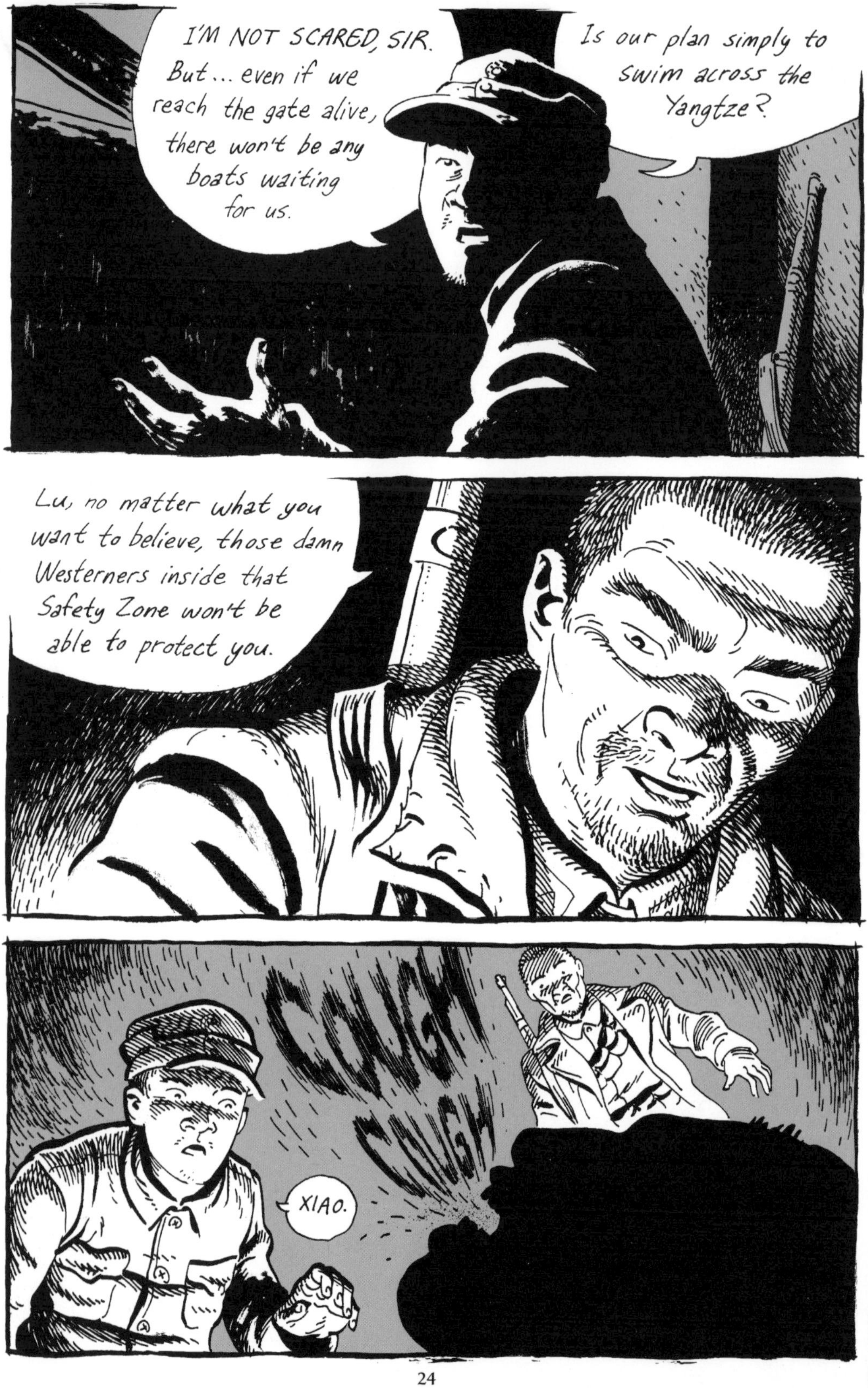
I'M NOT SCARED, SIR. But... even if we reach the gate alive, there won't be any boats waiting for us.
Is our plan simply to swim across the Yangtze?
Lu, no matter what you want to believe, those damn Westerners inside that Safety Zone won't be able to protect you.
COUGH
COUGH
XIAO.

...I'm really warm...

Don't struggle too much, Xiao. Here -- we have some more water.

How do you feel?

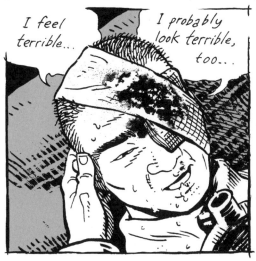

I feel terrible...

I probably look terrible, too...

NONSENSE. You're more handsome than ever.

Ha... you're funny, Captain...

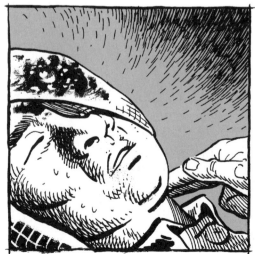

His father's farm was burned down by our own generals to keep it from the enemy. Now he dies like this.

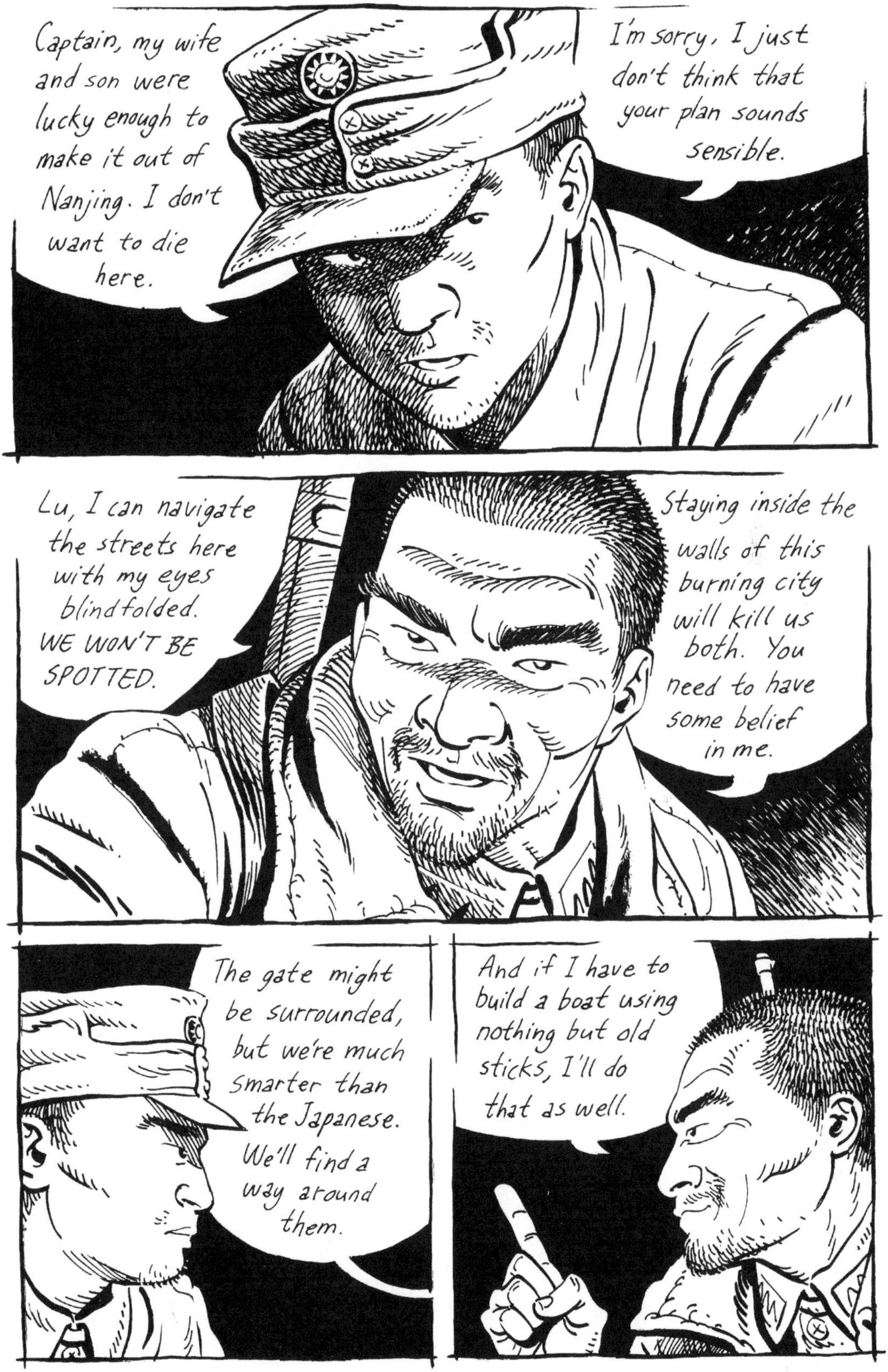

Captain, my wife and son were lucky enough to make it out of Nanjing. I don't want to die here.
I'm sorry. I just don't think that your plan sounds sensible.
Lu, I can navigate the streets here with my eyes blindfolded. WE WON'T BE SPOTTED.
Staying inside the walls of this burning city will kill us both. You need to have some belief in me.
The gate might be surrounded, but we're much smarter than the Japanese. We'll find a way around them.
And if I have to build a boat using nothing but old sticks, I'll do that as well.

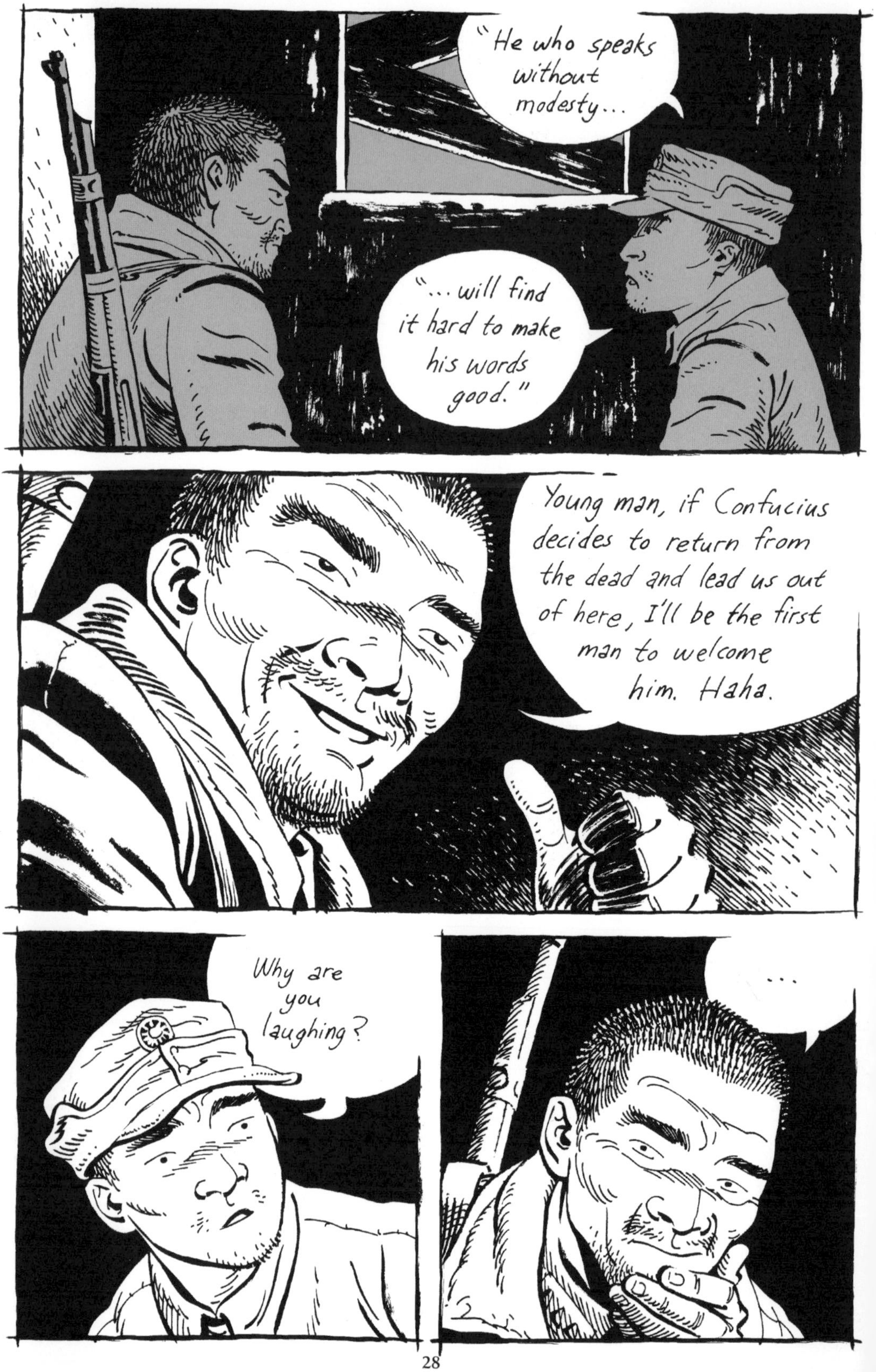
"He who speaks without modesty...
"...will find it hard to make his words good."
Young man, if Confucius decides to return from the dead and lead us out of here, I'll be the first man to welcome him. Haha.
Why are you laughing?
...

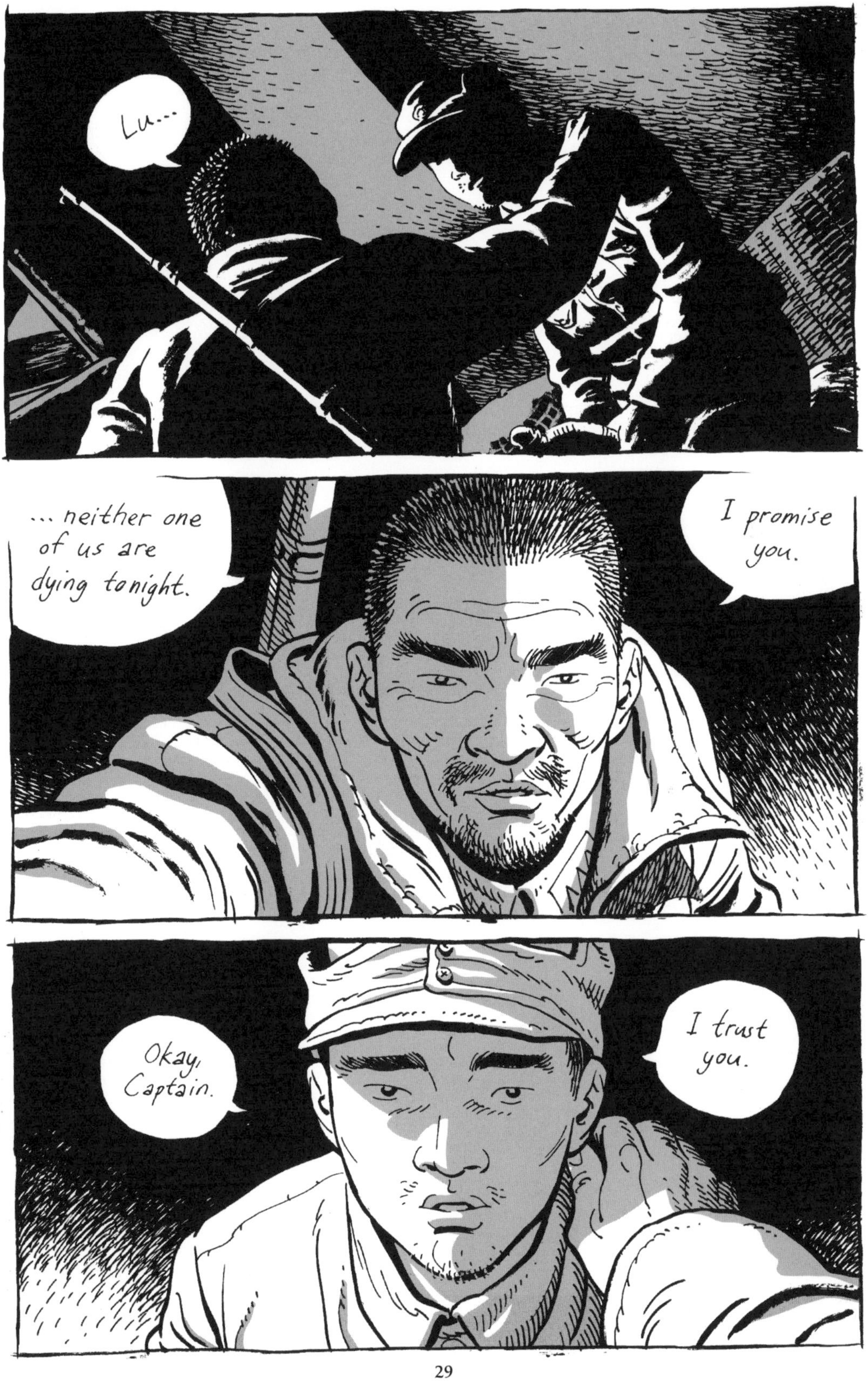
Lu...
... neither one of us are dying tonight.
I promise you.
Okay, Captain.
I trust you.

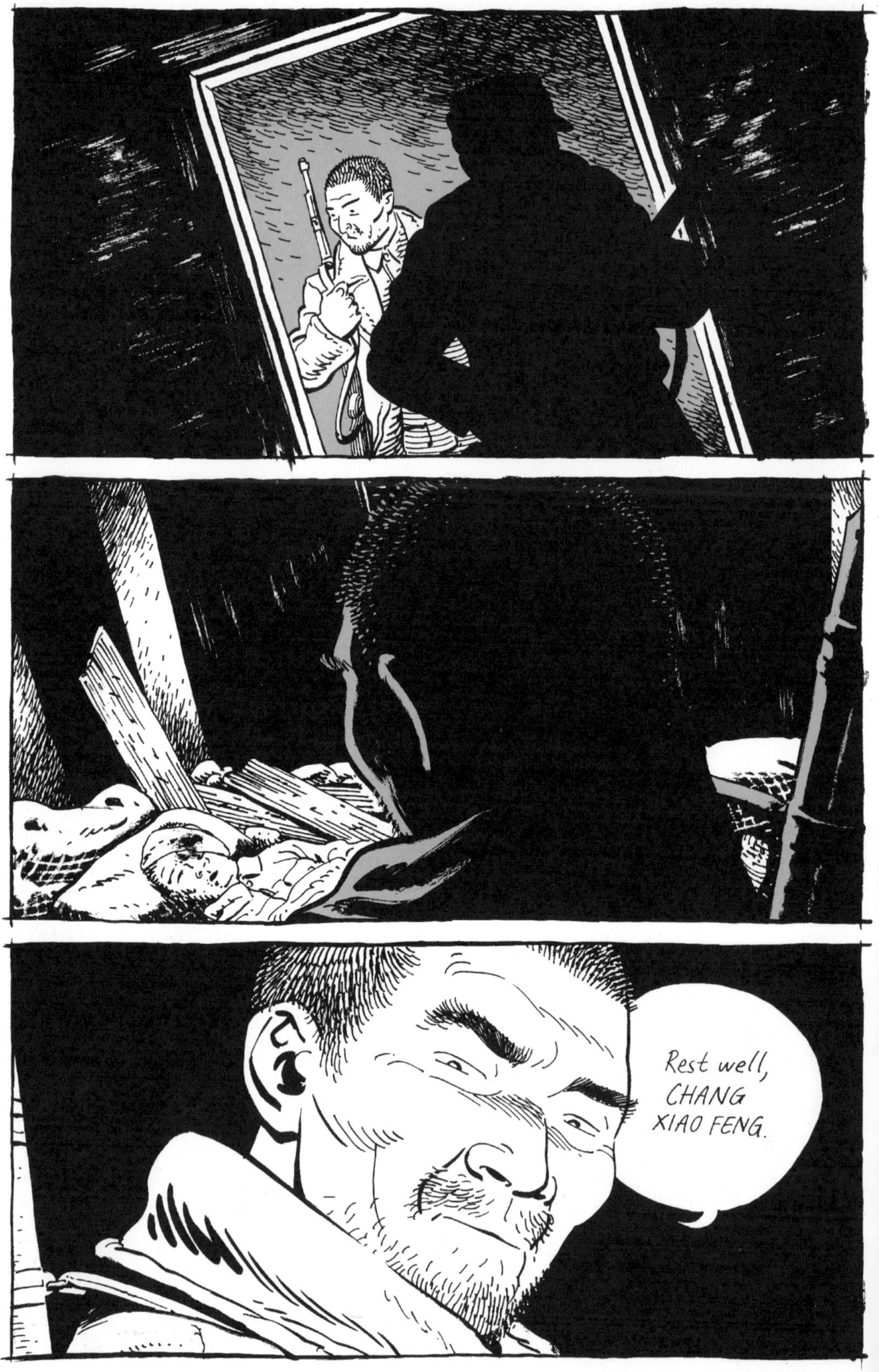
Rest well, CHANG XIAO FENG.

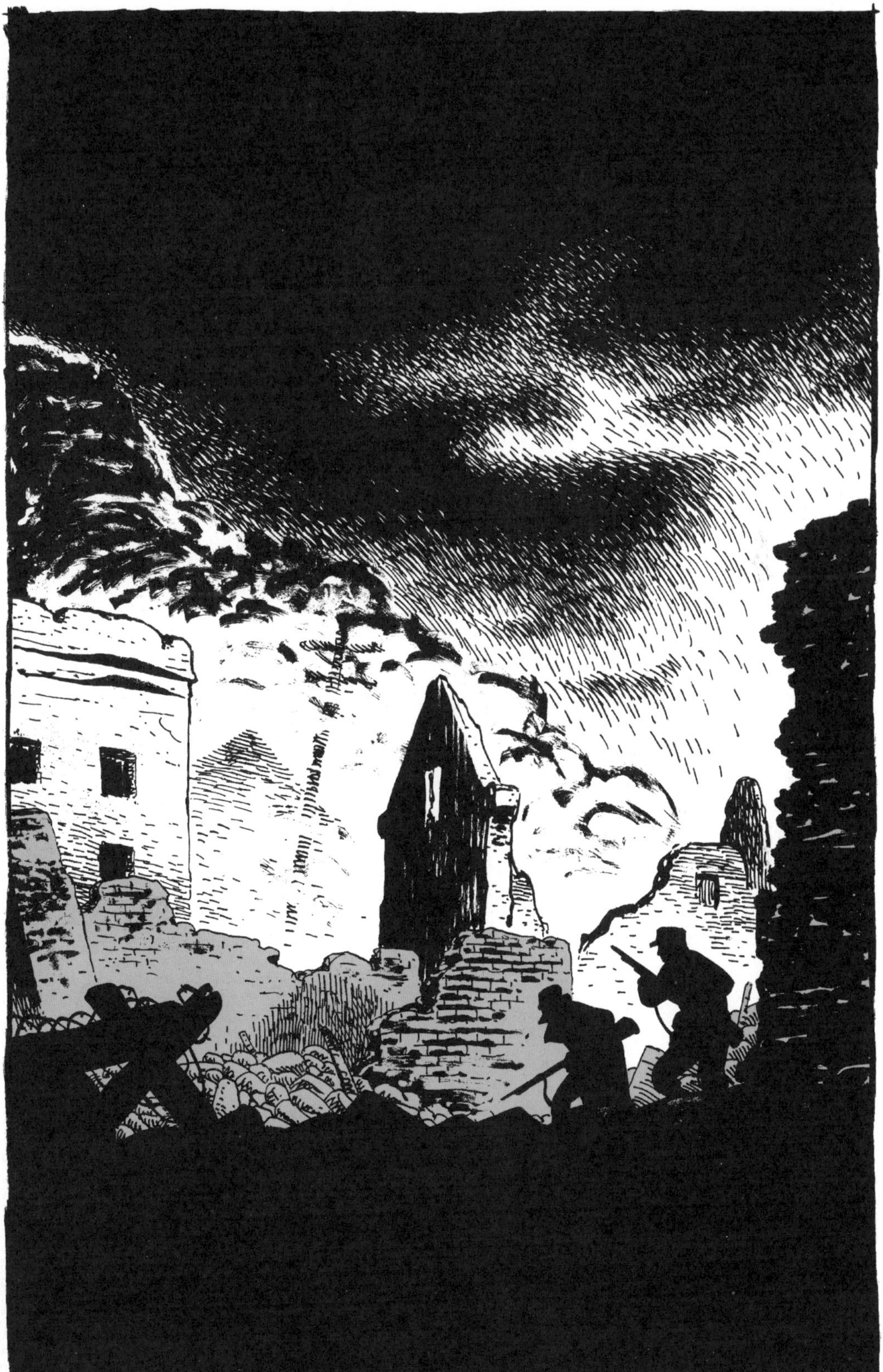

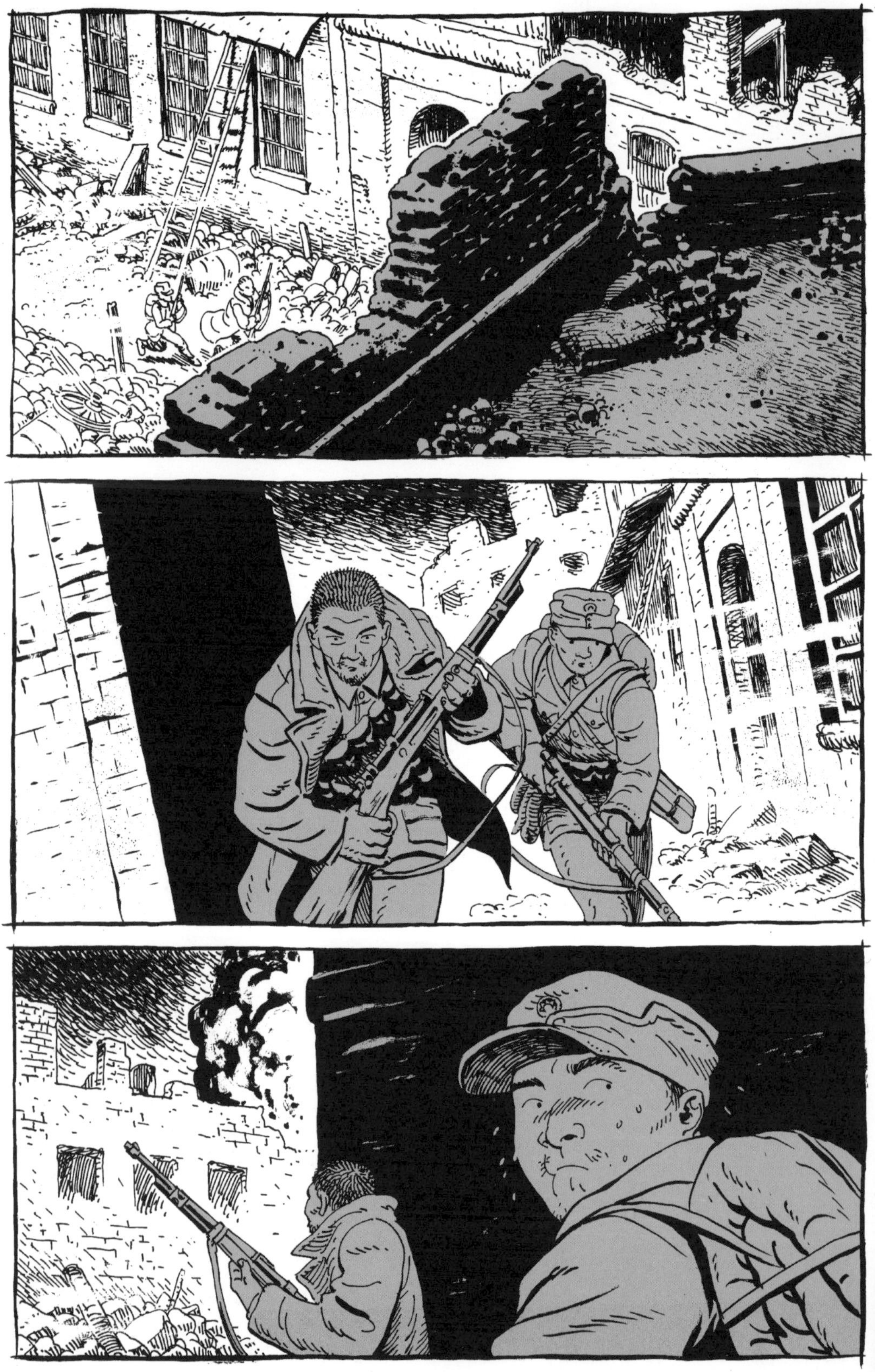

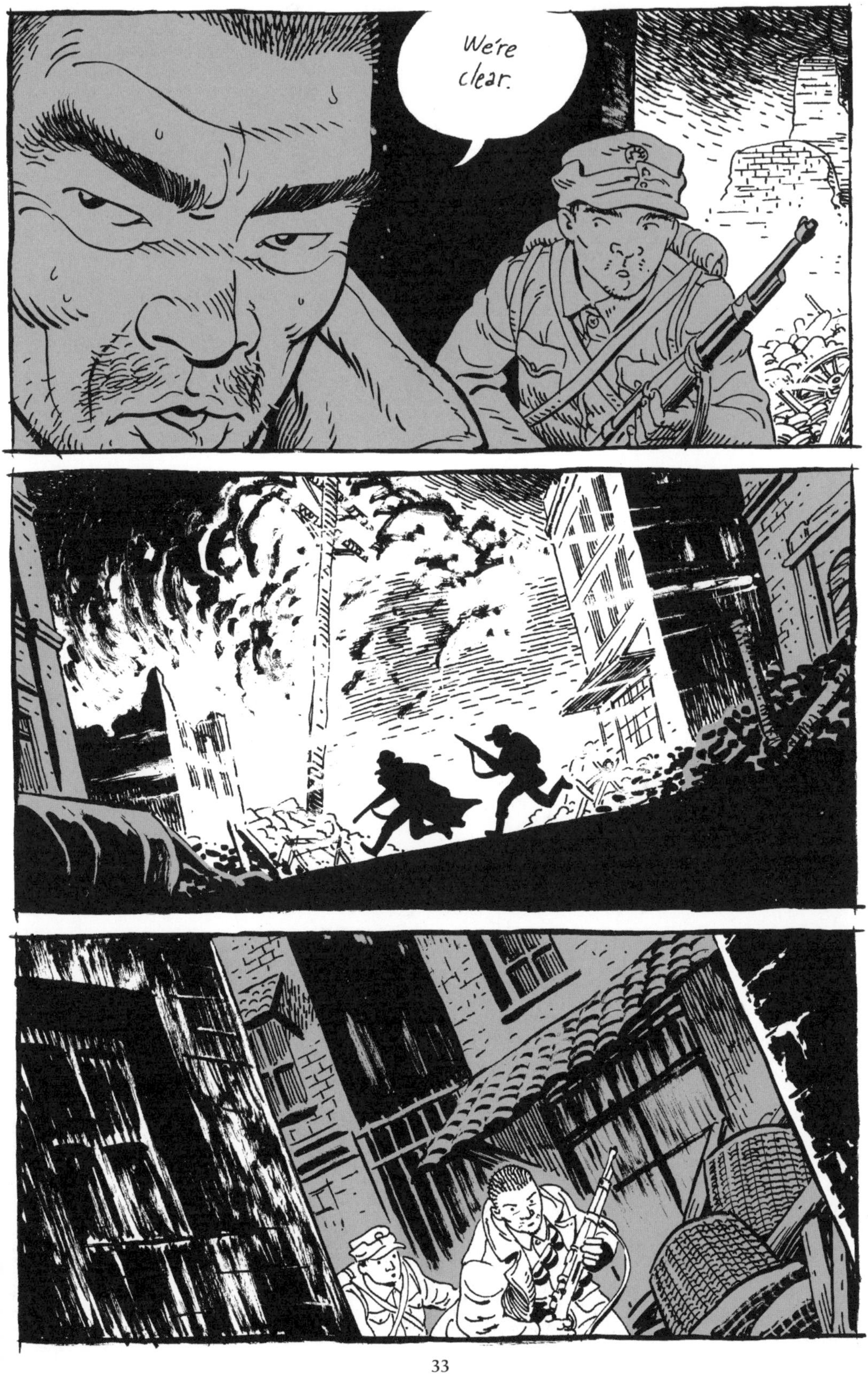
We're clear.

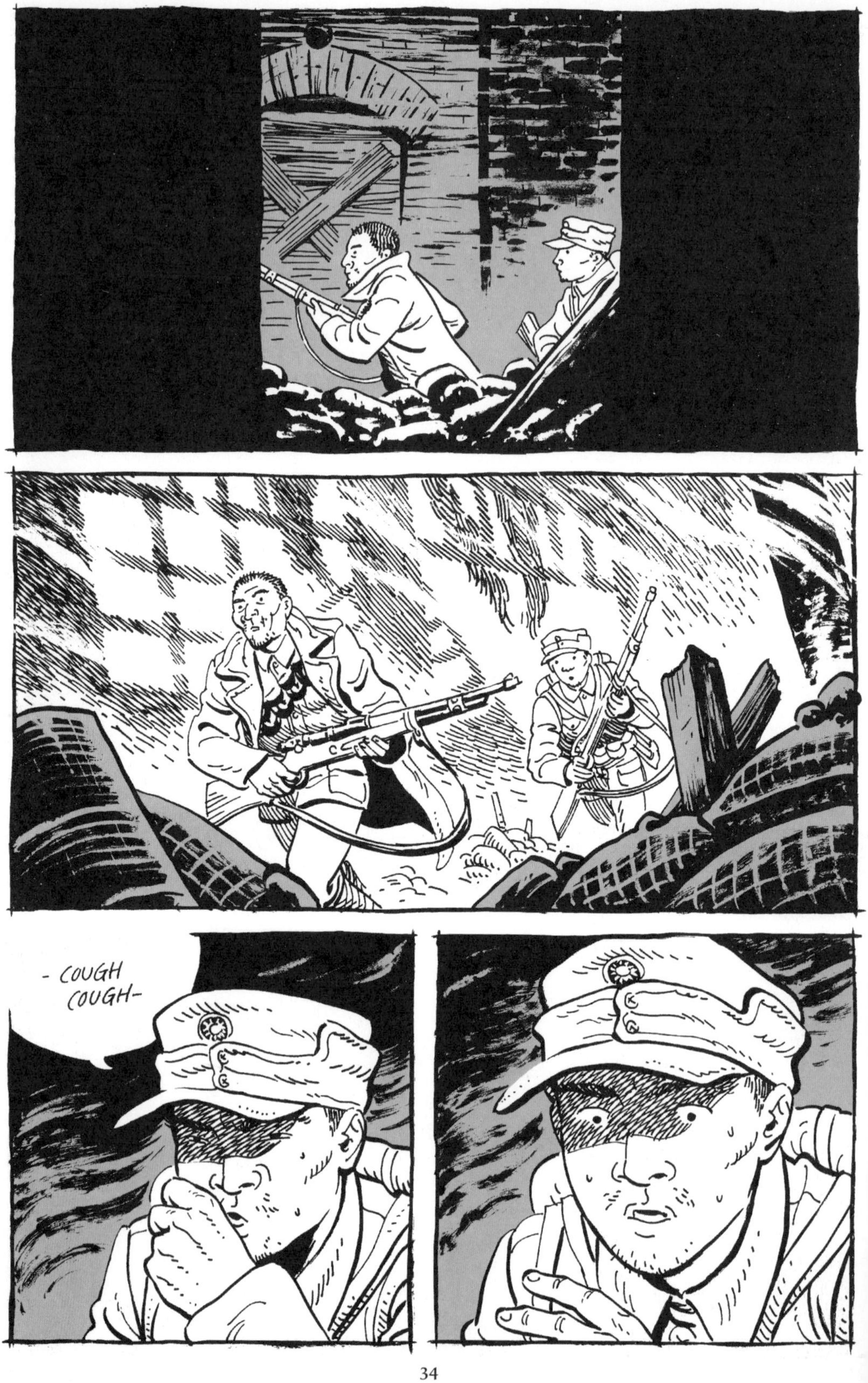
- COUGH COUGH-

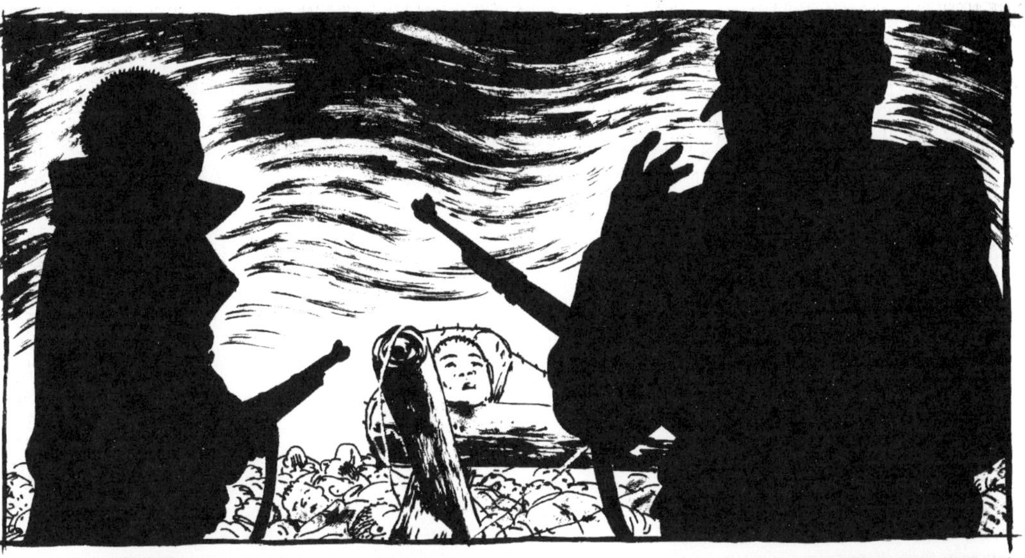

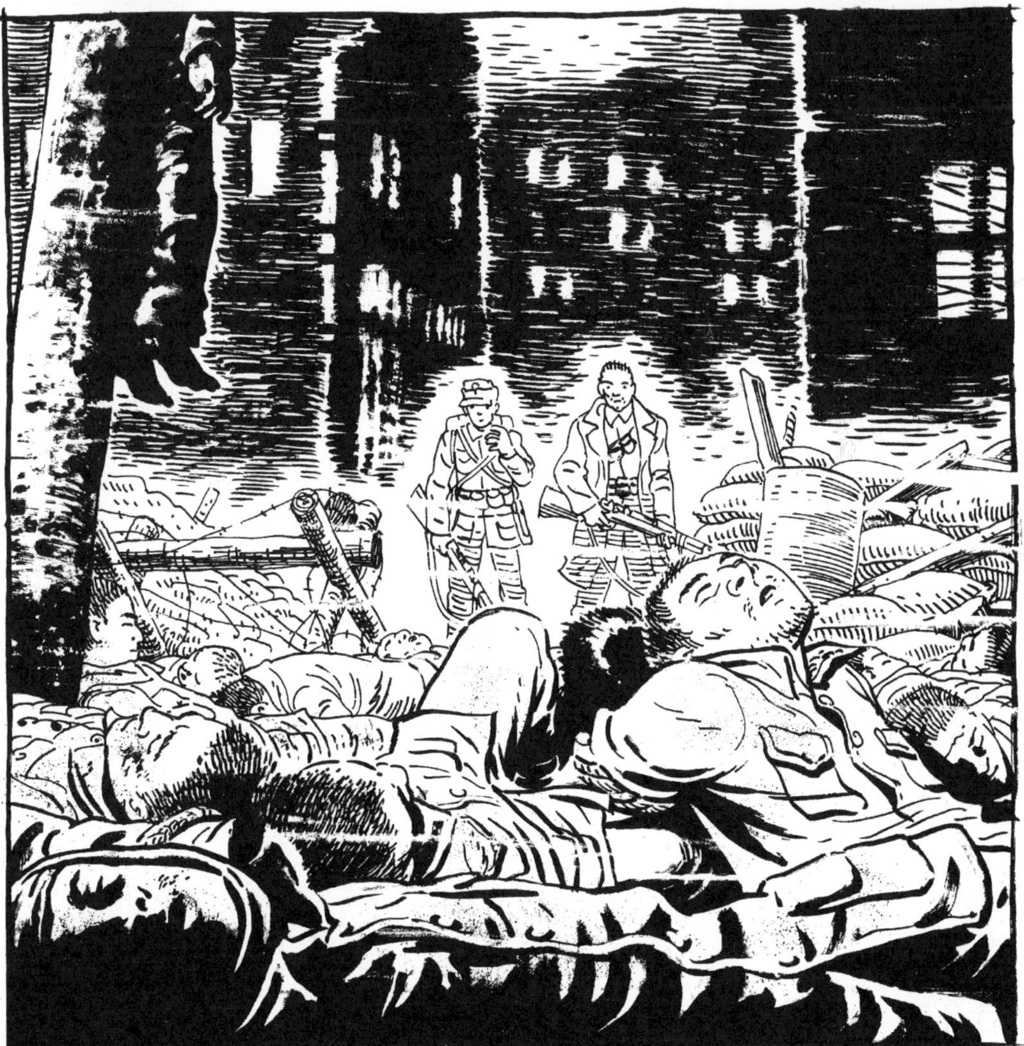

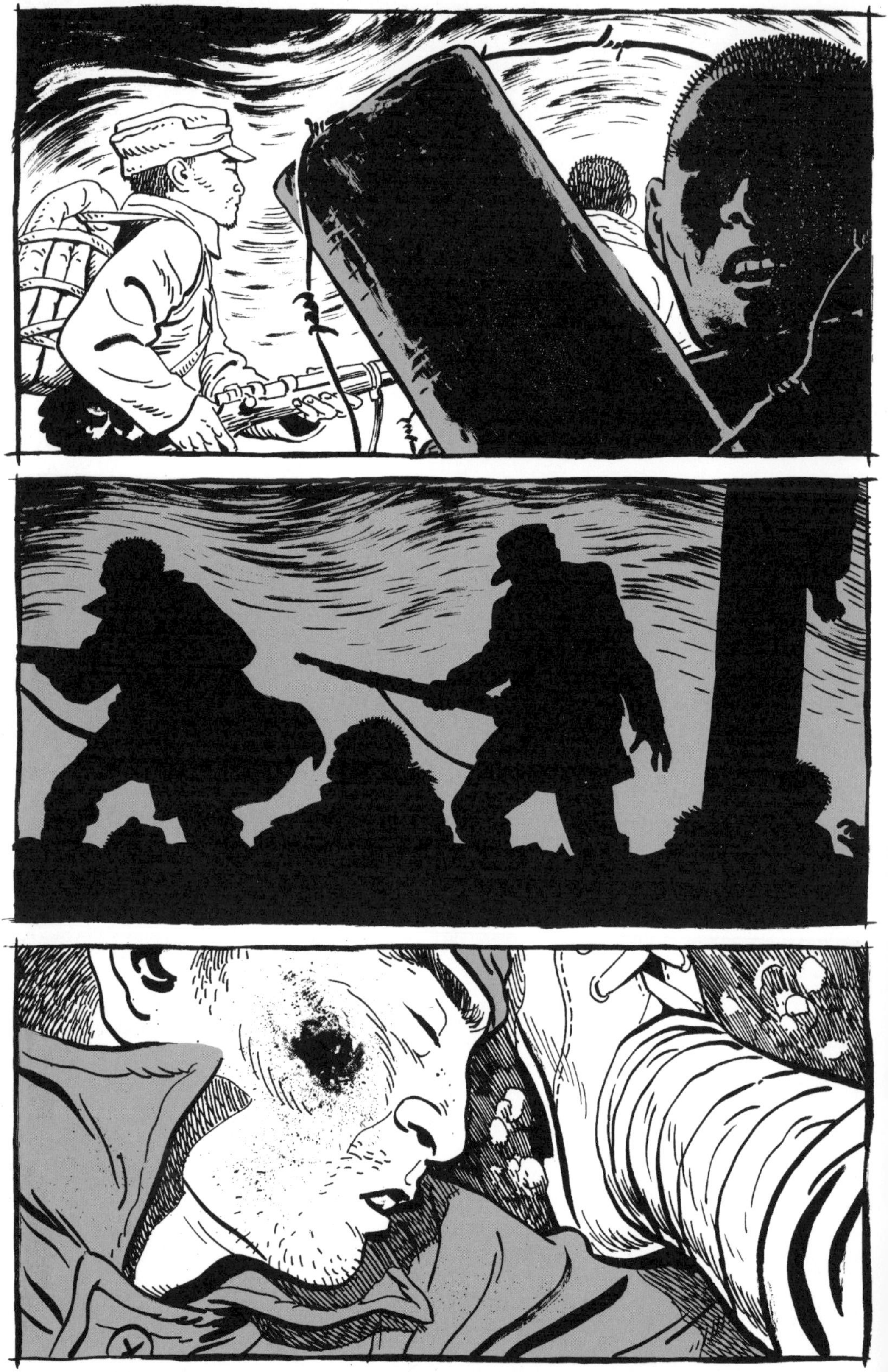

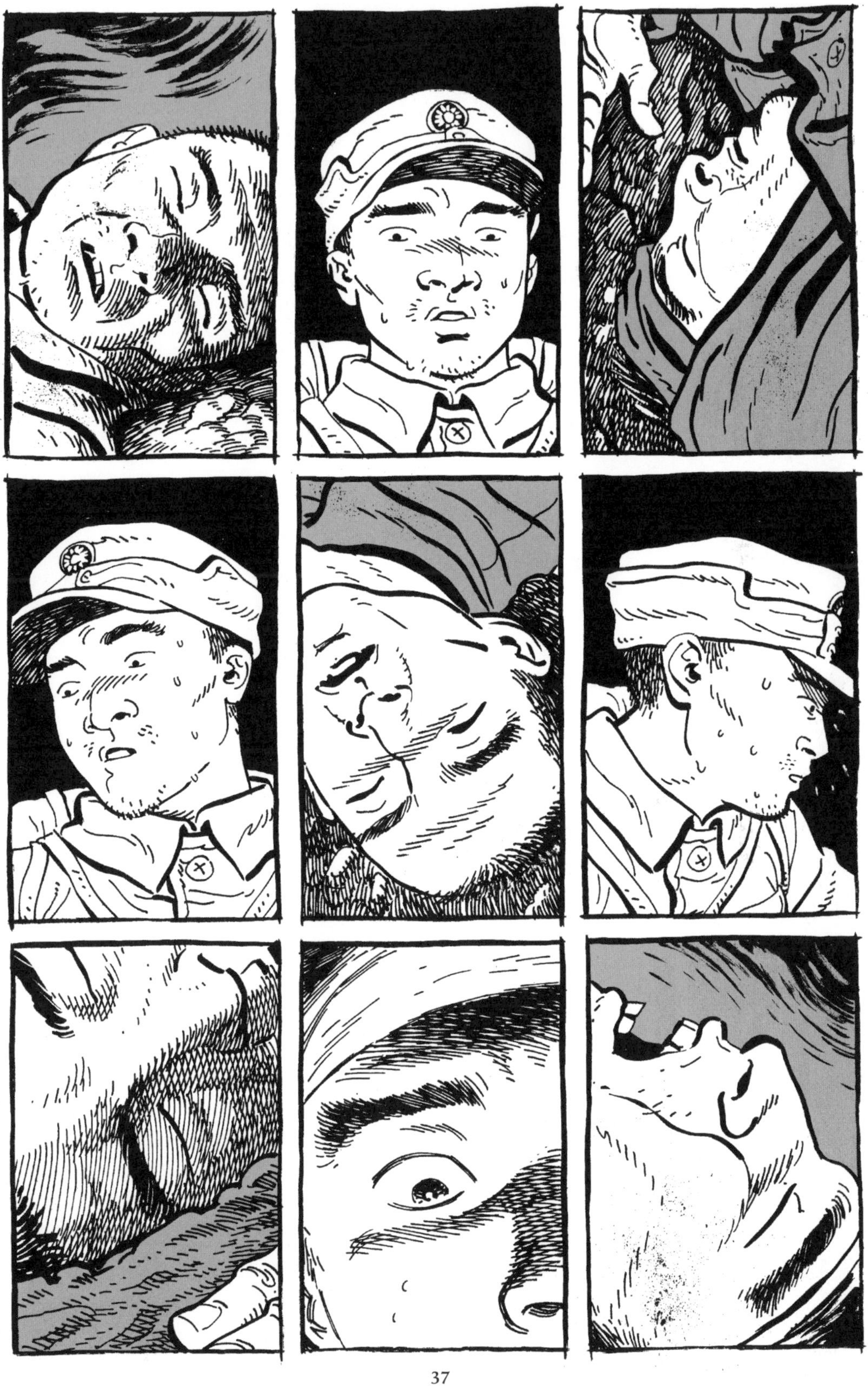

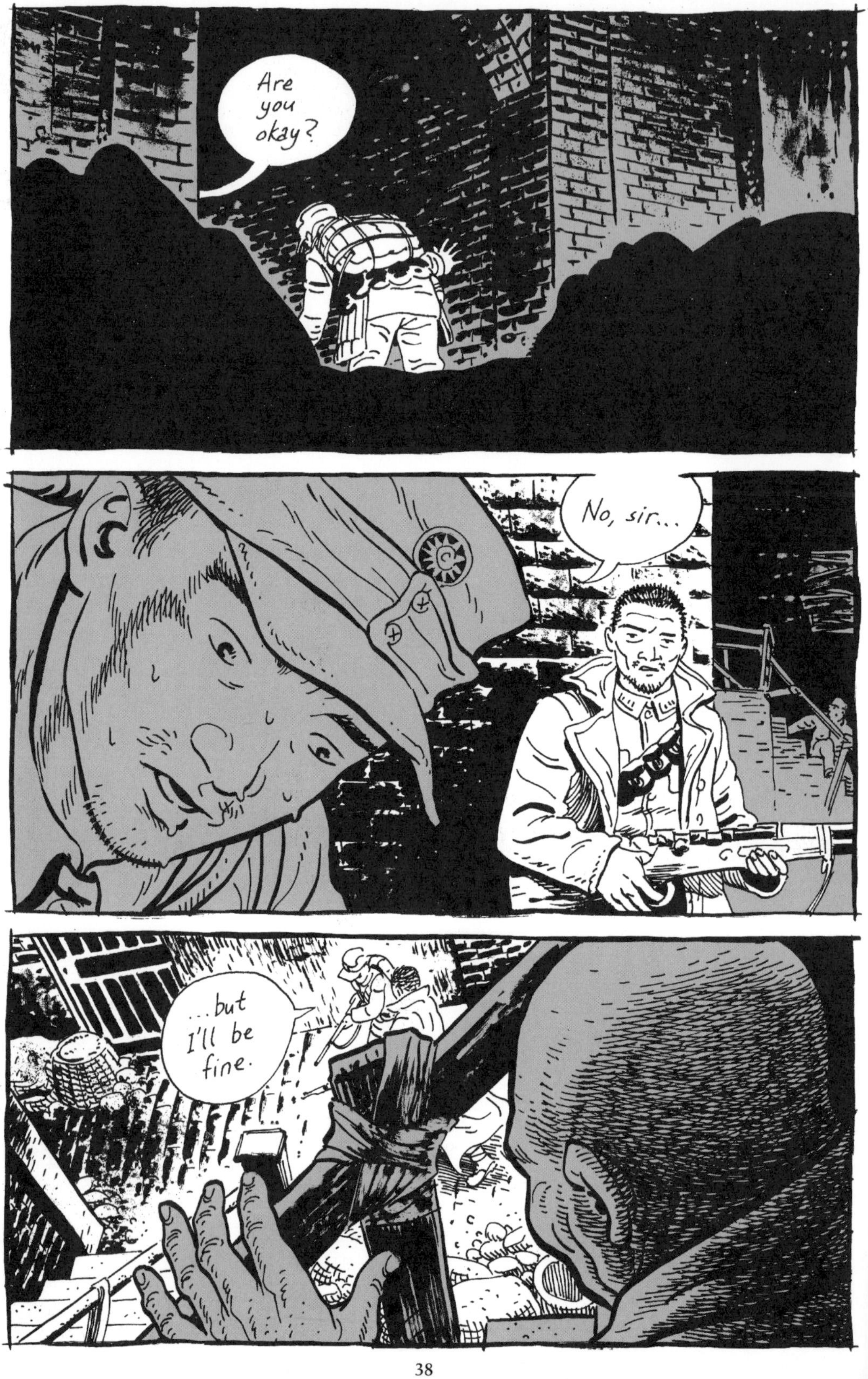
Are you okay?
No, sir...
...but I'll be fine.

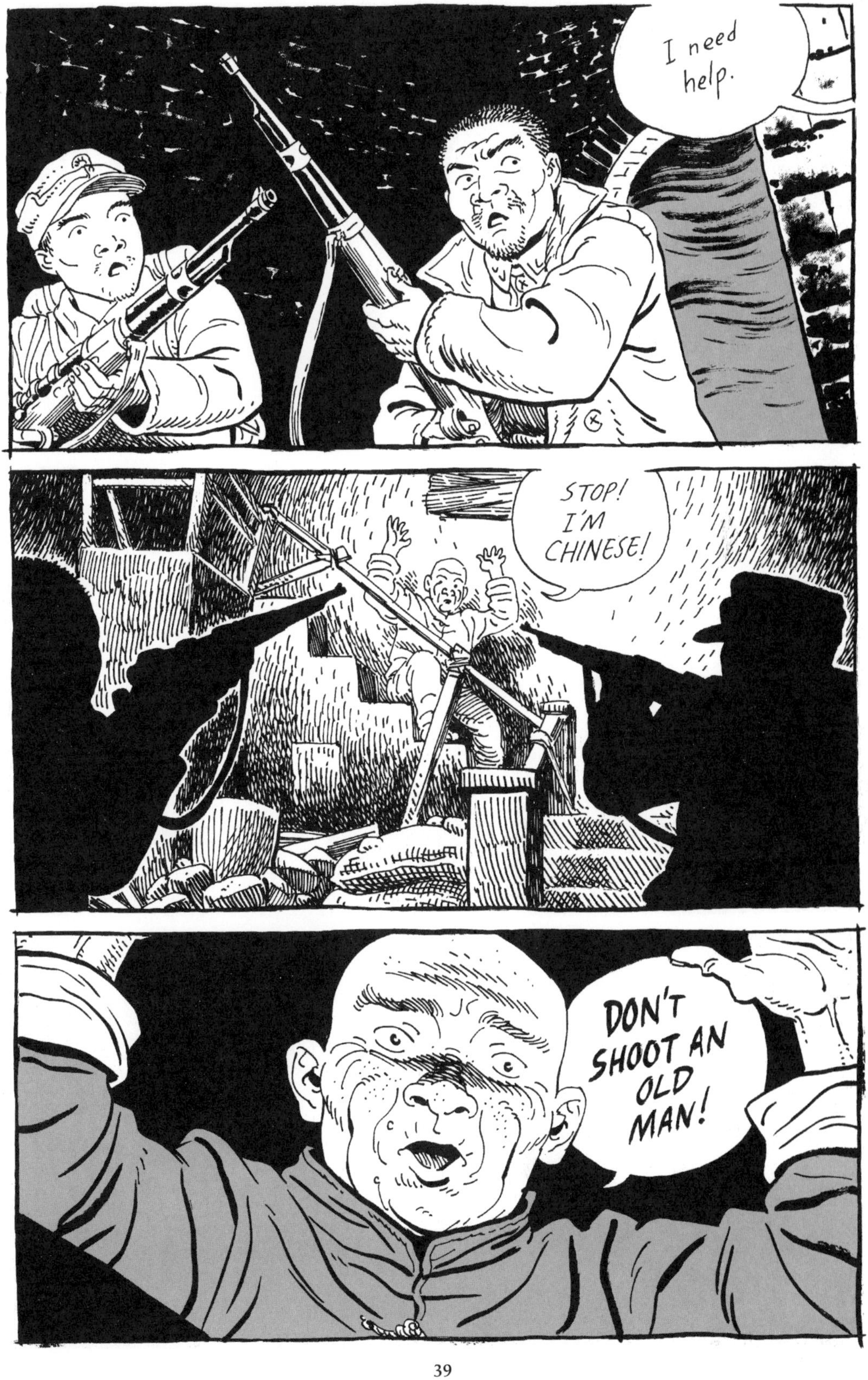
I need help.
STOP! I'M CHINESE!
DON'T SHOOT AN OLD MAN!

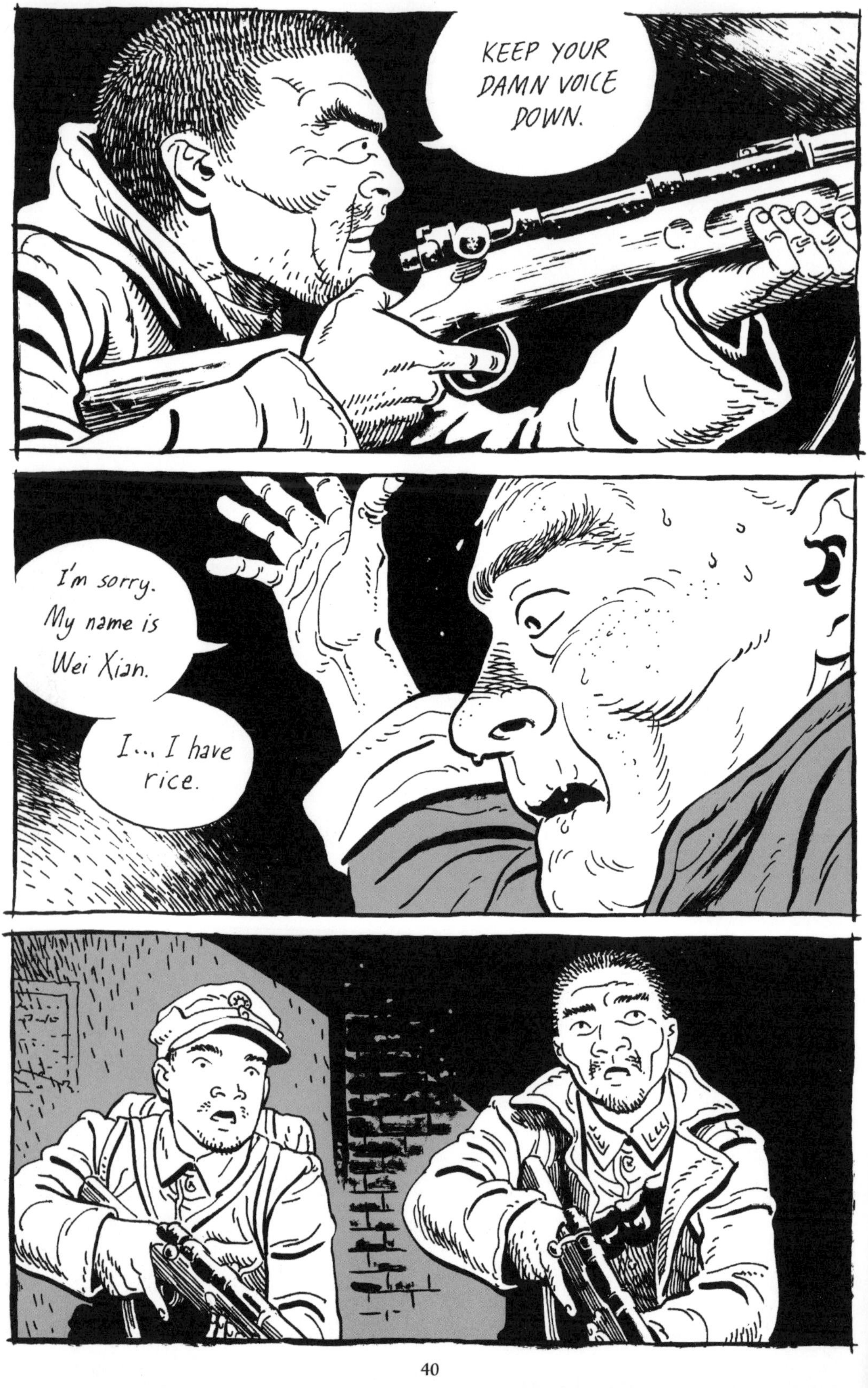
KEEP YOUR DAMN VOICE DOWN.
I'm sorry. My name is Wei Xian.
I... I have rice.

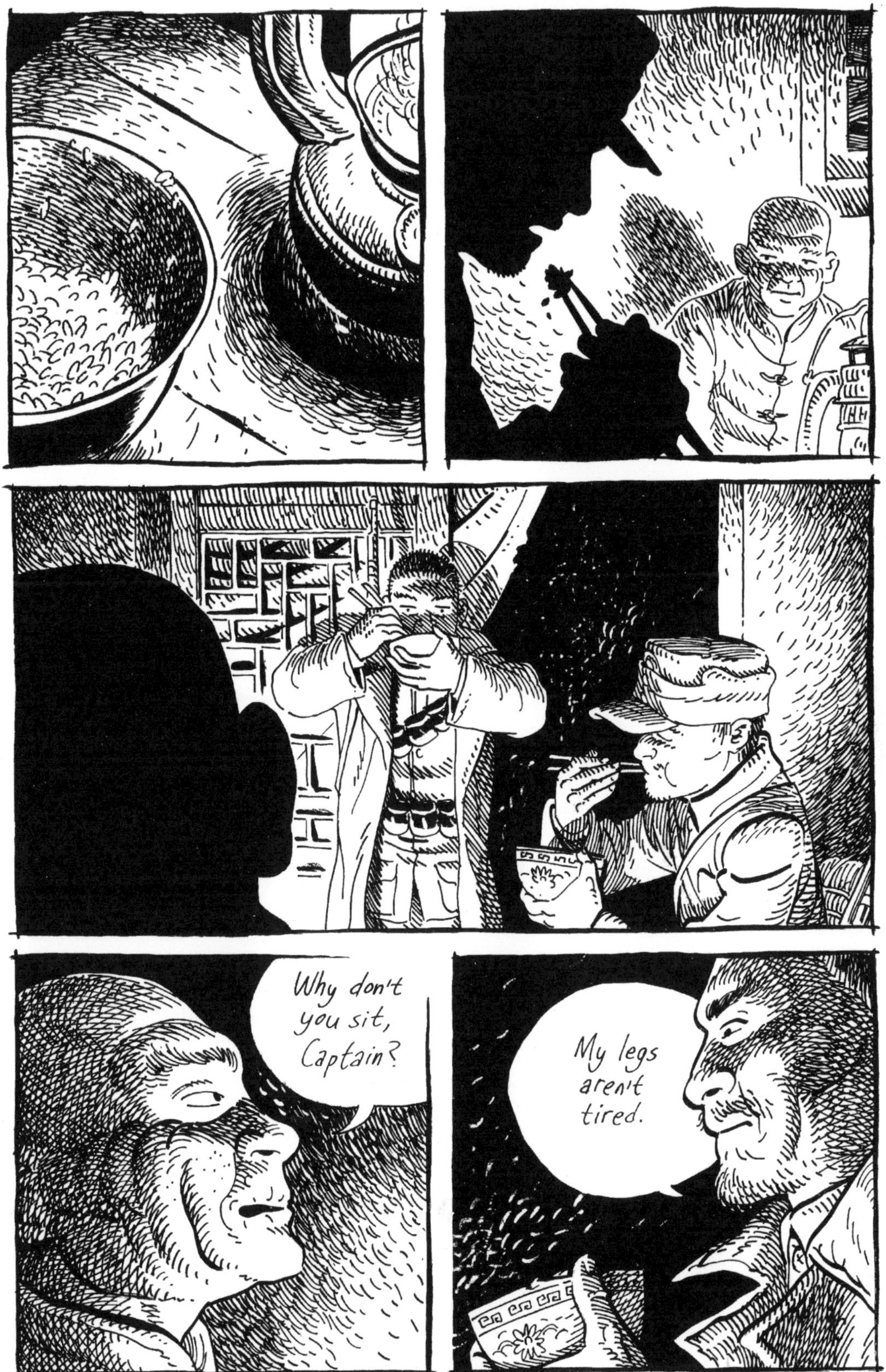
Why don't you sit, Captain?
My legs aren't tired.

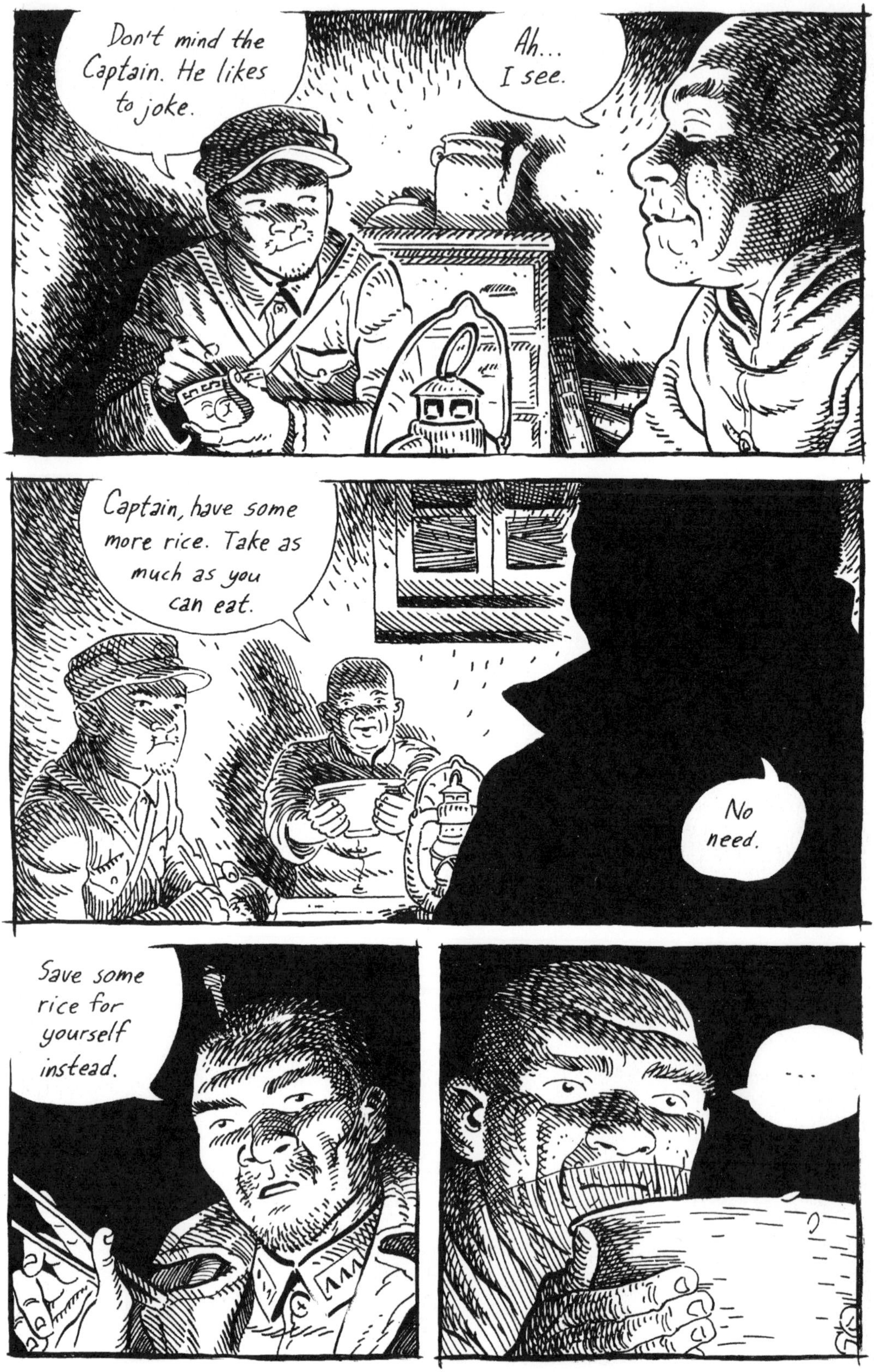
Don't mind the Captain. He likes to joke.
Ah... I see.
Captain, have some more rice. Take as much as you can eat.
No need.
Save some rice for yourself instead.
...

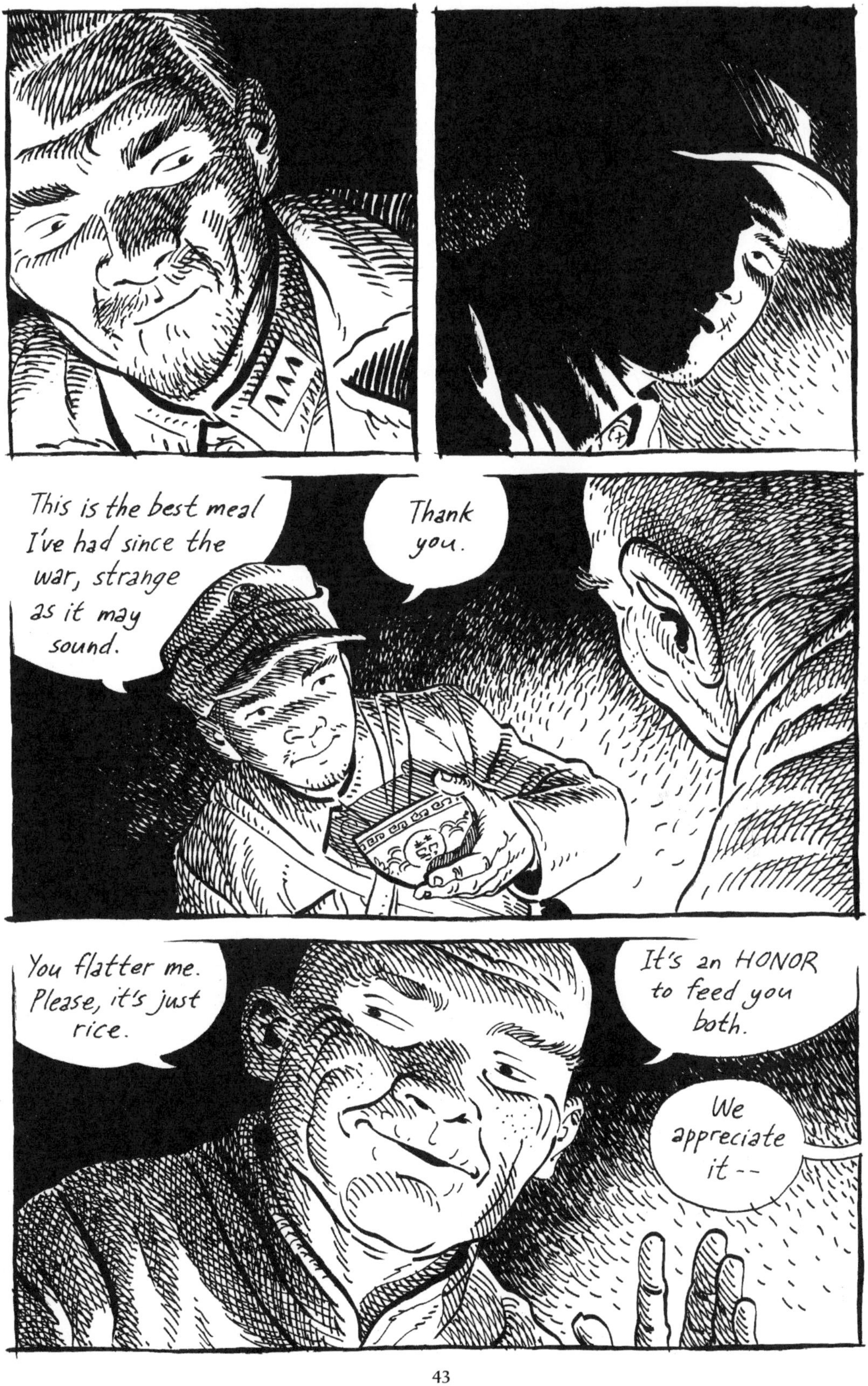
This is the best meal I've had since the war, strange as it may sound.
Thank you.
You flatter me. Please, it's just rice.
It's an HONOR to feed you both.
We appreciate it --

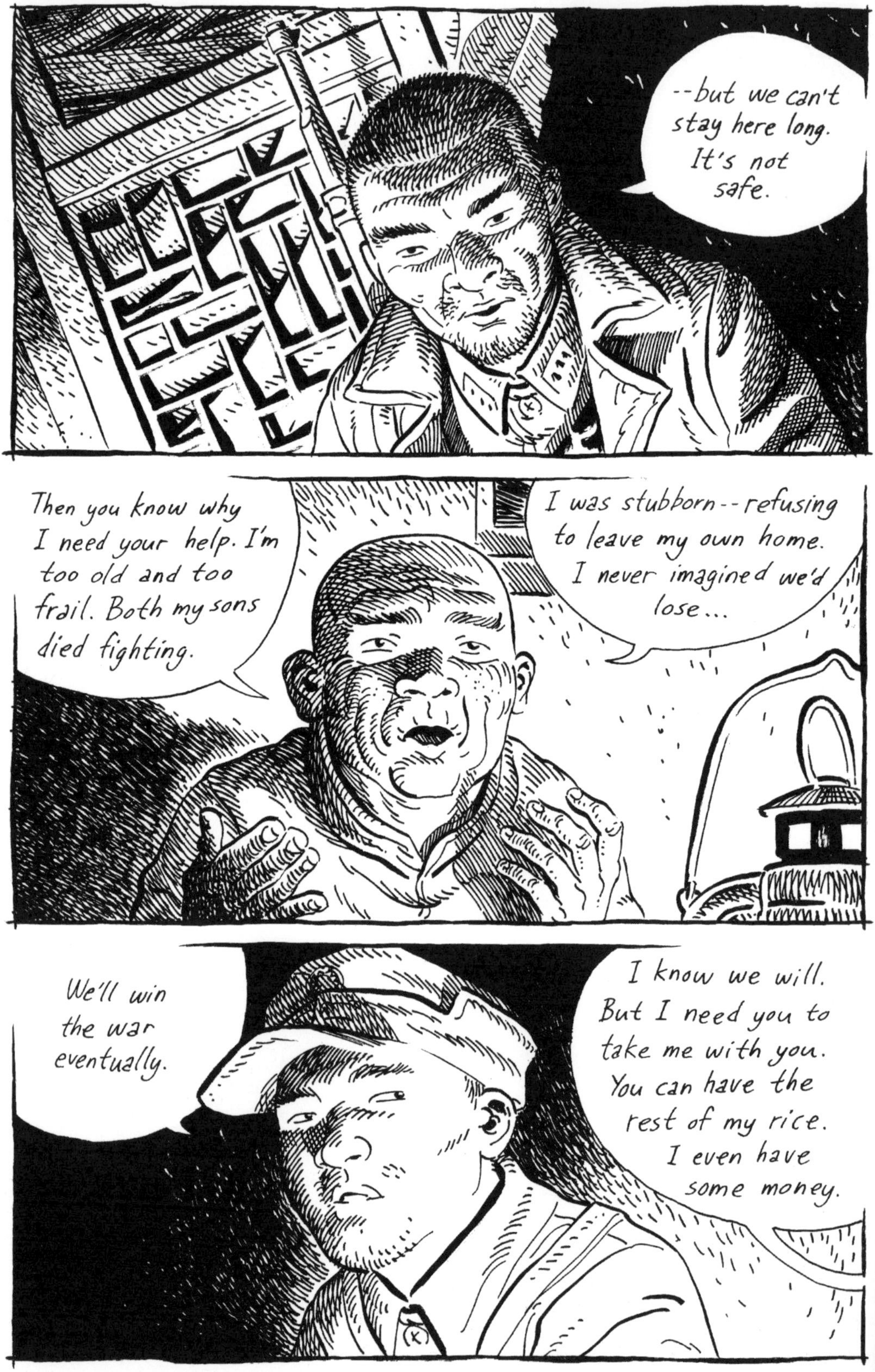
--but we can't stay here long. It's not safe.
Then you know why I need your help. I'm too old and too frail. Both my sons died fighting.
I was stubborn--refusing to leave my own home. I never imagined we'd lose...
We'll win the war eventually.
I know we will. But I need you to take me with you. You can have the rest of my rice. I even have some money.

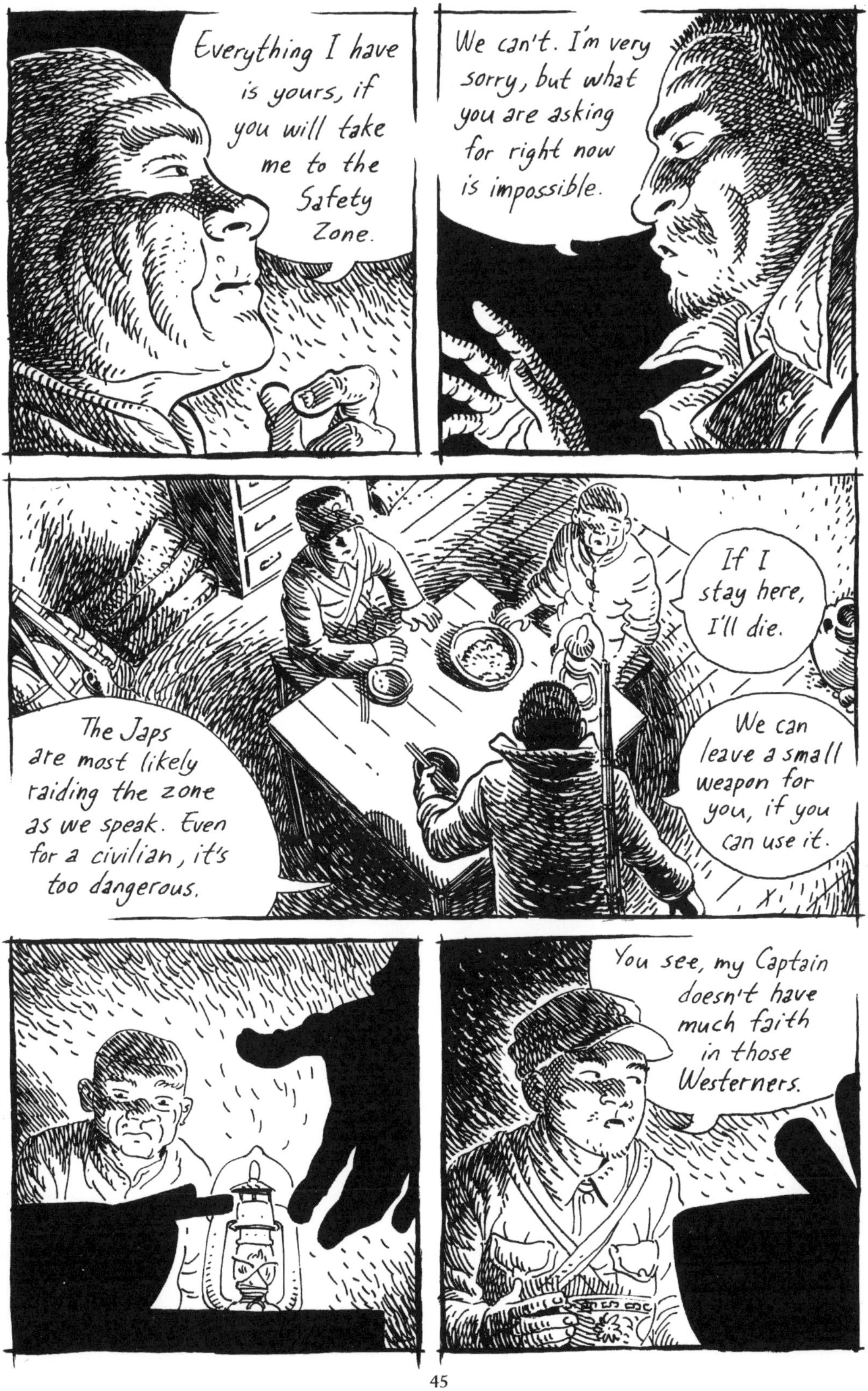
Everything I have is yours, if you will take me to the Safety Zone.
We can't. I'm very sorry, but what you are asking for right now is impossible.
If I stay here, I'll die.
The Japs are most likely raiding the zone as we speak. Even for a civilian, it's too dangerous.
We can leave a small weapon for you, if you can use it.
You see, my Captain doesn't have much faith in those Westerners.

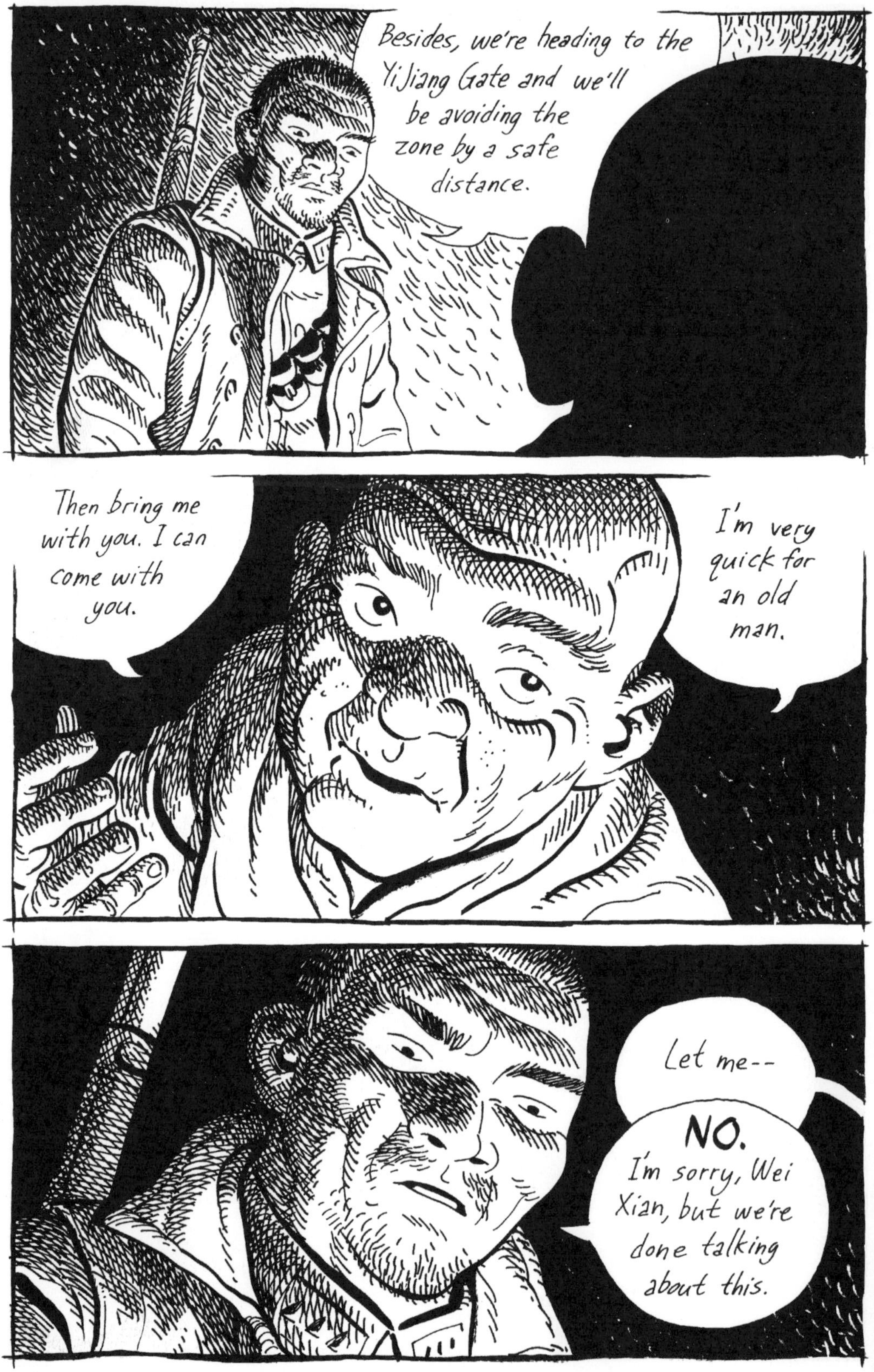
Besides, we're heading to the Yi Jiang Gate and we'll be avoiding the zone by a safe distance.
Then bring me with you. I can come with you.
I'm very quick for an old man.
Let me--
NO.
I'm sorry, Wei Xian, but we're done talking about this.

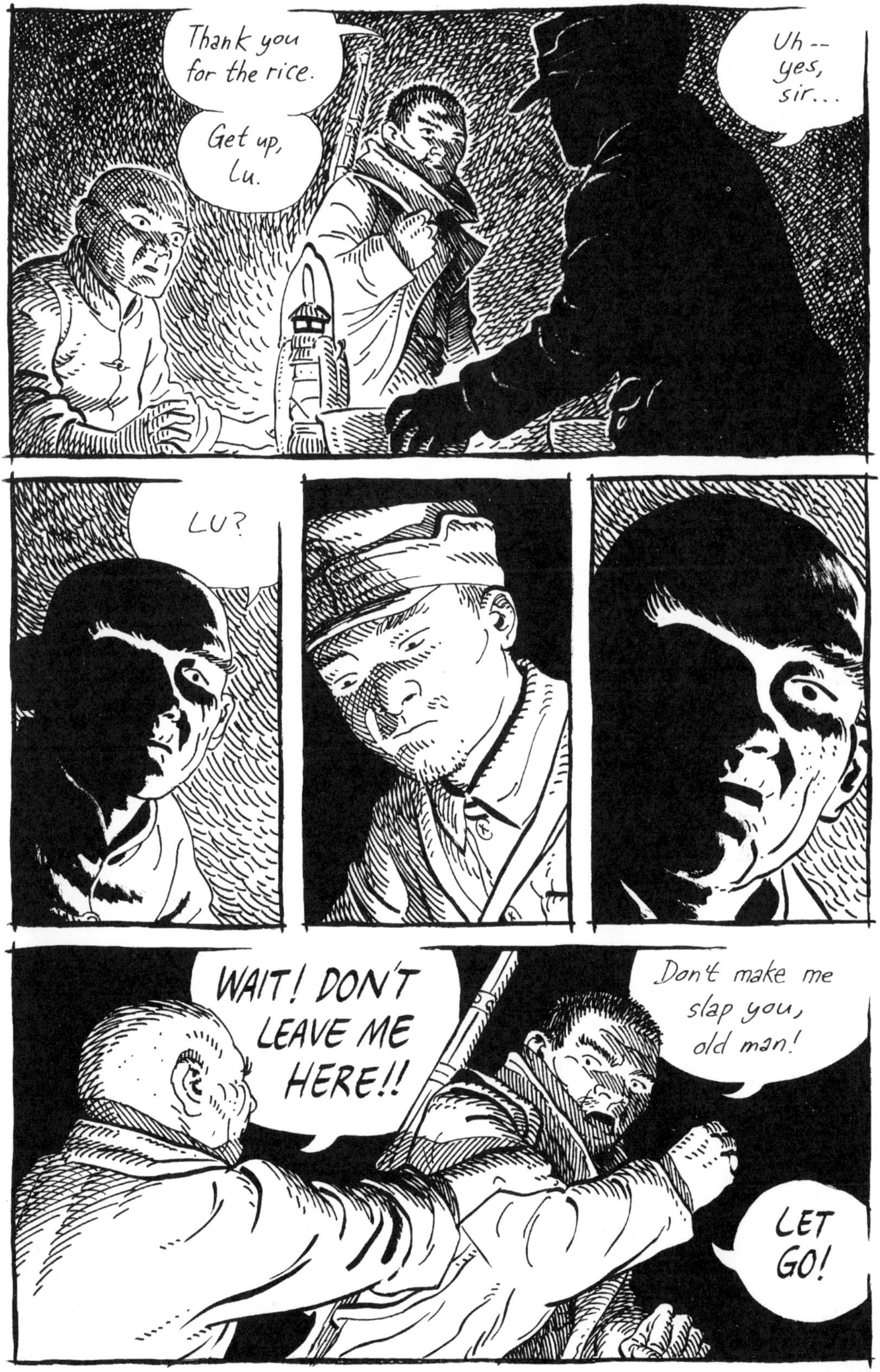
Thank you for the rice.
Get up, Lu.
Uh -- yes, sir...
LU?
WAIT! DON'T LEAVE ME HERE!!
Don't make me slap you, old man!
LET GO!

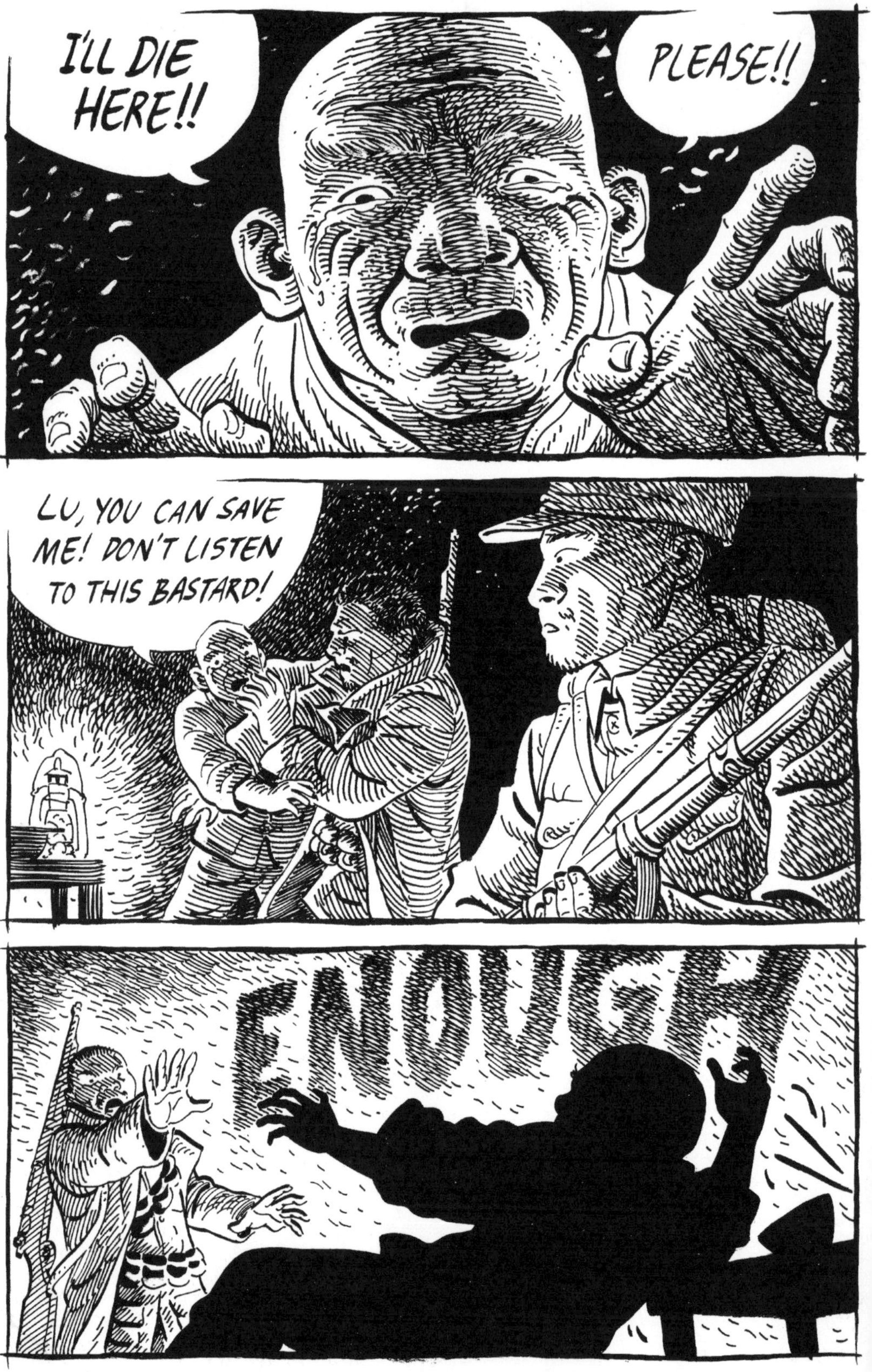
I'LL DIE HERE!!
PLEASE!!
LU, YOU CAN SAVE ME! DON'T LISTEN TO THIS BASTARD!
ENOUGH

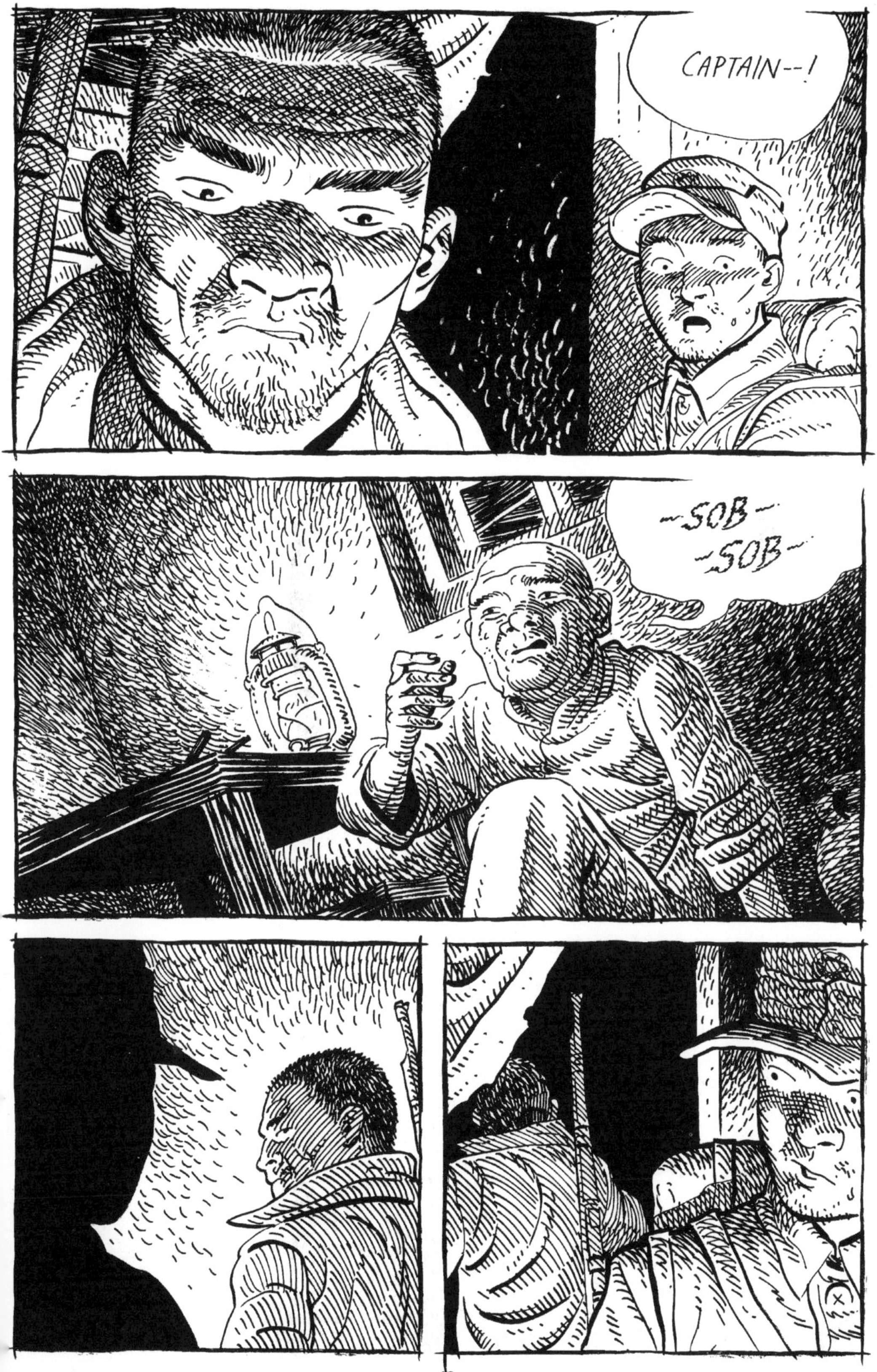
CAPTAIN--!
-SOB-
-SOB-

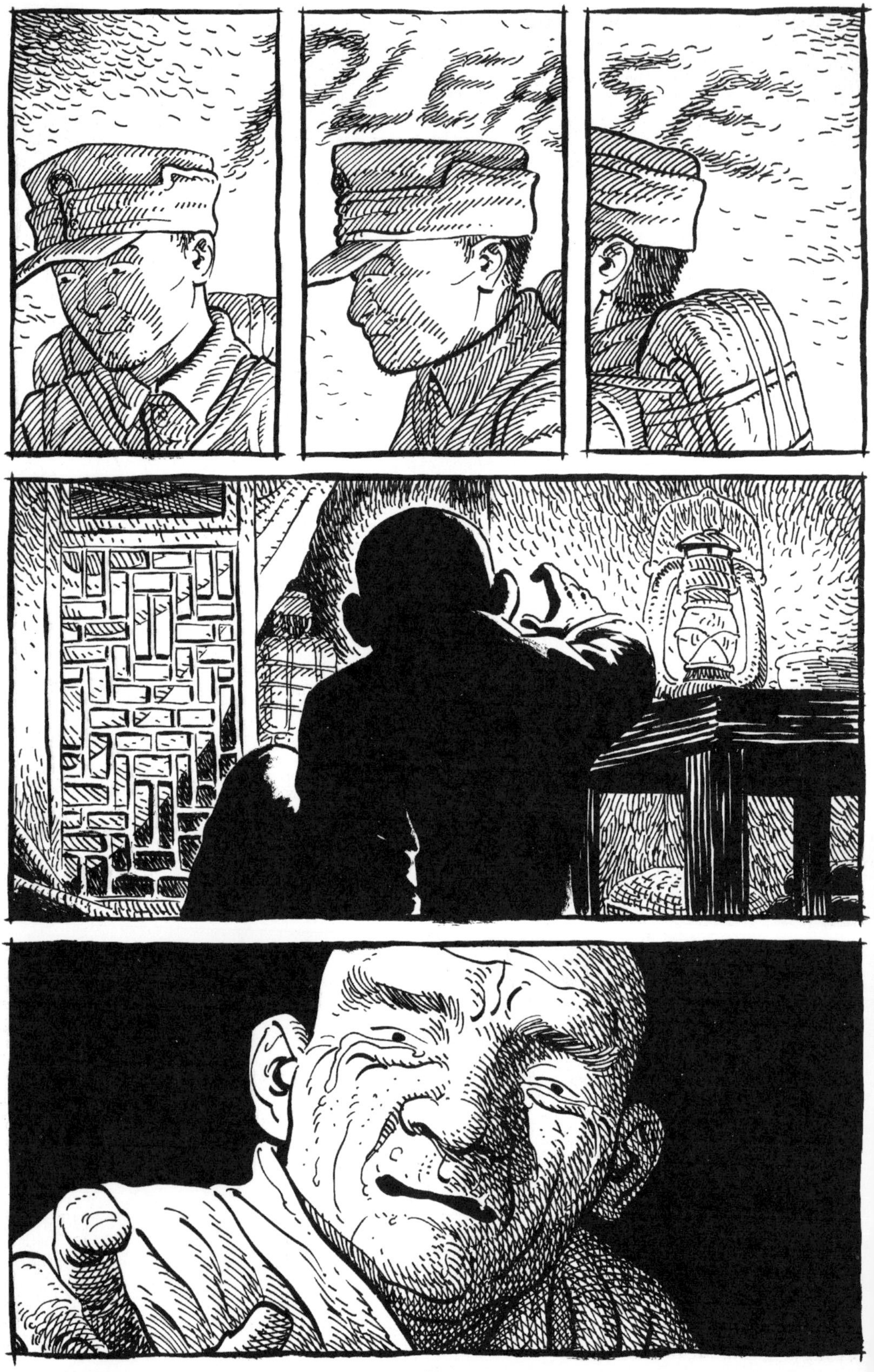
PLEASE

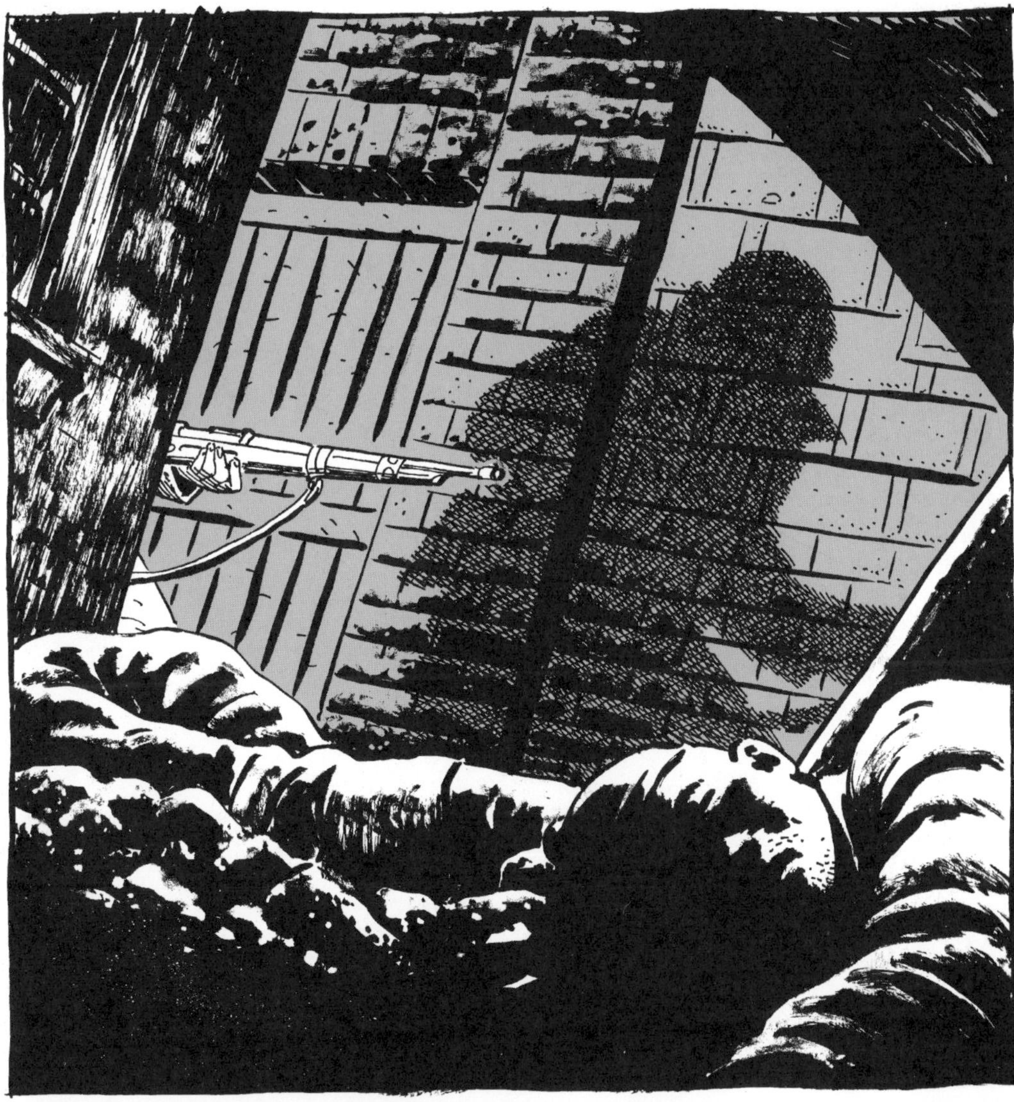

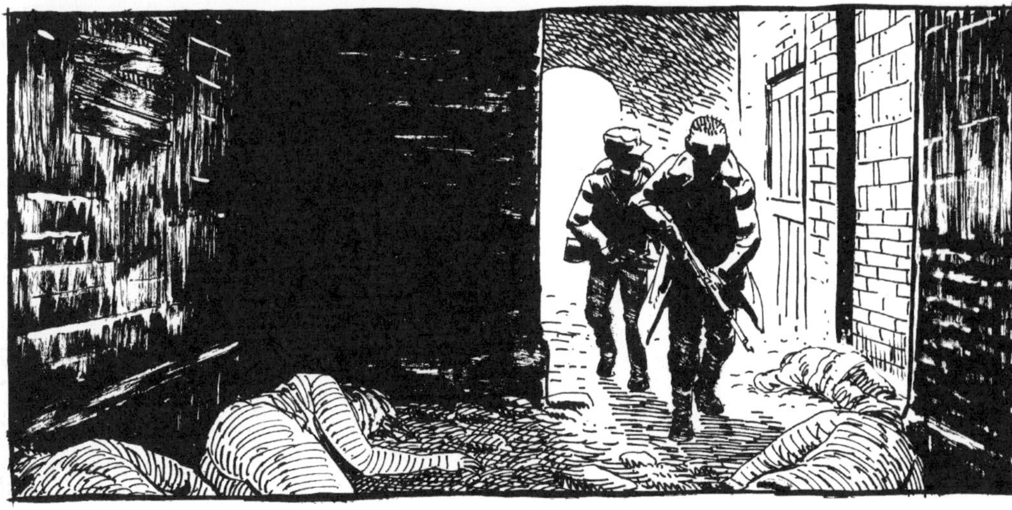

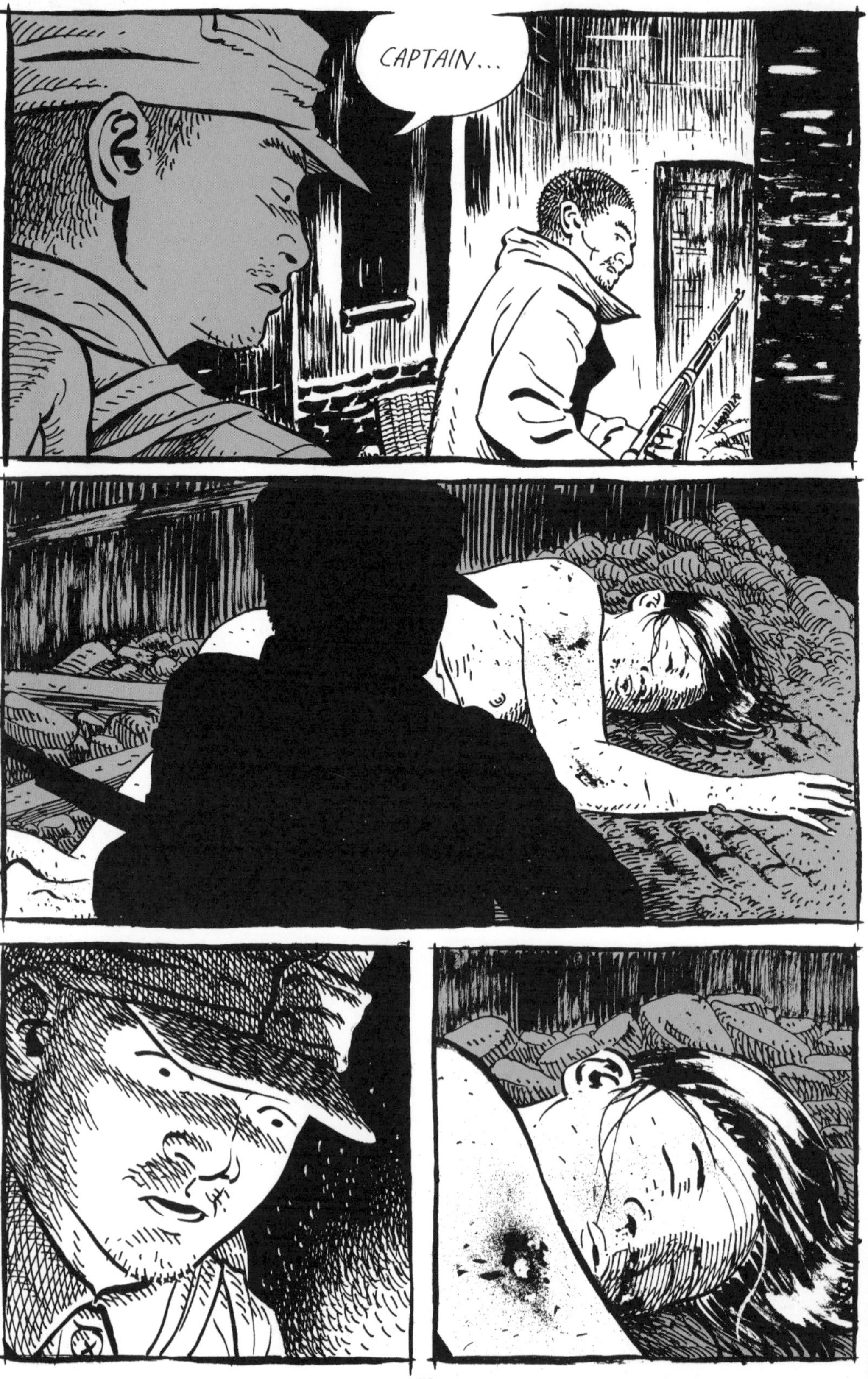
CAPTAIN...

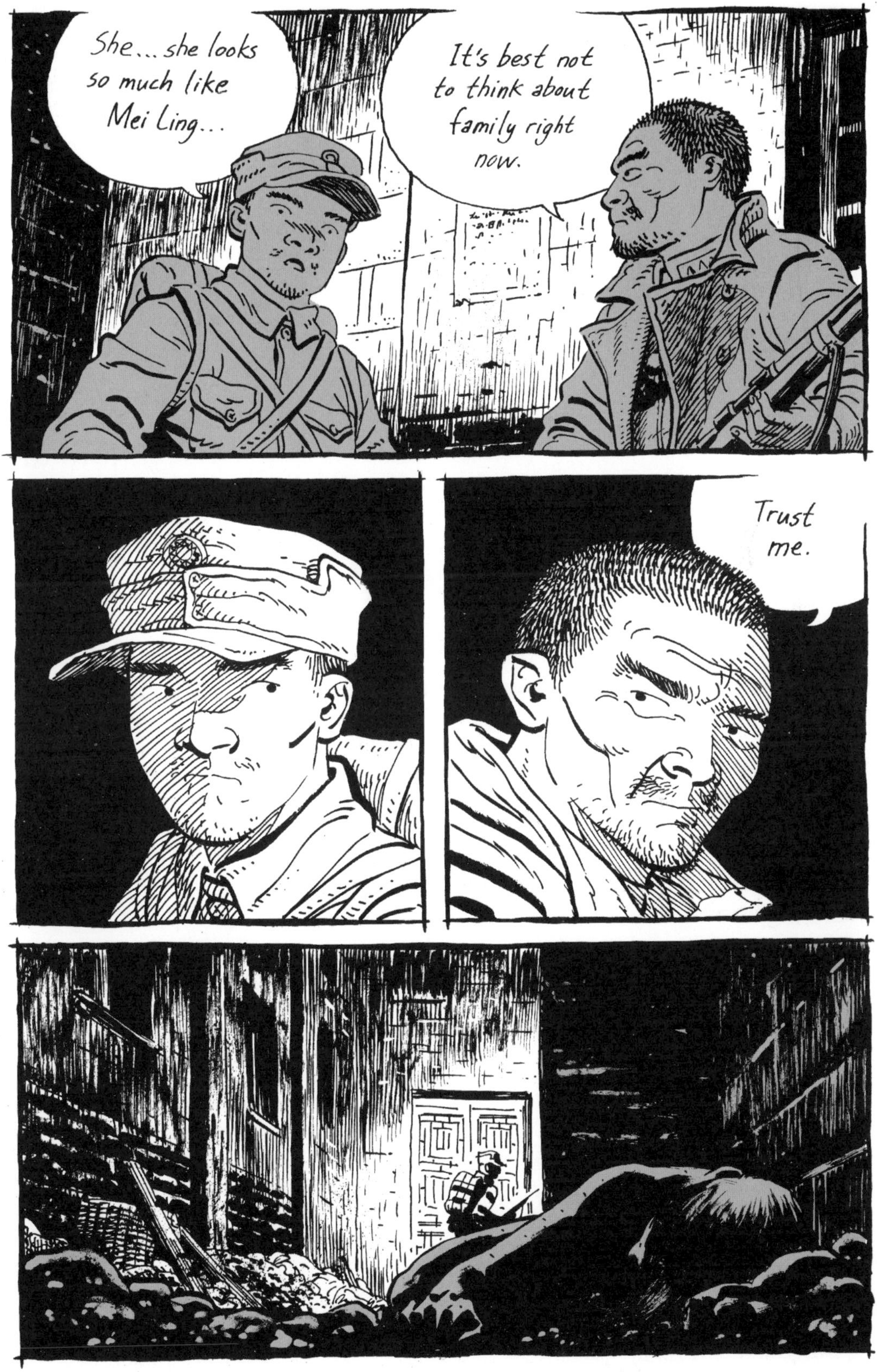
She... she looks so much like Mei Ling...
It's best not to think about family right now.
Trust me.

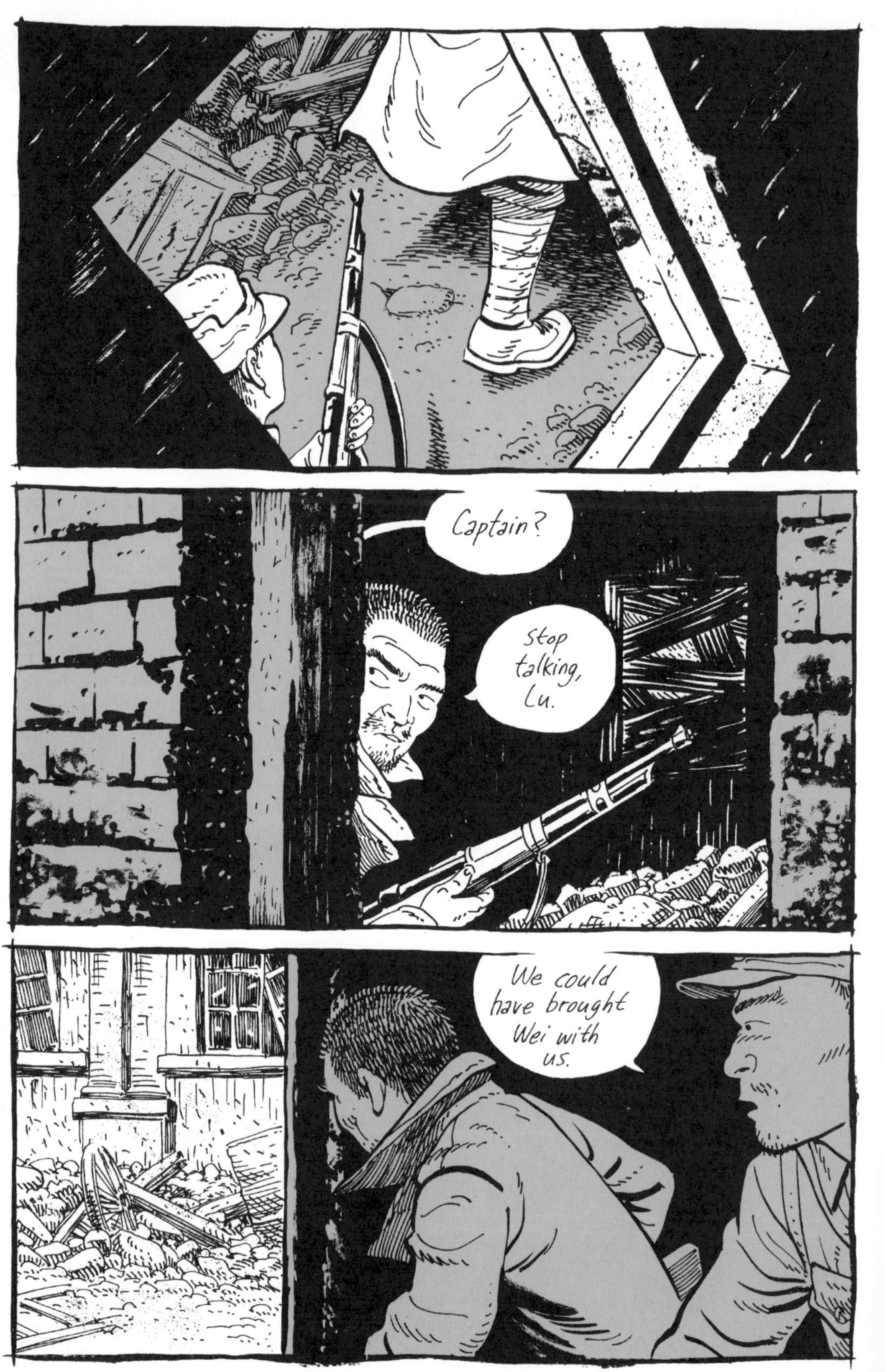
Captain?
Stop talking, Lu.
We could have brought Wei with us.

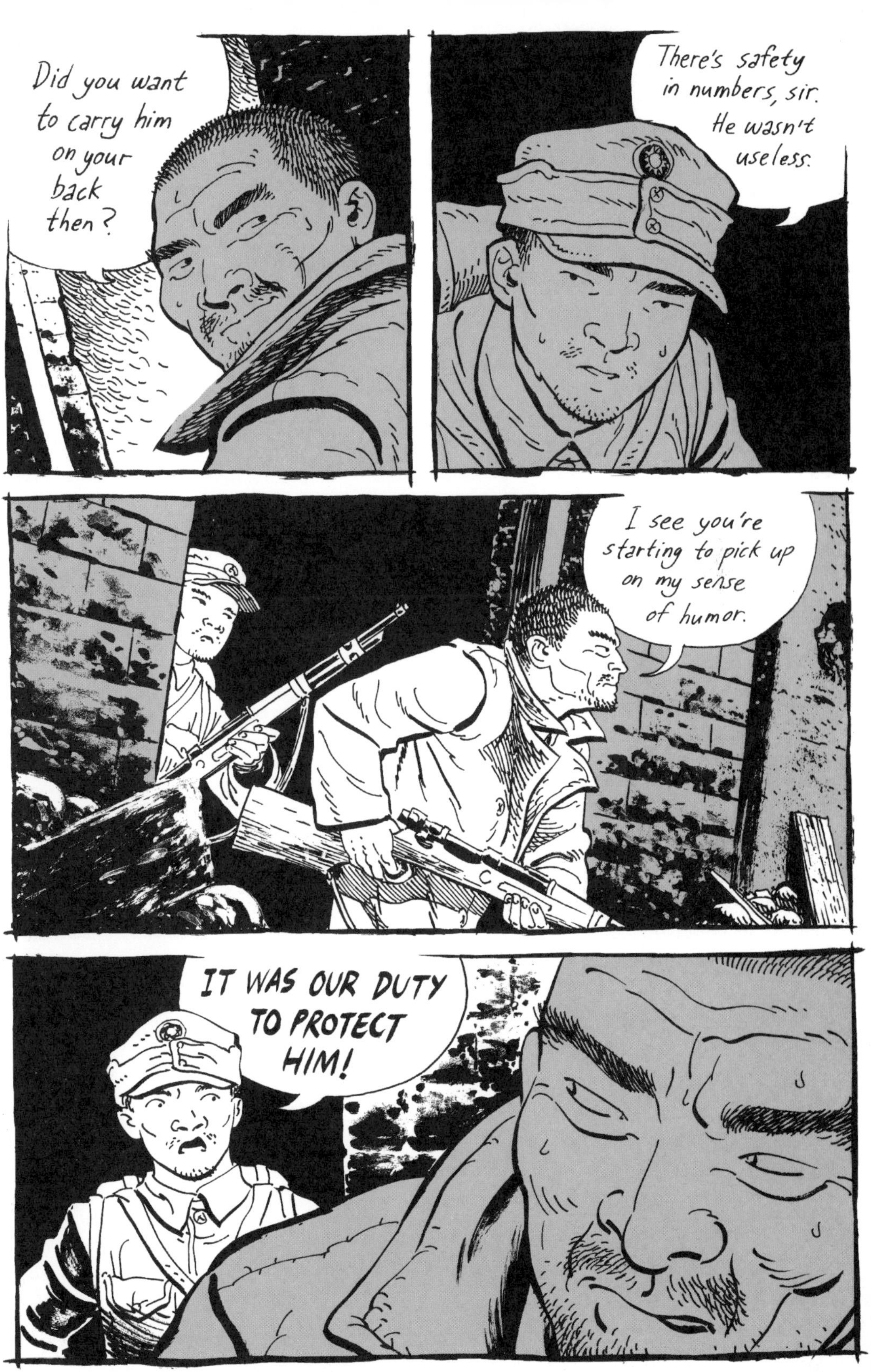

Did you want to carry him on your back then?
There's safety in numbers, sir. He wasn't useless.
I see you're starting to pick up on my sense of humor.
IT WAS OUR DUTY TO PROTECT HIM!

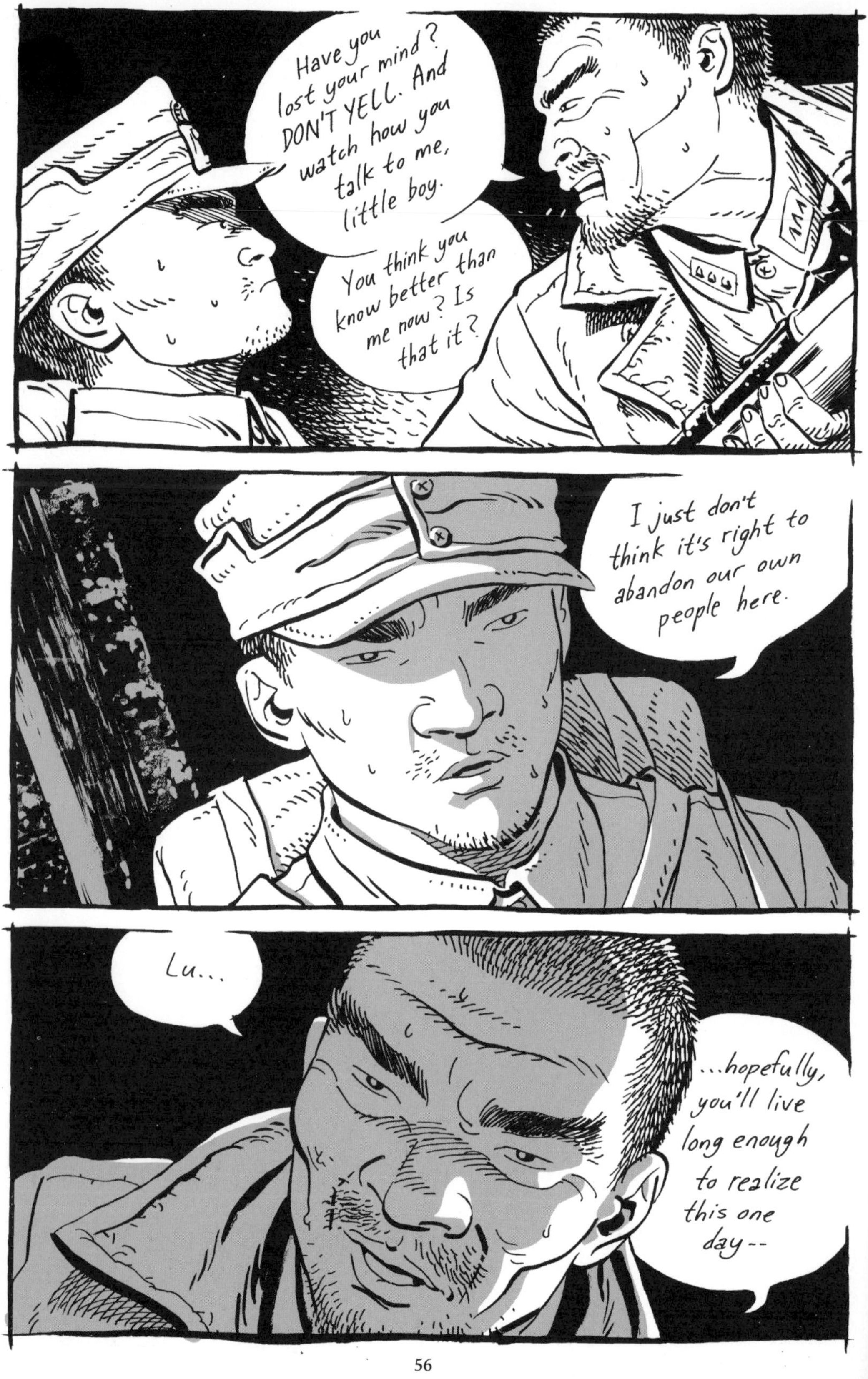
Have you lost your mind? DON'T YELL. And watch how you talk to me, little boy.
You think you know better than me now? Is that it?
I just don't think it's right to abandon our own people here.
Lu...
...hopefully, you'll live long enough to realize this one day--

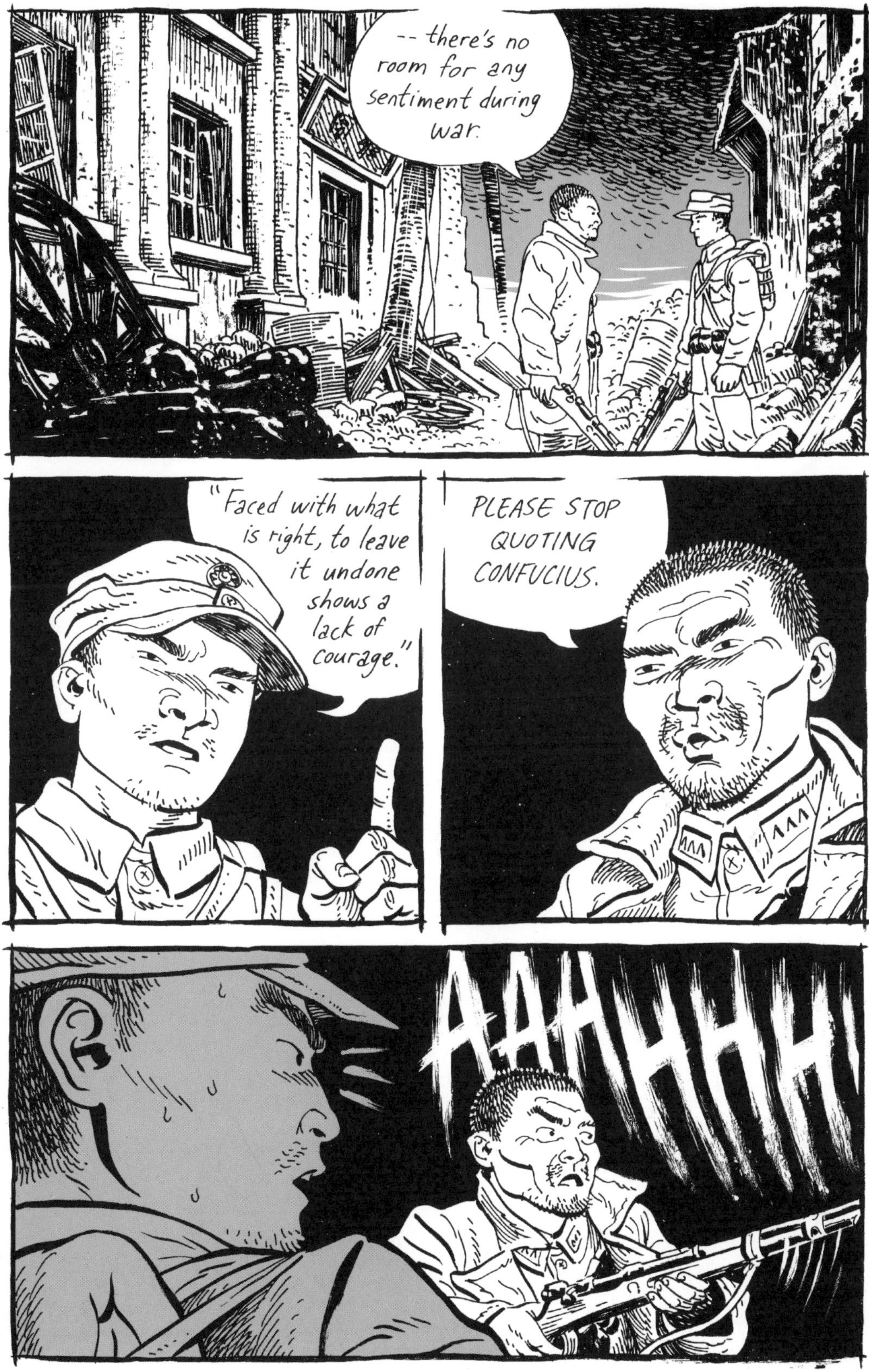
-- there's no room for any sentiment during war.
"Faced with what is right, to leave it undone shows a lack of courage."
PLEASE STOP QUOTING CONFUCIUS.
AAHHHH

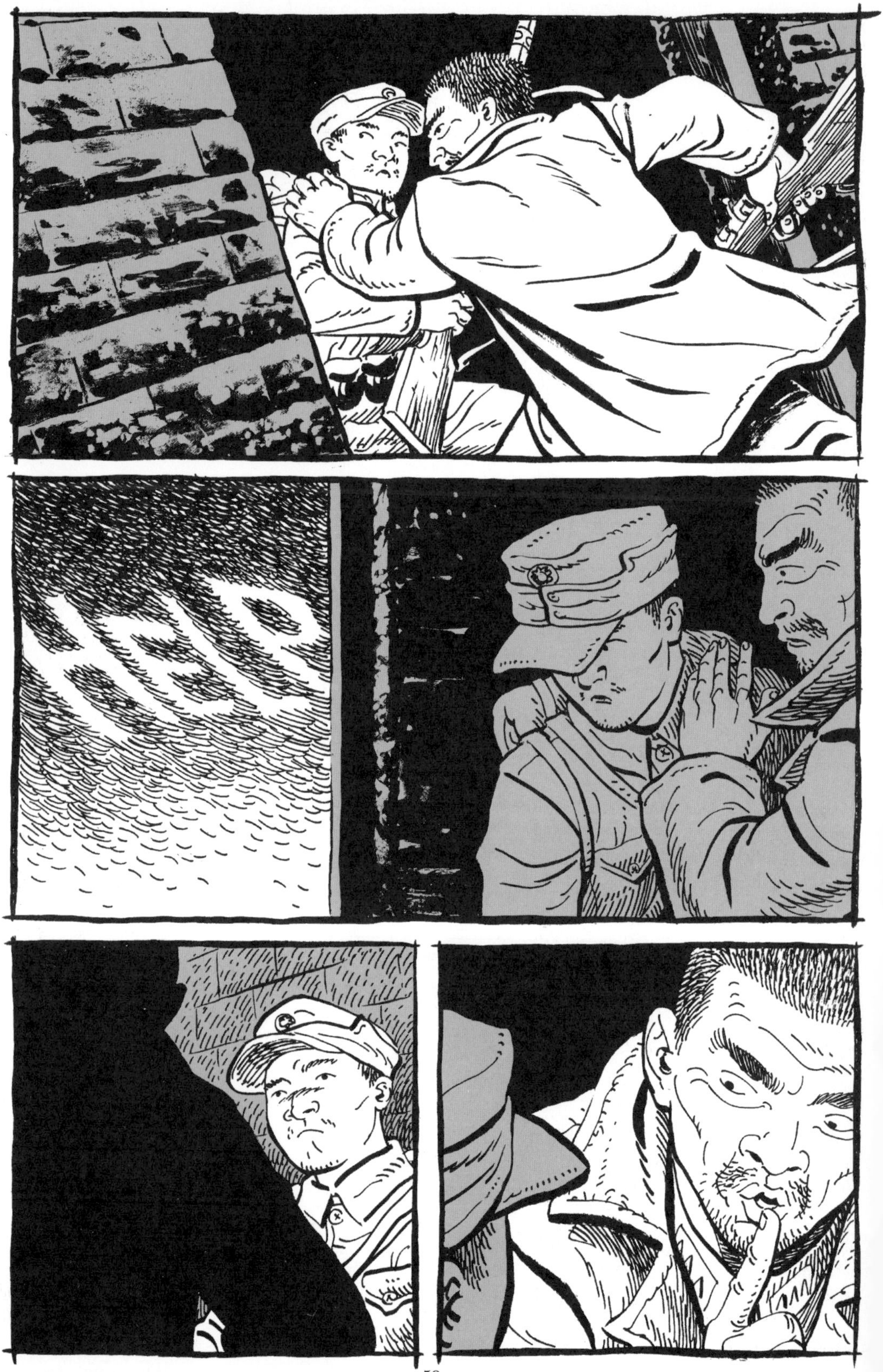

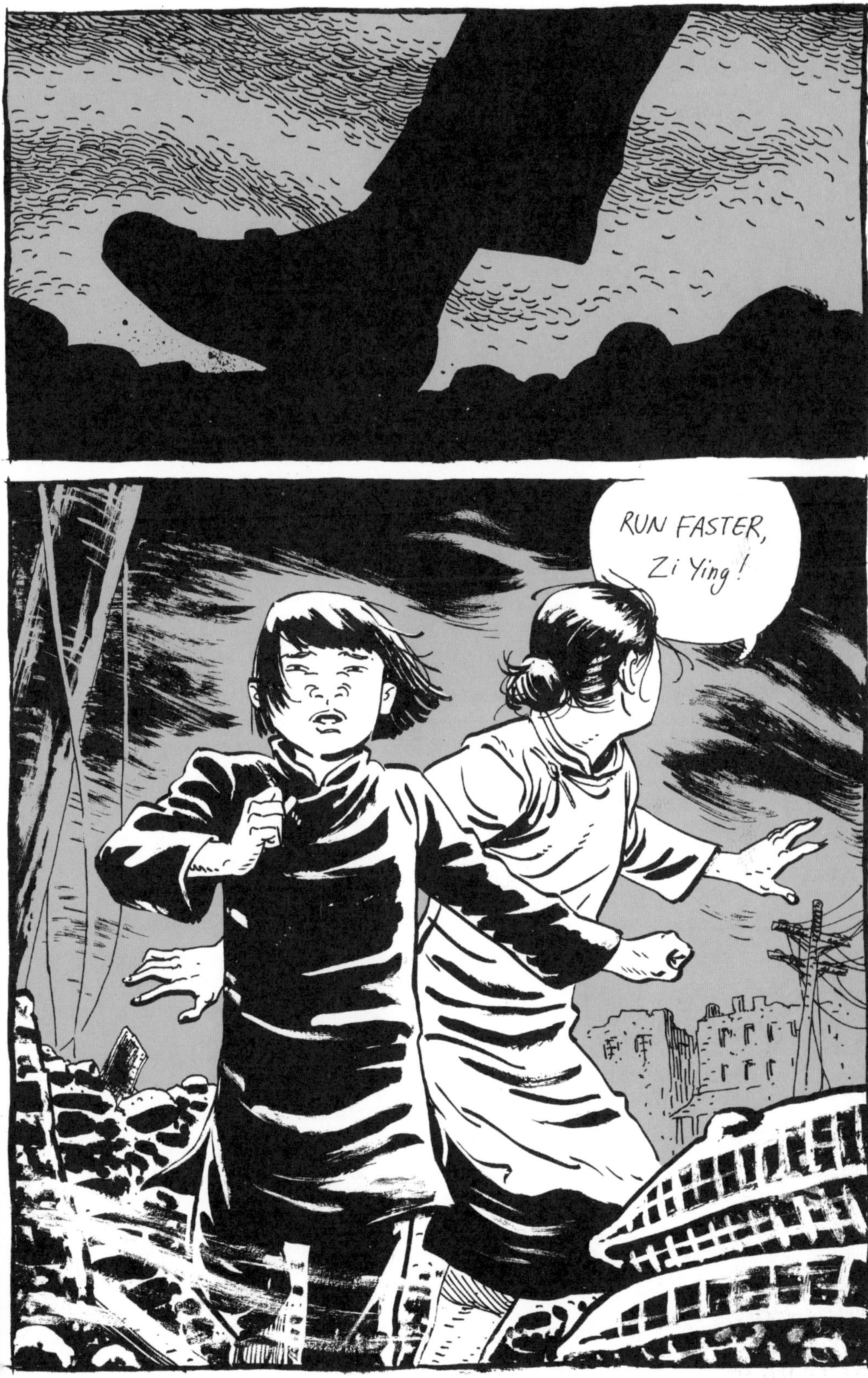
RUN FASTER, Zi Ying!

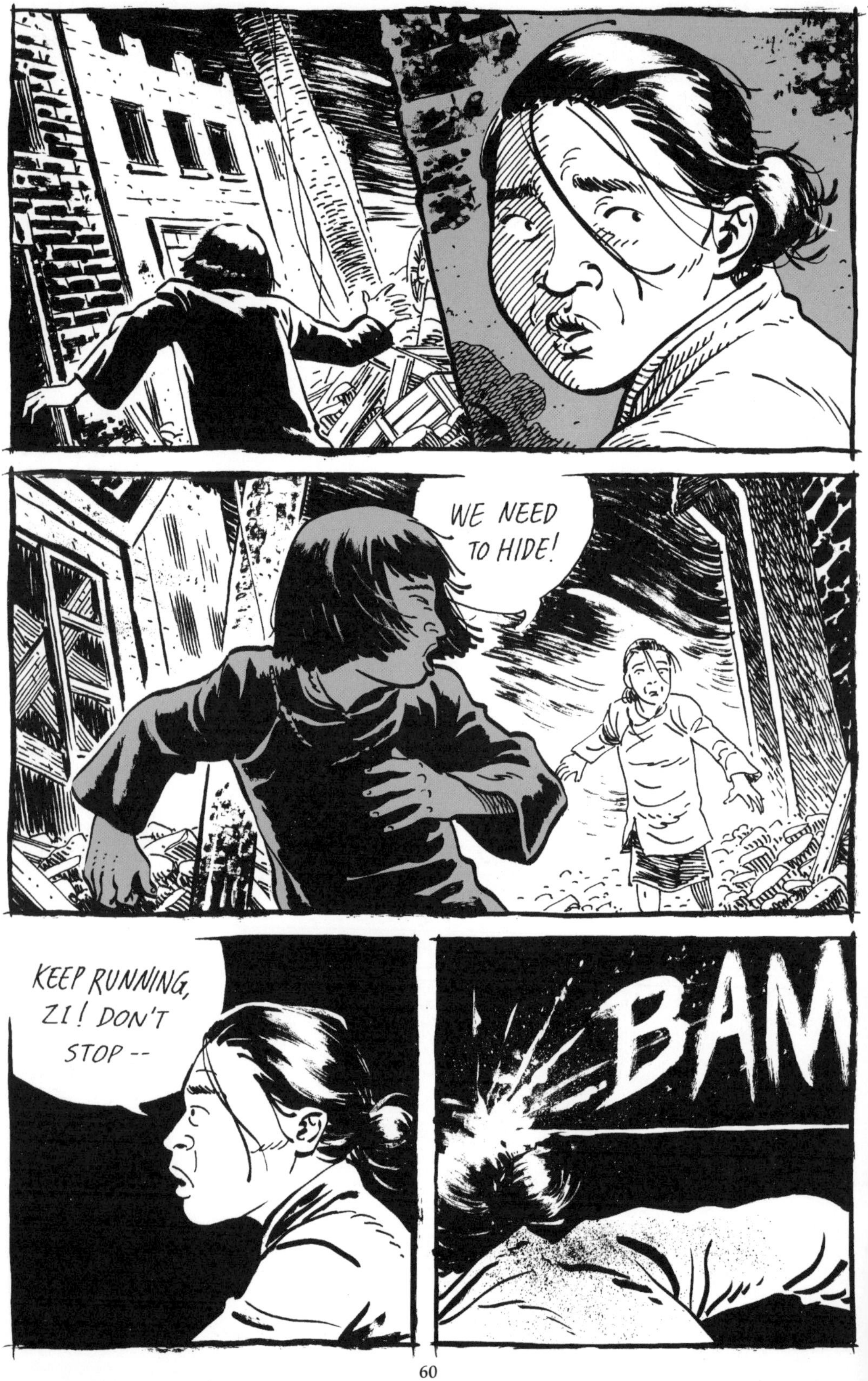
WE NEED TO HIDE!
KEEP RUNNING, ZI! DON'T STOP --
BAM

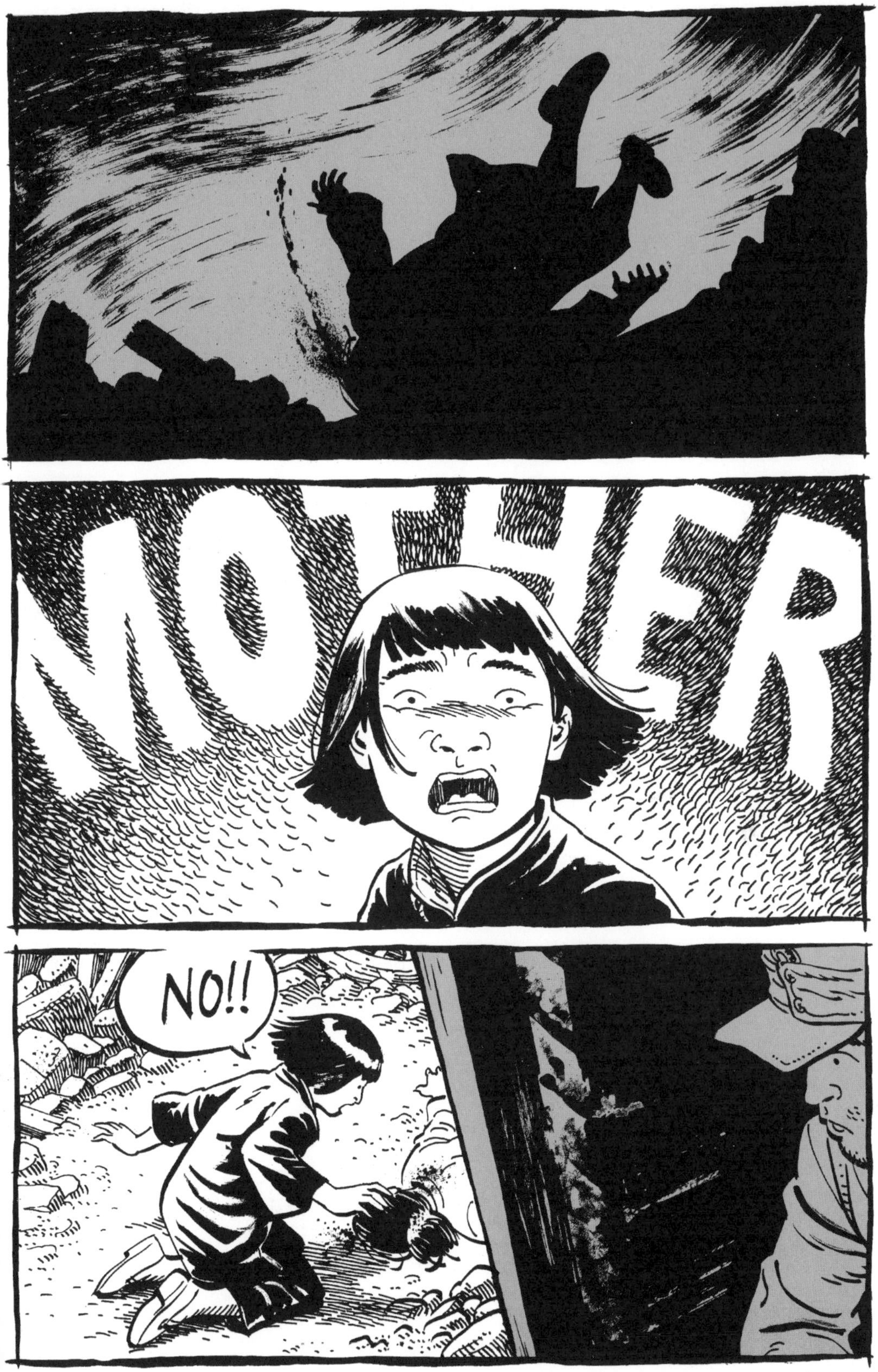
MOTHER
NO!!

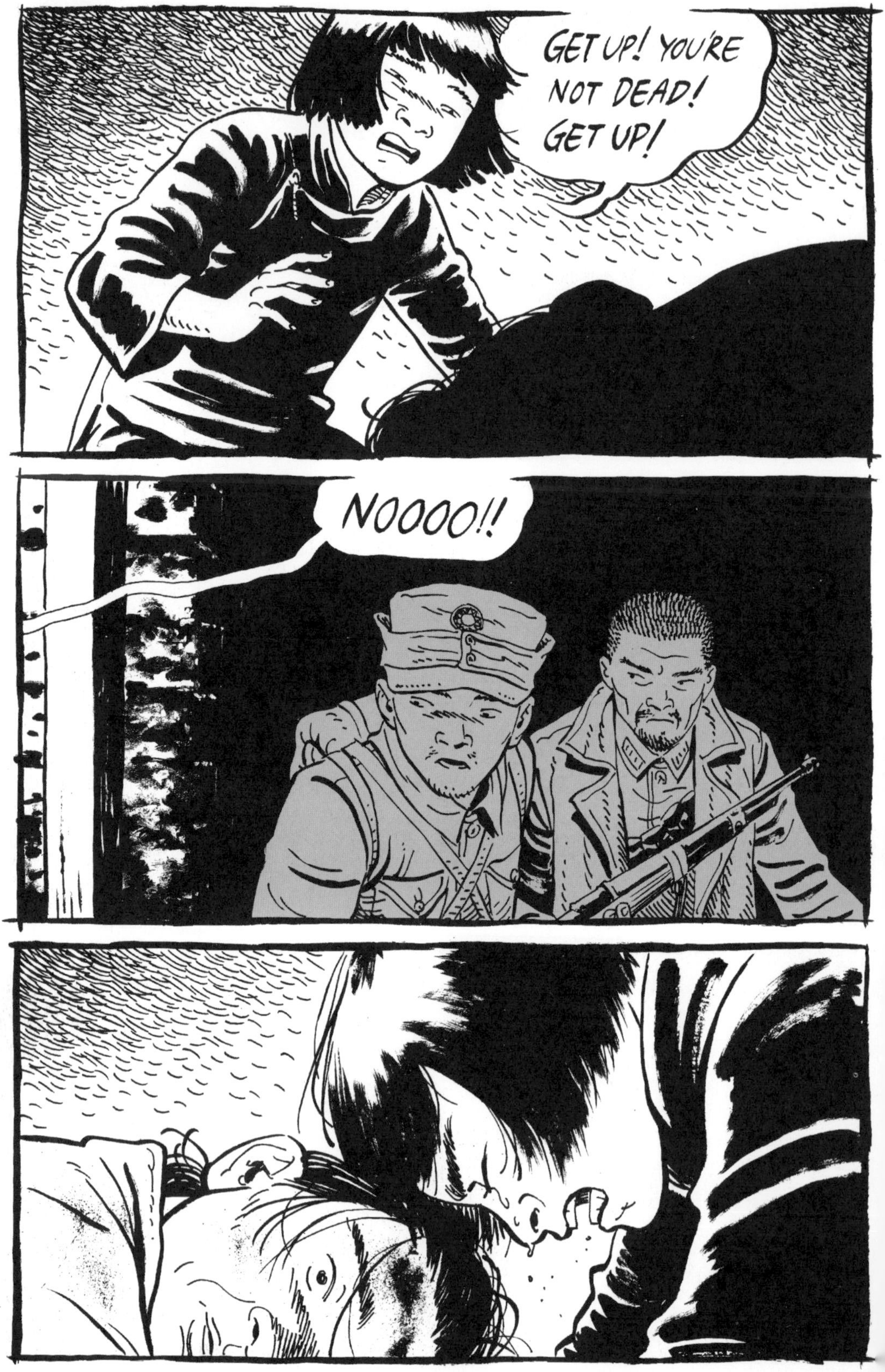
GET UP! YOU'RE NOT DEAD! GET UP!
NOOOO!!

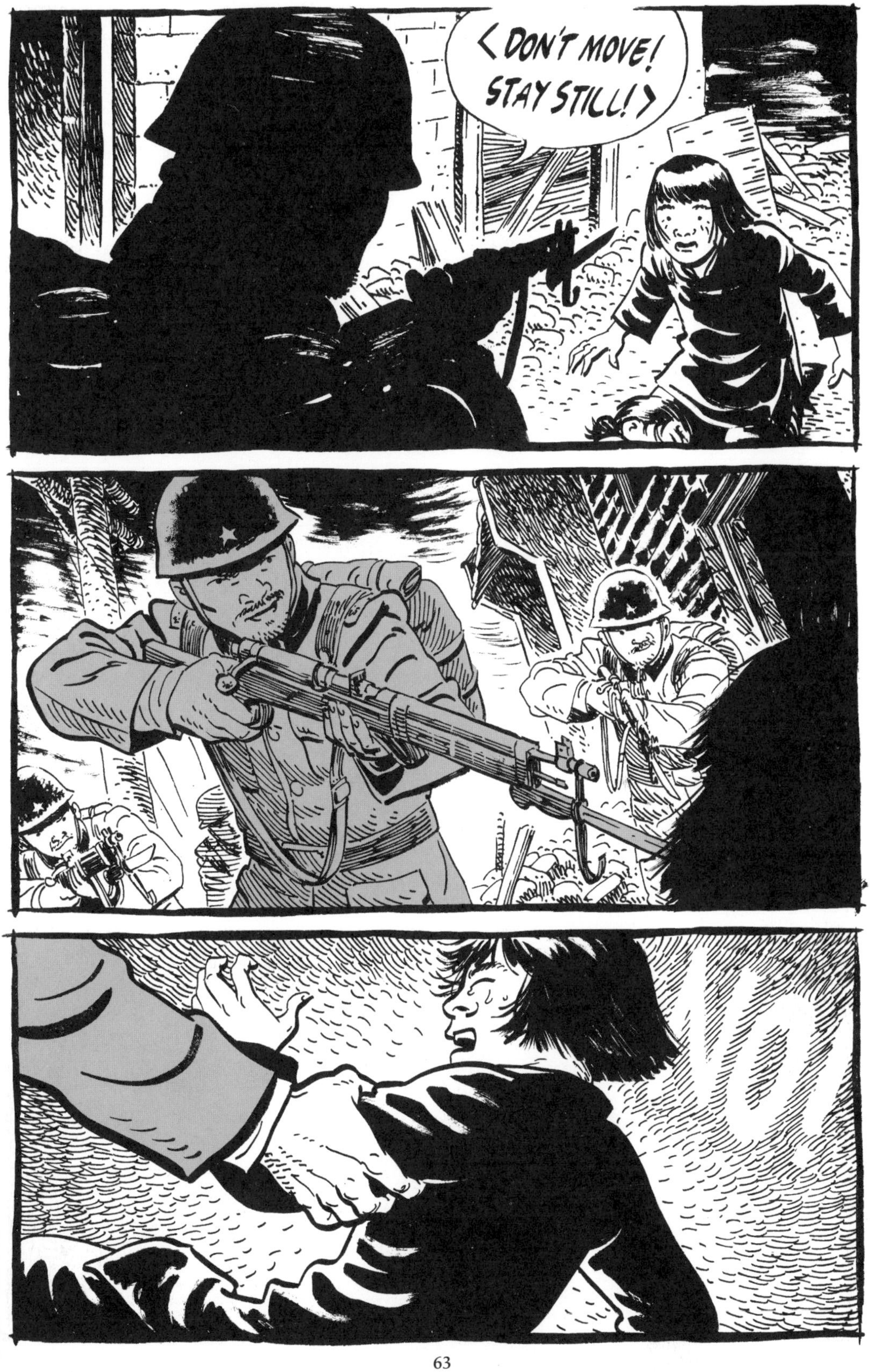
<DON'T MOVE! STAY STILL!>

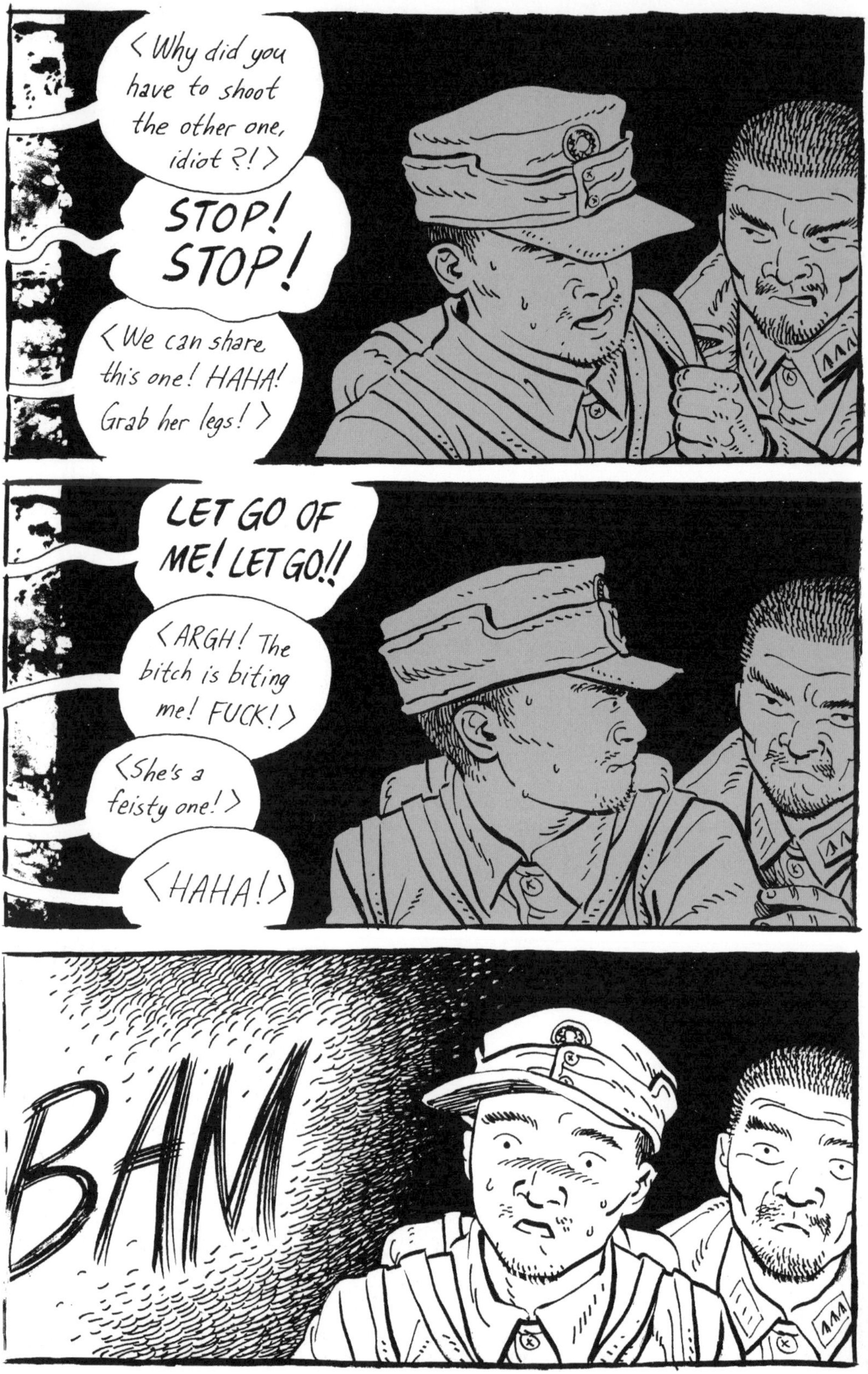

< Why did you have to shoot the other one, idiot ?! >
STOP! STOP!
< We can share this one! HAHA! Grab her legs! >
LET GO OF ME! LET GO!!
< ARGH! The bitch is biting me! FUCK! >
< She's a feisty one! >
< HAHA! >
BAM

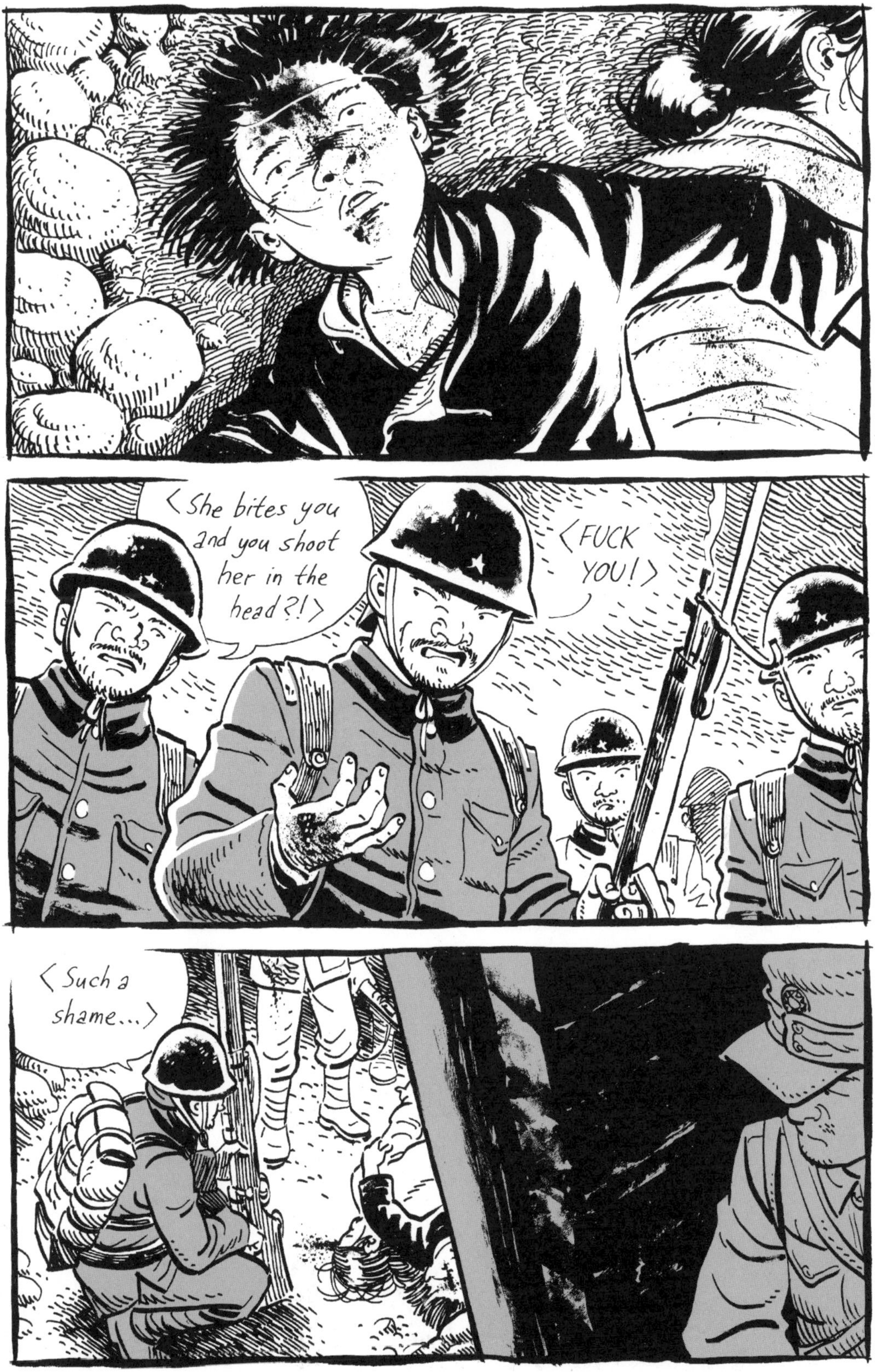

< She bites you and you shoot her in the head?! >
< FUCK YOU! >
< Such a shame... >

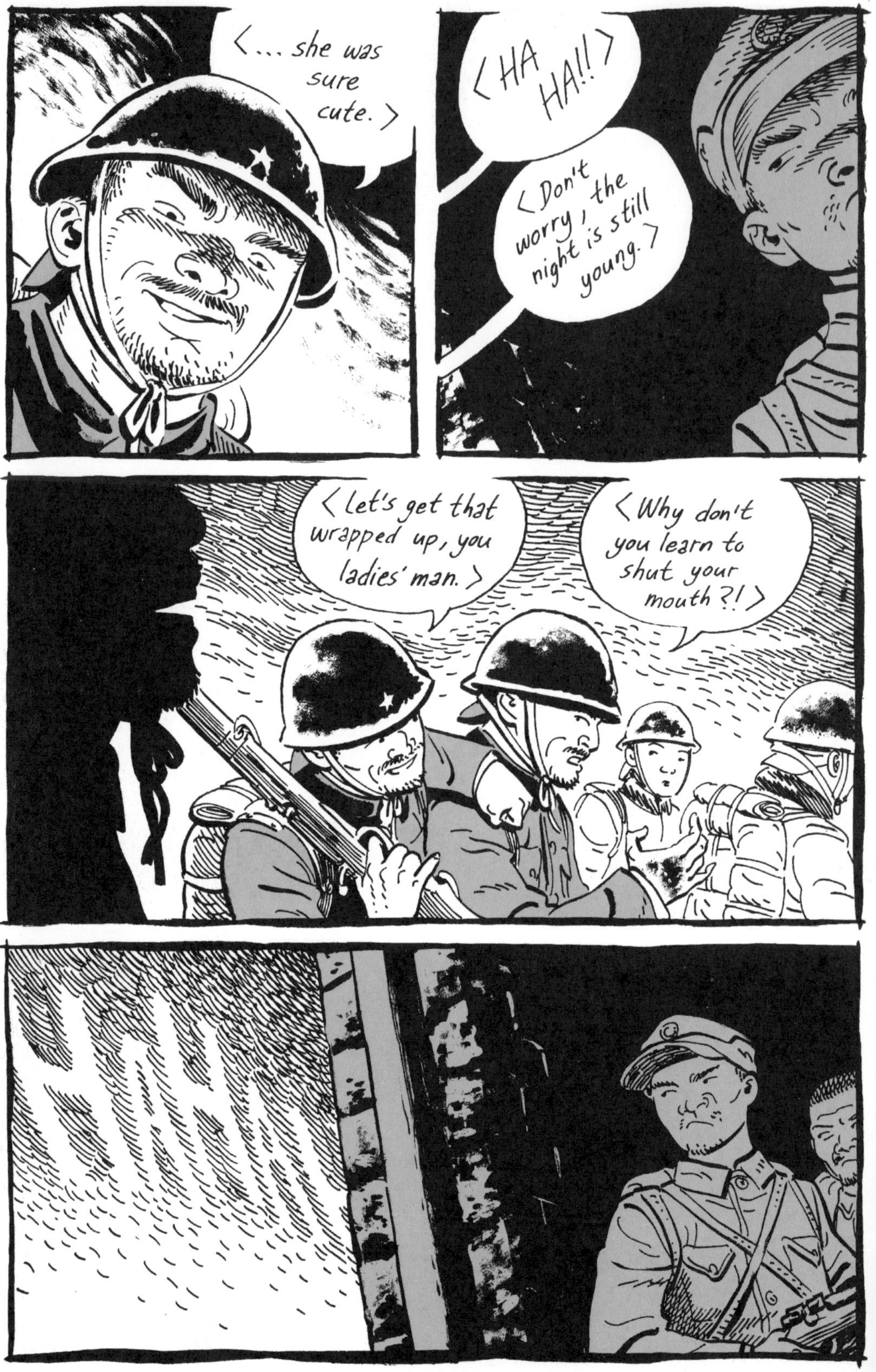

<... she was sure cute.>
<HA HA!!>
<Don't worry, the night is still young.>
<Let's get that wrapped up, you ladies' man.>
<Why don't you learn to shut your mouth?!>

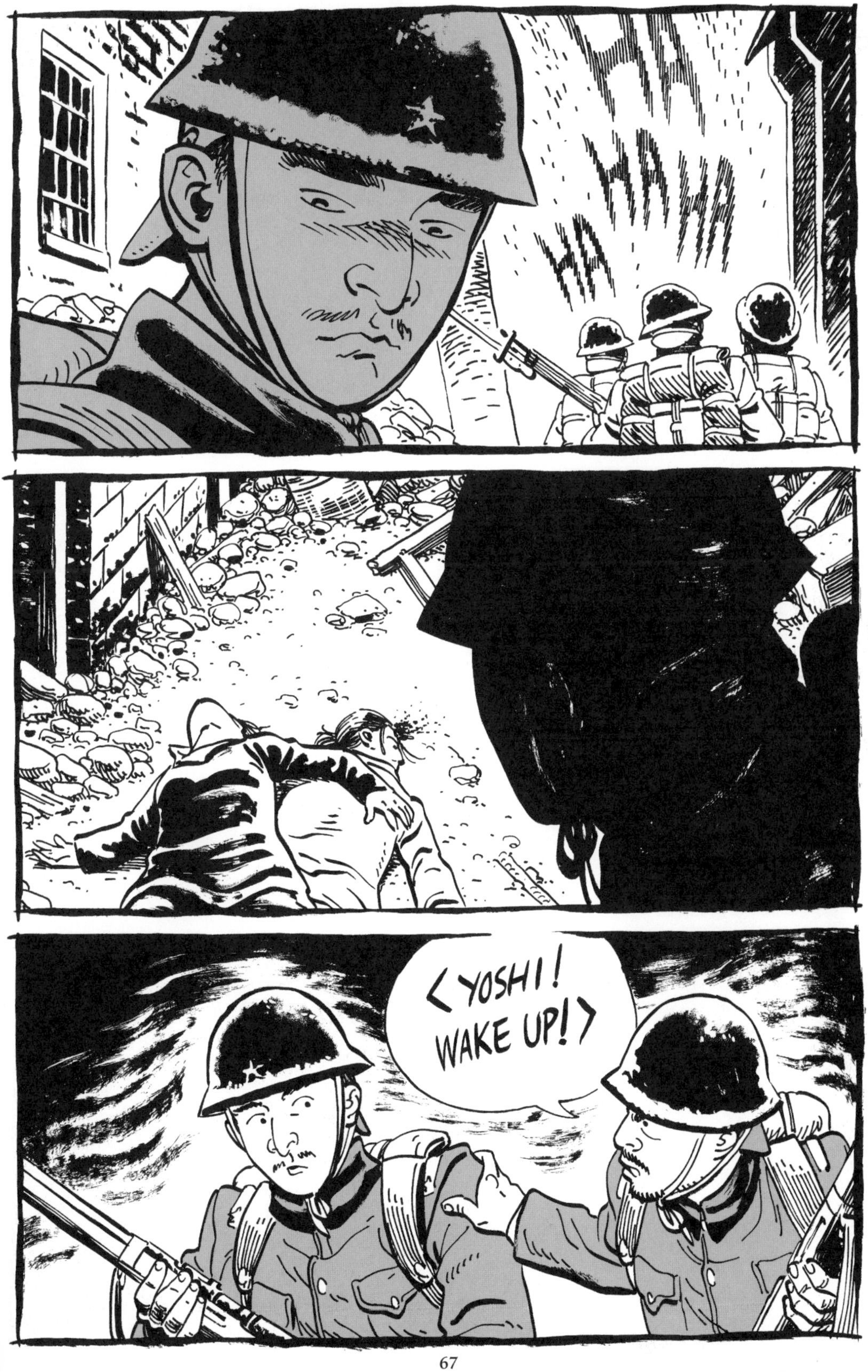
HA HA HA HA HA
<YOSHI! WAKE UP!>

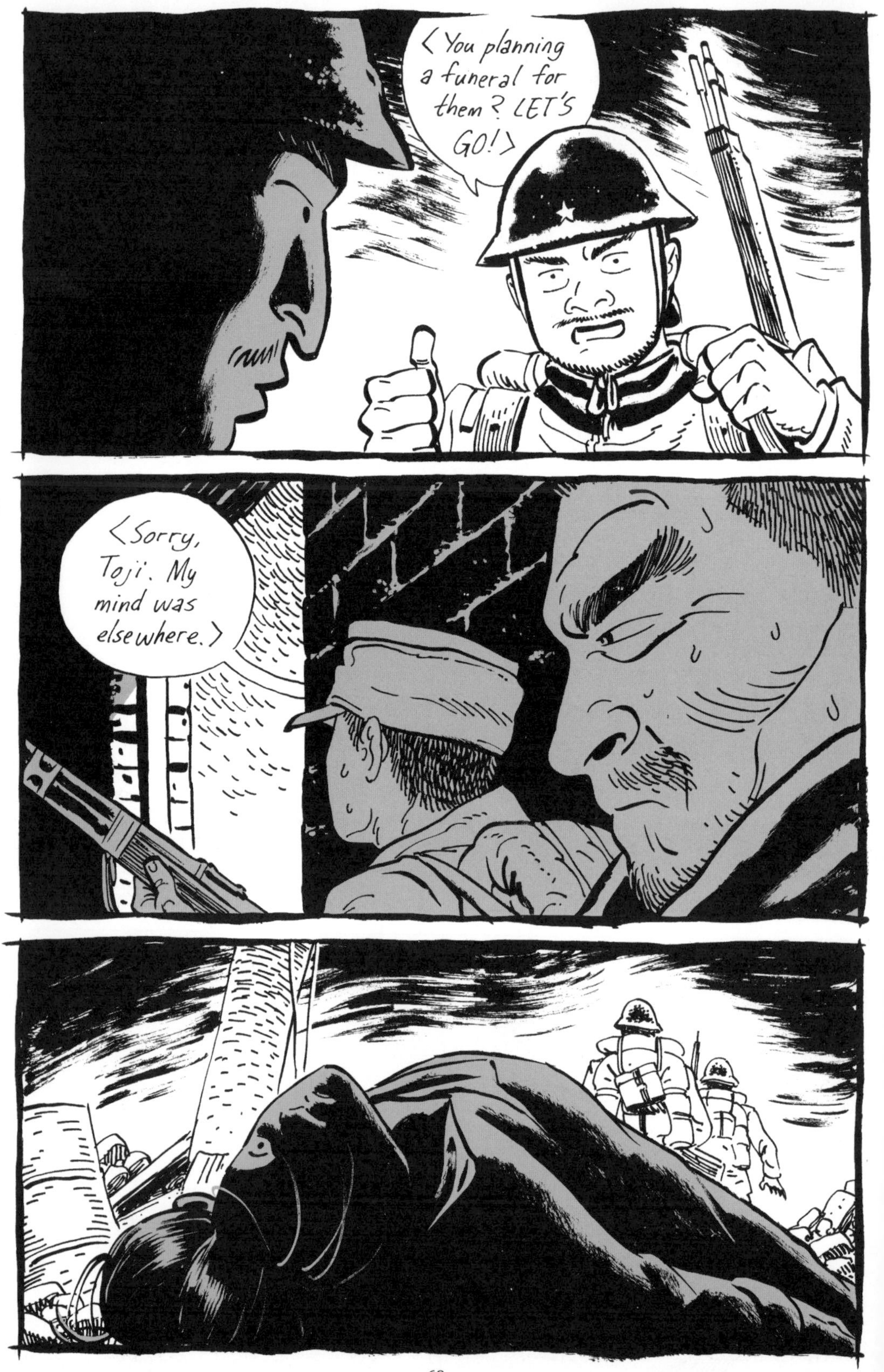
<You planning a funeral for them? LET'S GO!>
<Sorry, Toji. My mind was elsewhere.>

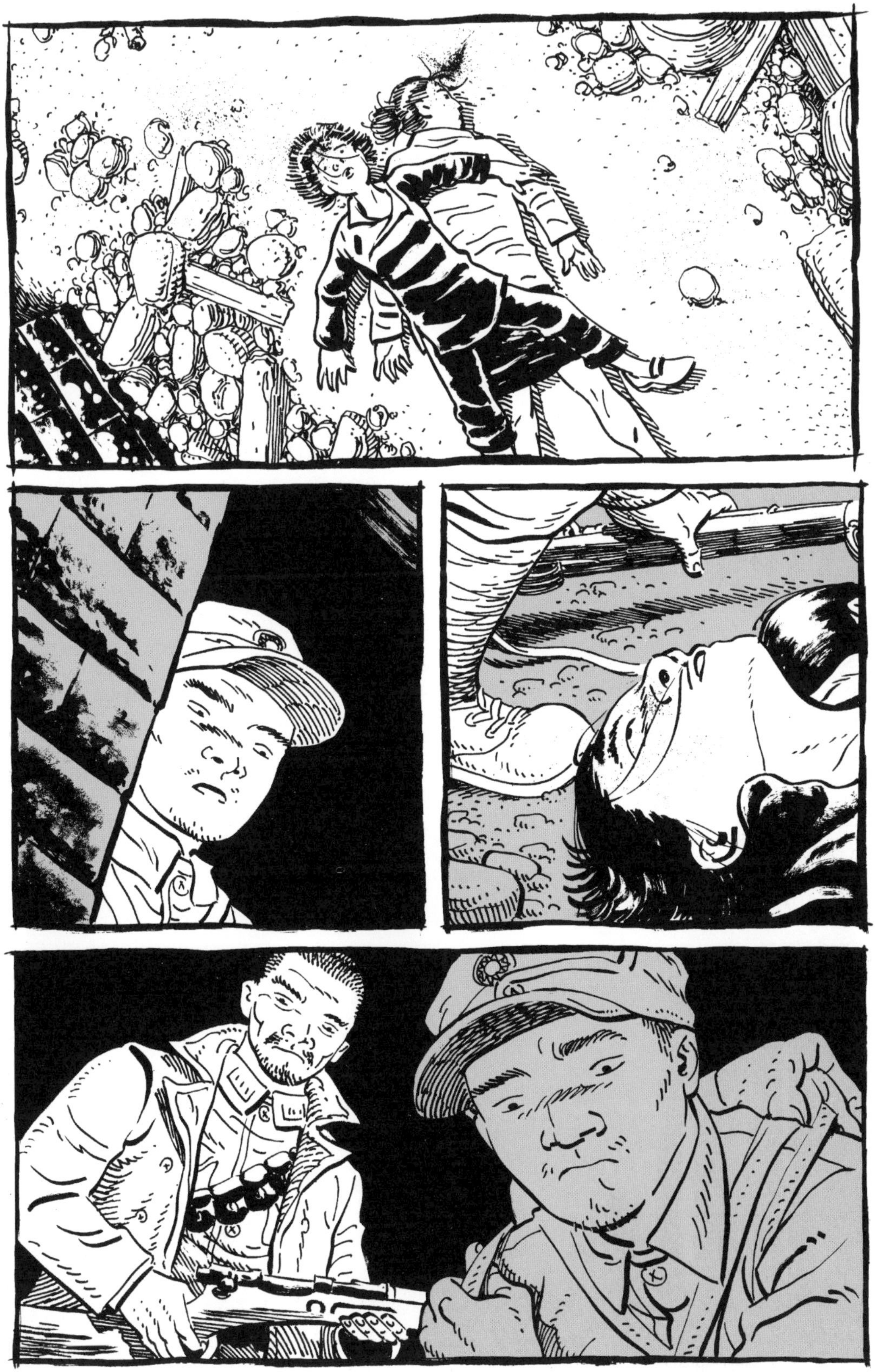

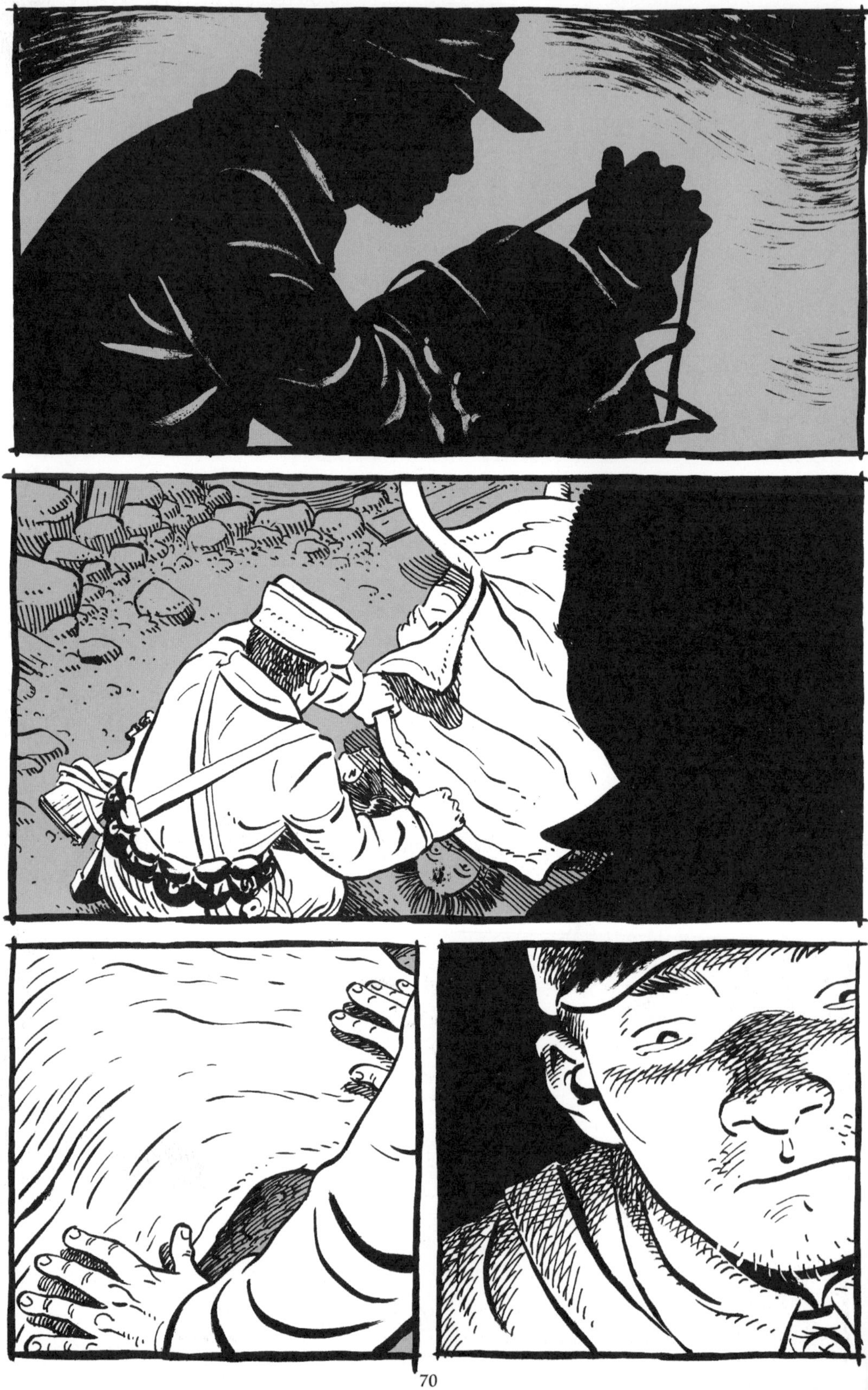

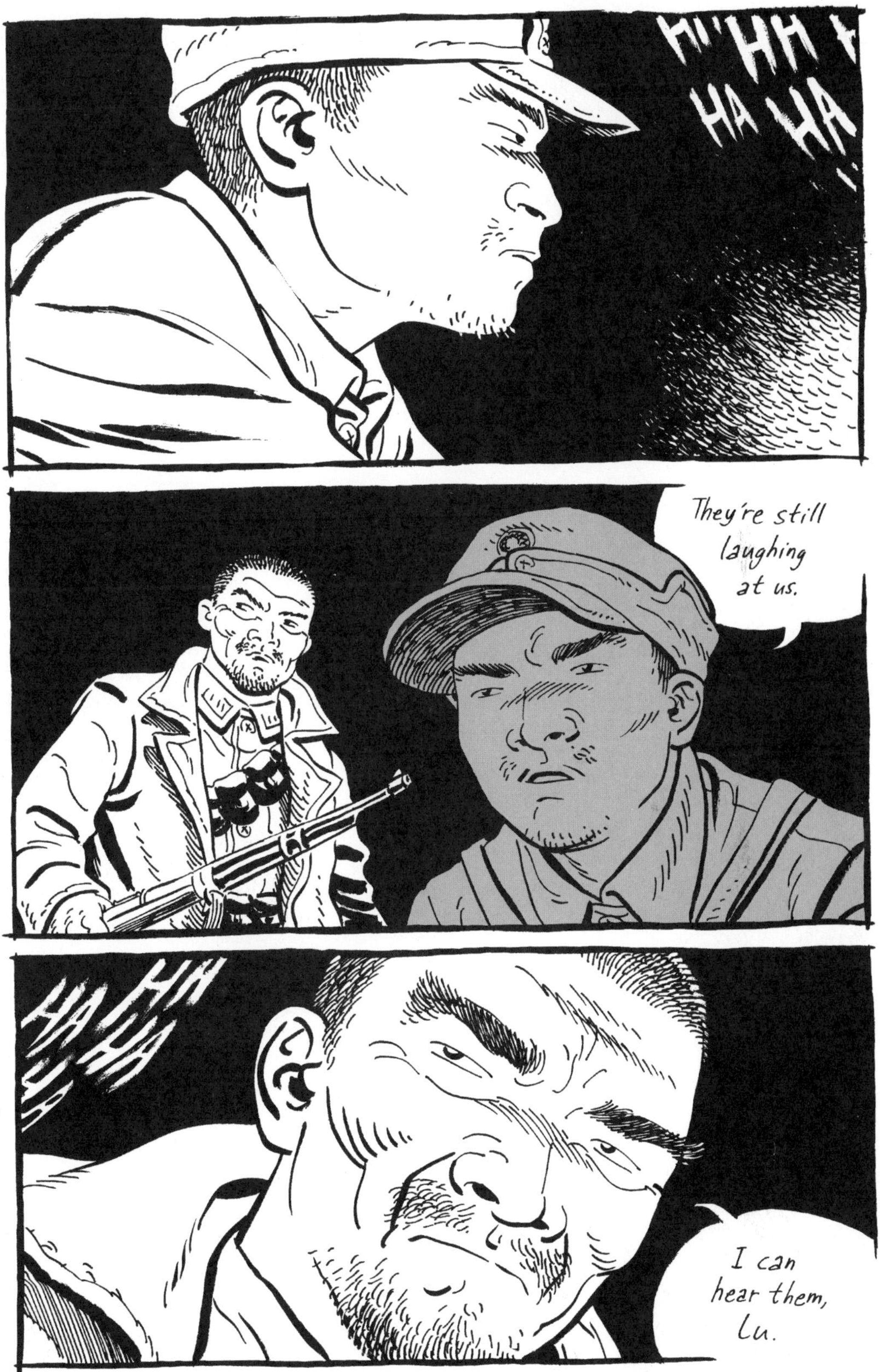
They're still laughing at us.
I can hear them, Lu.

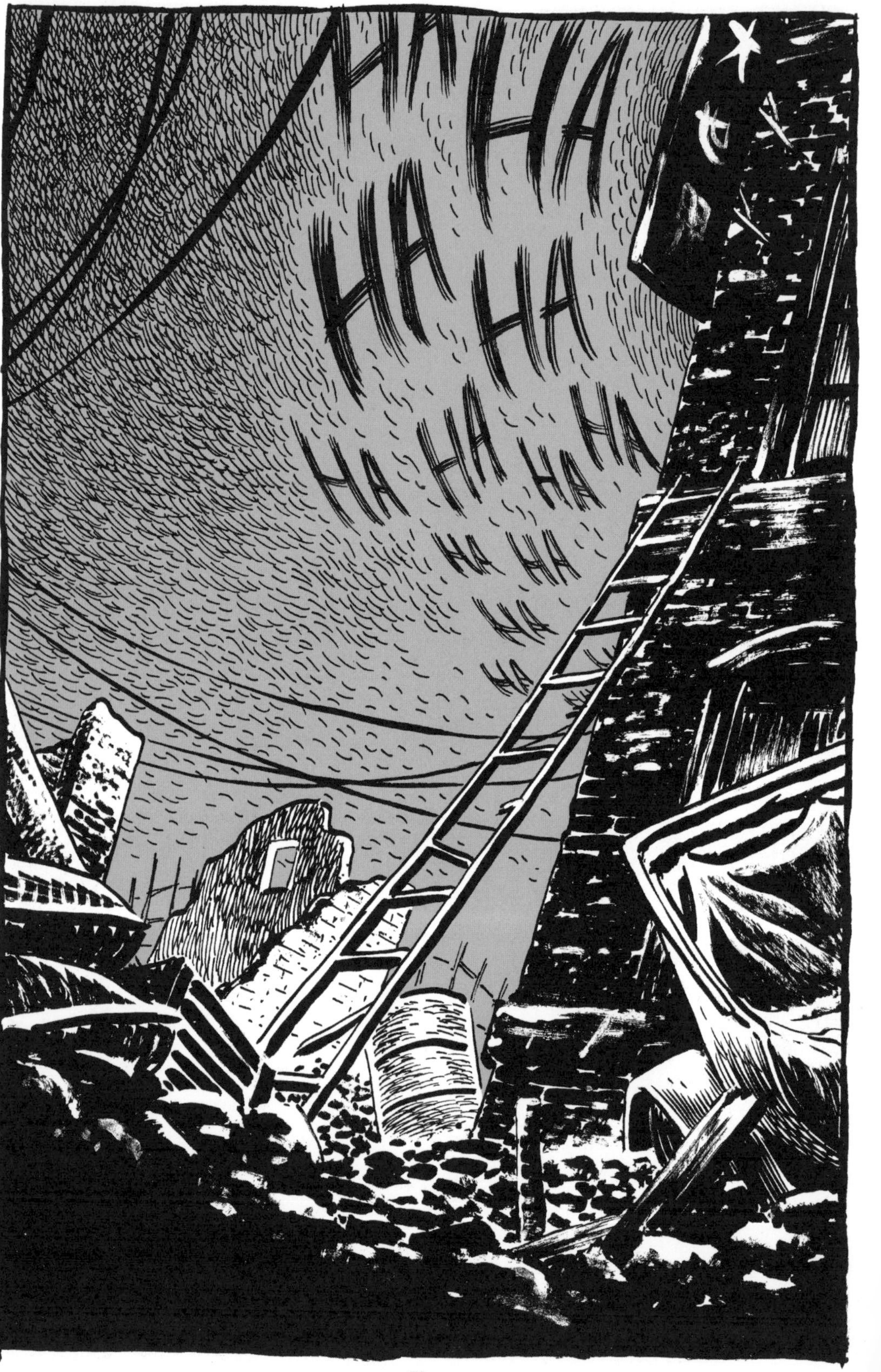
HA HA
HA HA
HA HA HA HA
HA HA
HA
HA

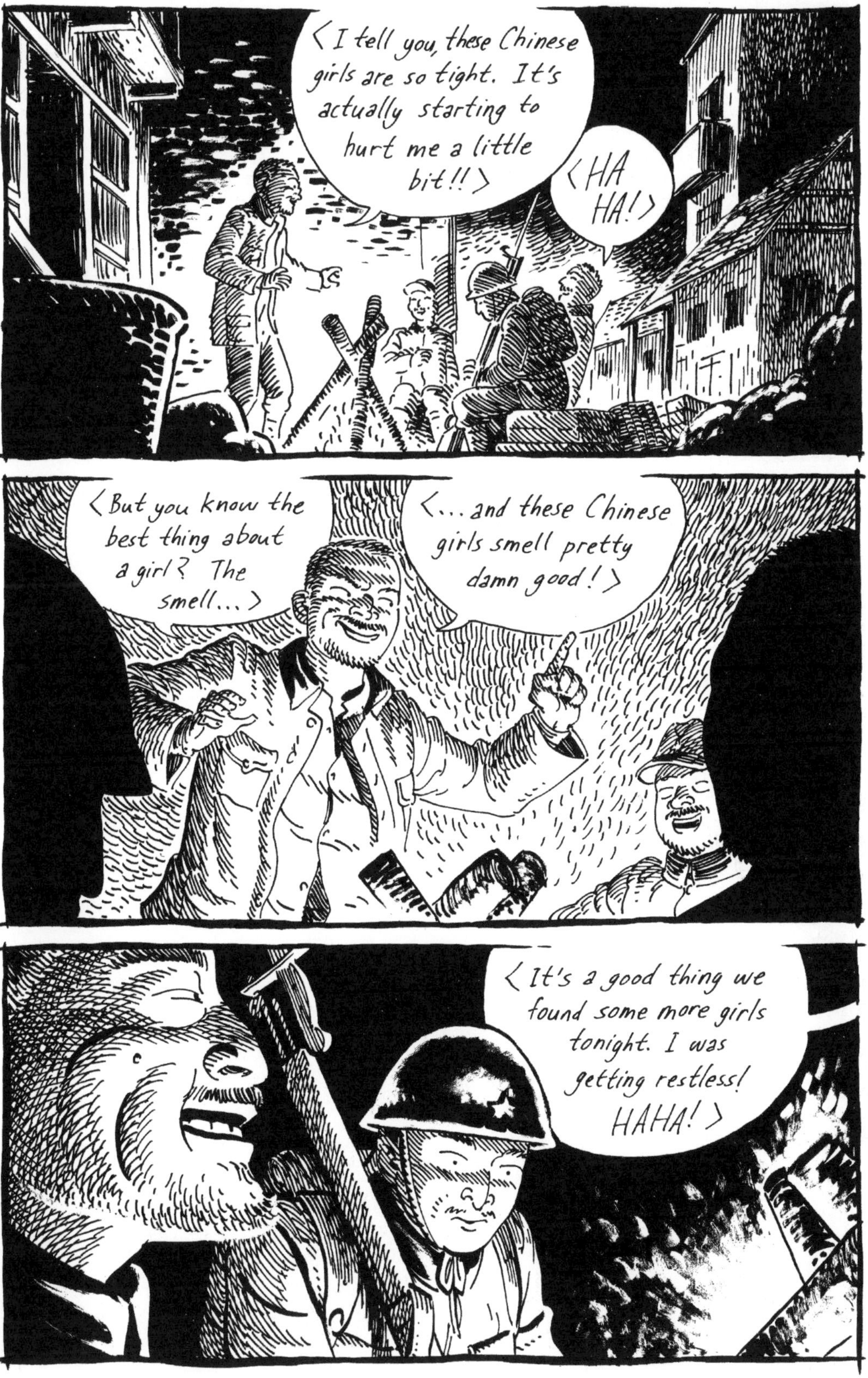
<I tell you, these Chinese girls are so tight. It's actually starting to hurt me a little bit!!>
<HA HA!>
<But you know the best thing about a girl? The smell...>
<...and these Chinese girls smell pretty damn good!>
<It's a good thing we found some more girls tonight. I was getting restless! HAHA!>

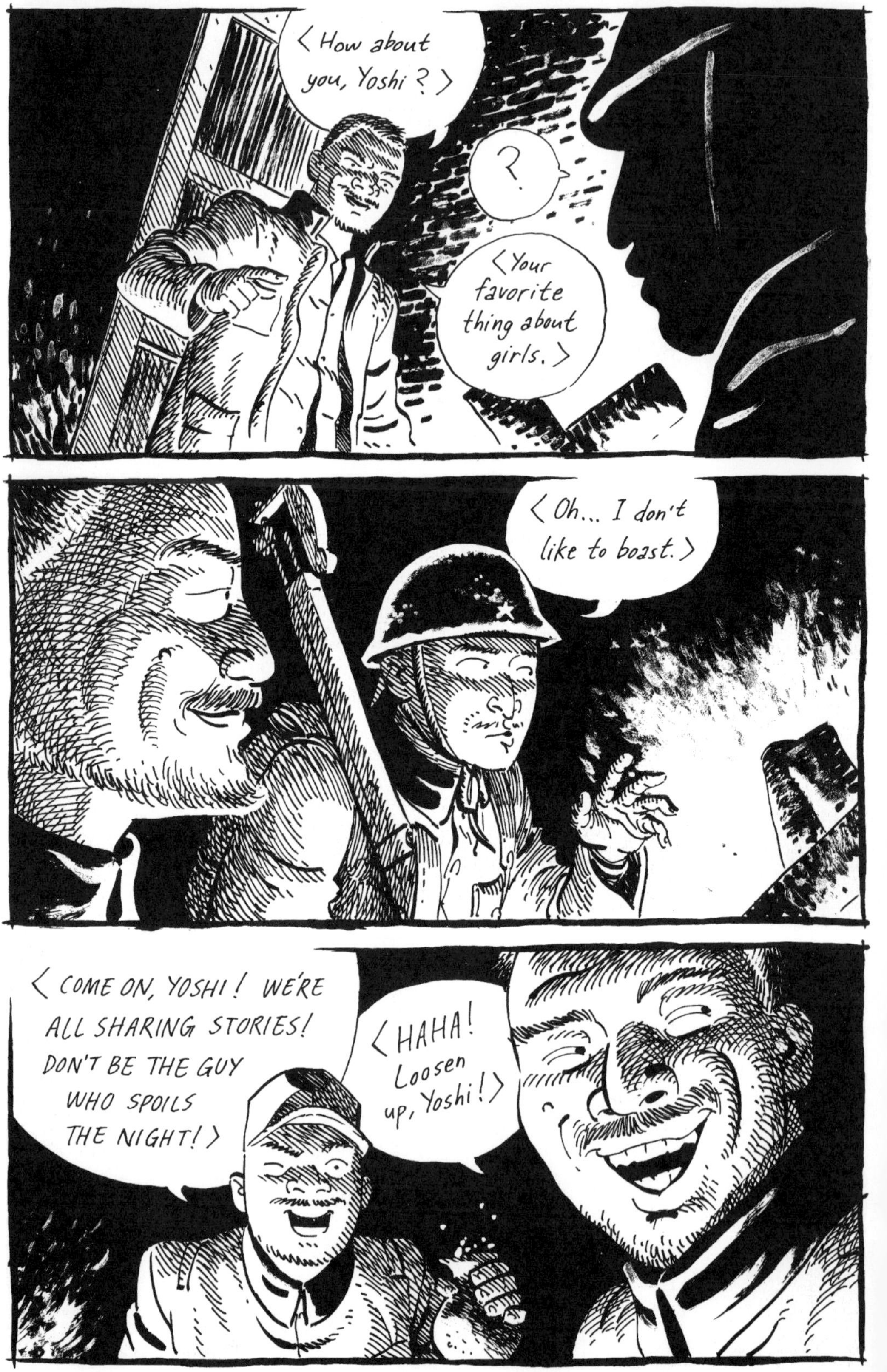
< How about you, Yoshi? >
?
< Your favorite thing about girls. >
< Oh... I don't like to boast. >
< COME ON, YOSHI! WE'RE ALL SHARING STORIES! DON'T BE THE GUY WHO SPOILS THE NIGHT! >
< HAHA! Loosen up, Yoshi! >

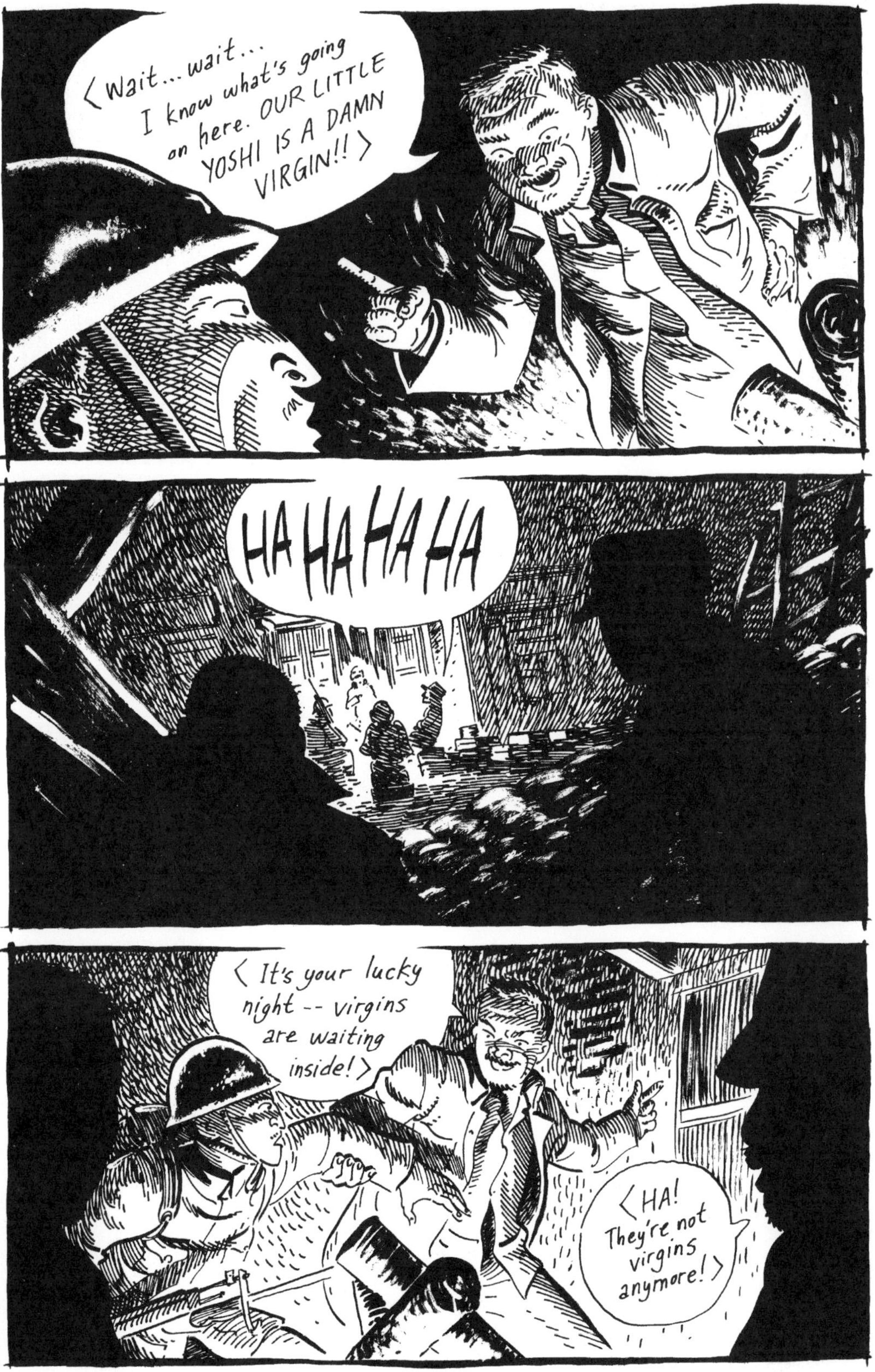
<Wait... wait... I know what's going on here. OUR LITTLE YOSHI IS A DAMN VIRGIN!!>
HA HA HA HA HA
<It's your lucky night -- virgins are waiting inside!>
<HA! They're not virgins anymore!>

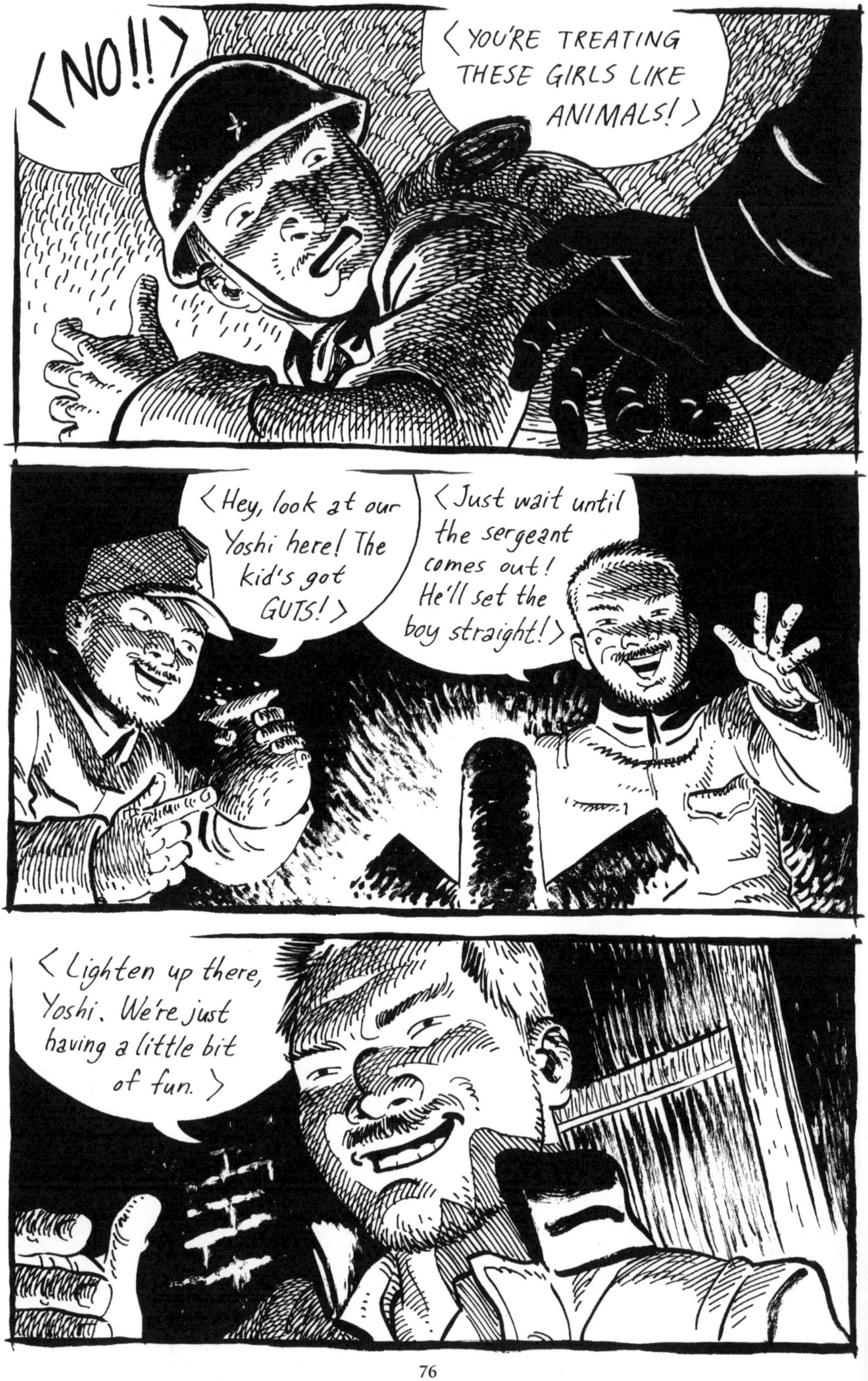
<NO!!>
<YOU'RE TREATING THESE GIRLS LIKE ANIMALS!>
<Hey, look at our Yoshi here! The kid's got GUTS!>
<Just wait until the sergeant comes out! He'll set the boy straight!>
<Lighten up there, Yoshi. We're just having a little bit of fun.>

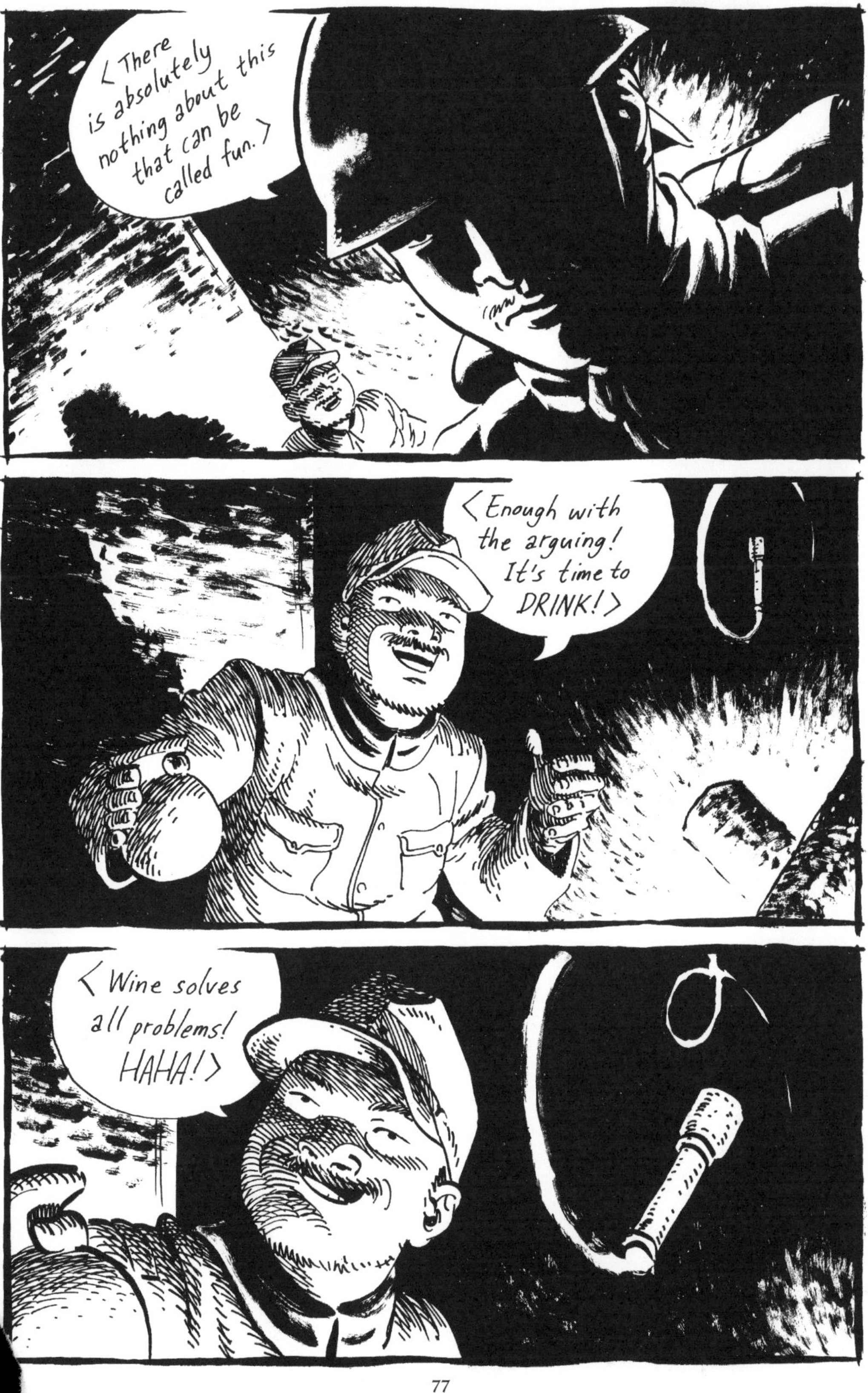
< There is absolutely nothing about this that can be called fun. >
< Enough with the arguing! It's time to DRINK! >
< Wine solves all problems! HAHA! >

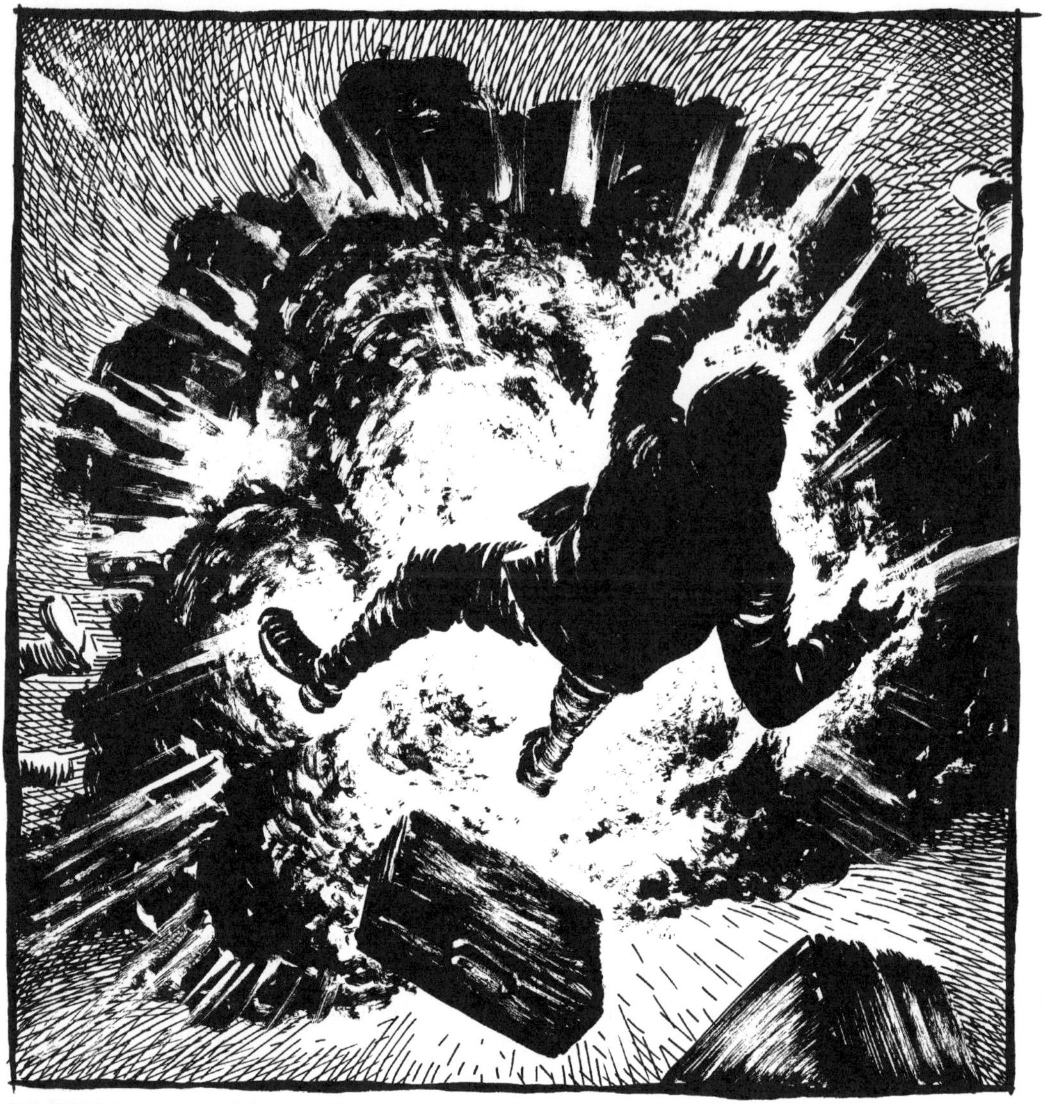

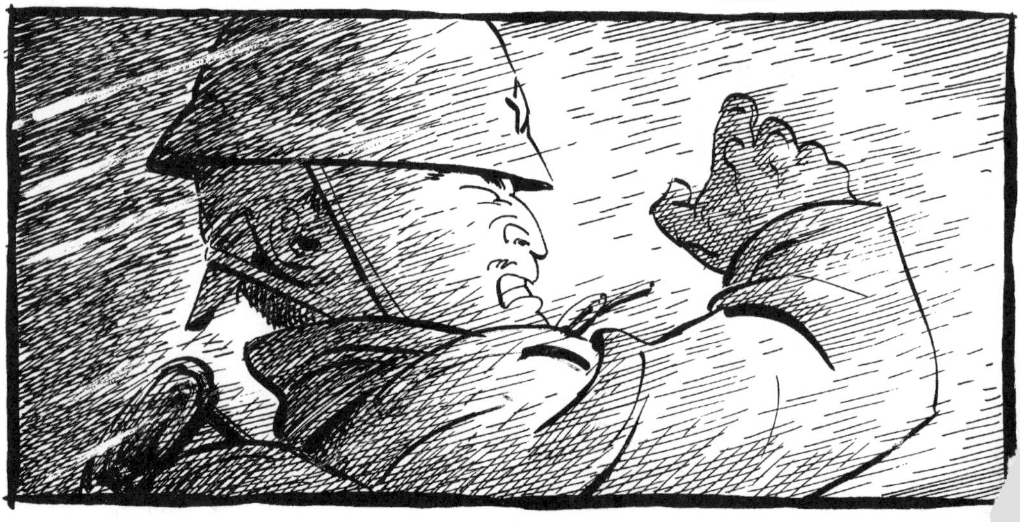

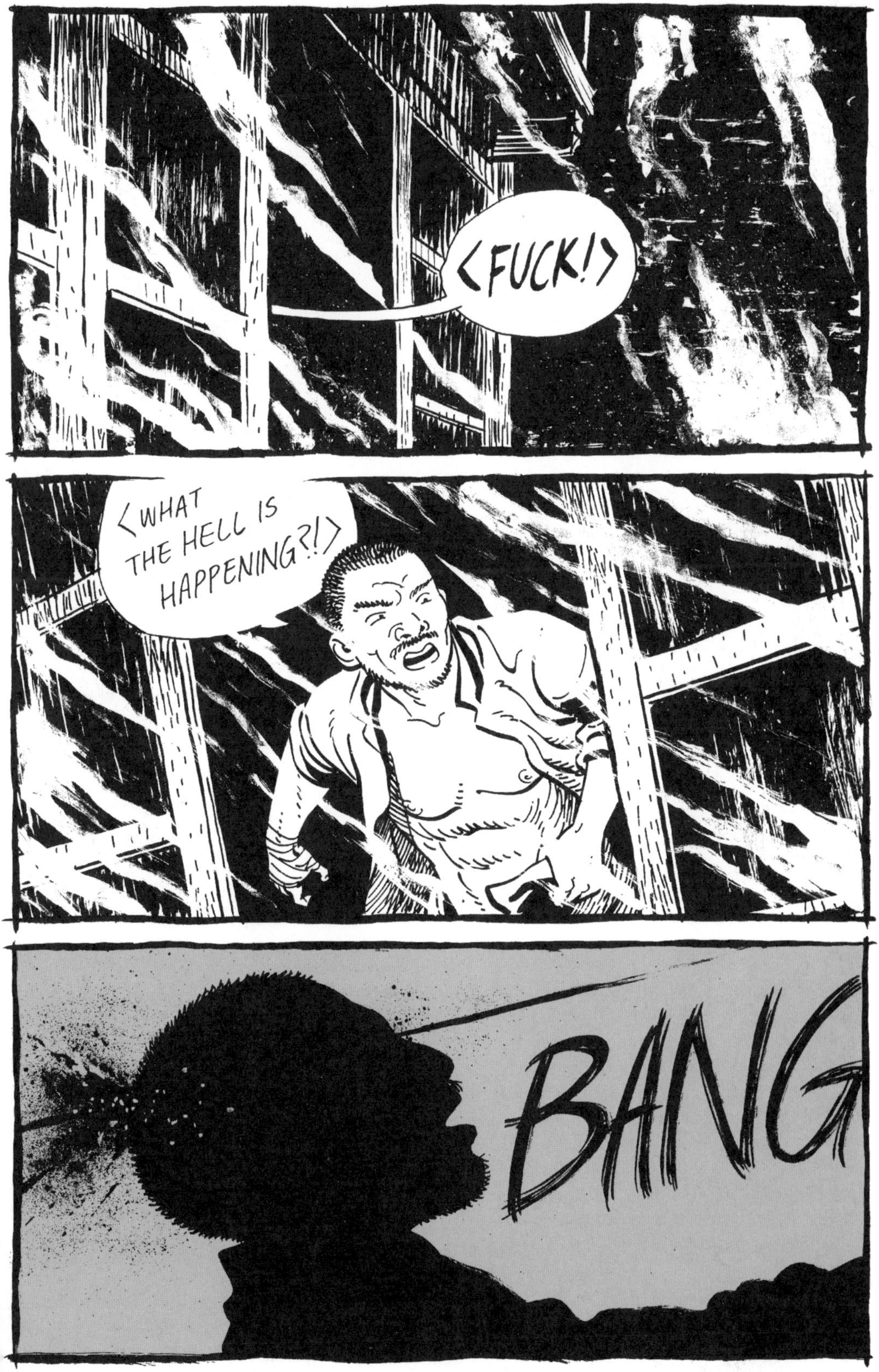
<FUCK!>
<WHAT THE HELL IS HAPPENING?!>
BANG

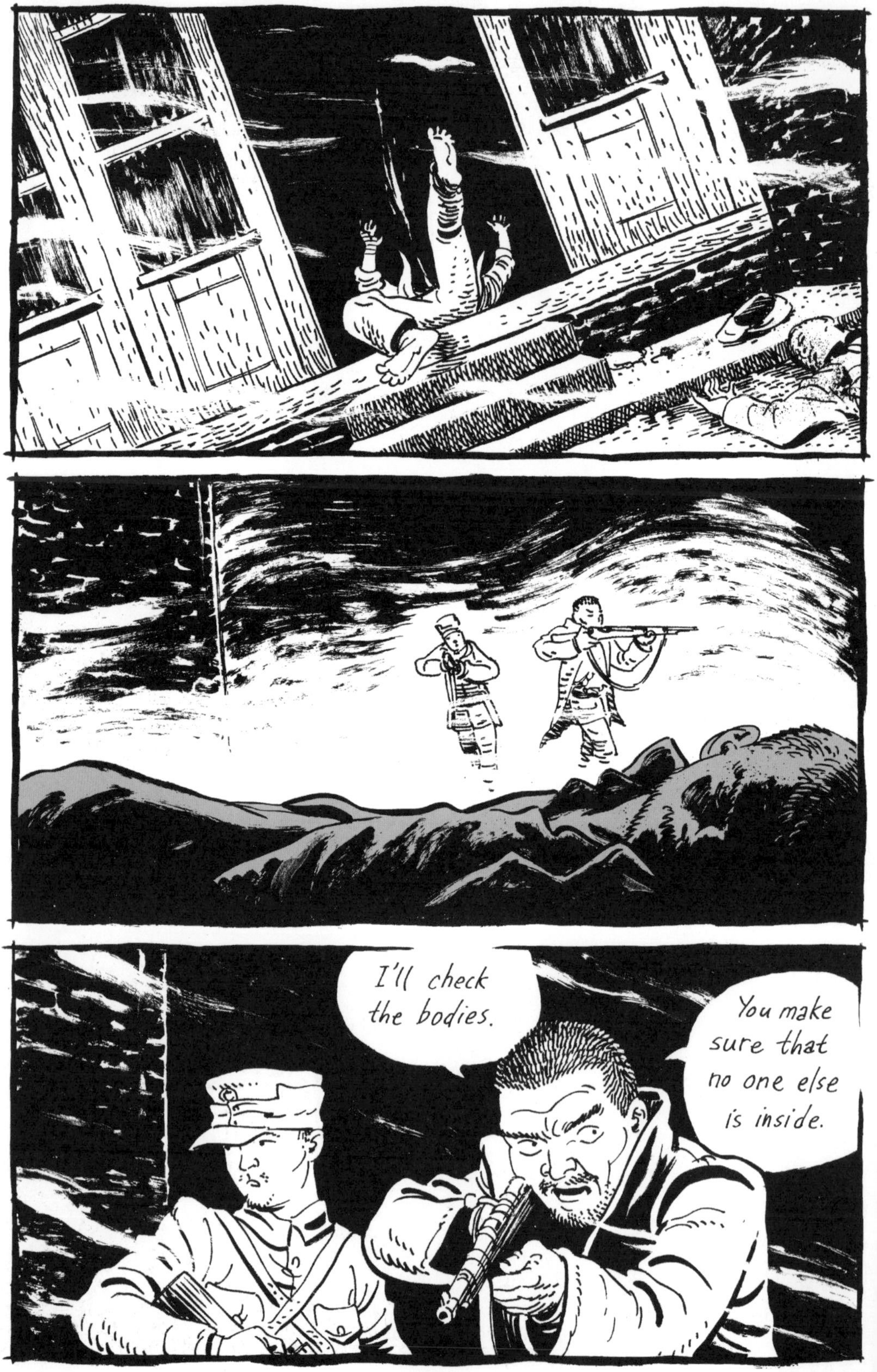
I'll check the bodies.
You make sure that no one else is inside.

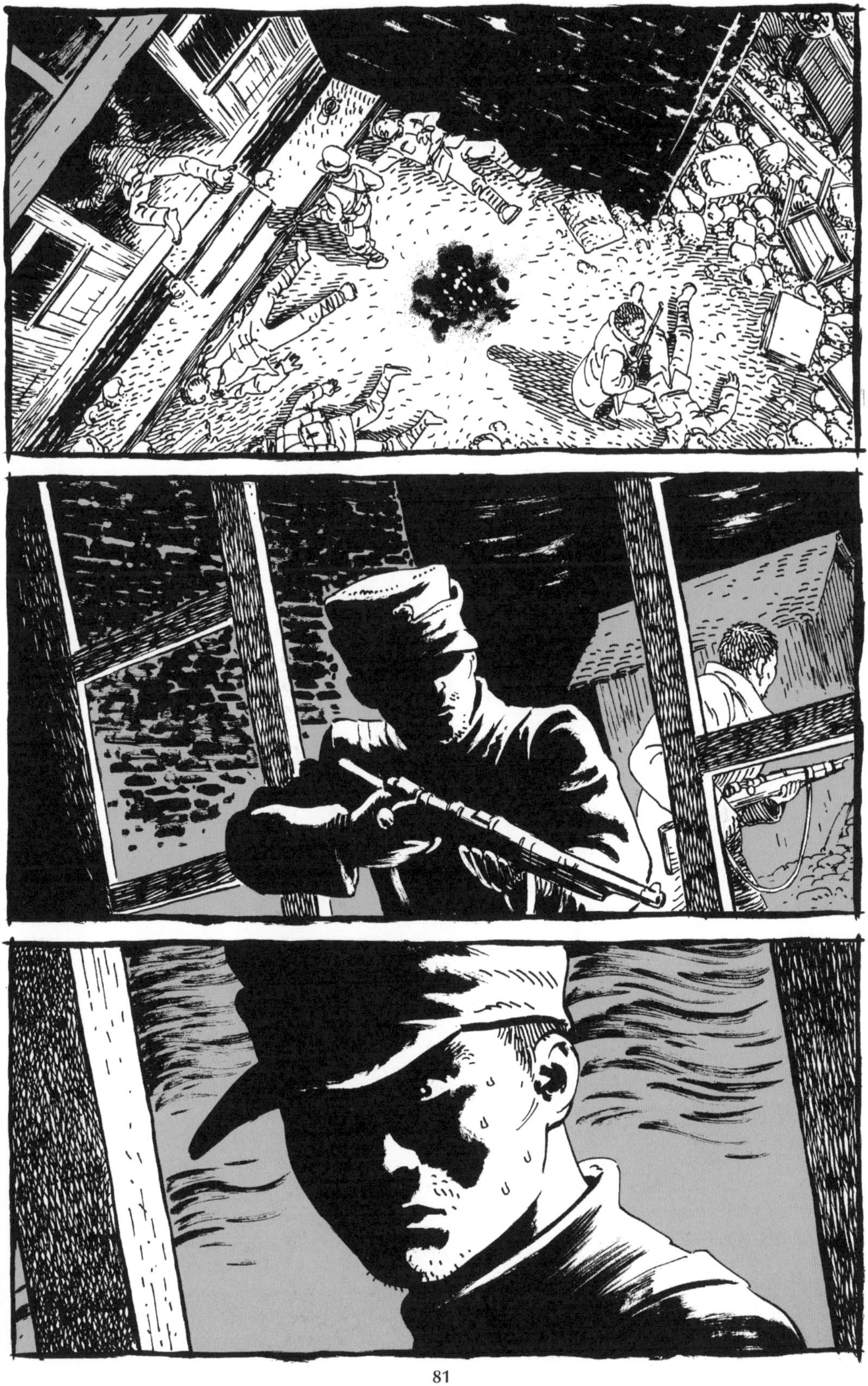

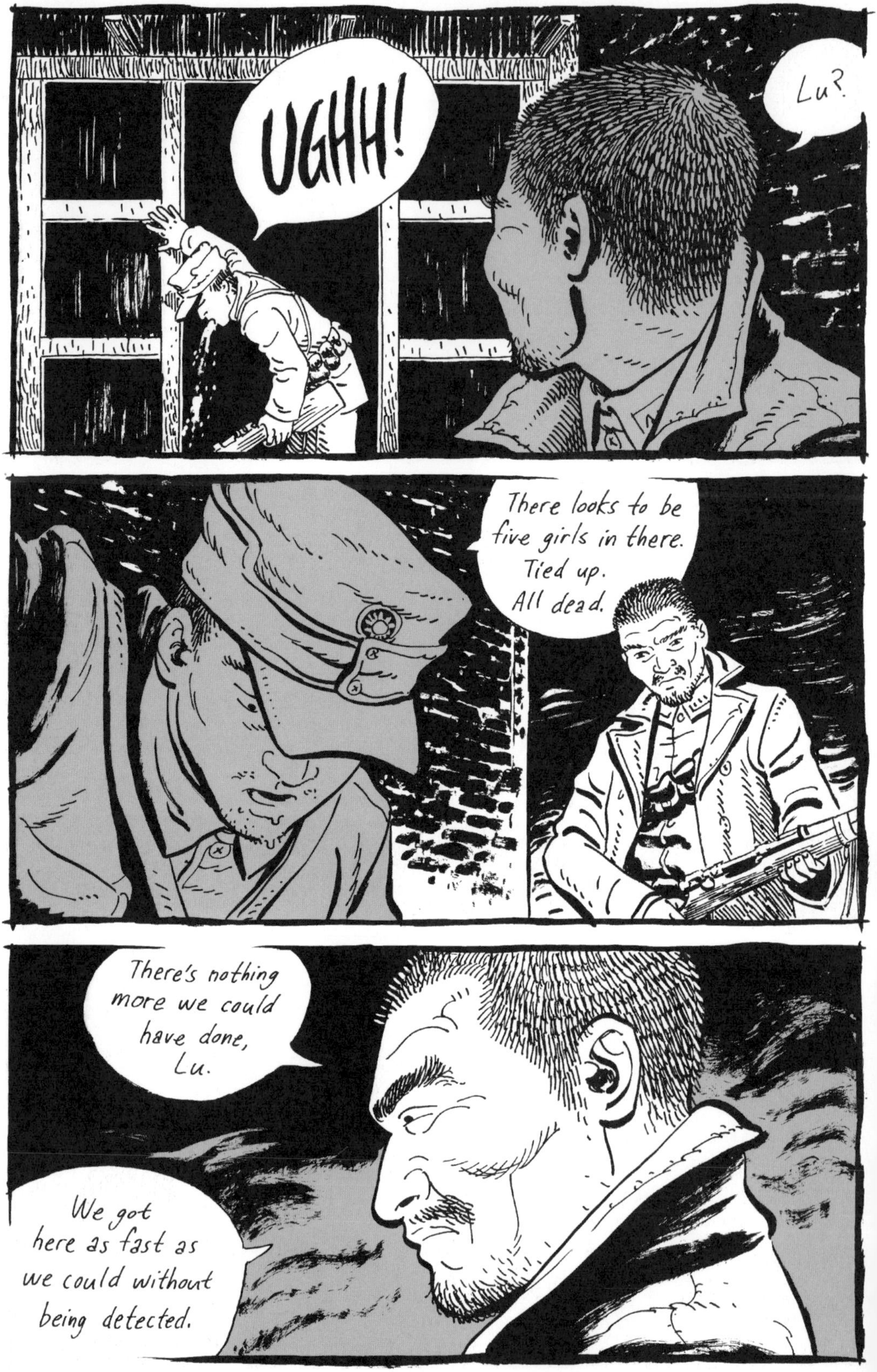
UGHH!
Lu?
There looks to be five girls in there. Tied up. All dead.
There's nothing more we could have done, Lu.
We got here as fast as we could without being detected.

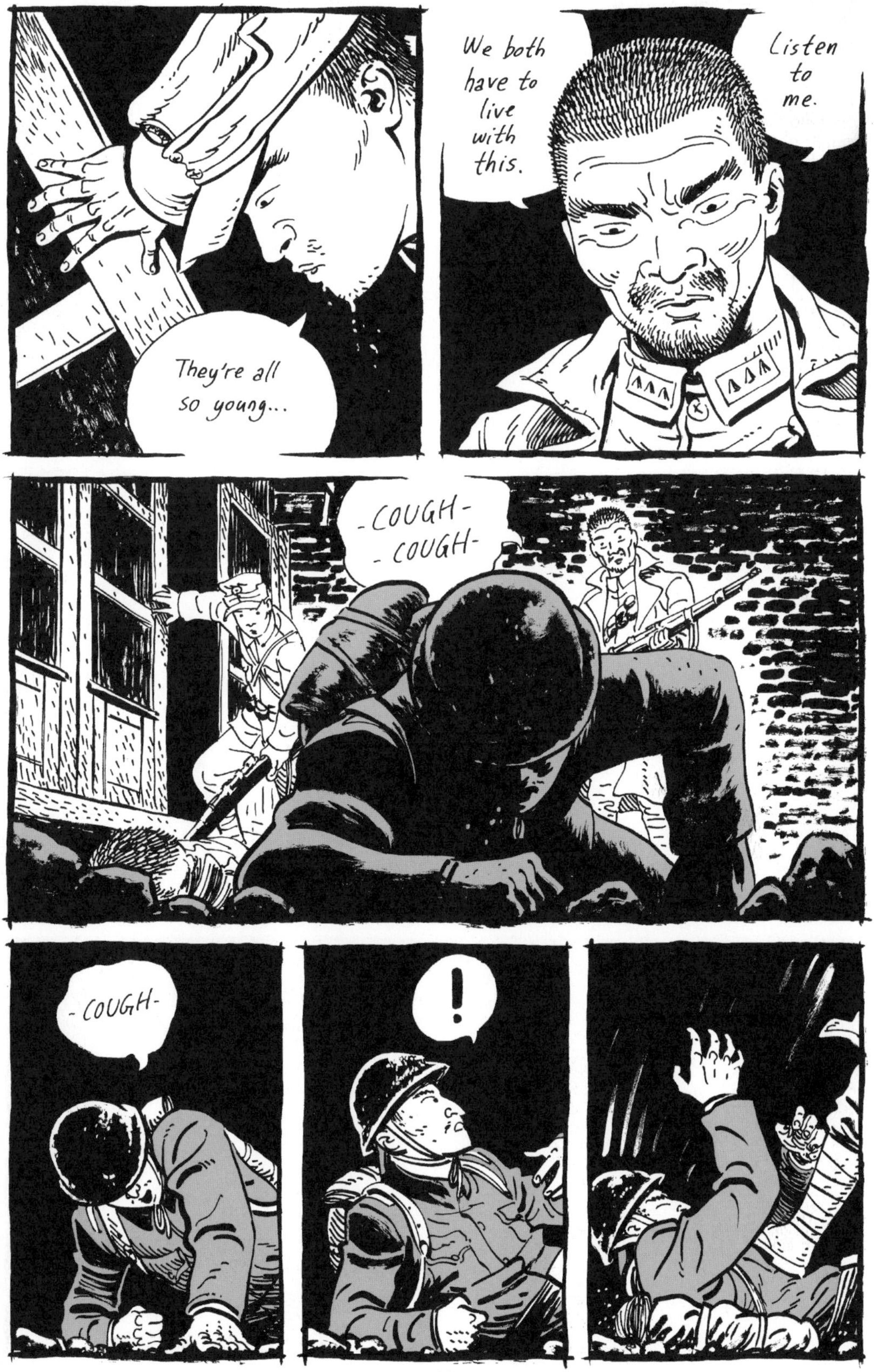
They're all so young...
We both have to live with this.
Listen to me.
-COUGH-
-COUGH-
-COUGH-
!

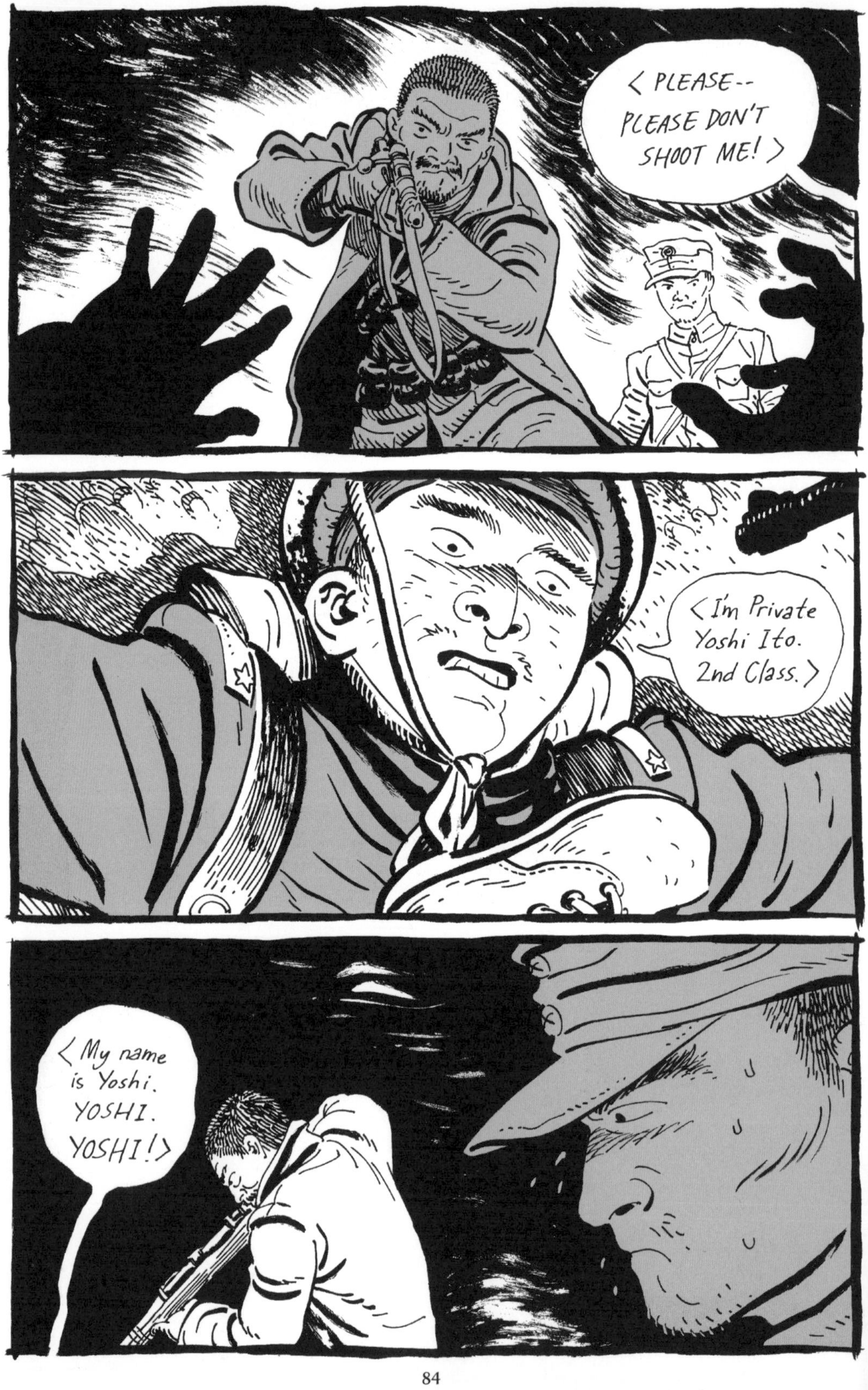
< PLEASE--
PLEASE DON'T
SHOOT ME! >
< I'm Private
Yoshi Ito.
2nd Class. >
< My name
is Yoshi.
YOSHI.
YOSHI! >

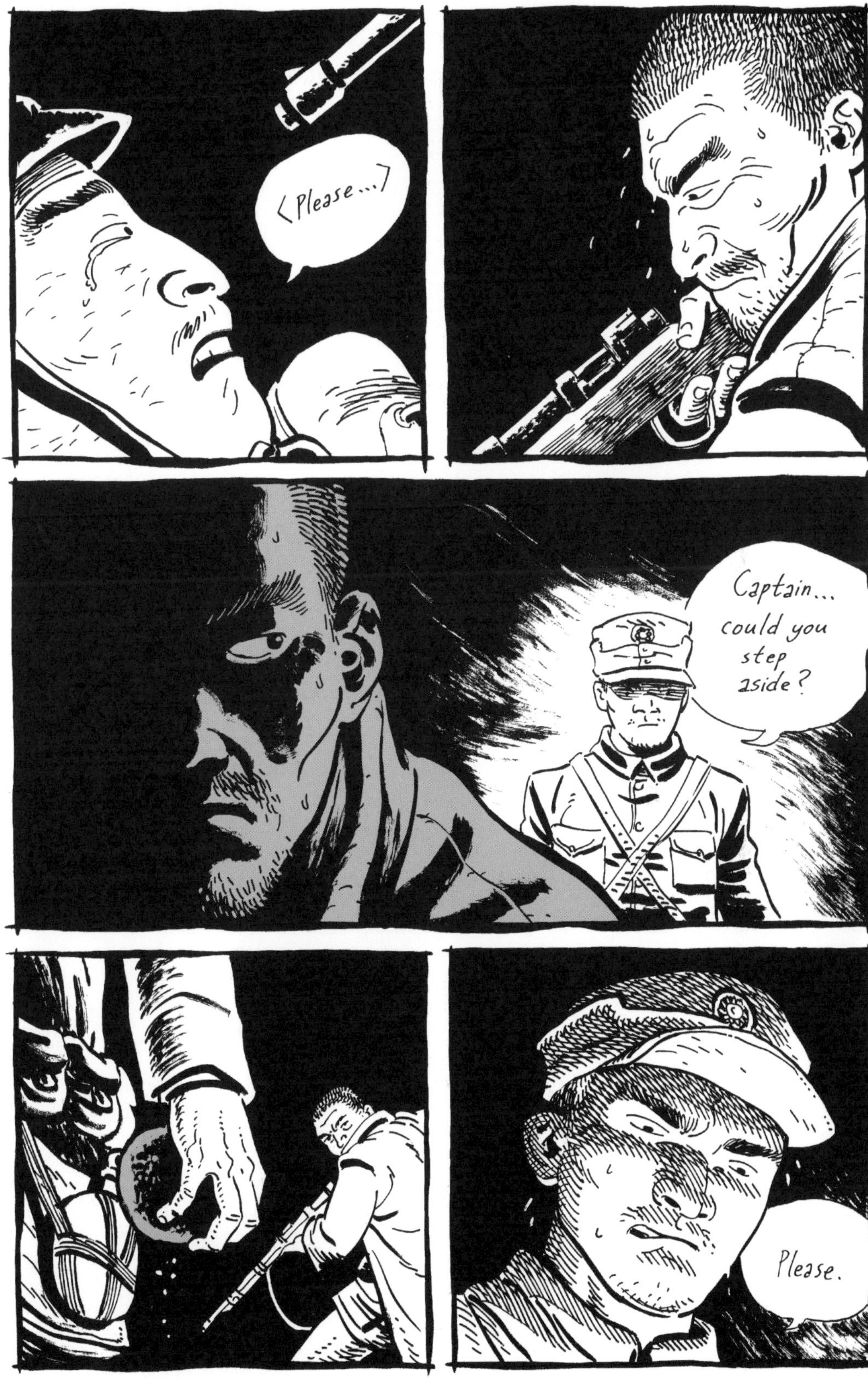

〈Please...〉
Captain... could you step aside?
Please.

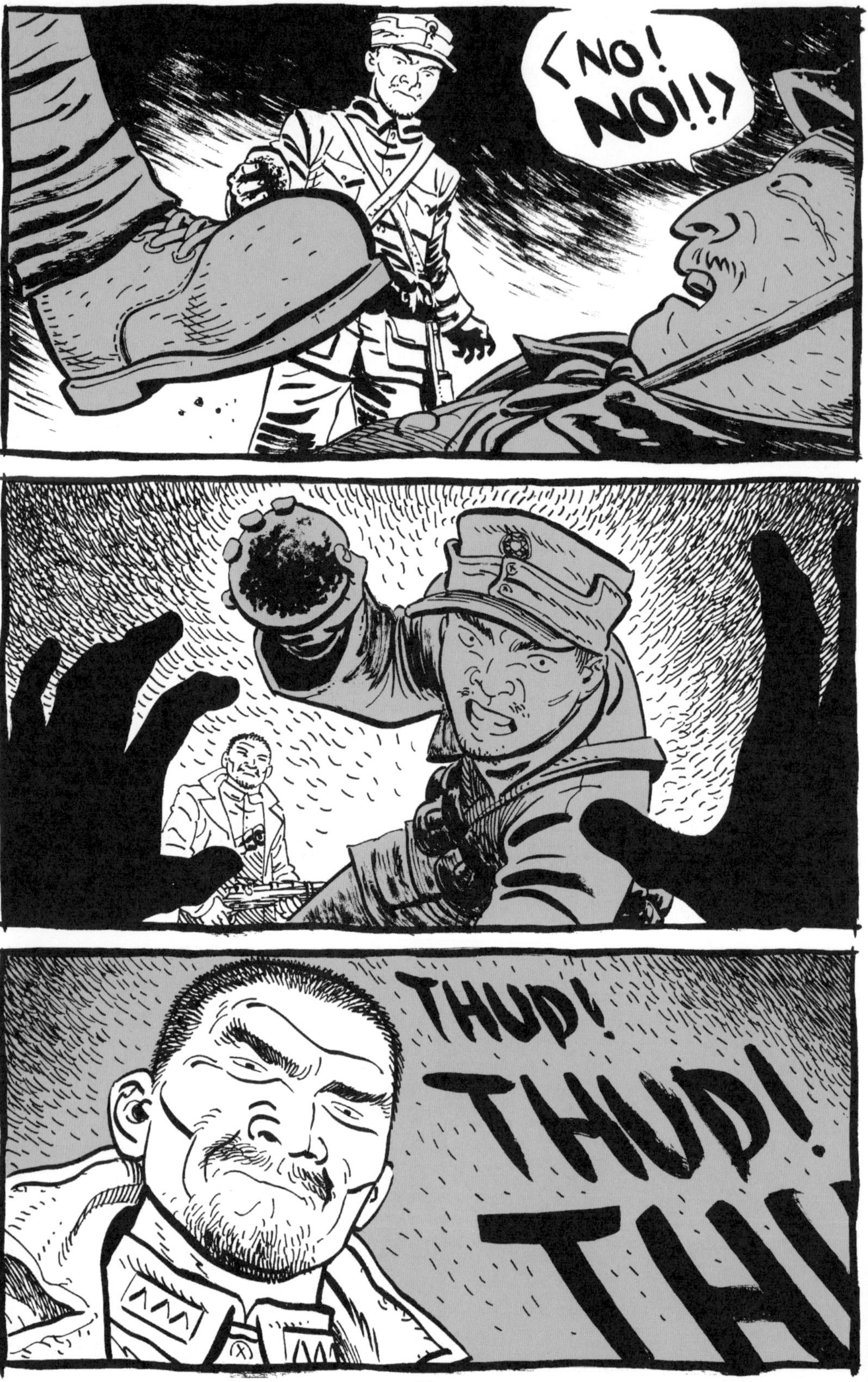

⟨NO!
NO!!⟩
THUD!
THUD!
THU

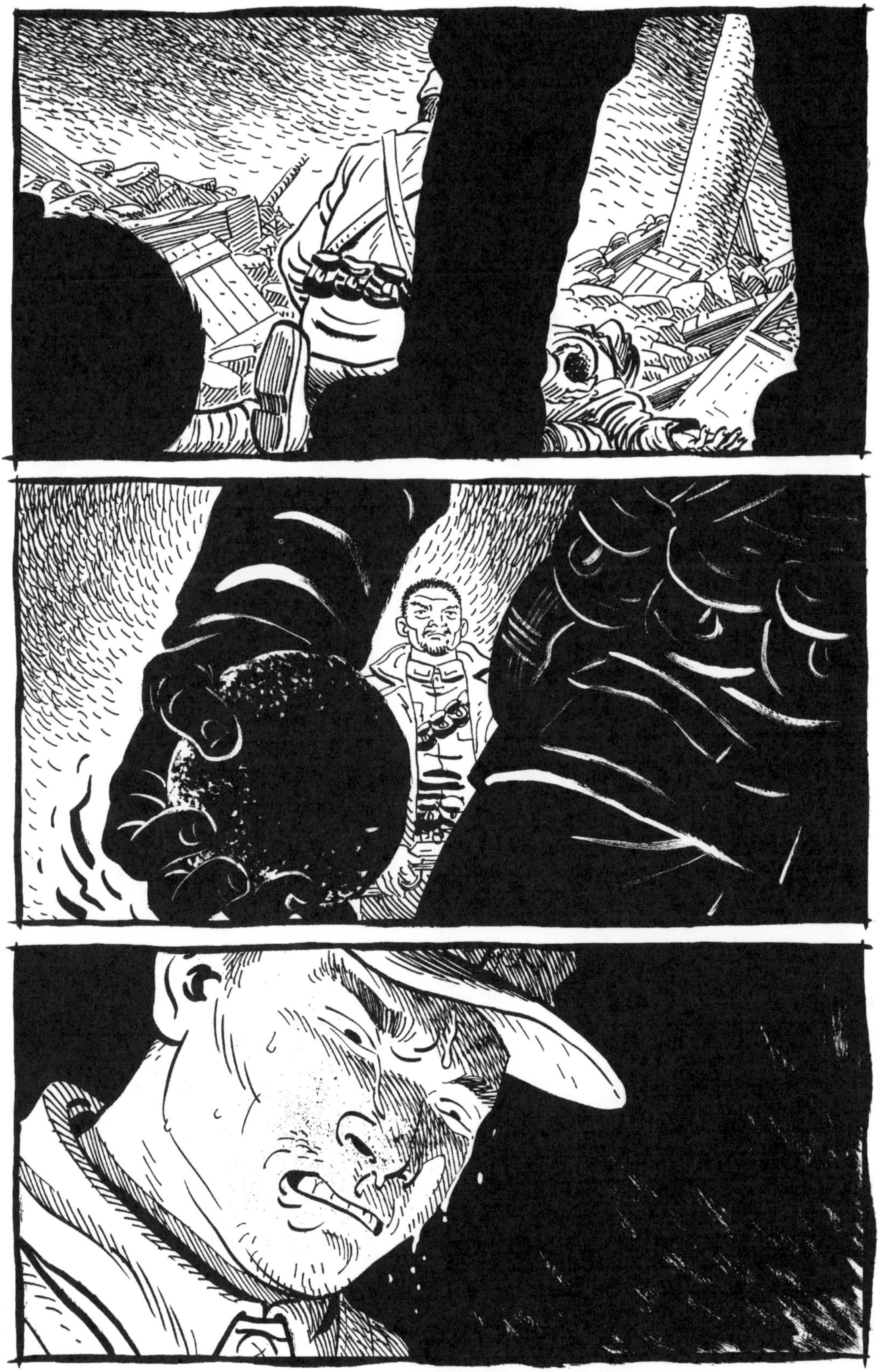

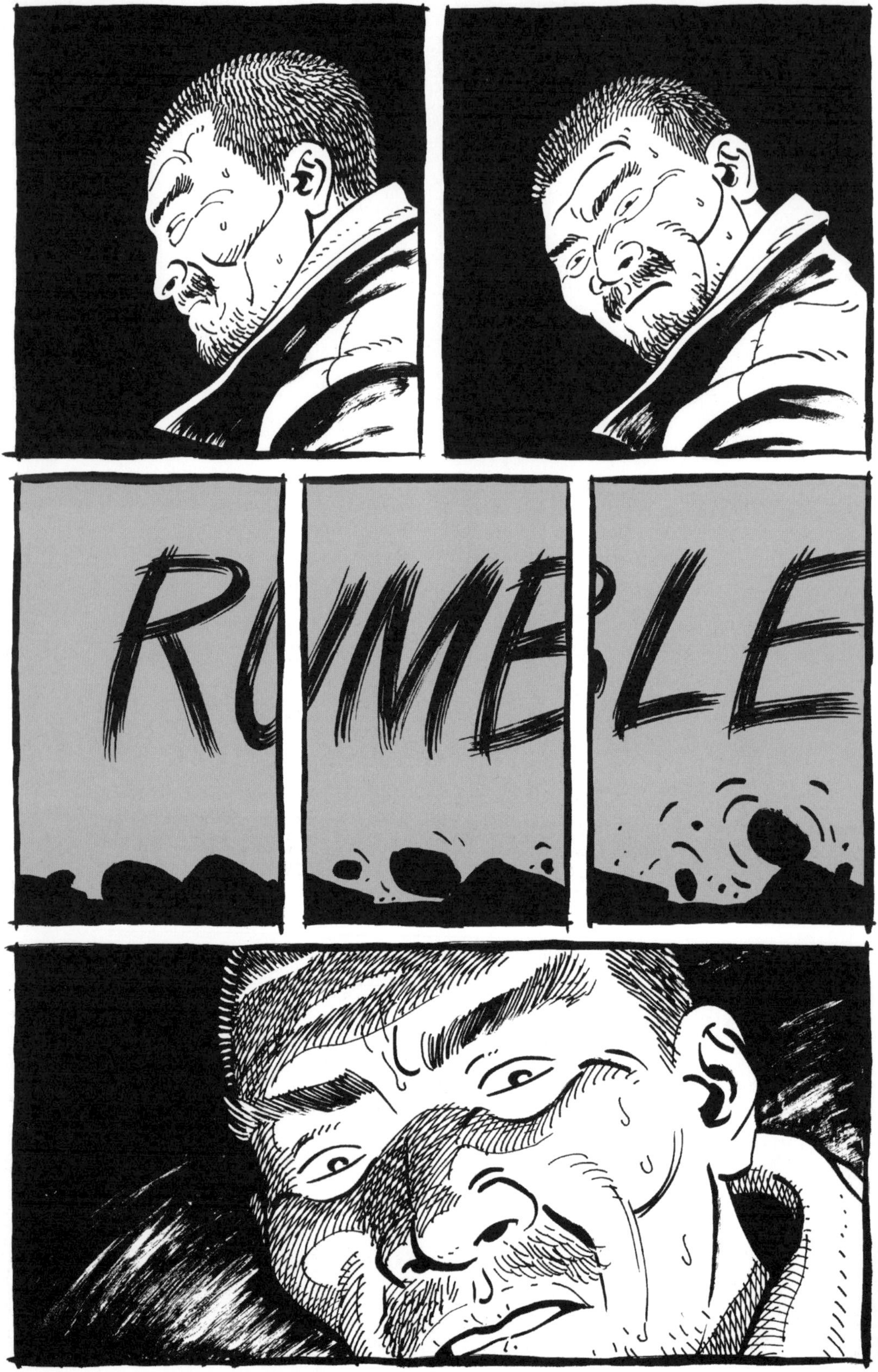
RUMBLE

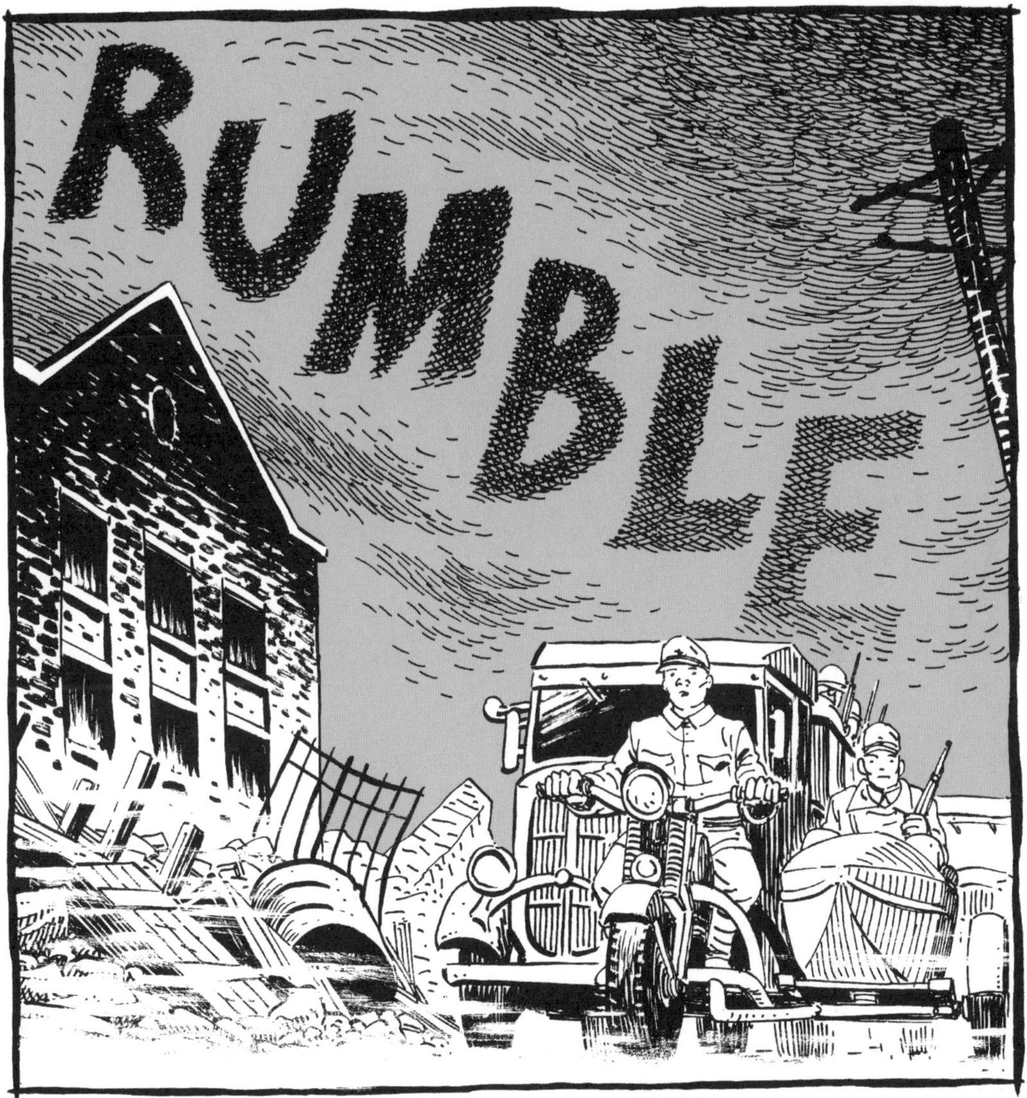
RUMBLE

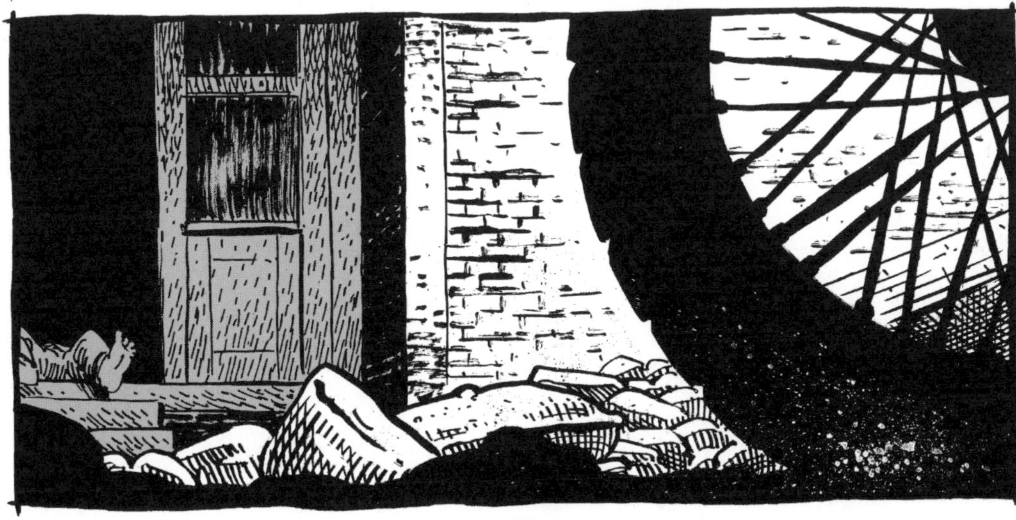

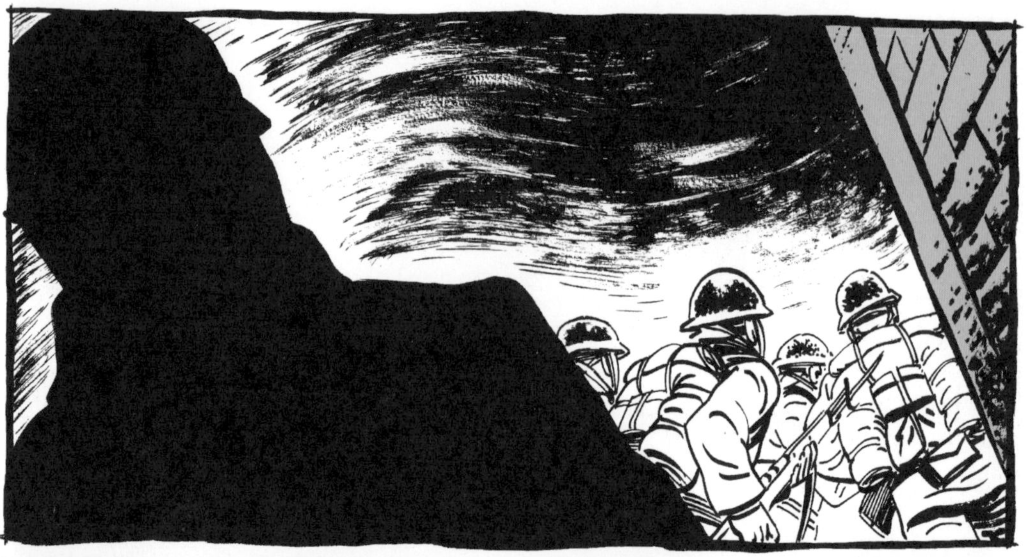

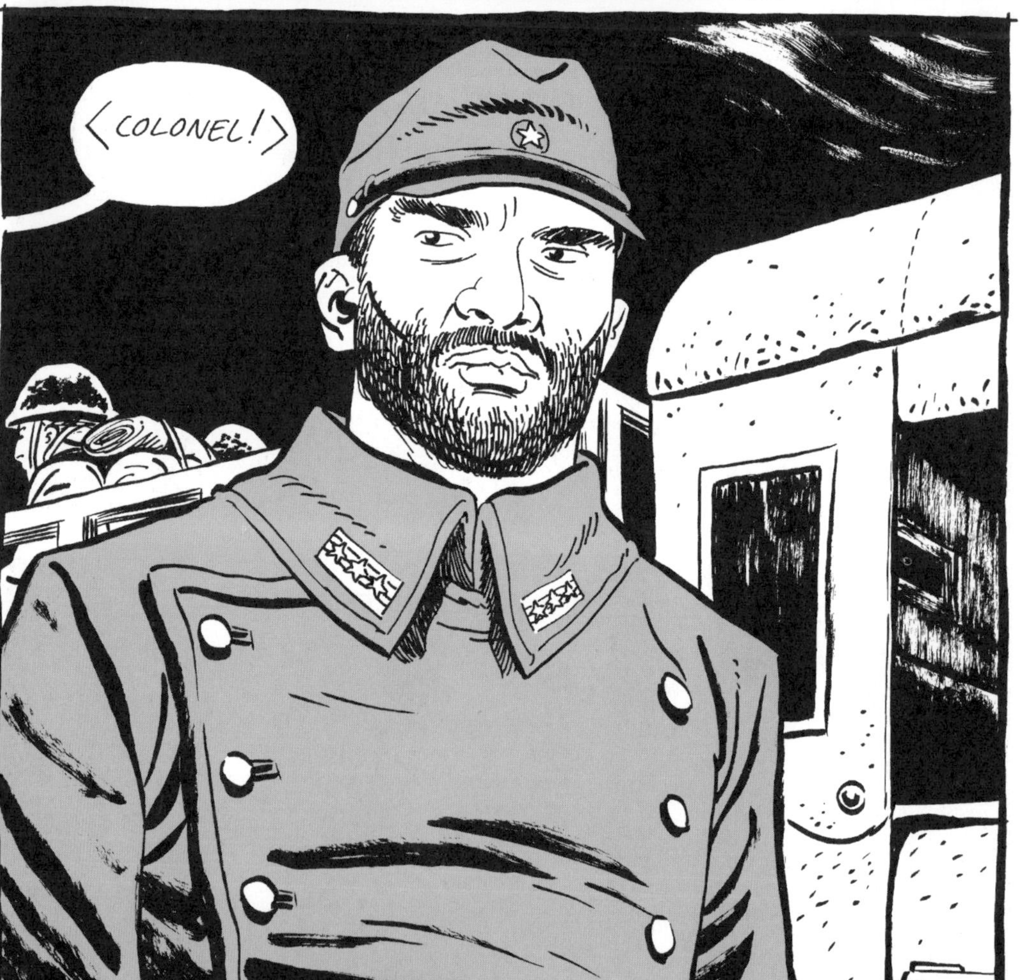
〈COLONEL!〉

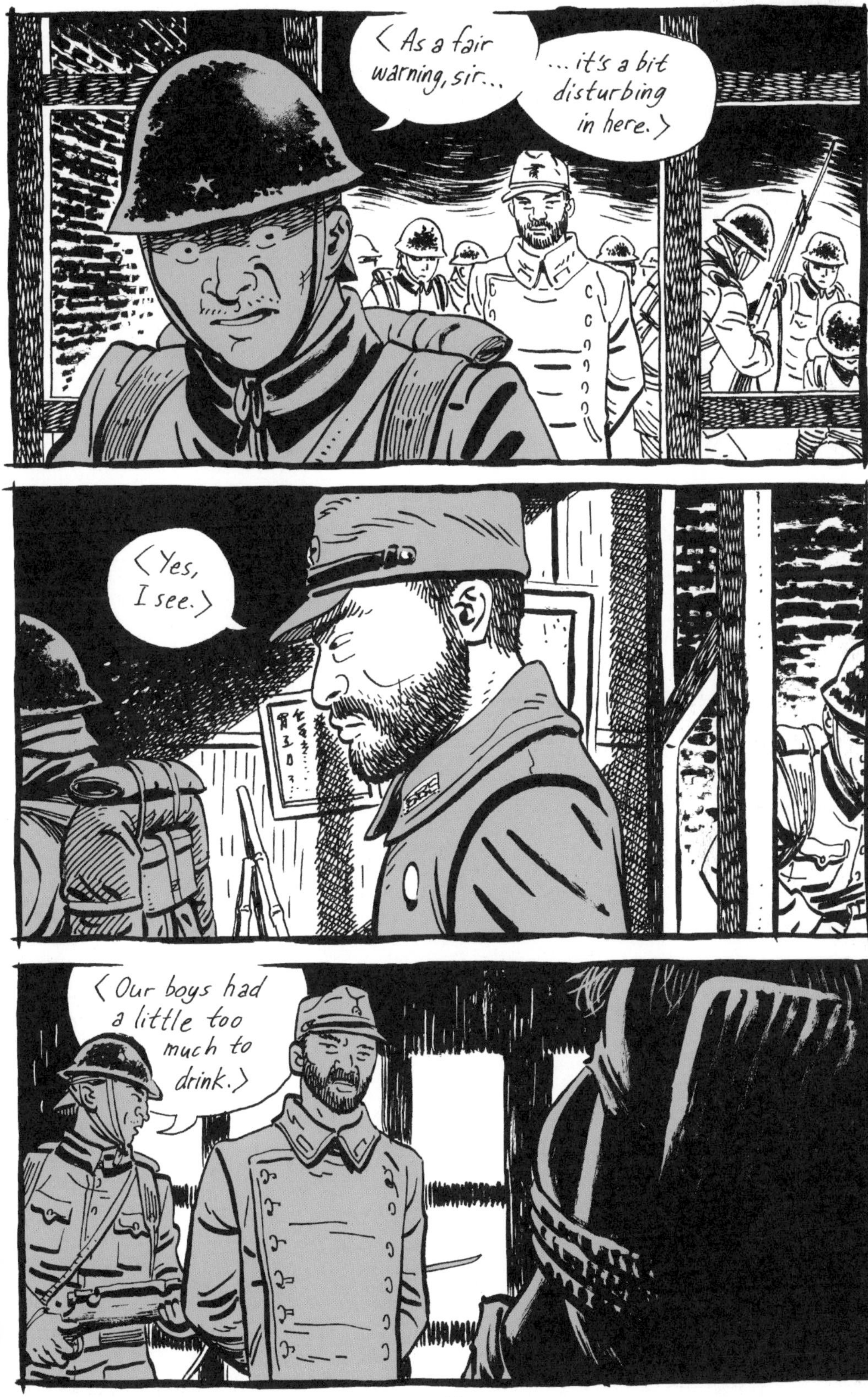
〈As a fair warning, sir...
...it's a bit disturbing in here.〉
〈Yes, I see.〉
〈Our boys had a little too much to drink.〉

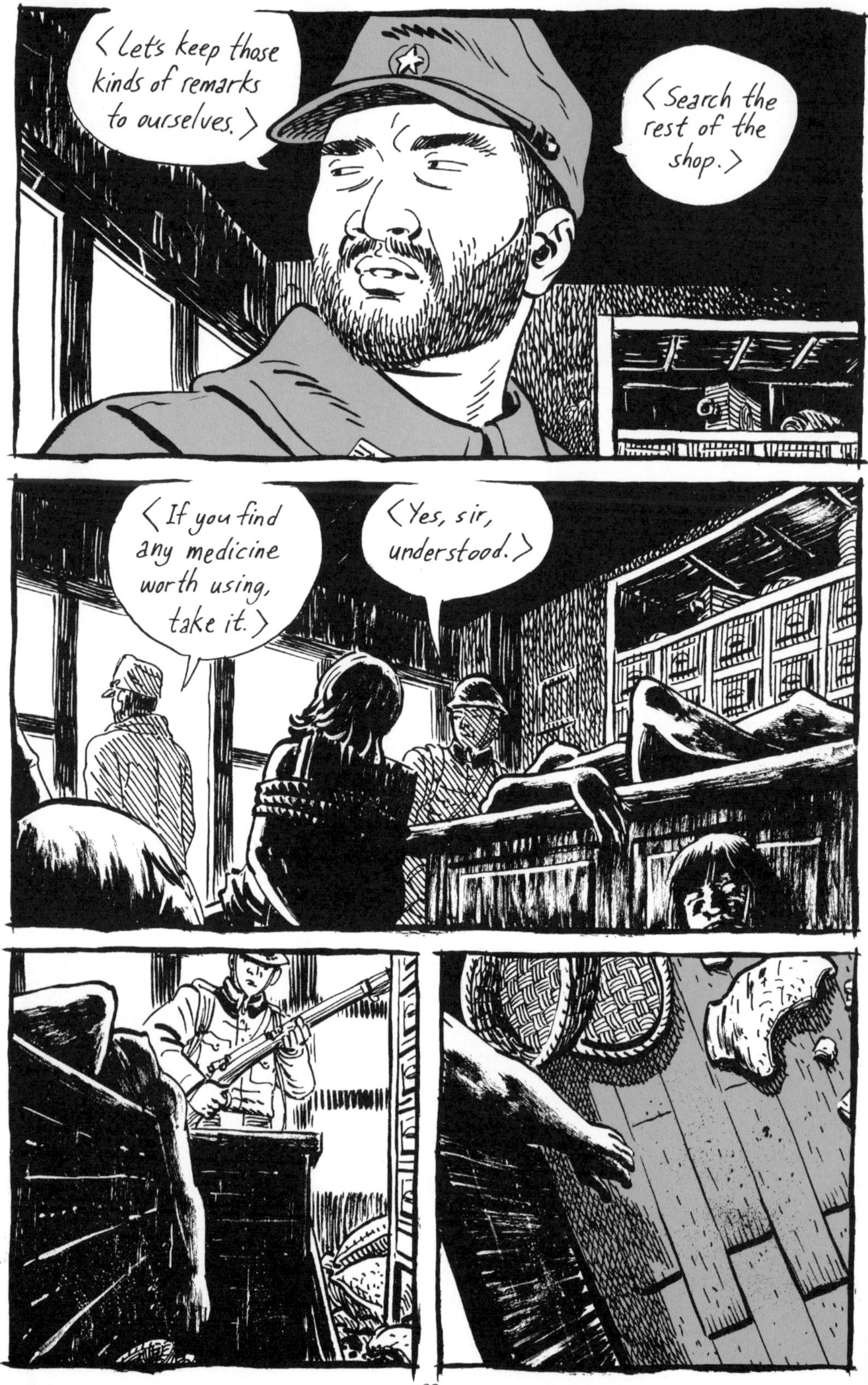

< Let's keep those kinds of remarks to ourselves. >
< Search the rest of the shop. >
< If you find any medicine worth using, take it. >
< Yes, sir, understood. >

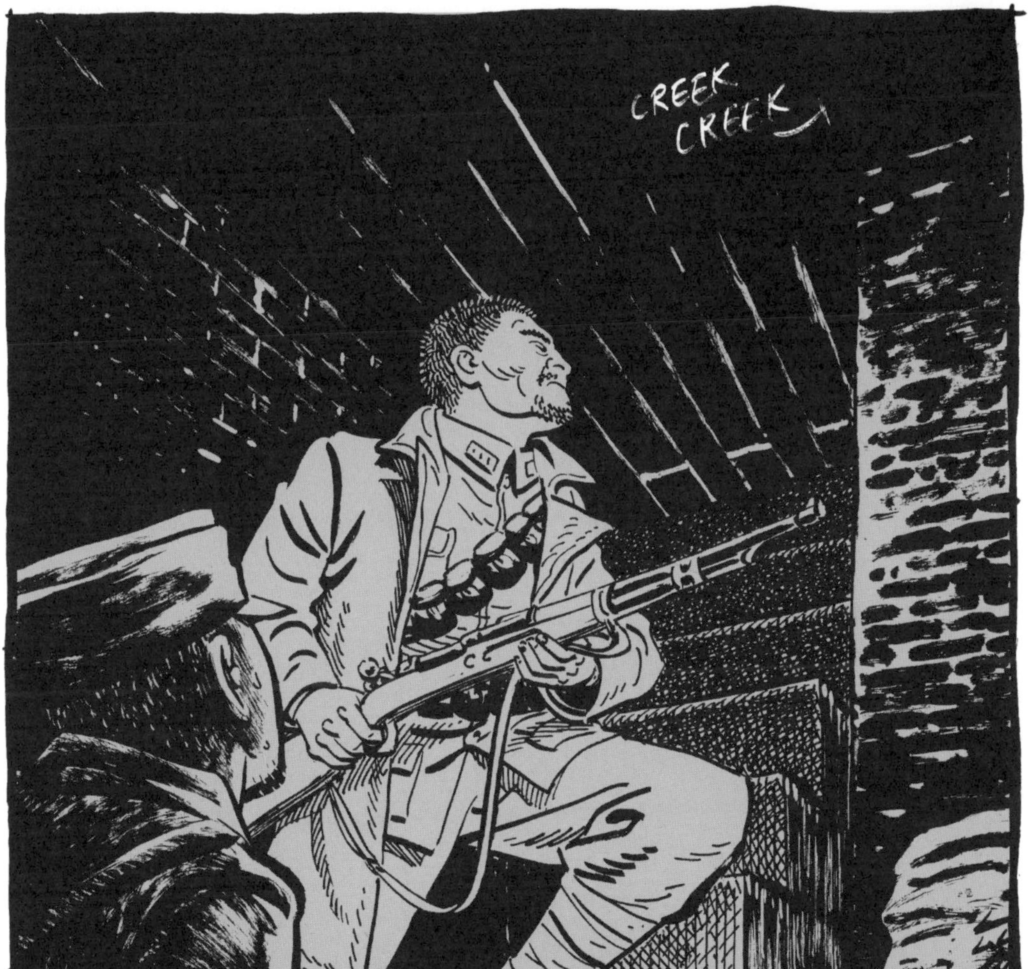
CREEK
CREEK
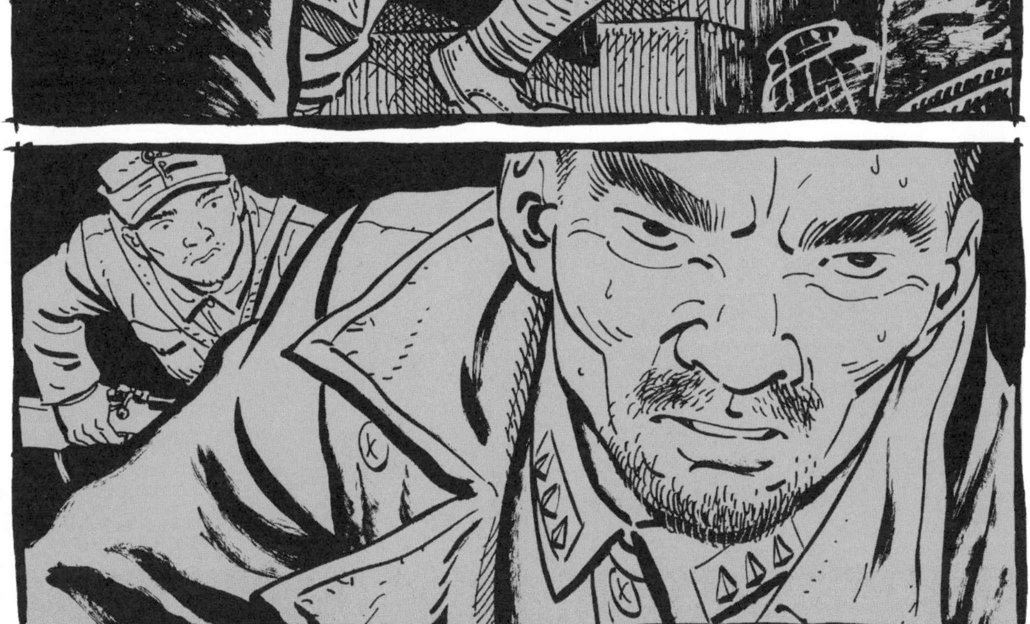

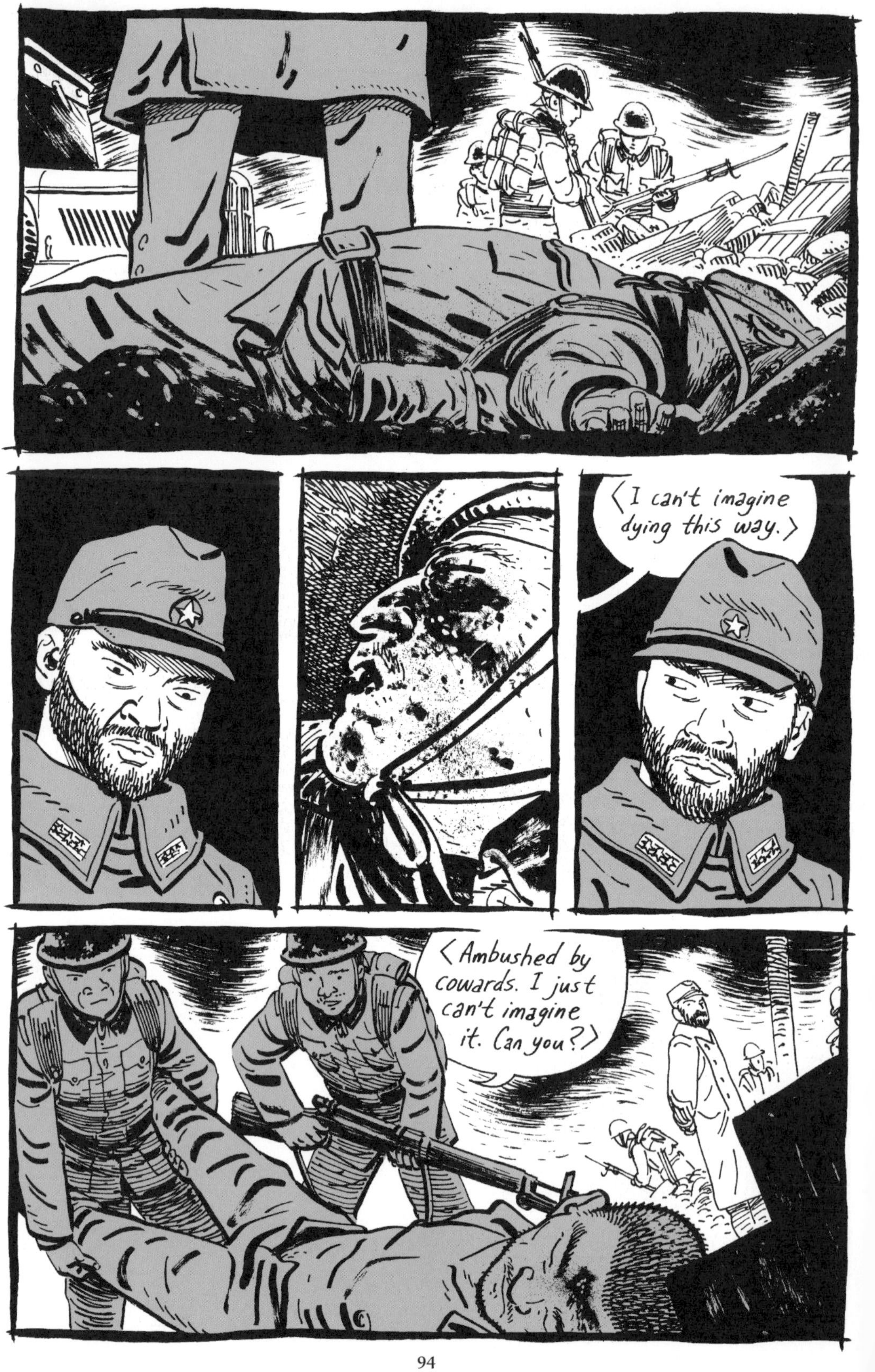
〈I can't imagine dying this way.〉
〈Ambushed by cowards. I just can't imagine it. Can you?〉

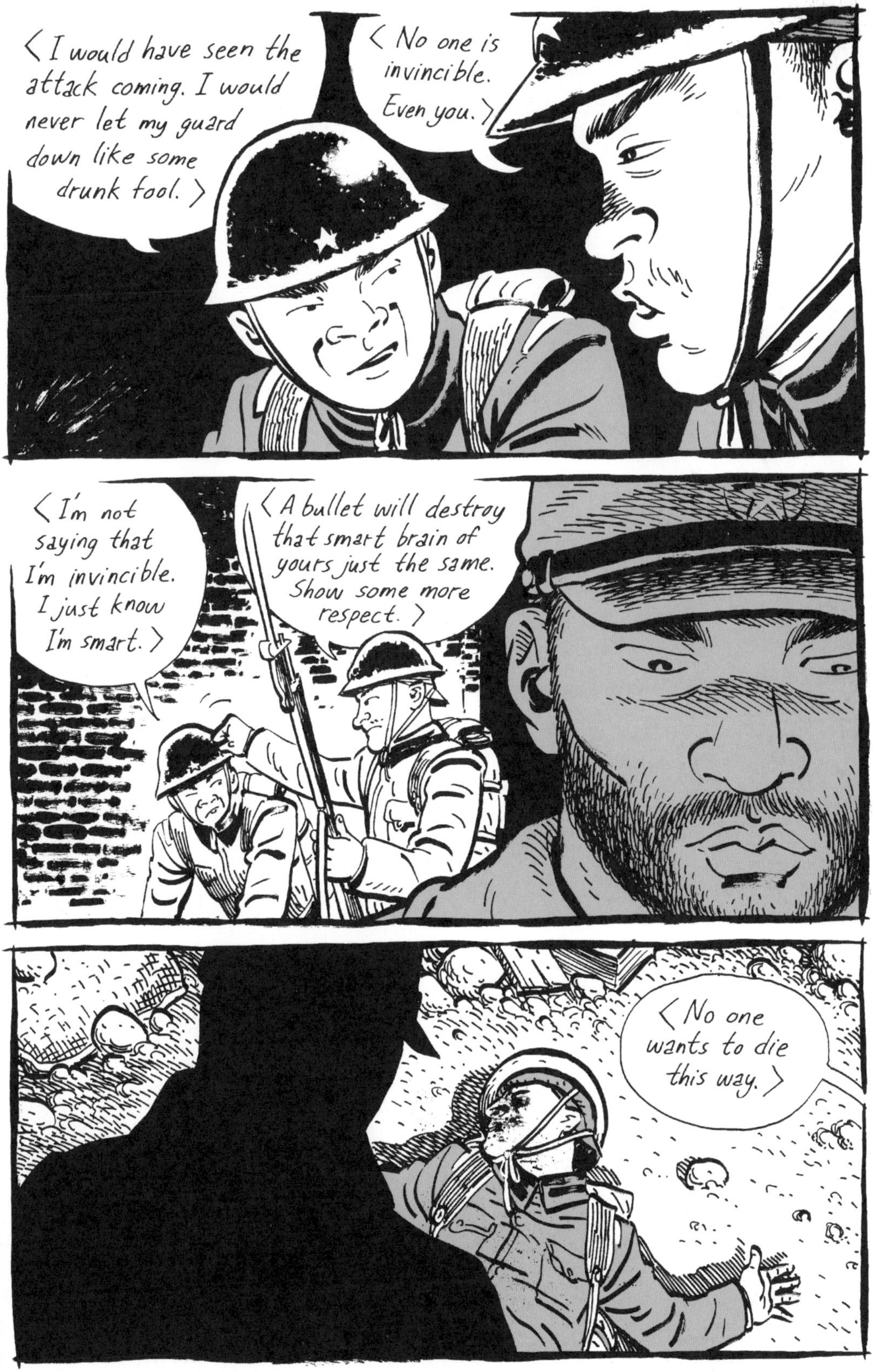

< I would have seen the attack coming. I would never let my guard down like some drunk fool. >
< No one is invincible. Even you. >
< I'm not saying that I'm invincible. I just know I'm smart. >
< A bullet will destroy that smart brain of yours just the same. Show some more respect. >
< No one wants to die this way. >

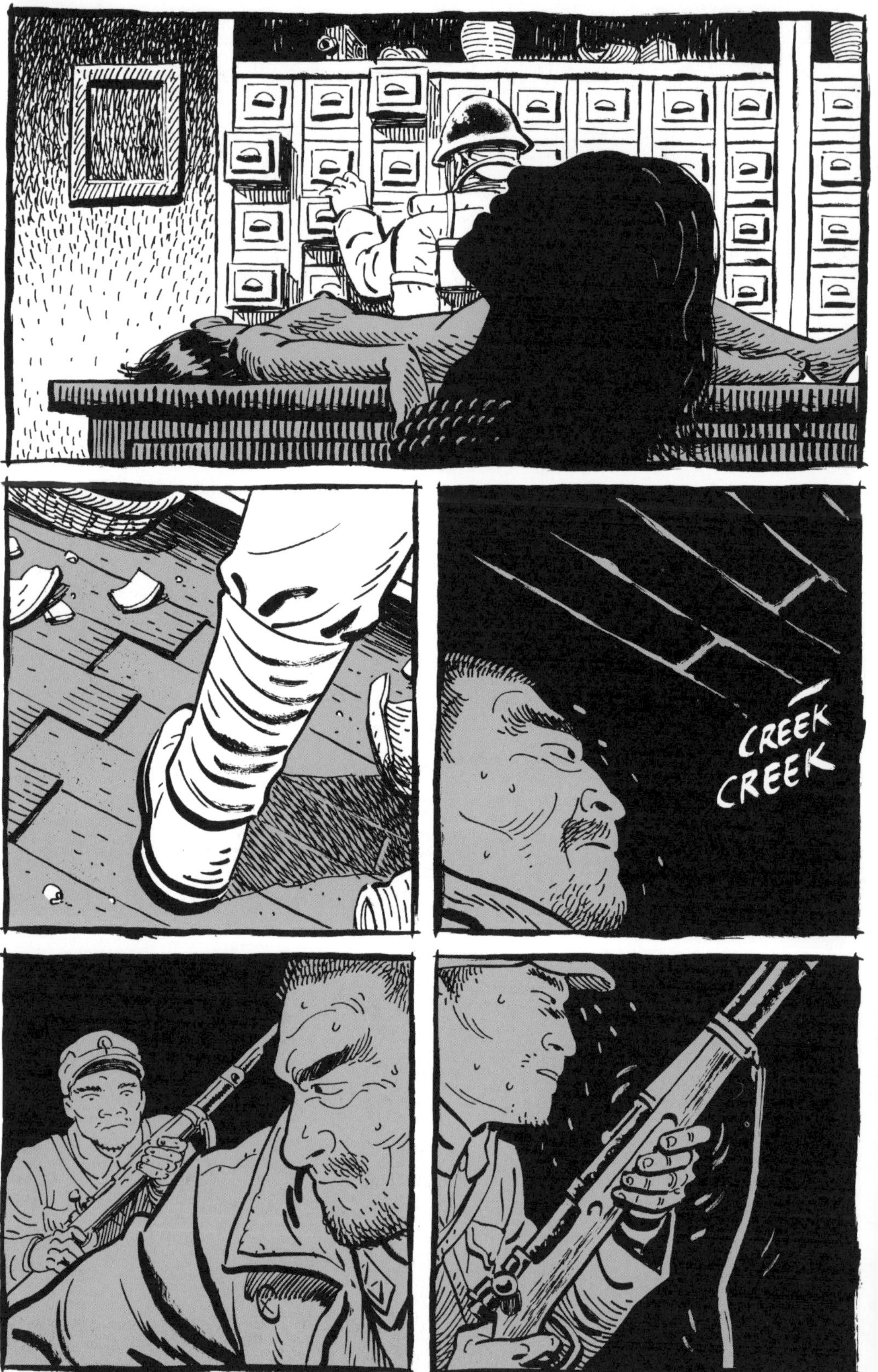
CREEK
CREEK

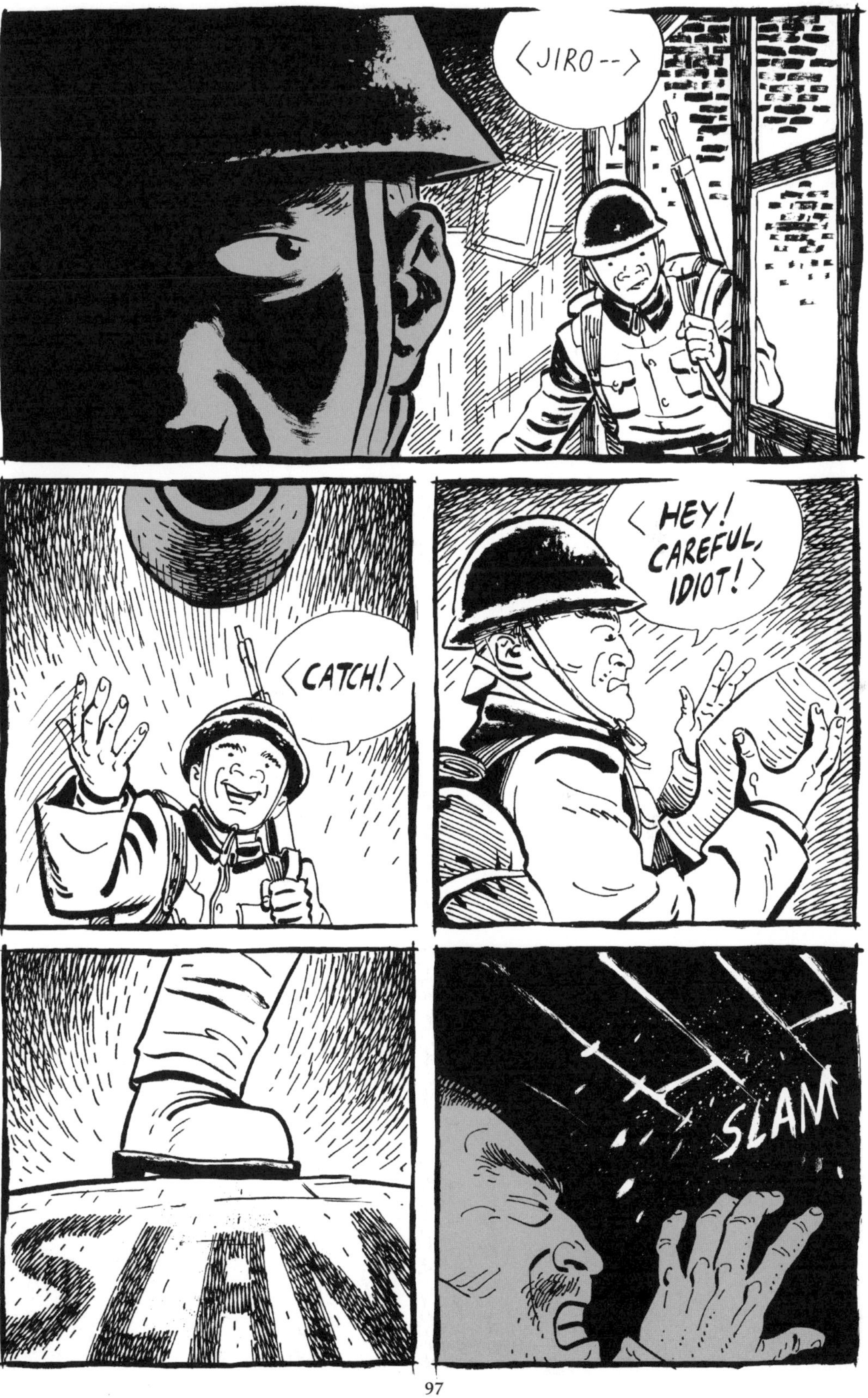
〈JIRO--〉
〈CATCH!〉
〈HEY! CAREFUL, IDIOT!〉
SLAM
SLAM

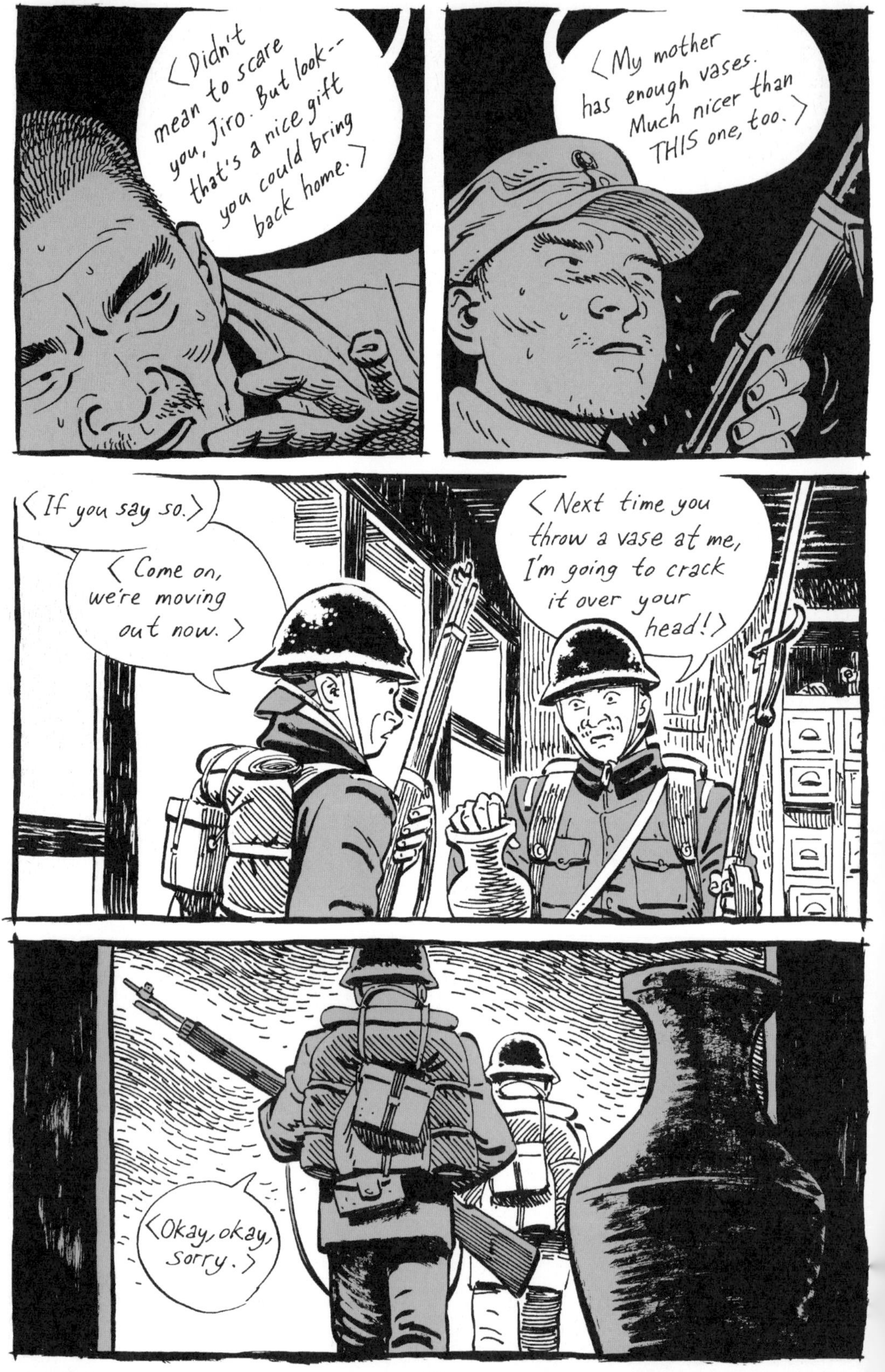

< Didn't mean to scare you, Jiro. But look-- that's a nice gift you could bring back home. >
< My mother has enough vases. Much nicer than THIS one, too. >
< If you say so. >
< Come on, we're moving out now. >
< Next time you throw a vase at me, I'm going to crack it over your head! >
< Okay, okay, sorry. >

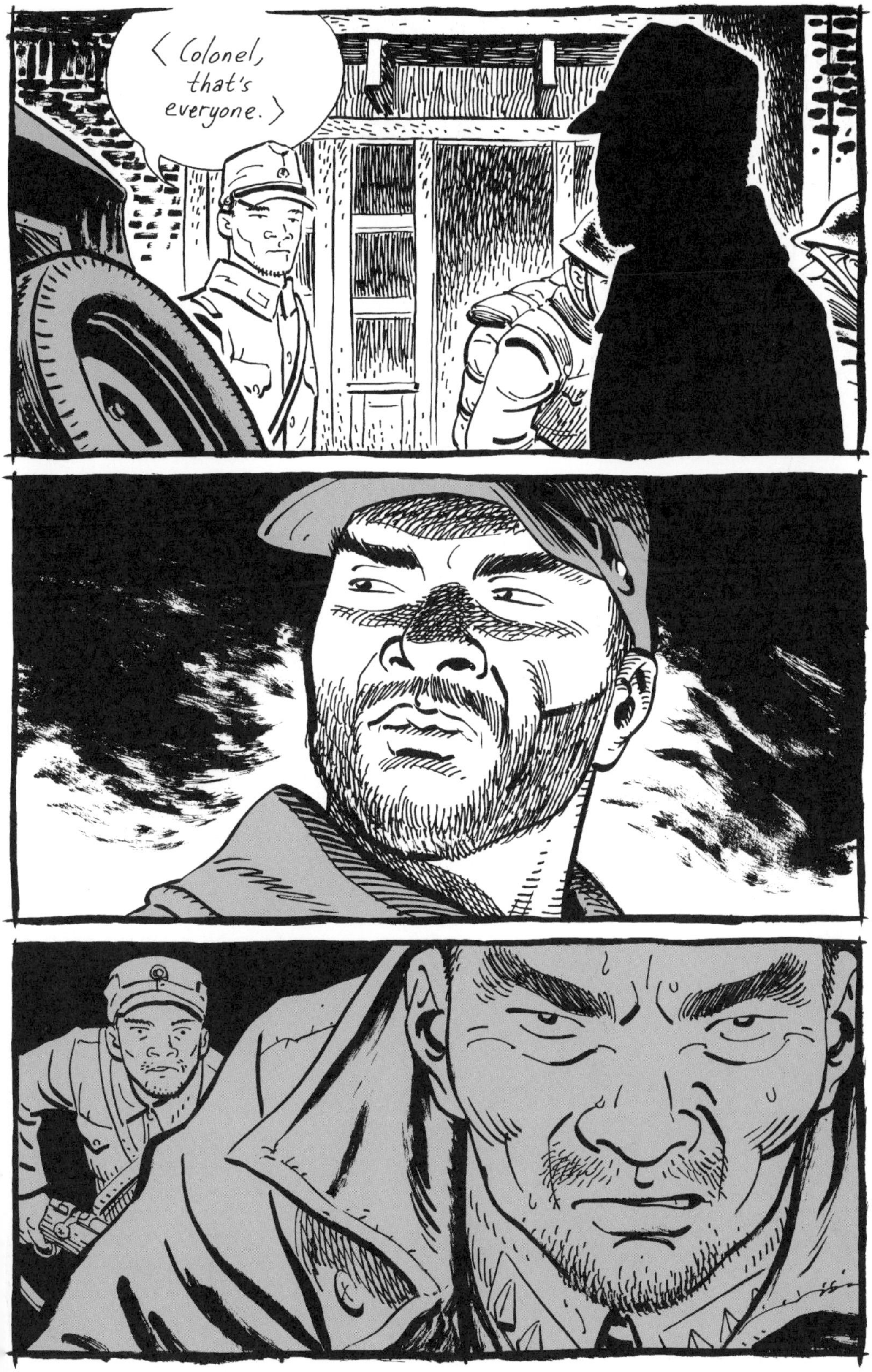

〈 Colonel, that's everyone. 〉

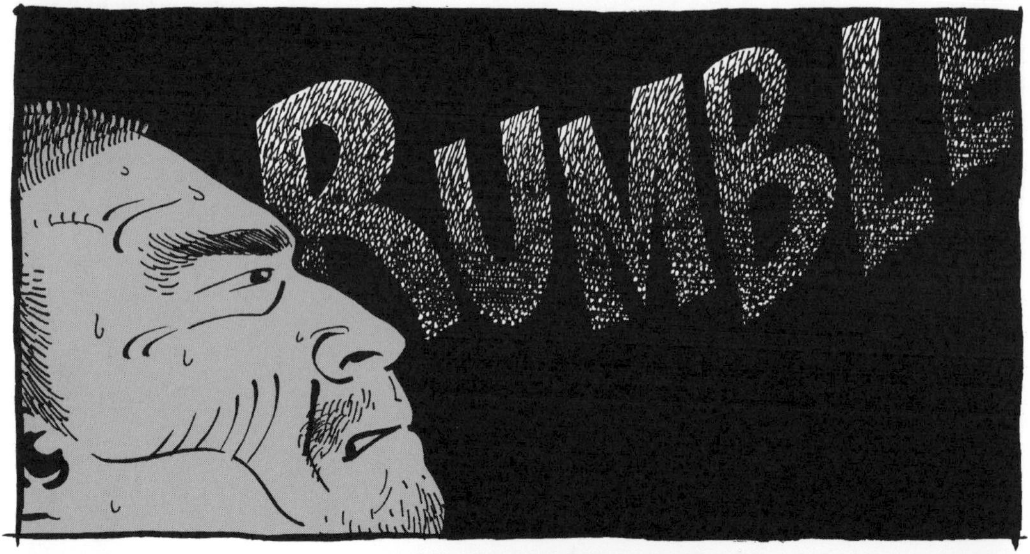
RUMBLE
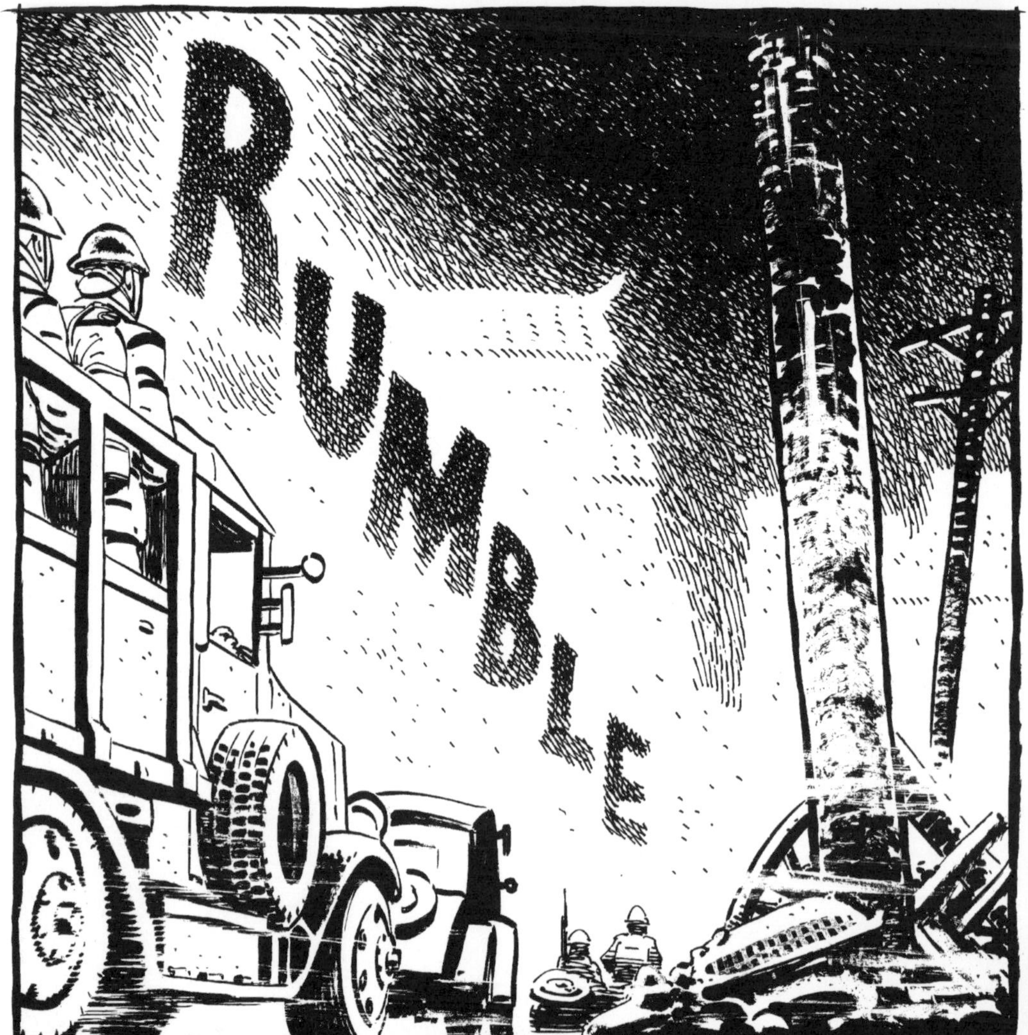
RUMBLE

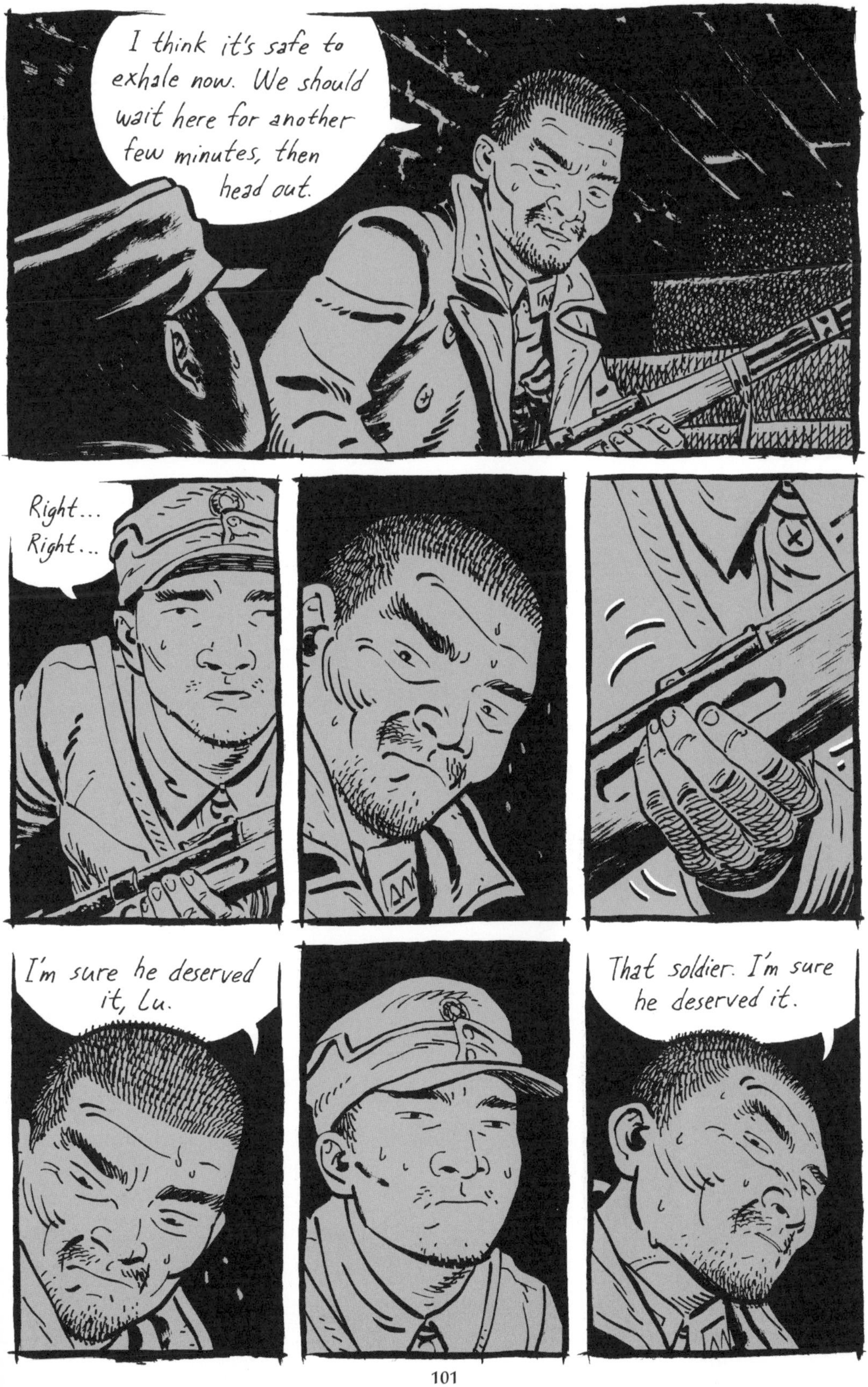
I think it's safe to exhale now. We should wait here for another few minutes, then head out.
Right... Right...
I'm sure he deserved it, Lu.
That soldier. I'm sure he deserved it.

In case you were thinking about it.

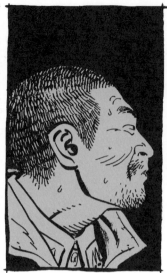

It's been longer than three hours...

What was that?

You said it would only take three hours to reach the YiJiang Gate.

...

... I lost track of the time.

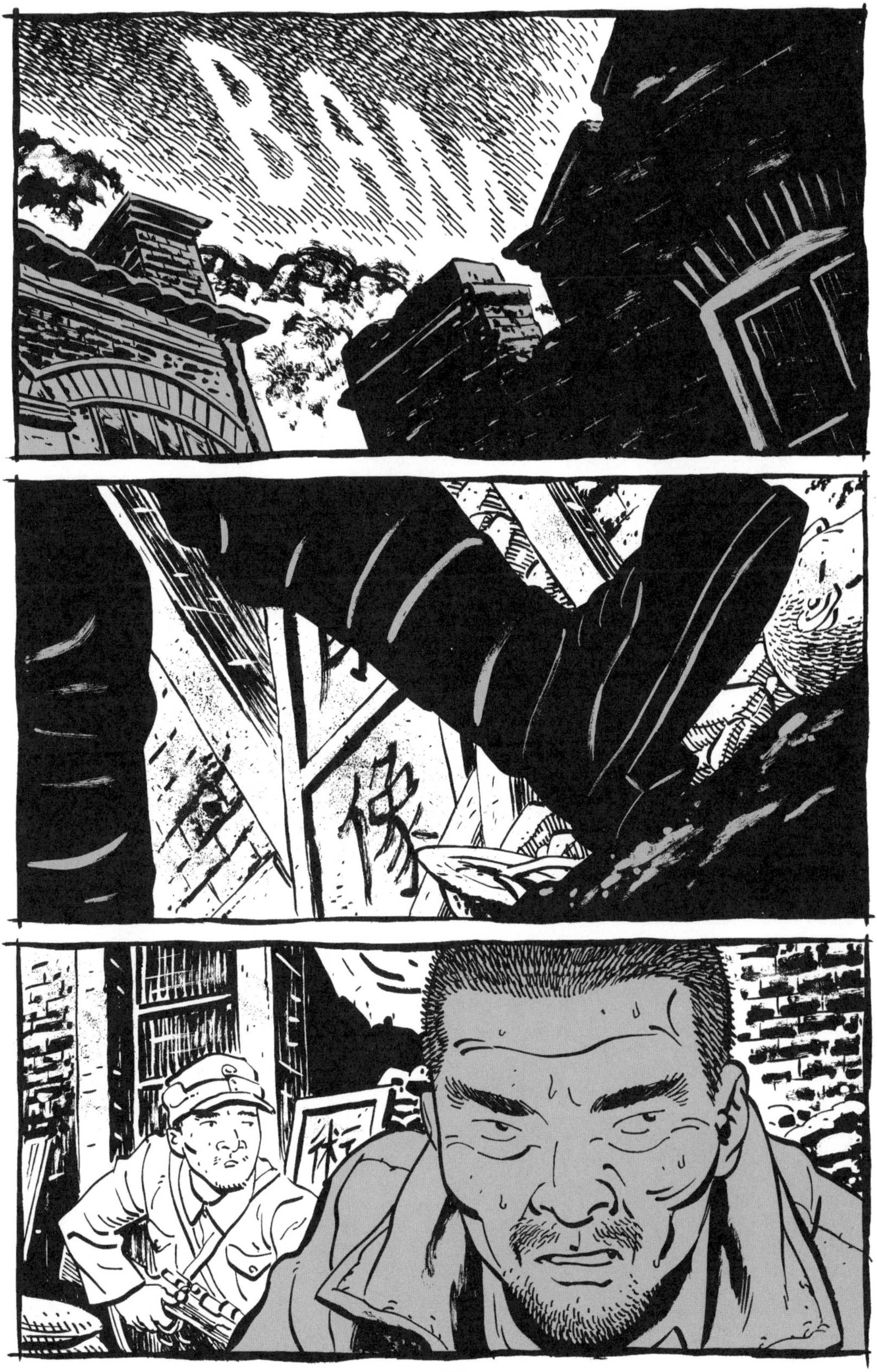
像

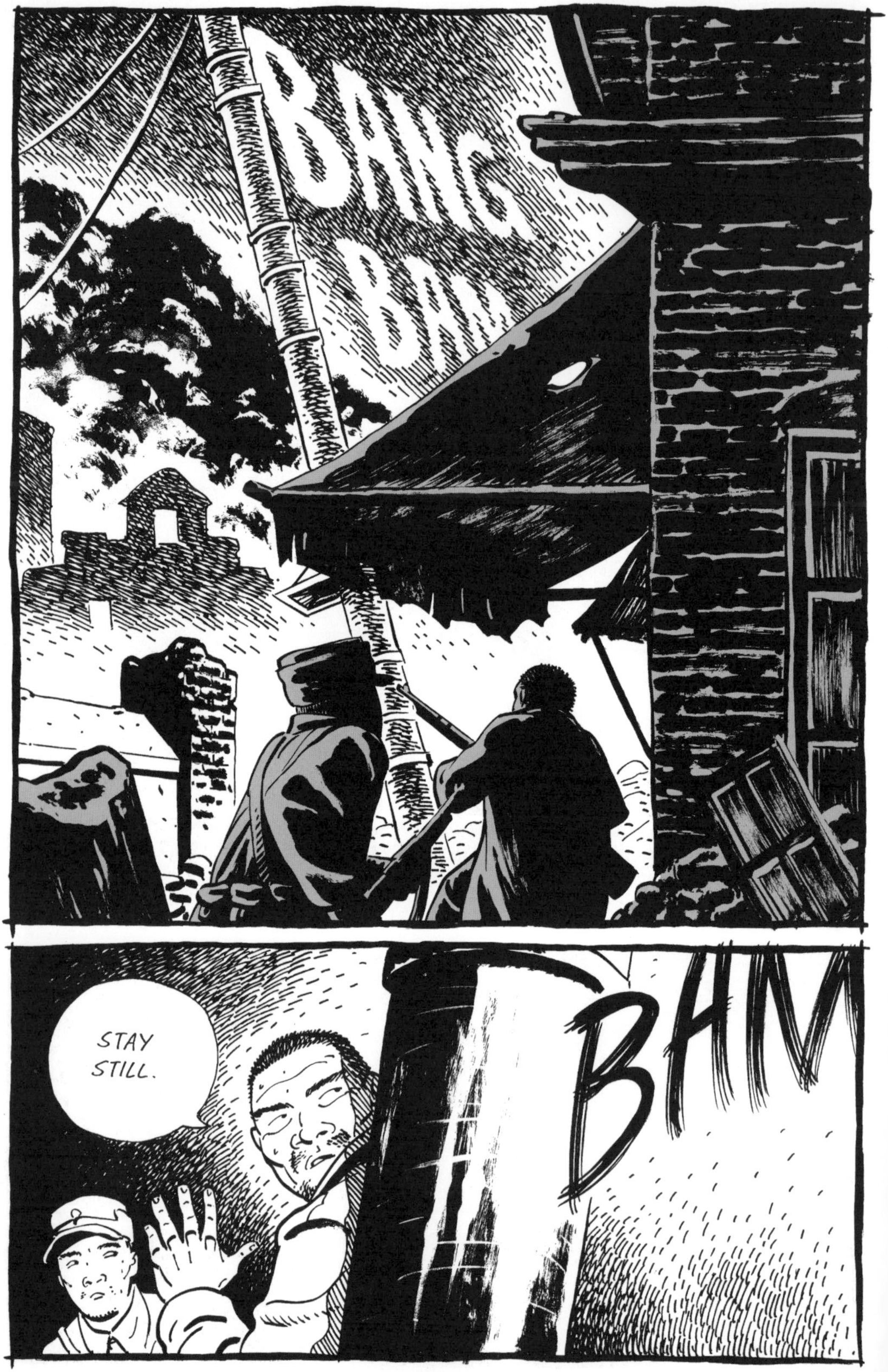
BANG
STAY STILL.
BAM

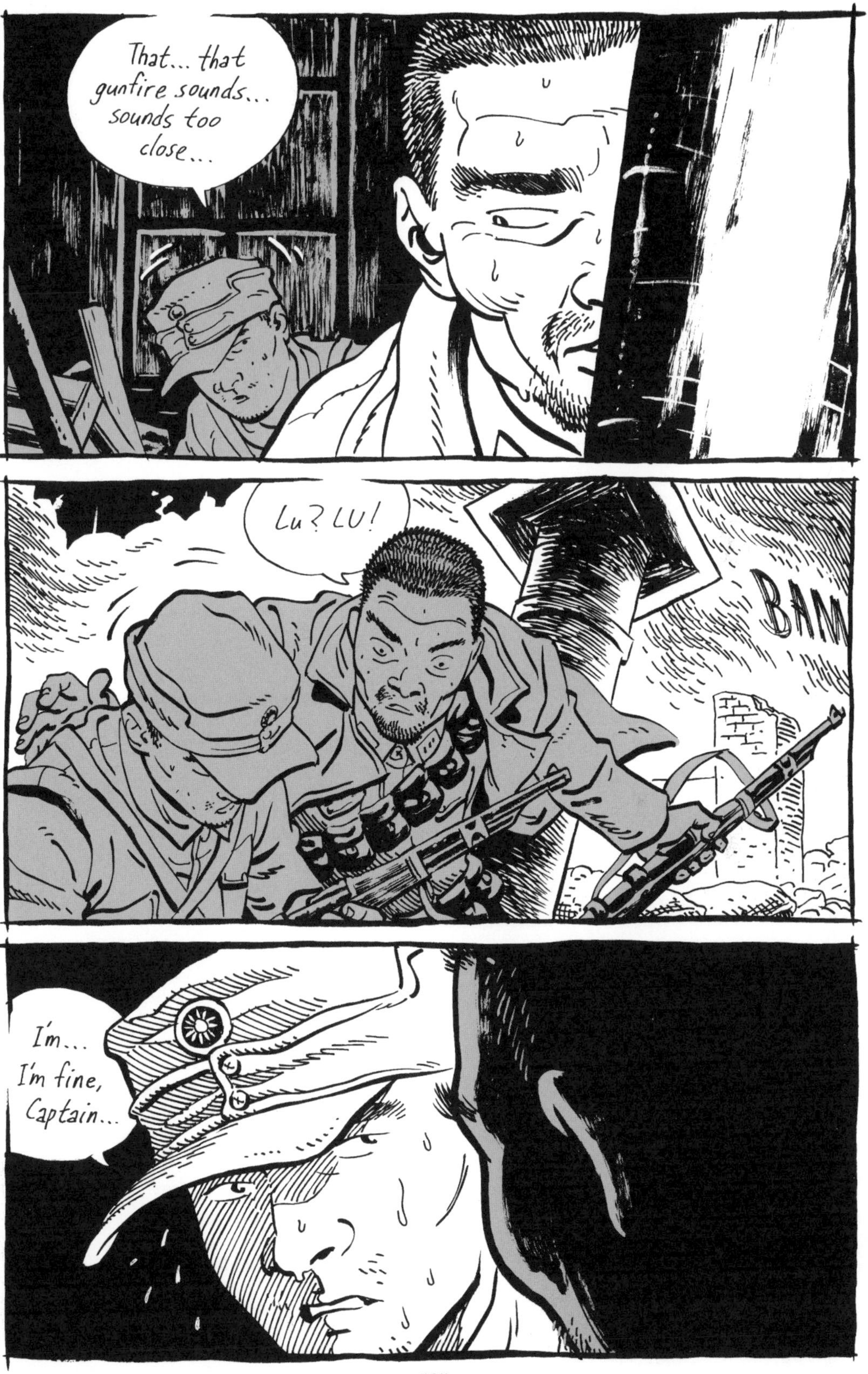
That... that gunfire sounds... sounds too close...
Lu? LU!
BAM
I'm... I'm fine, Captain...

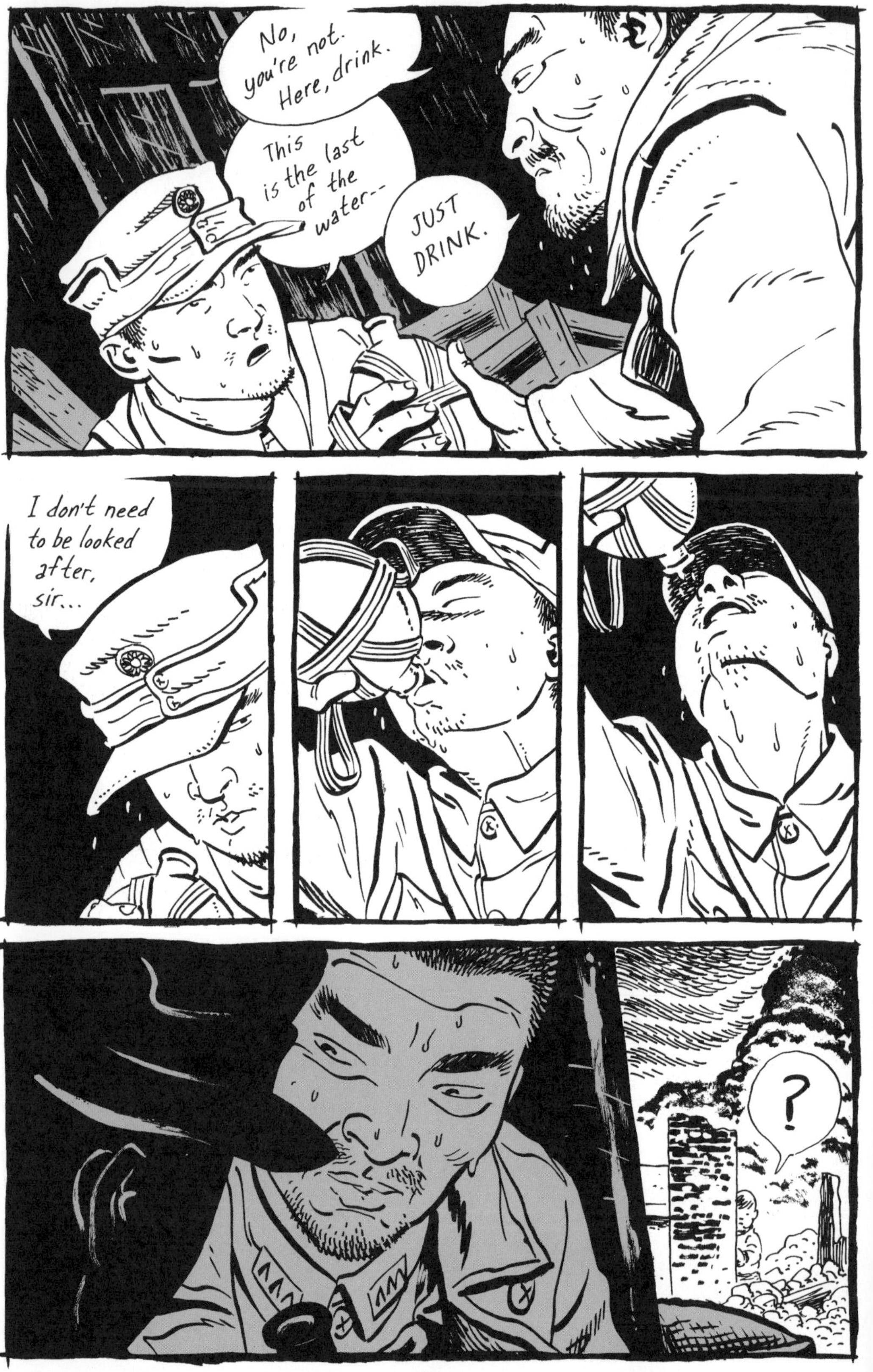
No, you're not. Here, drink.
This is the last of the water...
JUST DRINK.
I don't need to be looked after, sir...
?

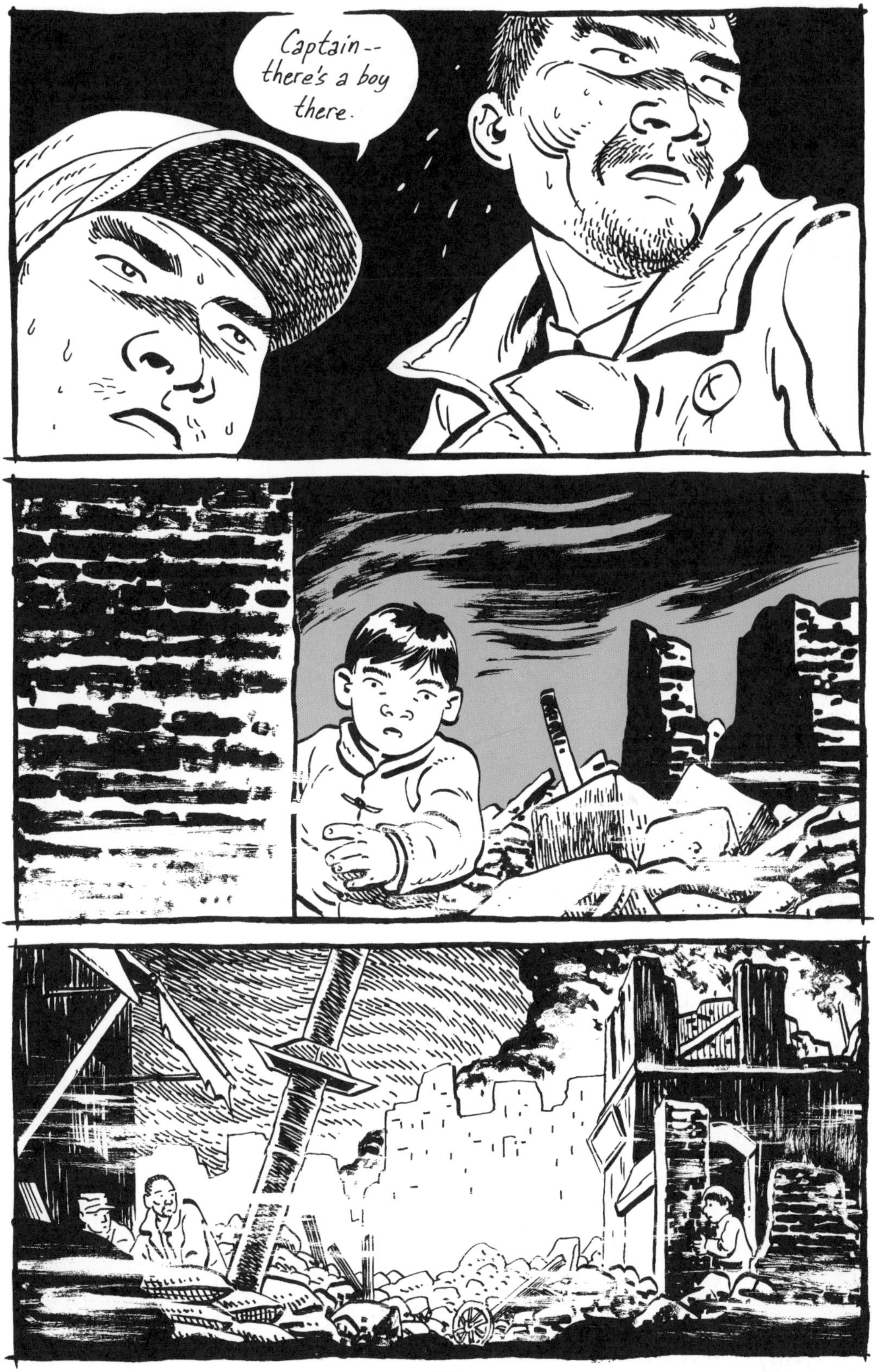
Captain-- there's a boy there.

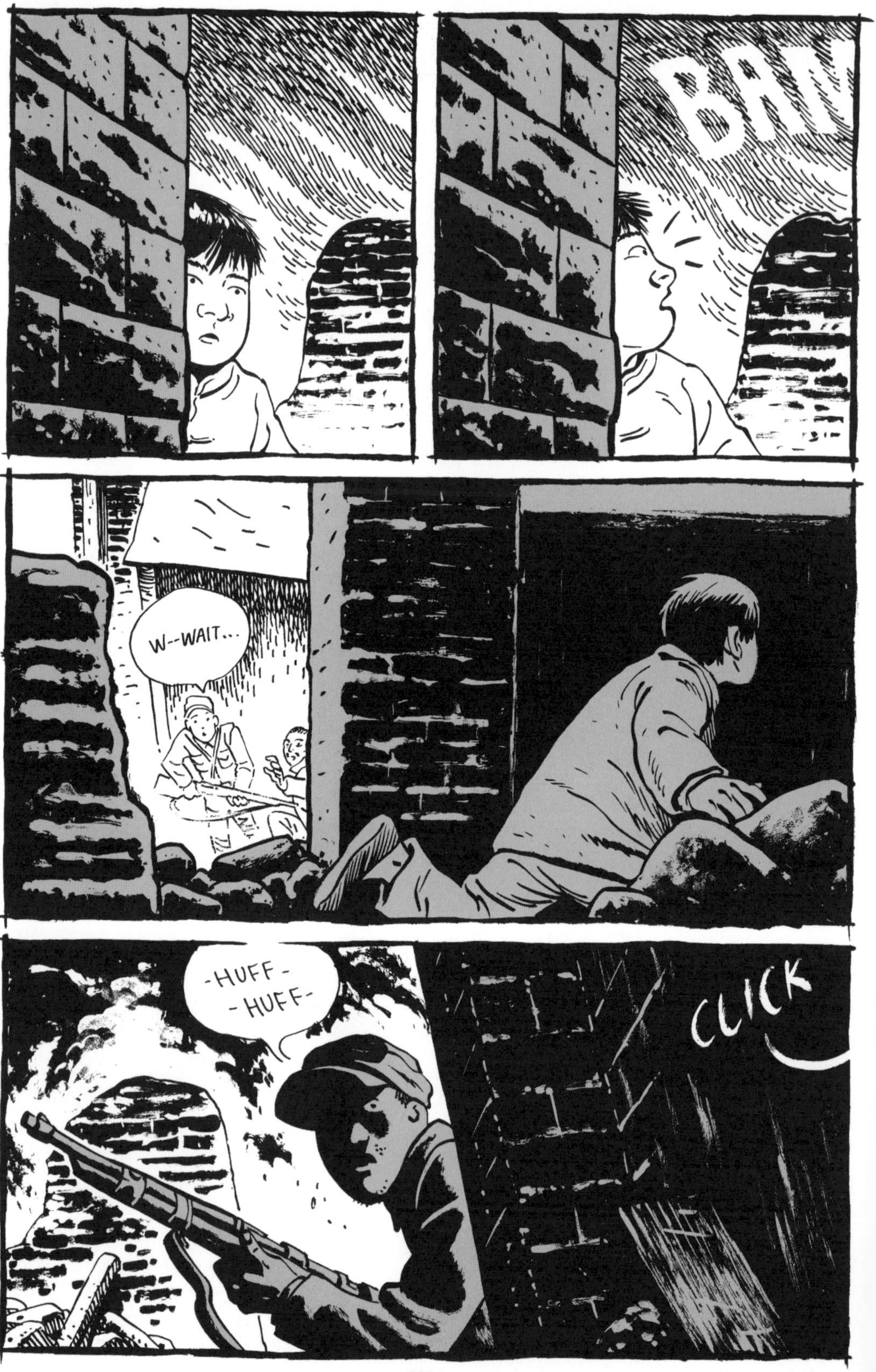
BRA
W--WAIT...
-HUFF-
-HUFF-
CLICK

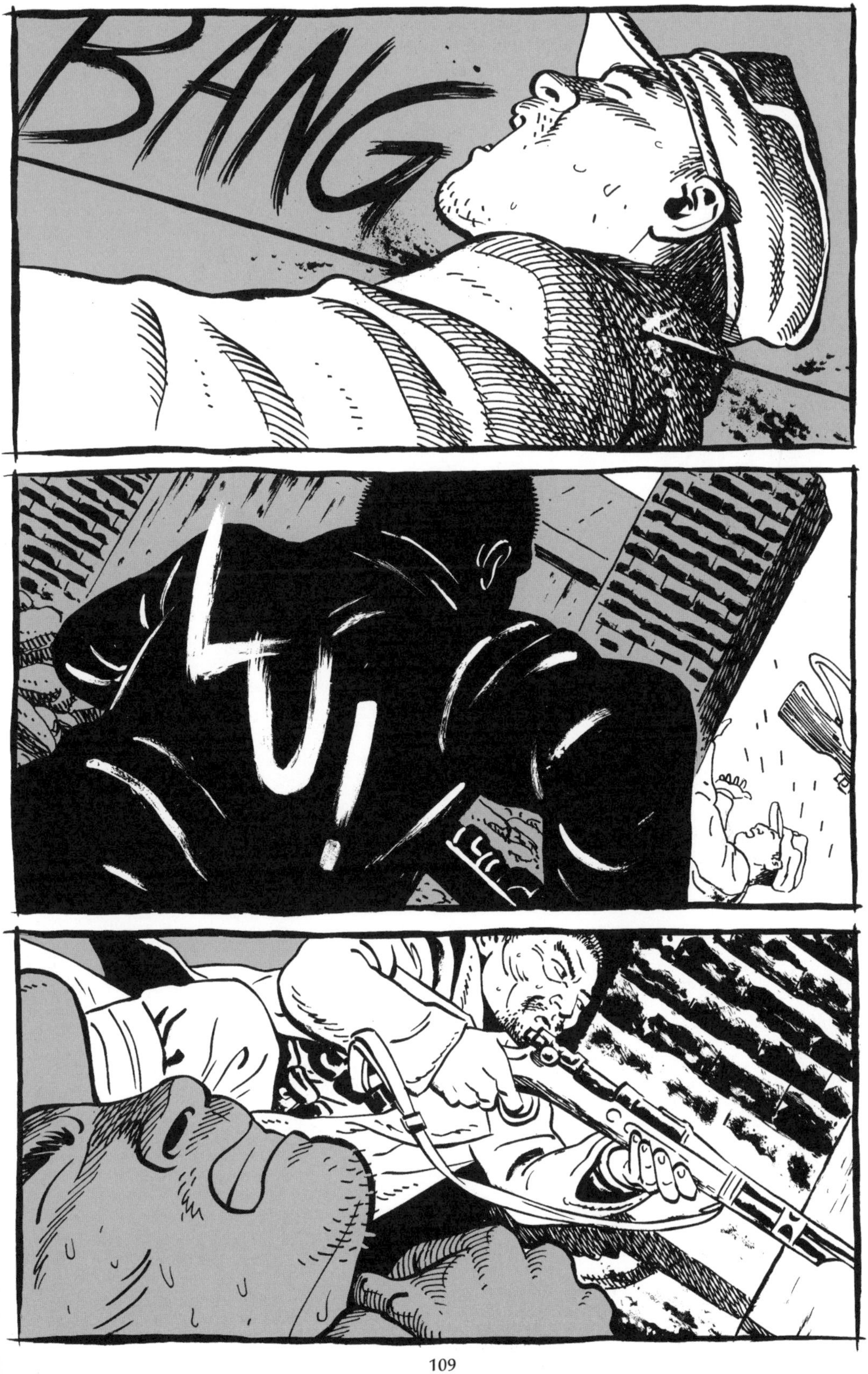
BANG
LUI!

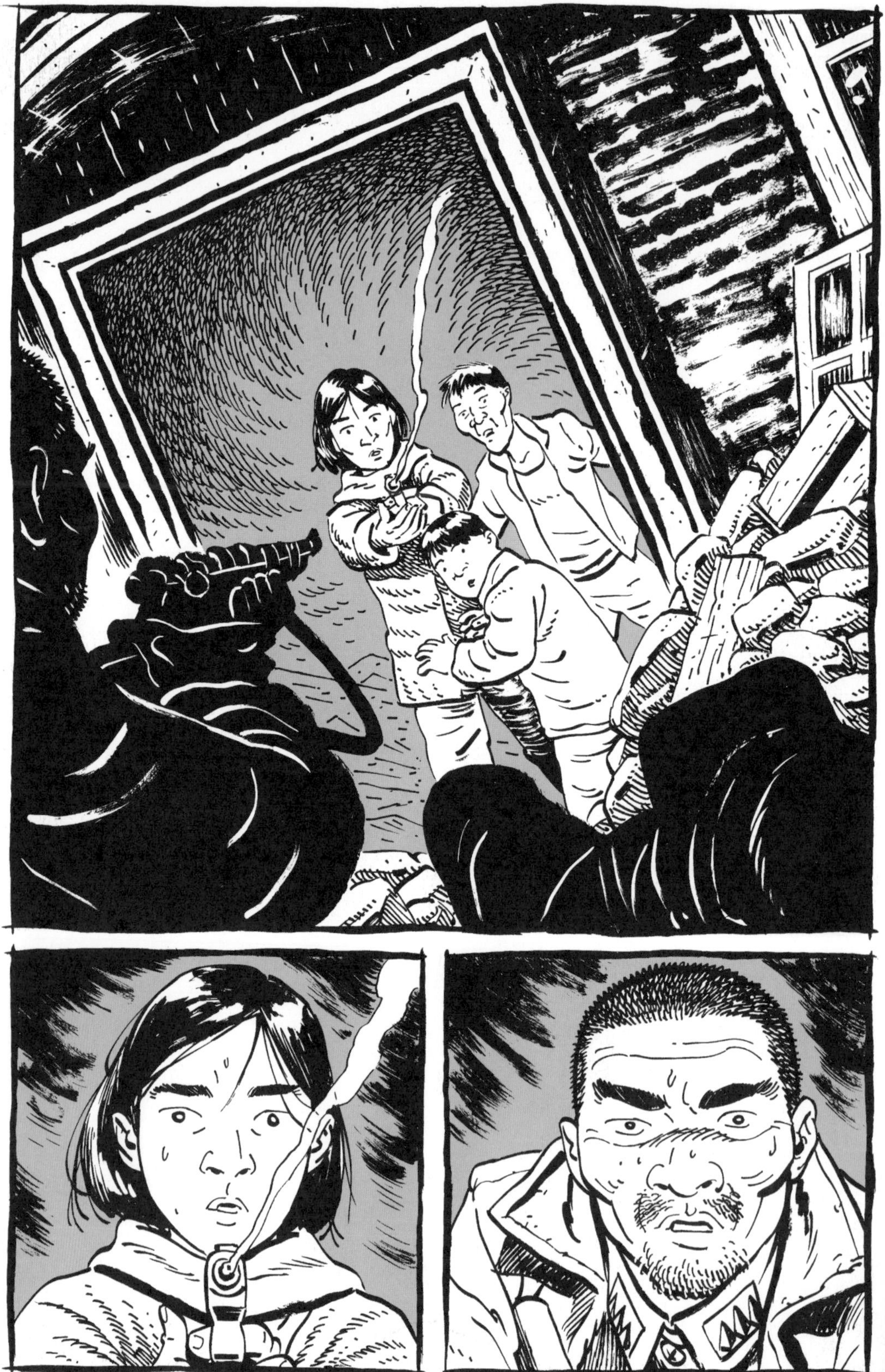

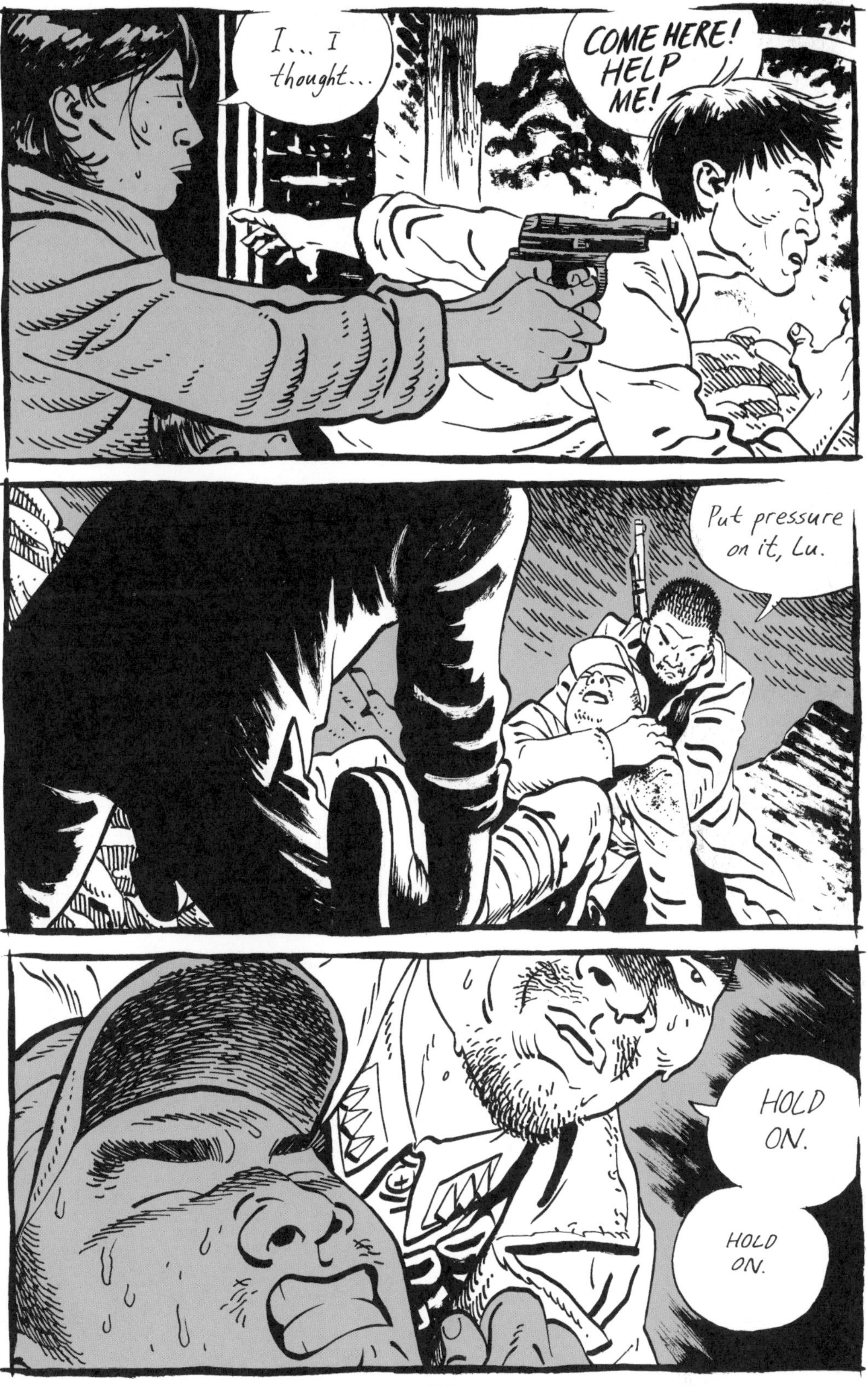
I... I thought...
COME HERE! HELP ME!
Put pressure on it, Lu.
HOLD ON.
HOLD ON.

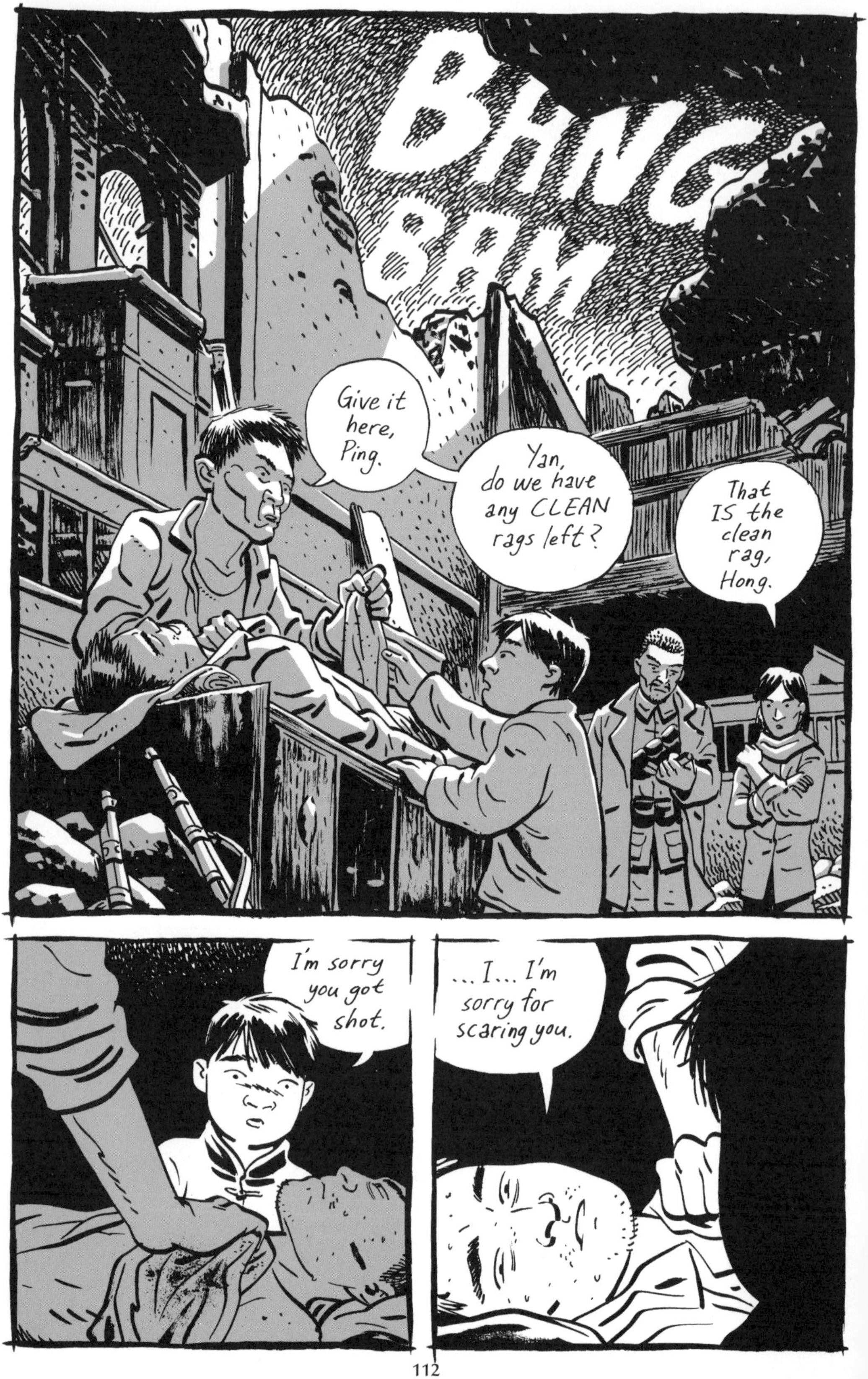
BANG
BAM
Give it here, Ping.
Yan, do we have any CLEAN rags left?
That IS the clean rag, Hong.
I'm sorry you got shot.
...I... I'm sorry for scaring you.

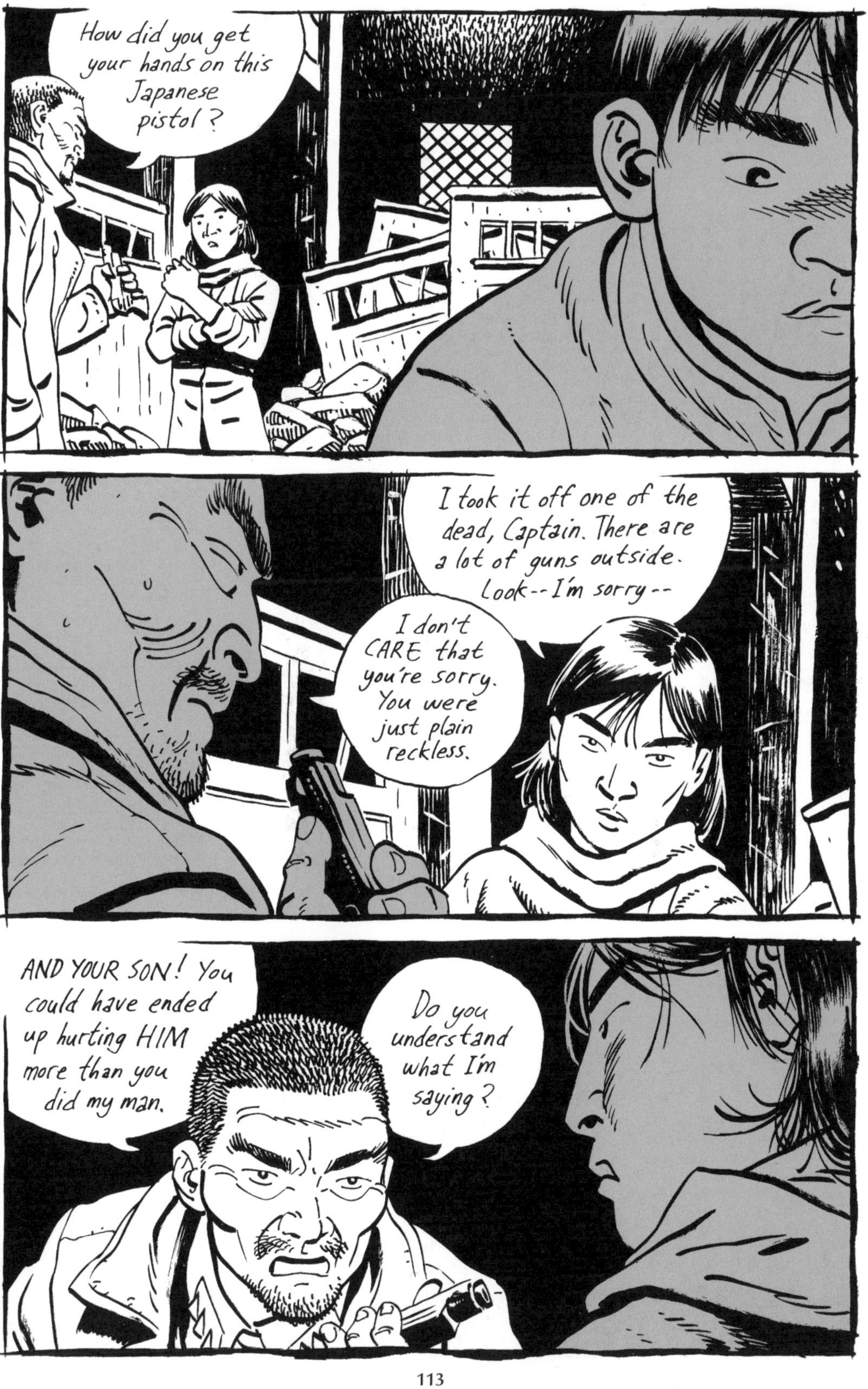
How did you get your hands on this Japanese pistol?
I took it off one of the dead, Captain. There are a lot of guns outside. Look--I'm sorry--
I don't CARE that you're sorry. You were just plain reckless.
AND YOUR SON! You could have ended up hurting HIM more than you did my man.
Do you understand what I'm saying?

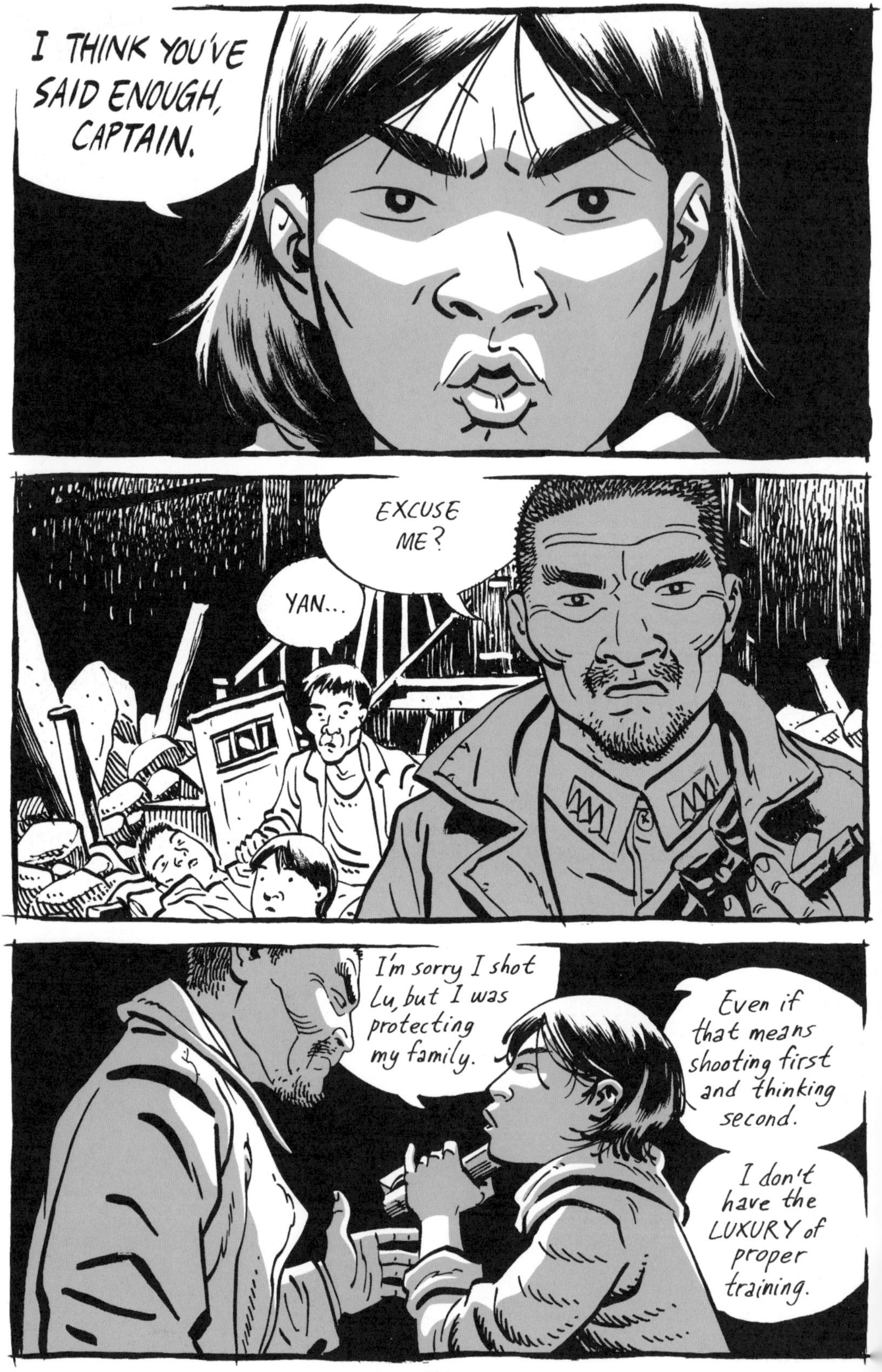
I THINK YOU'VE SAID ENOUGH, CAPTAIN.
EXCUSE ME?
YAN...
I'm sorry I shot Lu, but I was protecting my family.
Even if that means shooting first and thinking second.
I don't have the LUXURY of proper training.

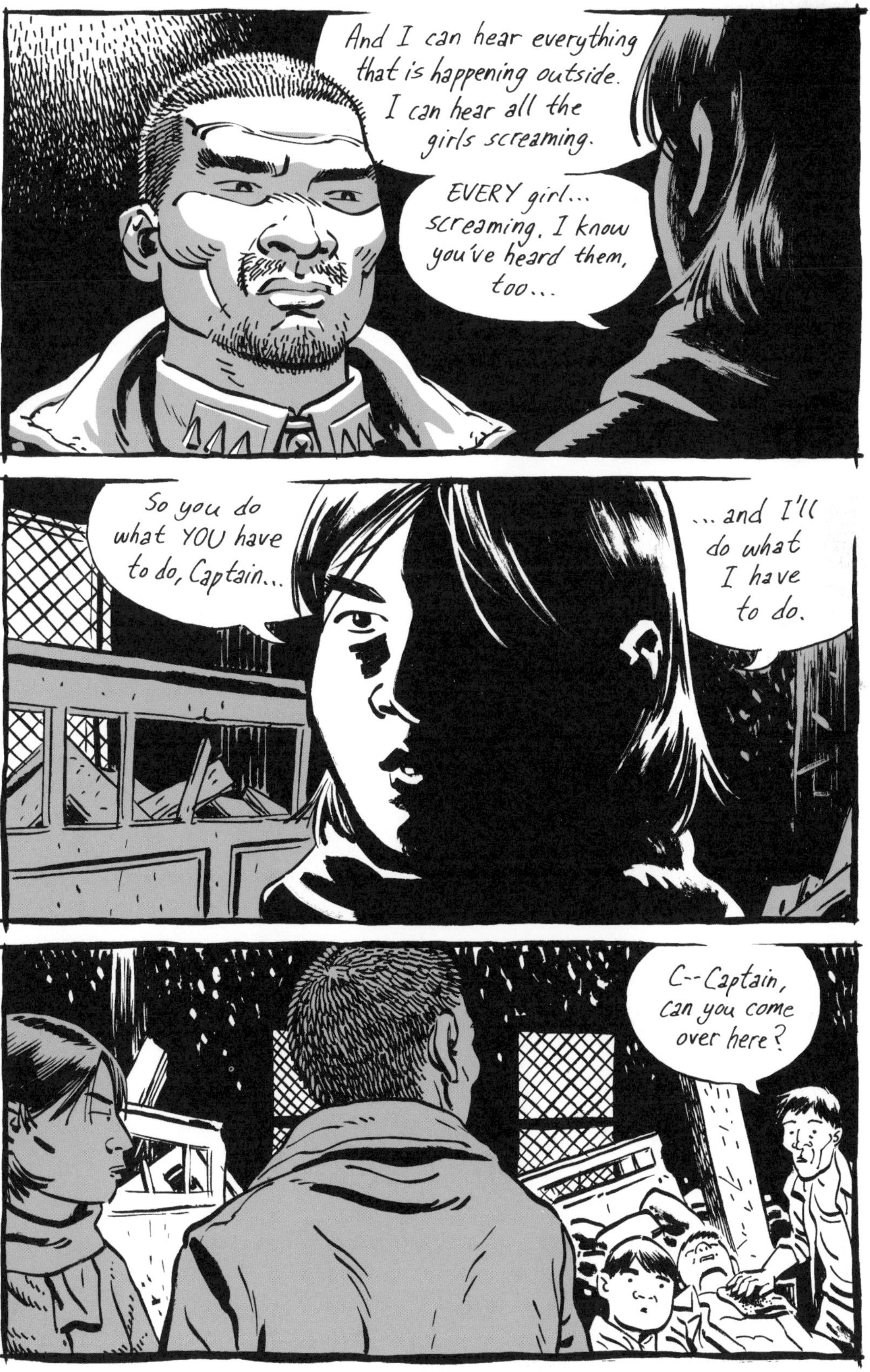
And I can hear everything that is happening outside. I can hear all the girls screaming.
EVERY girl... screaming. I know you've heard them, too...
So you do what YOU have to do, Captain...
...and I'll do what I have to do.
C--Captain, can you come over here?

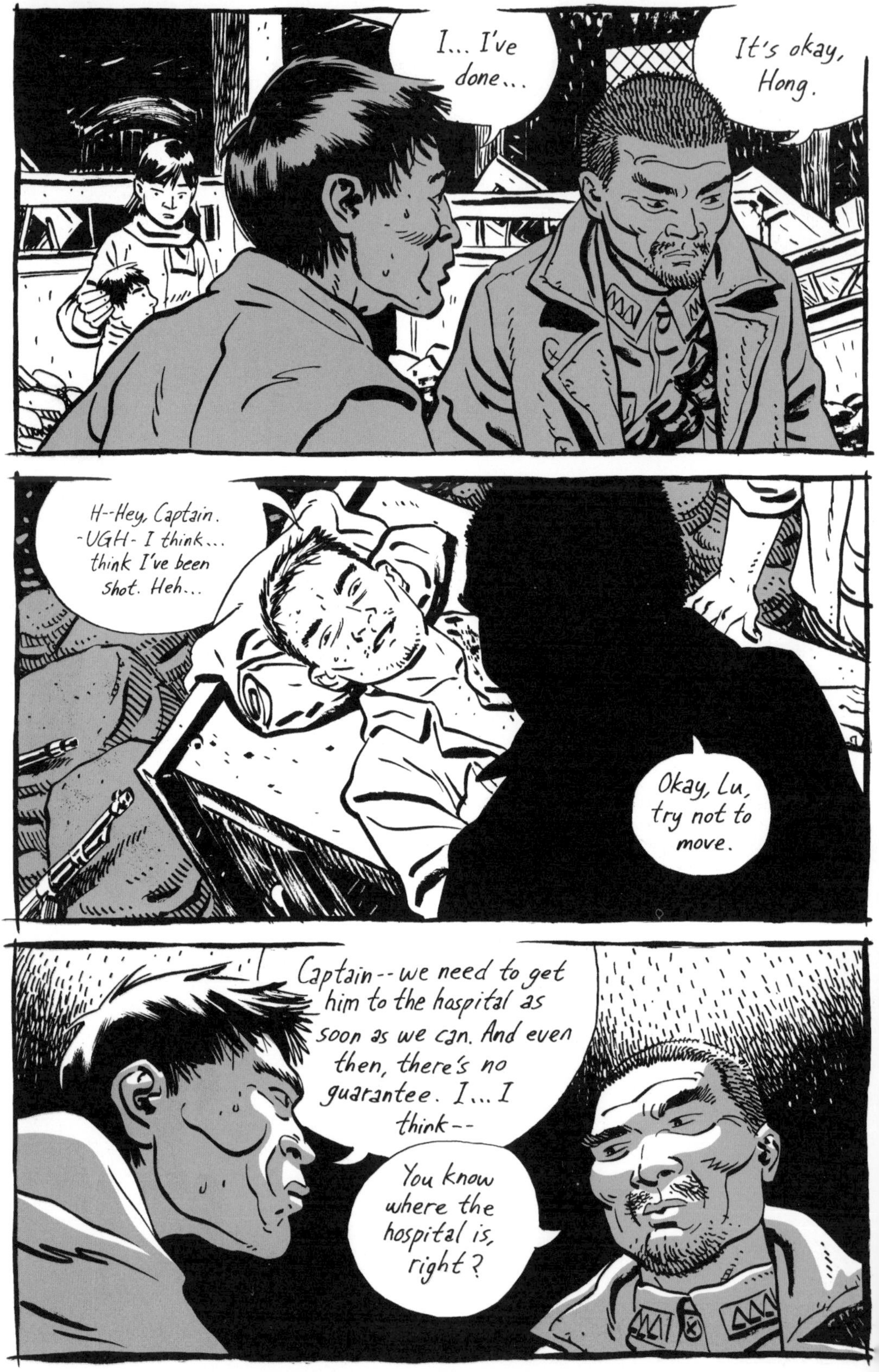

I... I've done...
It's okay, Hong.
H--Hey, Captain. -UGH- I think... think I've been shot. Heh...
Okay, Lu, try not to move.
Captain--we need to get him to the hospital as soon as we can. And even then, there's no guarantee. I... I think--
You know where the hospital is, right?

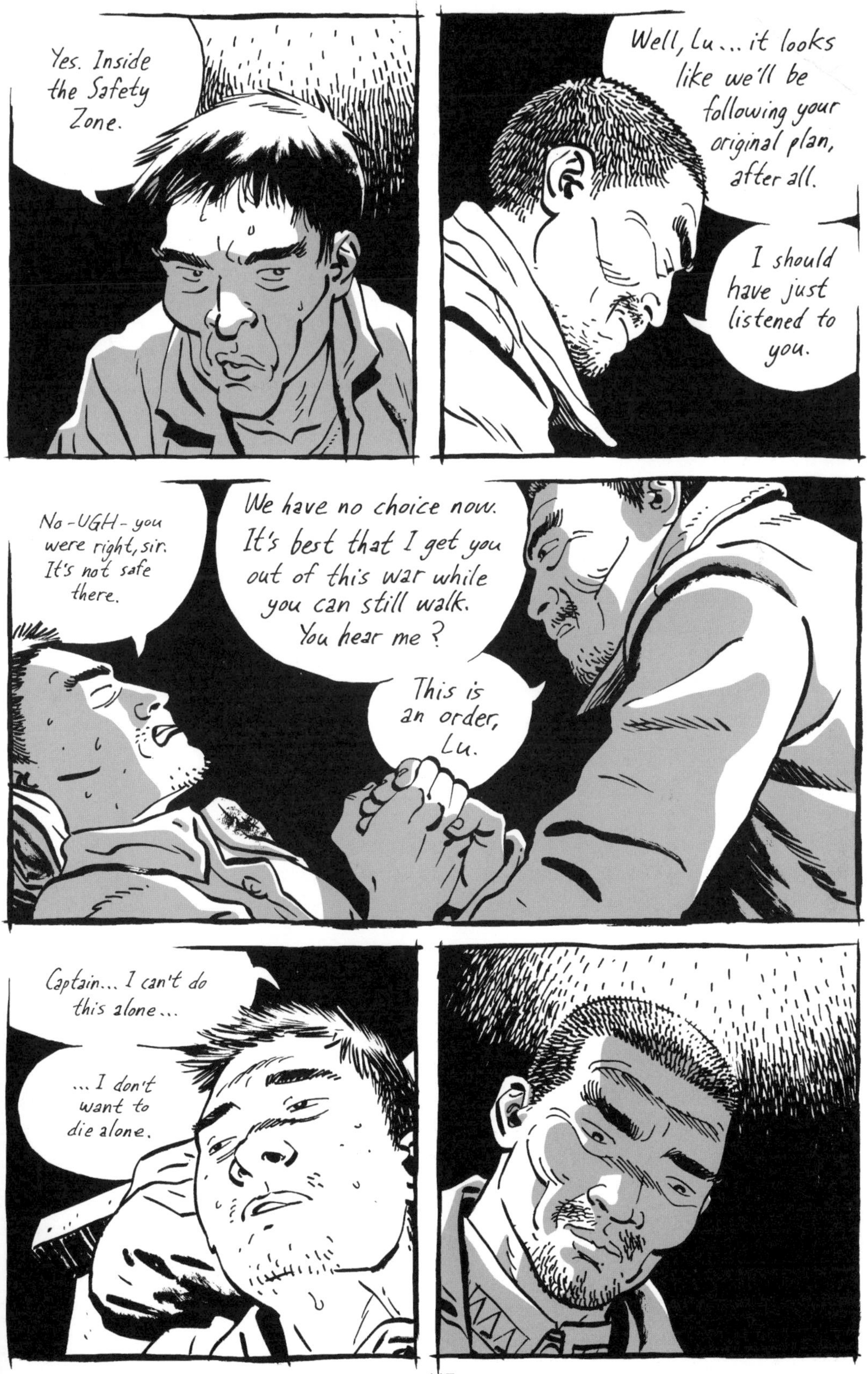
Yes. Inside the Safety Zone.
Well, Lu... it looks like we'll be following your original plan, after all.
I should have just listened to you.
No-UGH-you were right, sir. It's not safe there.
We have no choice now. It's best that I get you out of this war while you can still walk. You hear me?
This is an order, Lu.
Captain... I can't do this alone...
...I don't want to die alone.

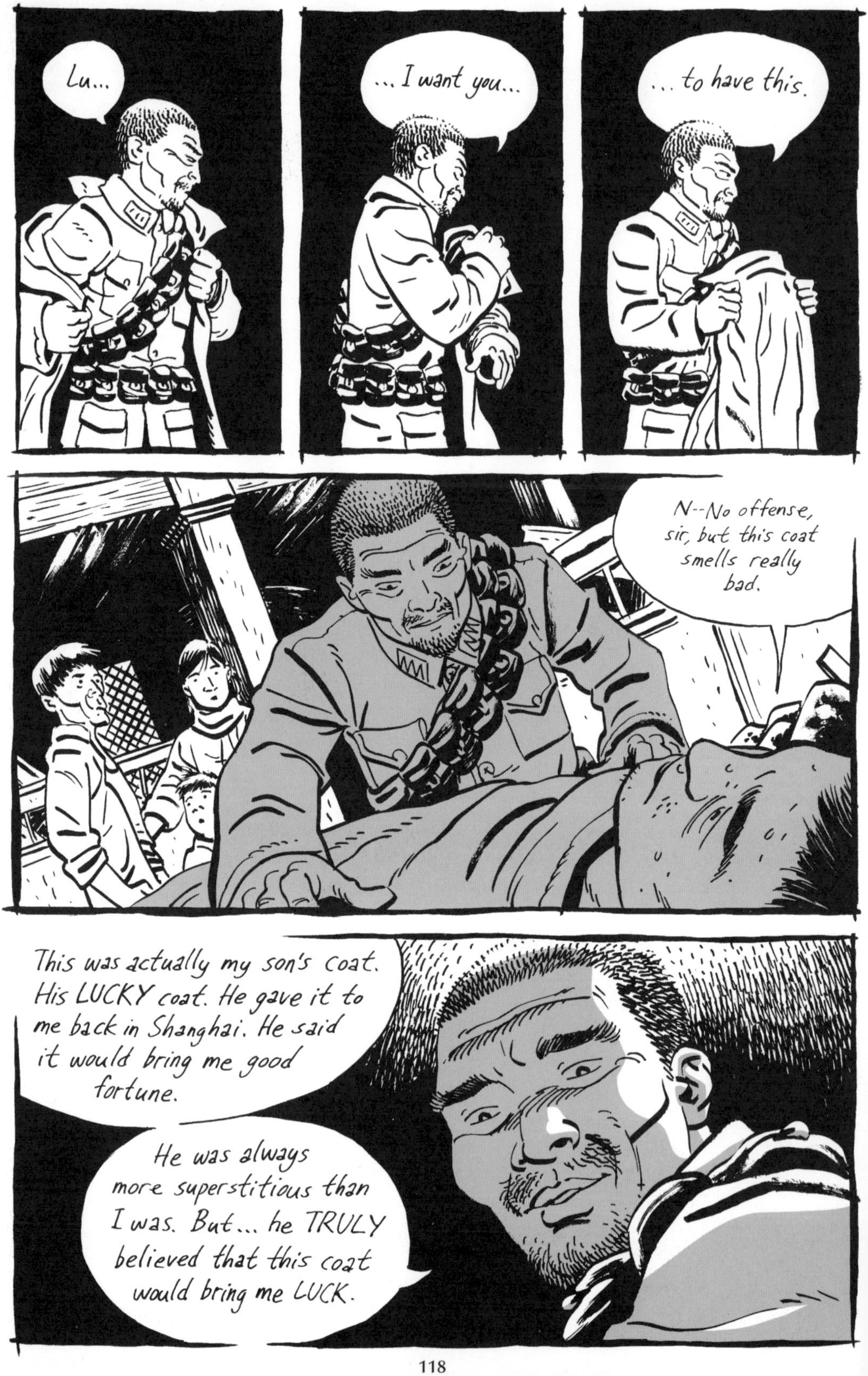
Lu...
...I want you...
...to have this.
N--No offense, sir, but this coat smells really bad.
This was actually my son's coat. His LUCKY coat. He gave it to me back in Shanghai. He said it would bring me good fortune.
He was always more superstitious than I was. But... he TRULY believed that this coat would bring me LUCK.

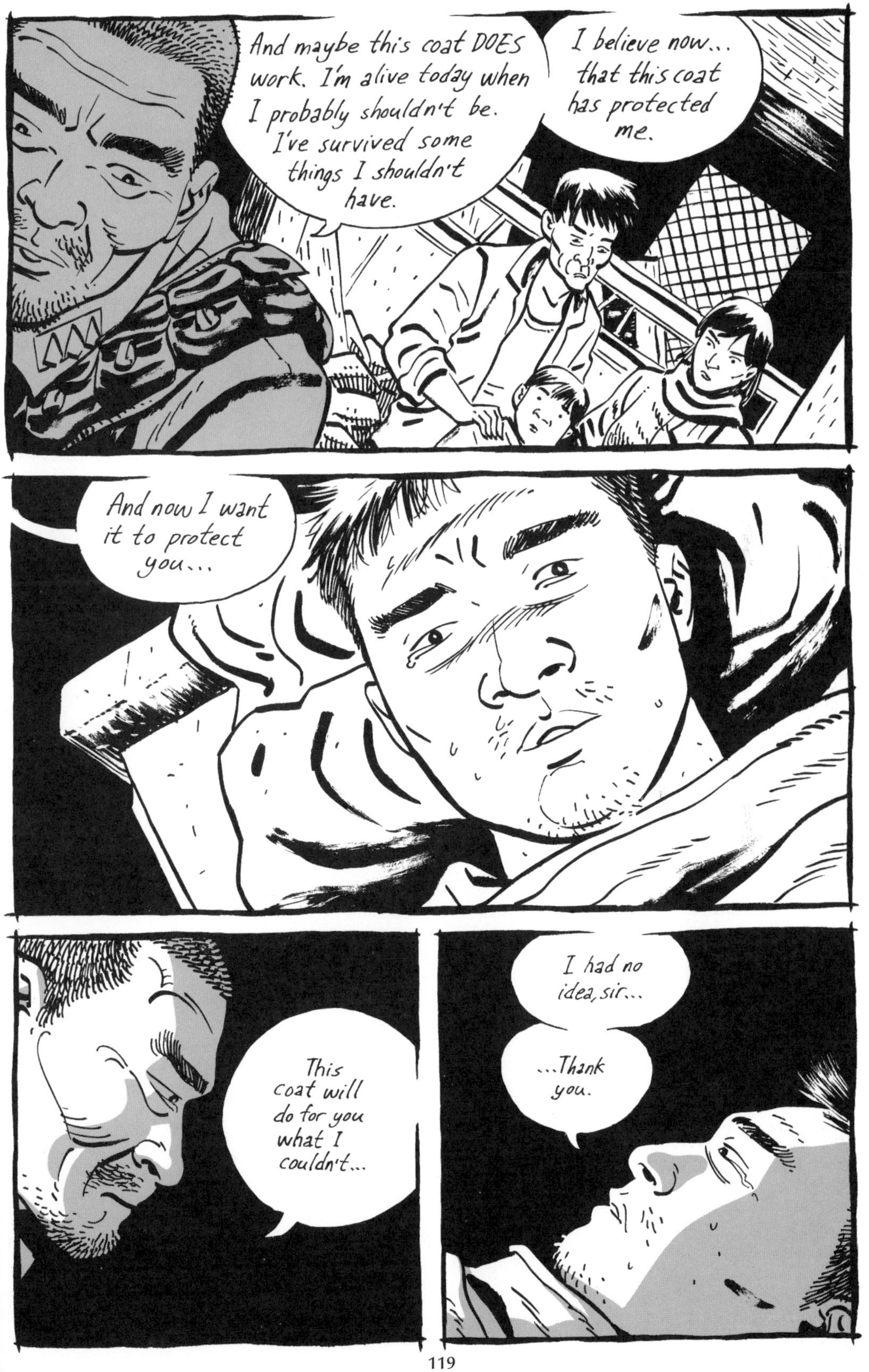
And maybe this coat DOES work. I'm alive today when I probably shouldn't be. I've survived some things I shouldn't have.
I believe now... that this coat has protected me.
And now I want it to protect you...
This coat will do for you what I couldn't...
I had no idea, sir...
...Thank you.

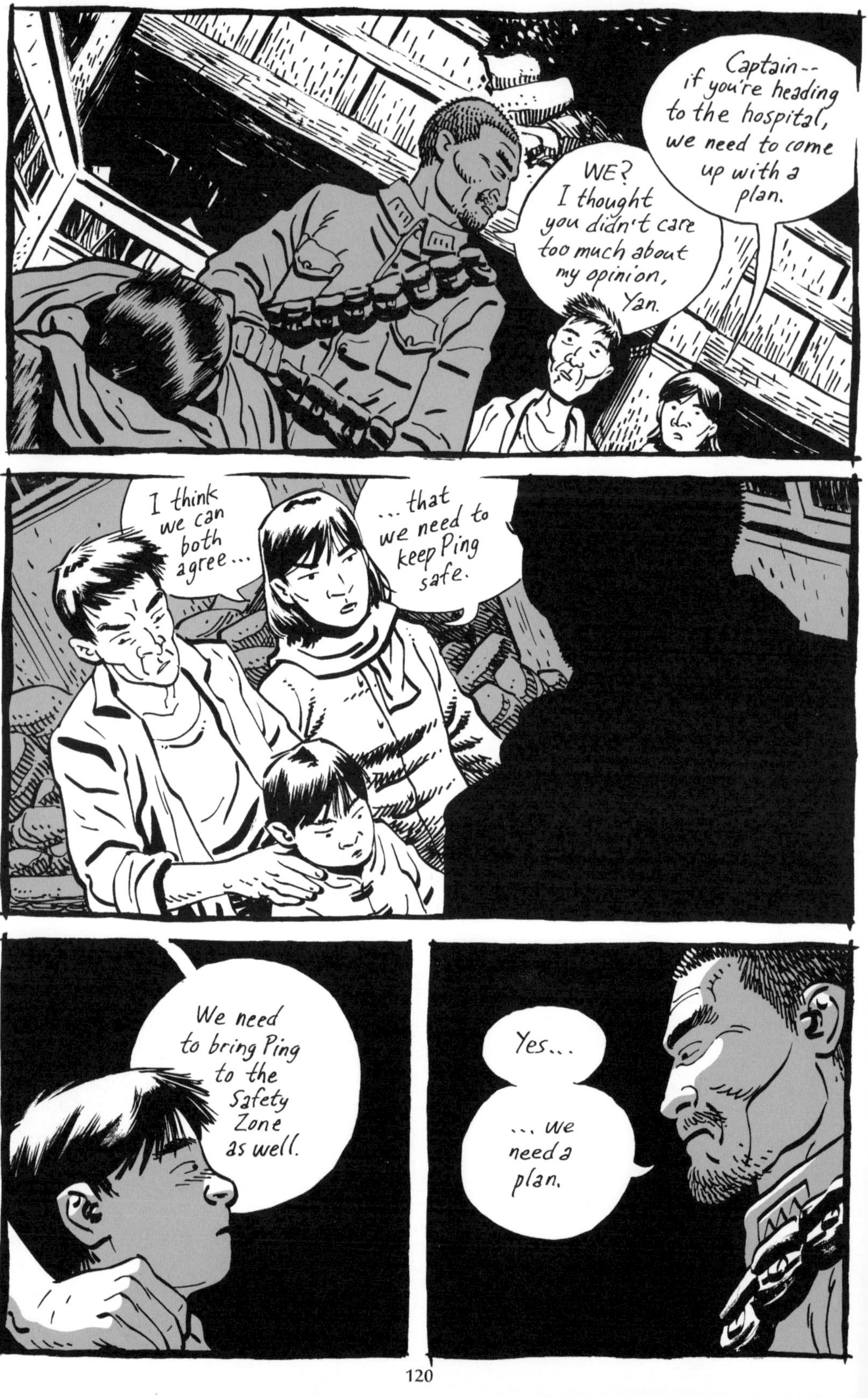
Captain-- if you're heading to the hospital, we need to come up with a plan.
WE? I thought you didn't care too much about my opinion, Yan.
I think we can both agree...
... that we need to keep Ping safe.
We need to bring Ping to the Safety Zone as well.
Yes...
... we need a plan.

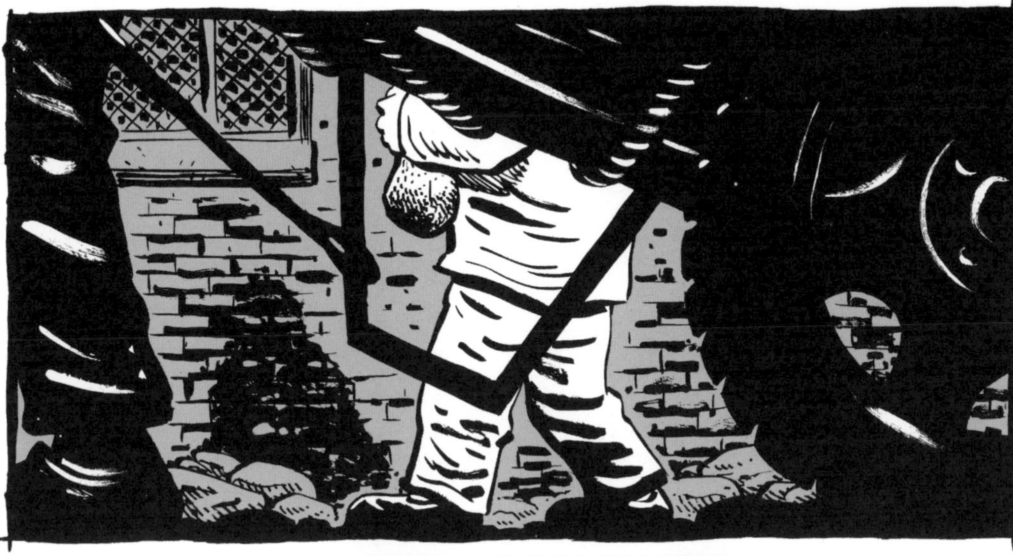

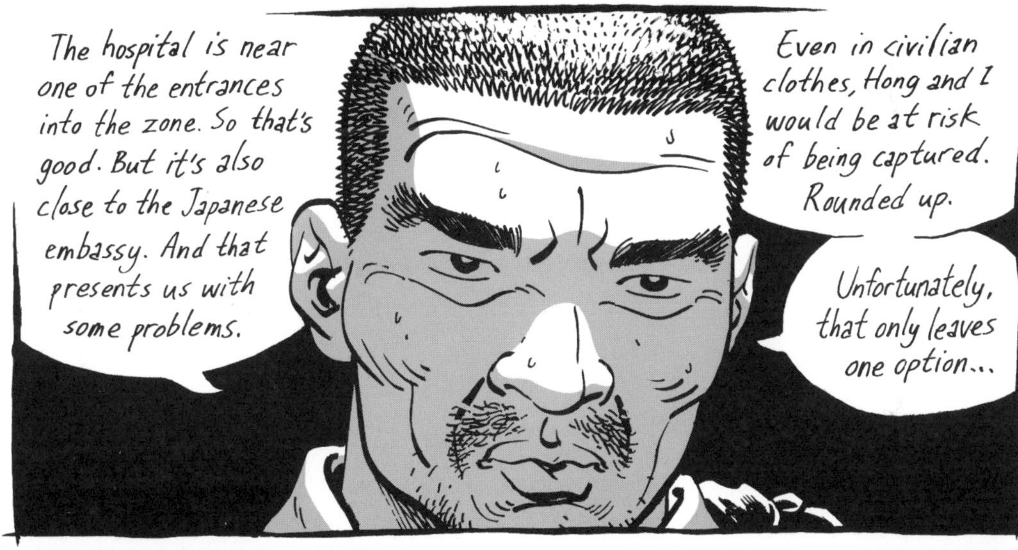
The hospital is near one of the entrances into the zone. So that's good. But it's also close to the Japanese embassy. And that presents us with some problems.
Even in civilian clothes, Hong and I would be at risk of being captured. Rounded up.
Unfortunately, that only leaves one option...

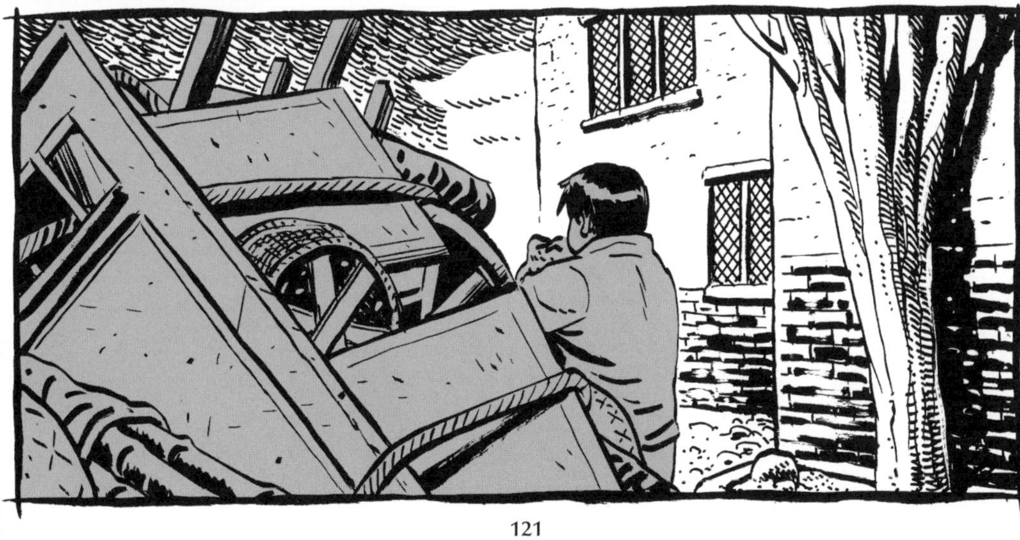

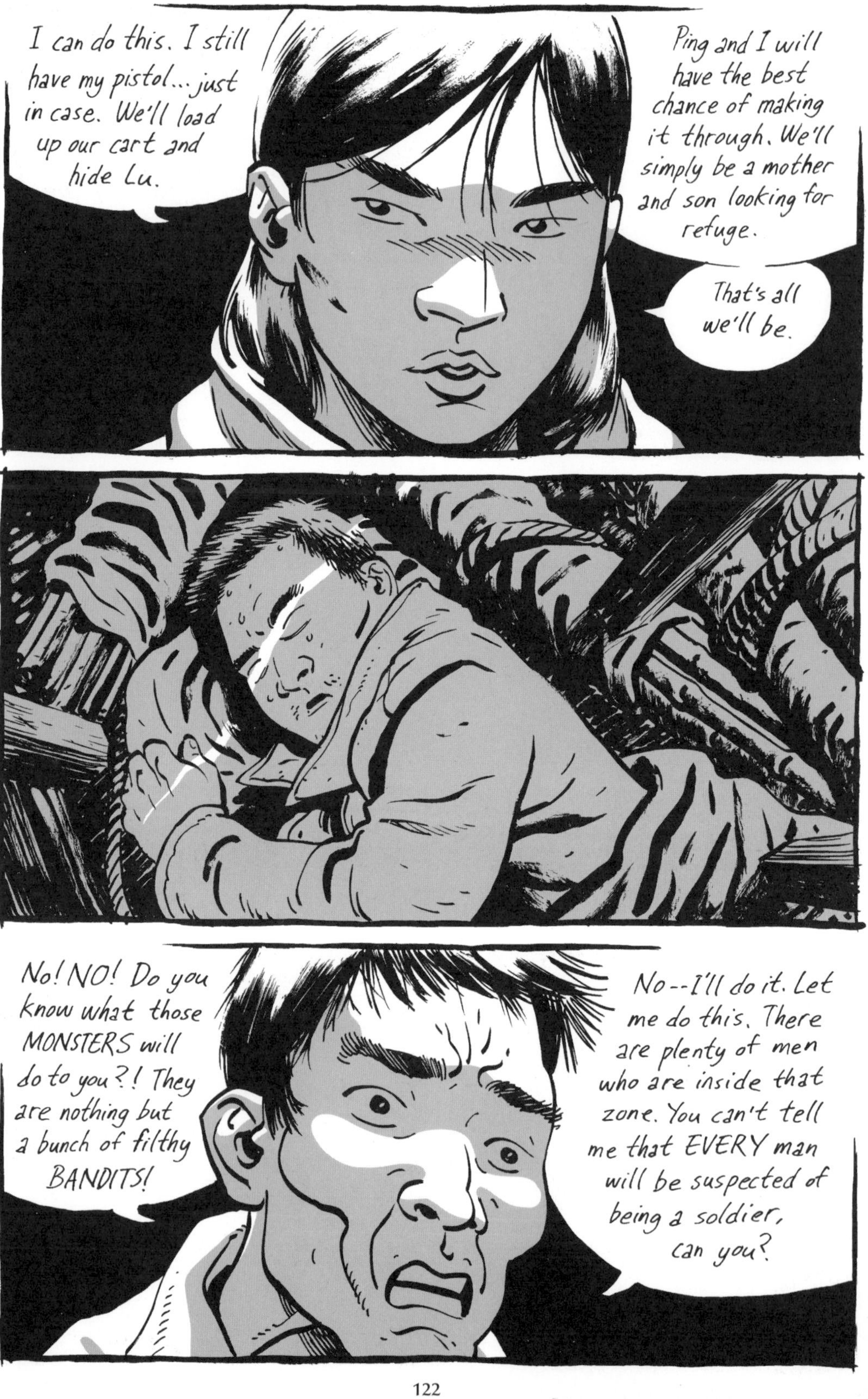
I can do this. I still have my pistol... just in case. We'll load up our cart and hide Lu.
Ping and I will have the best chance of making it through. We'll simply be a mother and son looking for refuge.
That's all we'll be.
No! NO! Do you know what those MONSTERS will do to you?! They are nothing but a bunch of filthy BANDITS!
No--I'll do it. Let me do this. There are plenty of men who are inside that zone. You can't tell me that EVERY man will be suspected of being a soldier, can you?

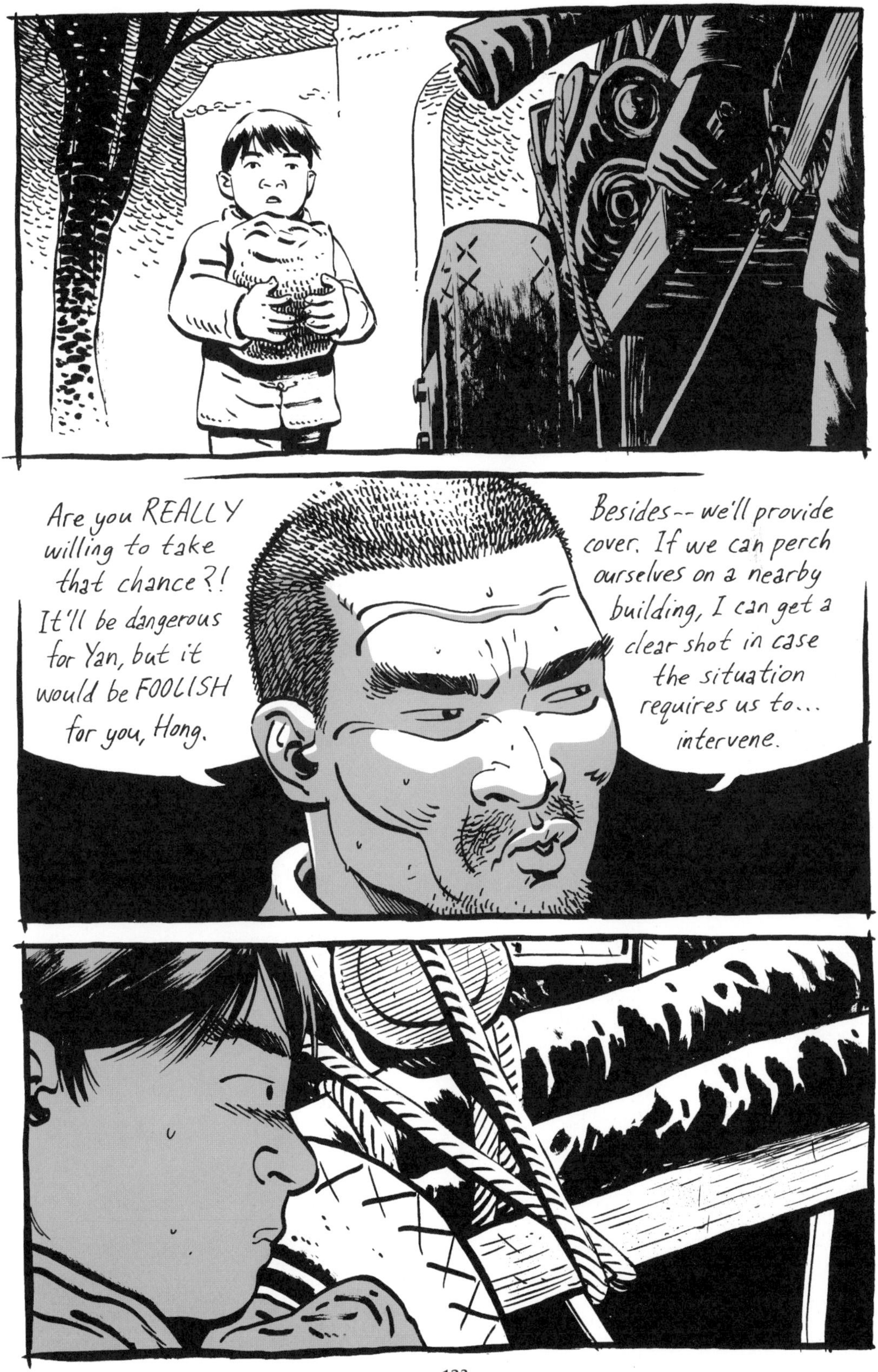
Are you REALLY willing to take that chance?! It'll be dangerous for Yan, but it would be FOOLISH for you, Hong.
Besides-- we'll provide cover. If we can perch ourselves on a nearby building, I can get a clear shot in case the situation requires us to... intervene.

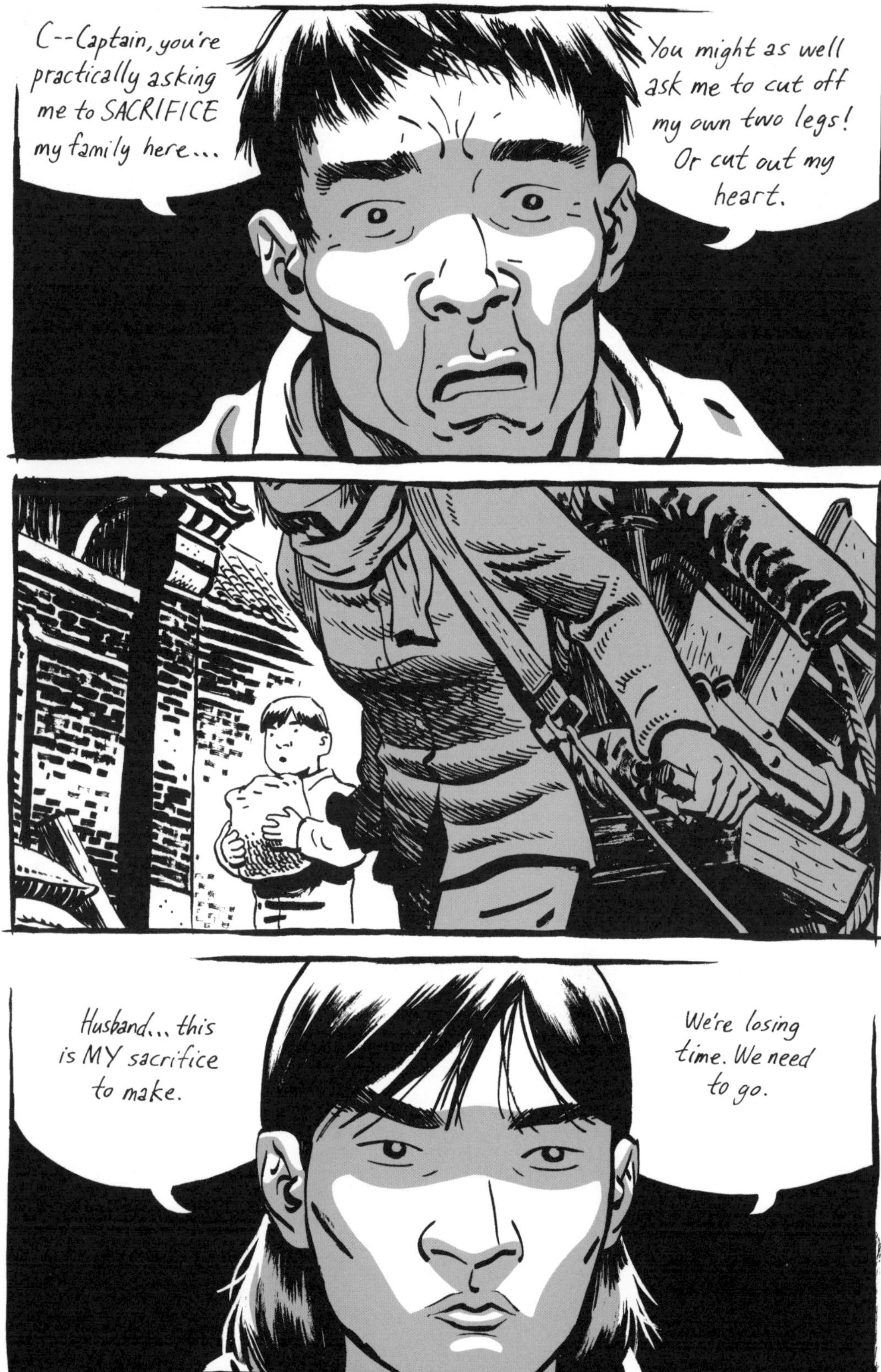
C--Captain, you're practically asking me to SACRIFICE my family here...
You might as well ask me to cut off my own two legs! Or cut out my heart.
Husband... this is MY sacrifice to make.
We're losing time. We need to go.

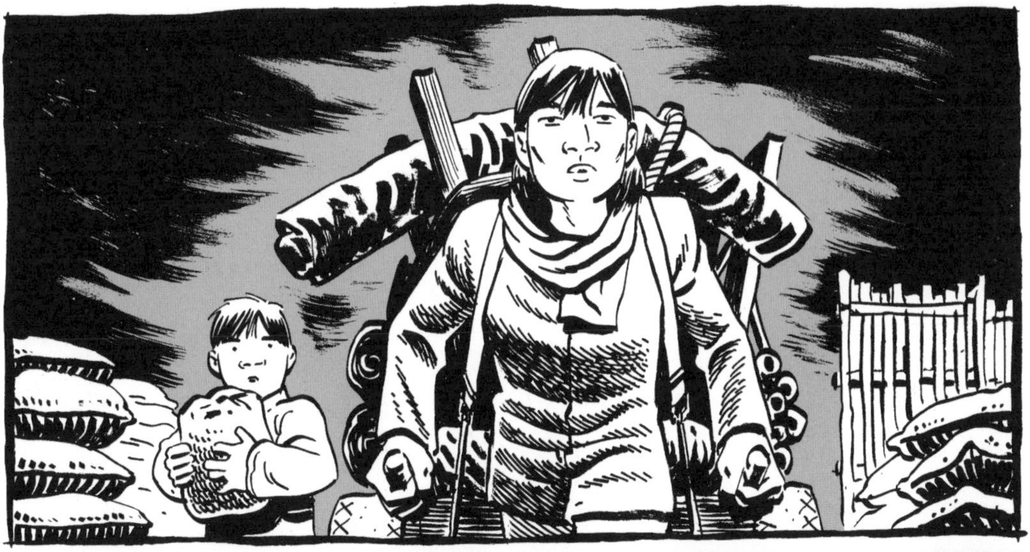

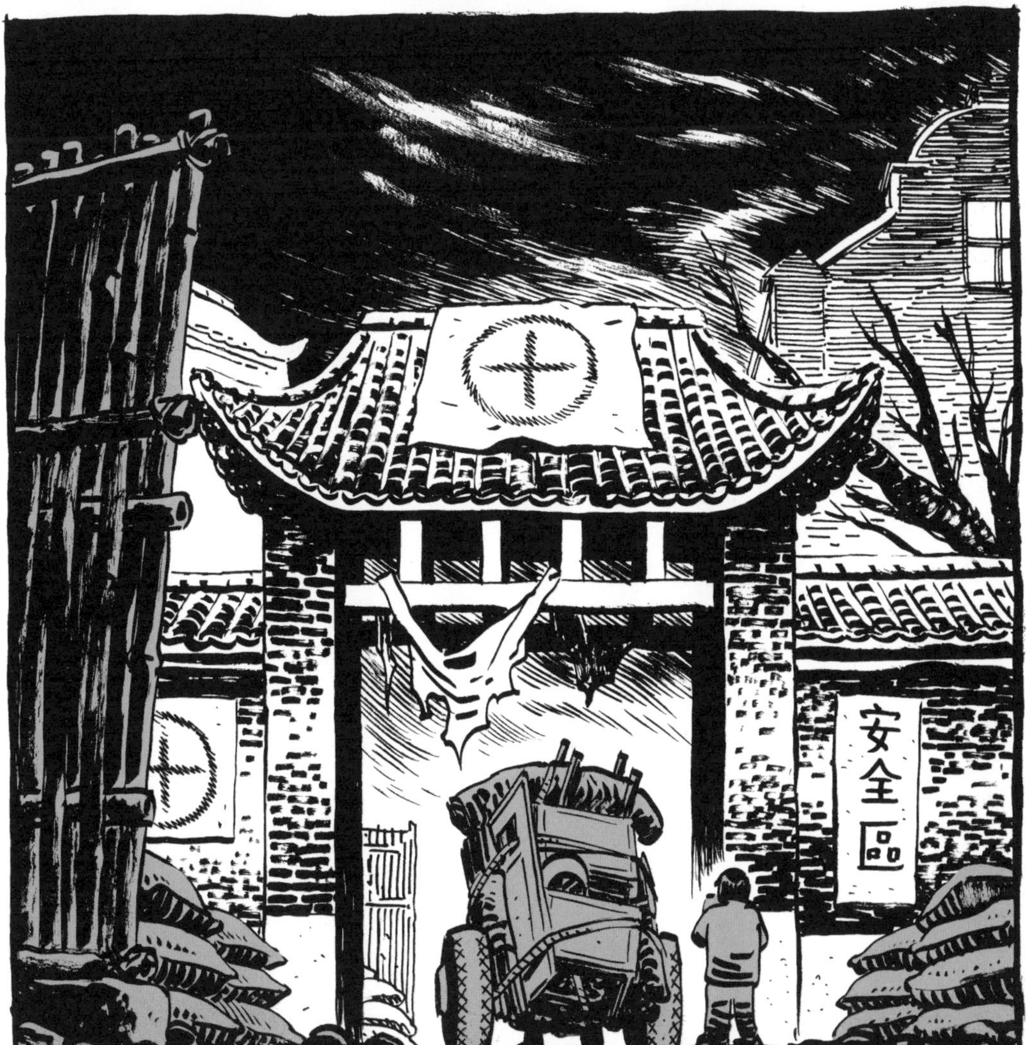
安全區

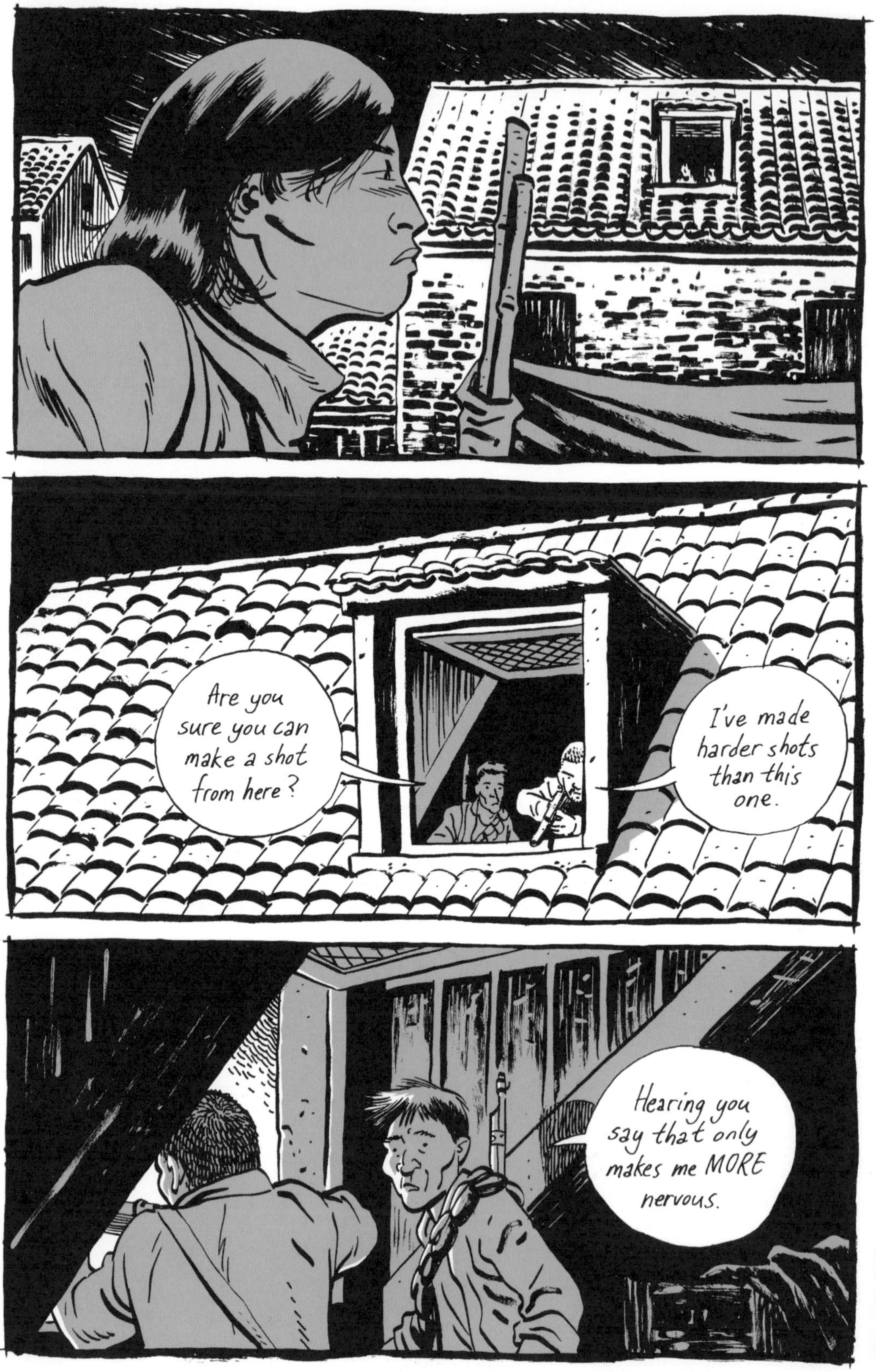
Are you sure you can make a shot from here?
I've made harder shots than this one.
Hearing you say that only makes me MORE nervous.

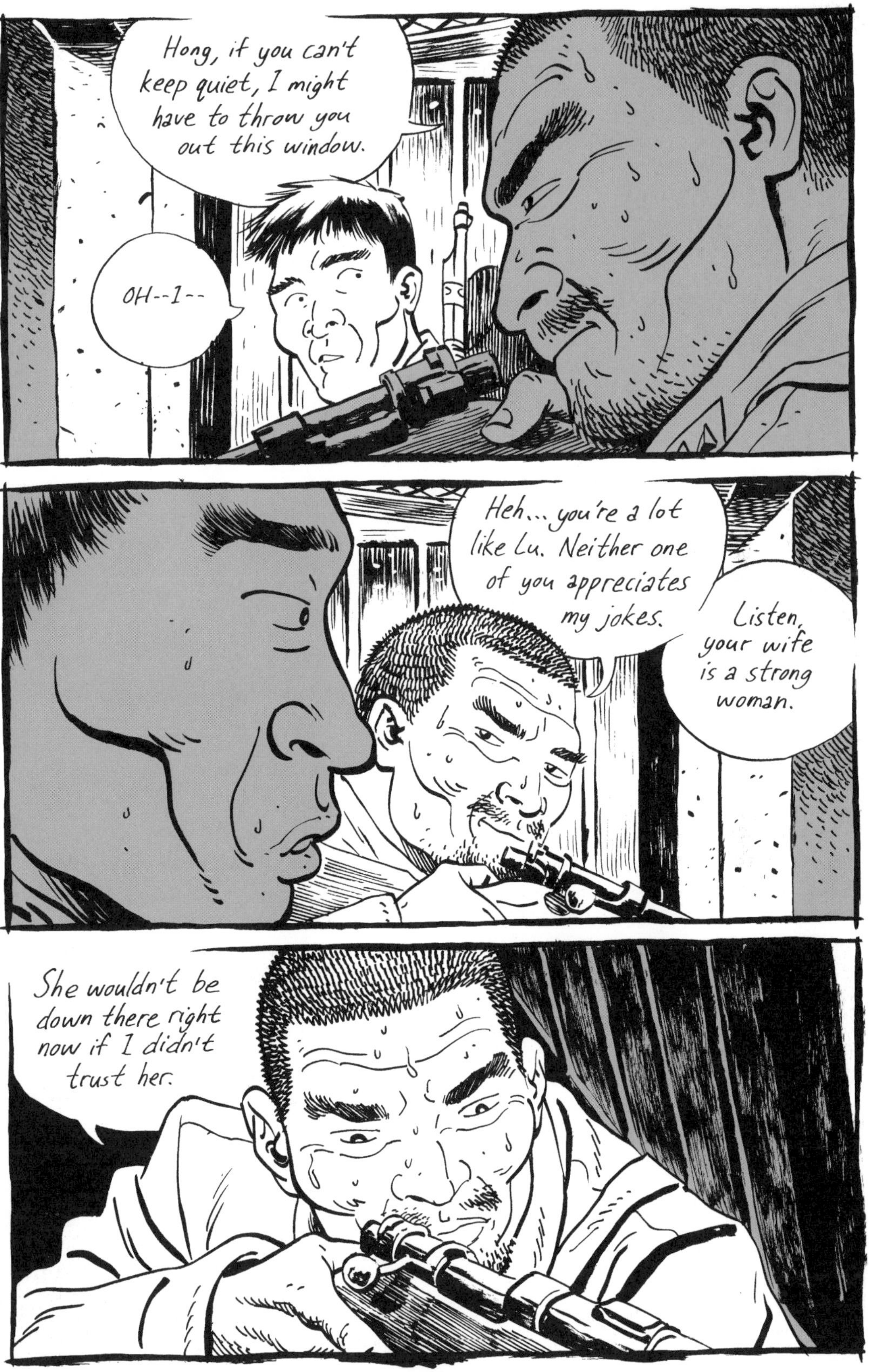
Hong, if you can't keep quiet, I might have to throw you out this window.
OH--I--
Heh... you're a lot like Lu. Neither one of you appreciates my jokes.
Listen, your wife is a strong woman.
She wouldn't be down there right now if I didn't trust her.

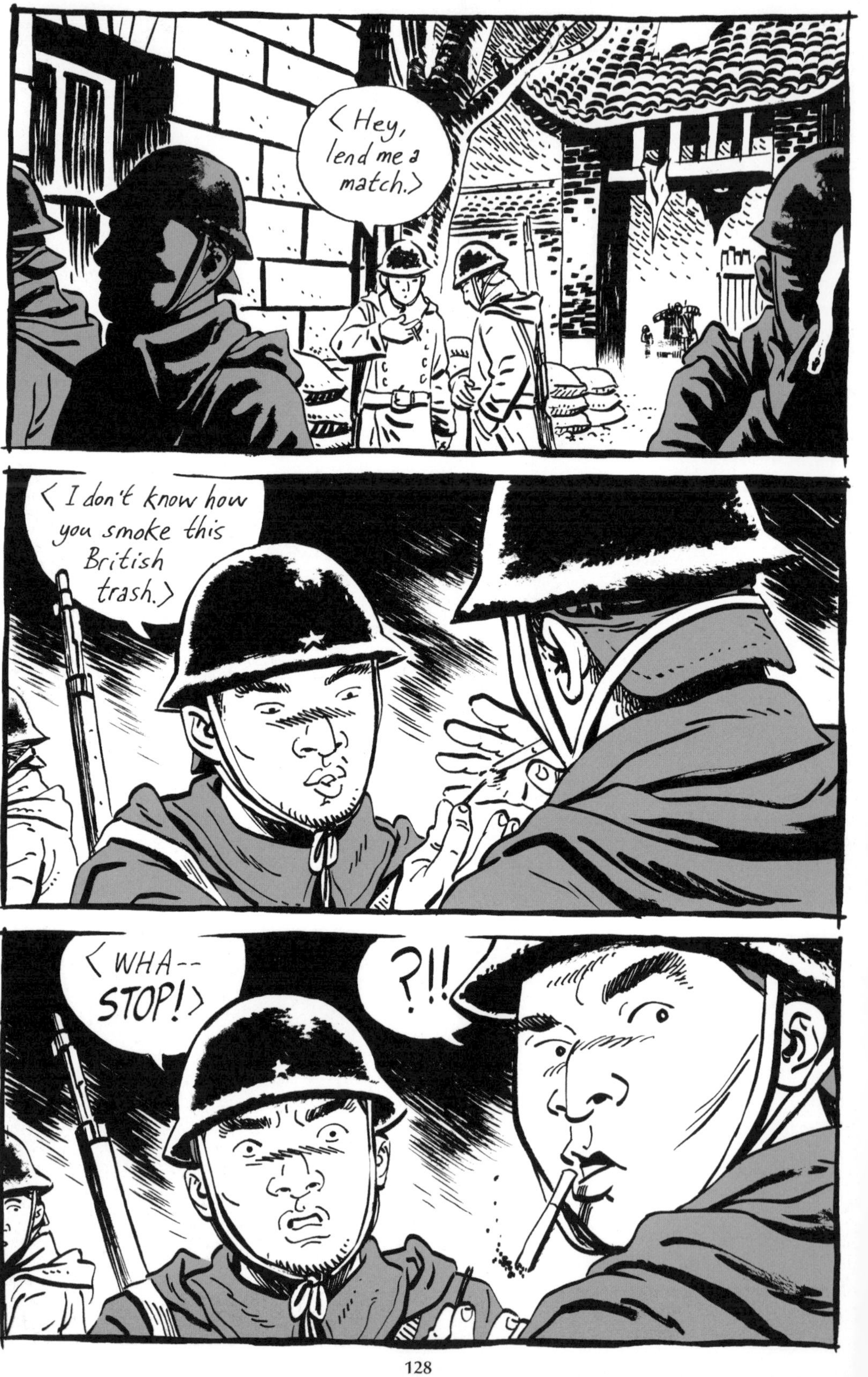
<Hey, lend me a match.>
<I don't know how you smoke this British trash.>
<WHA-- STOP!>
?!!

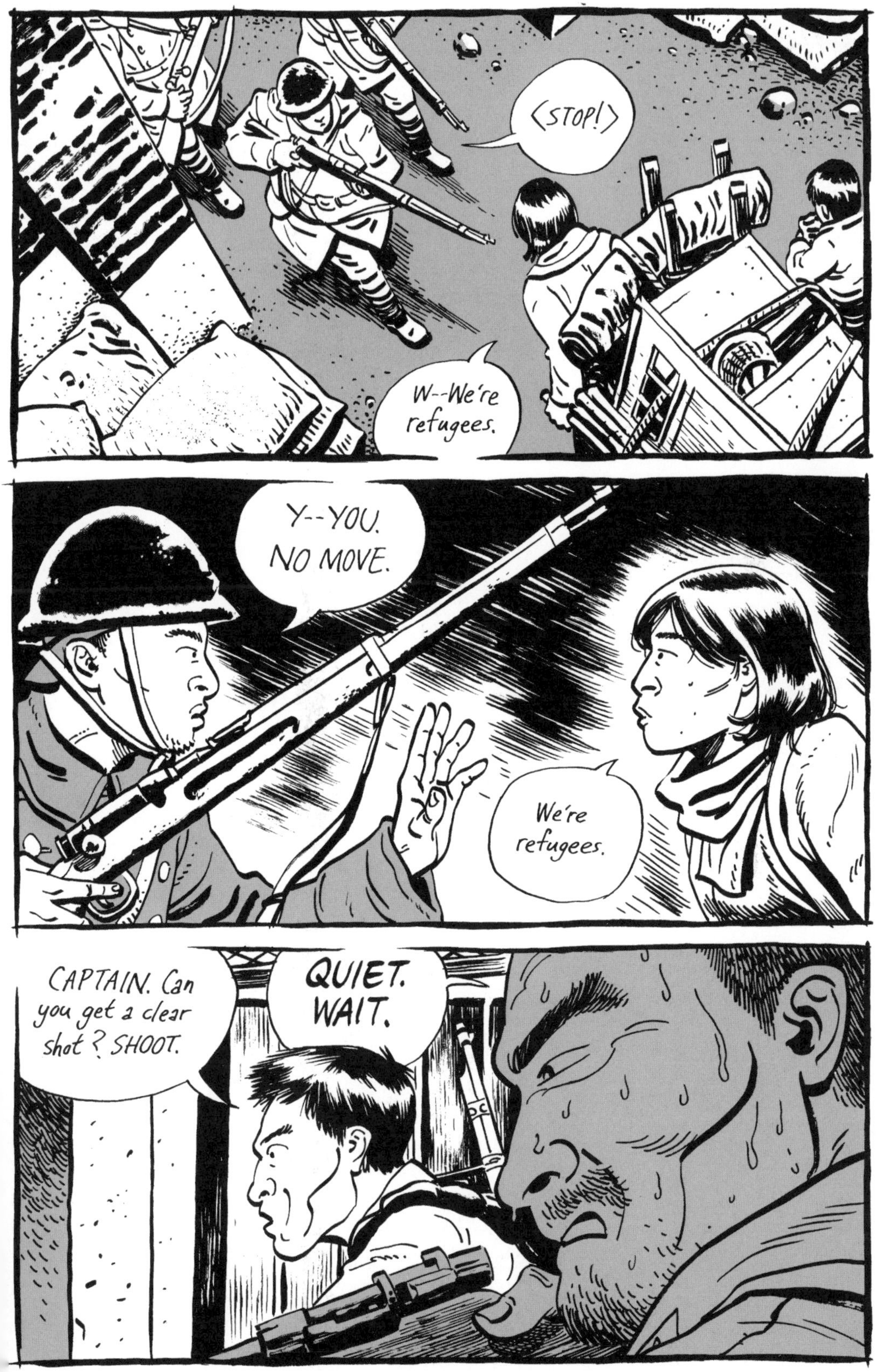
⟨STOP!⟩
W--We're refugees.
Y--YOU. NO MOVE.
We're refugees.
CAPTAIN. Can you get a clear shot? SHOOT.
QUIET. WAIT.

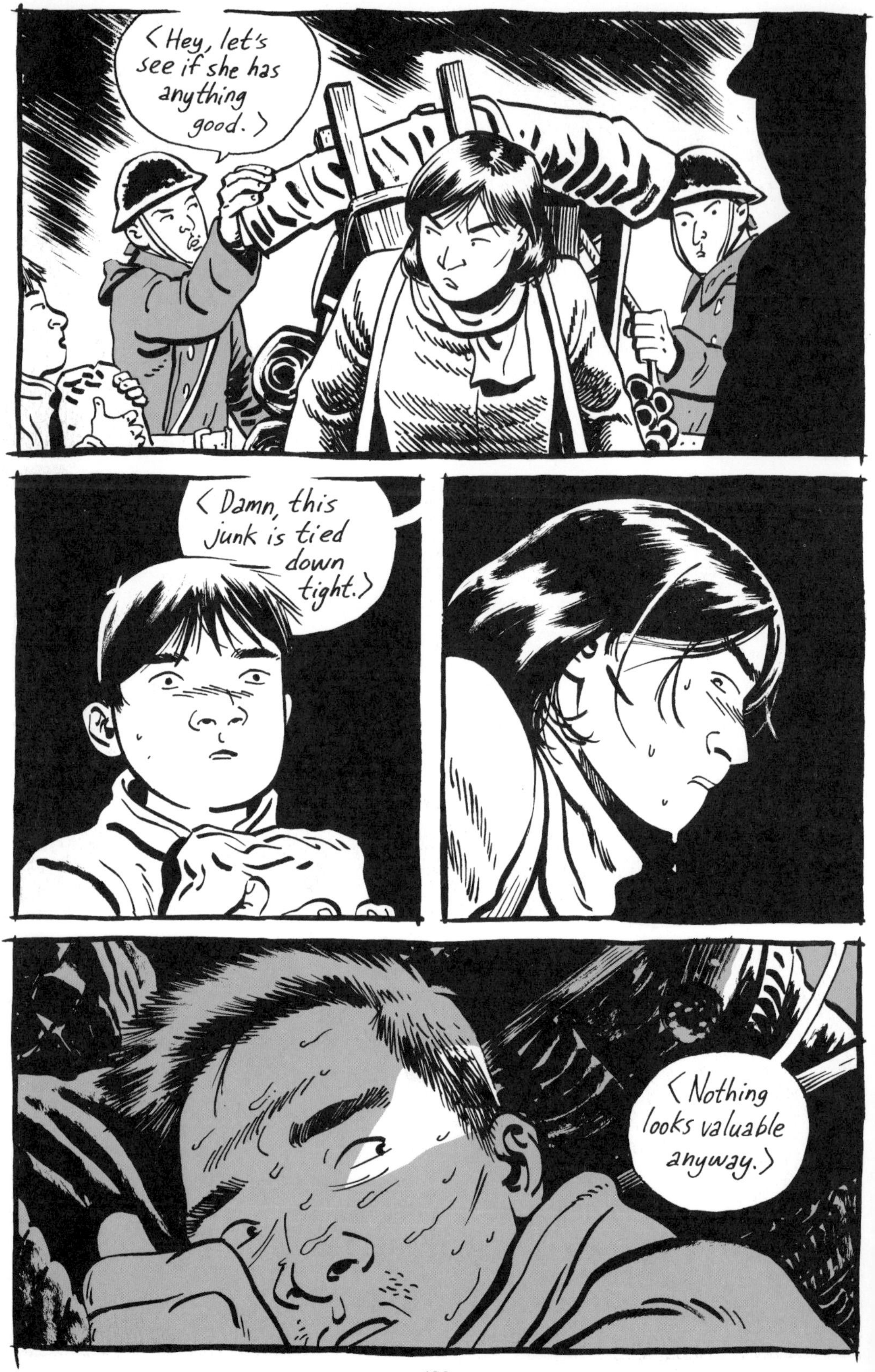
< Hey, let's see if she has anything good. >
< Damn, this junk is tied down tight. >
< Nothing looks valuable anyway. >

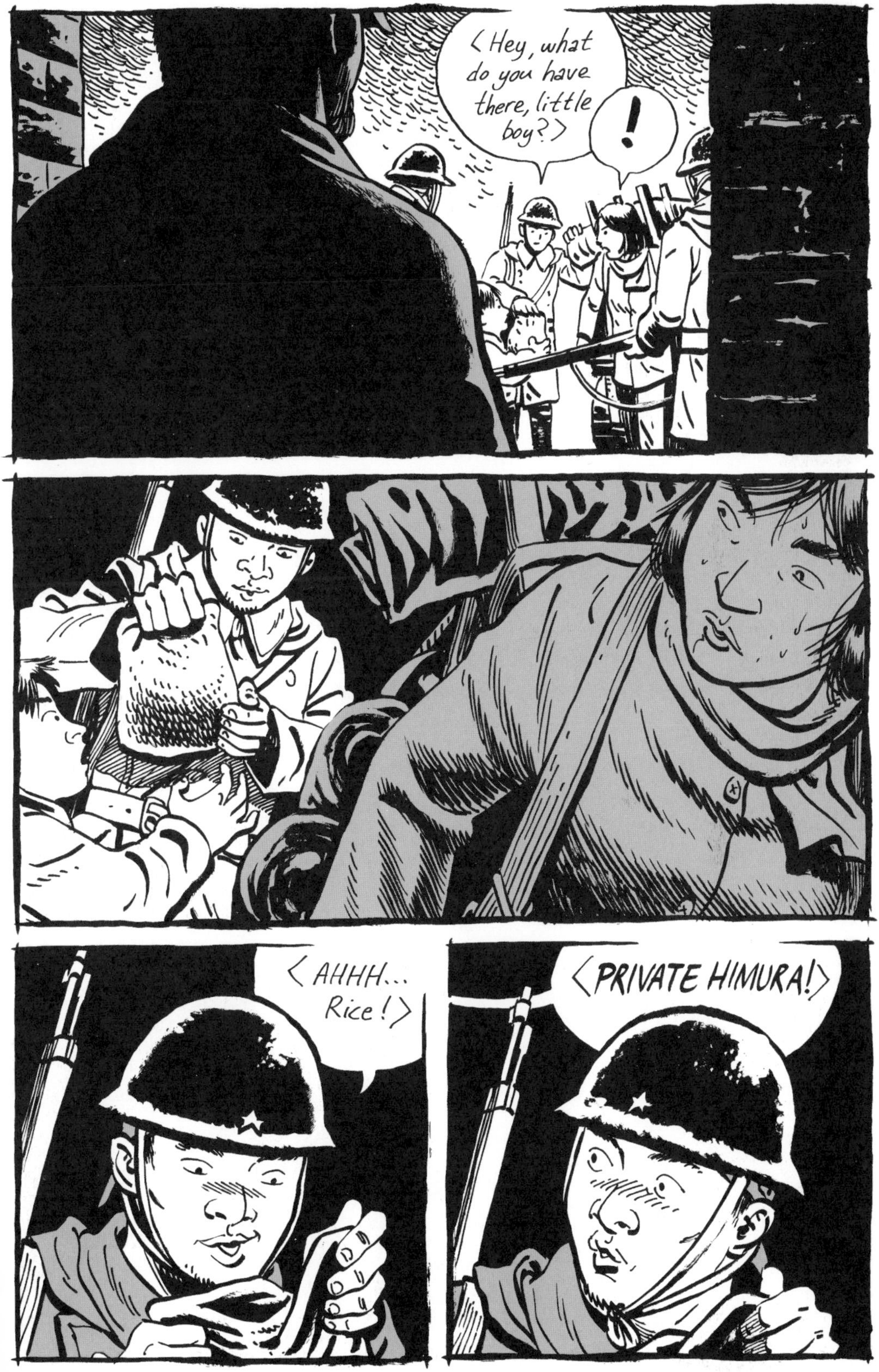

⟨Hey, what do you have there, little boy?⟩
!
⟨AHHH... Rice!⟩
⟨PRIVATE HIMURA!⟩

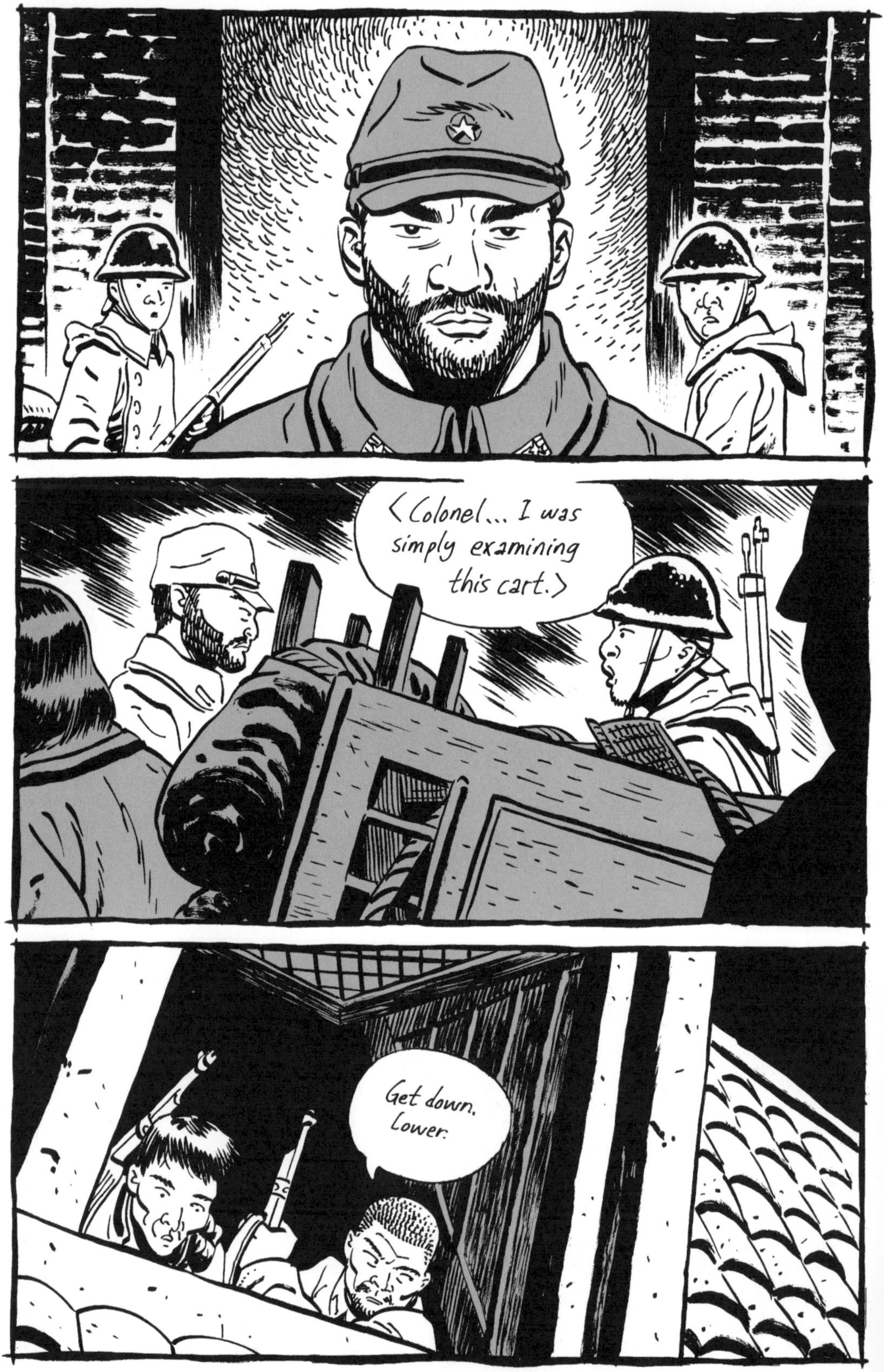

<Colonel... I was simply examining this cart.>
Get down. Lower.

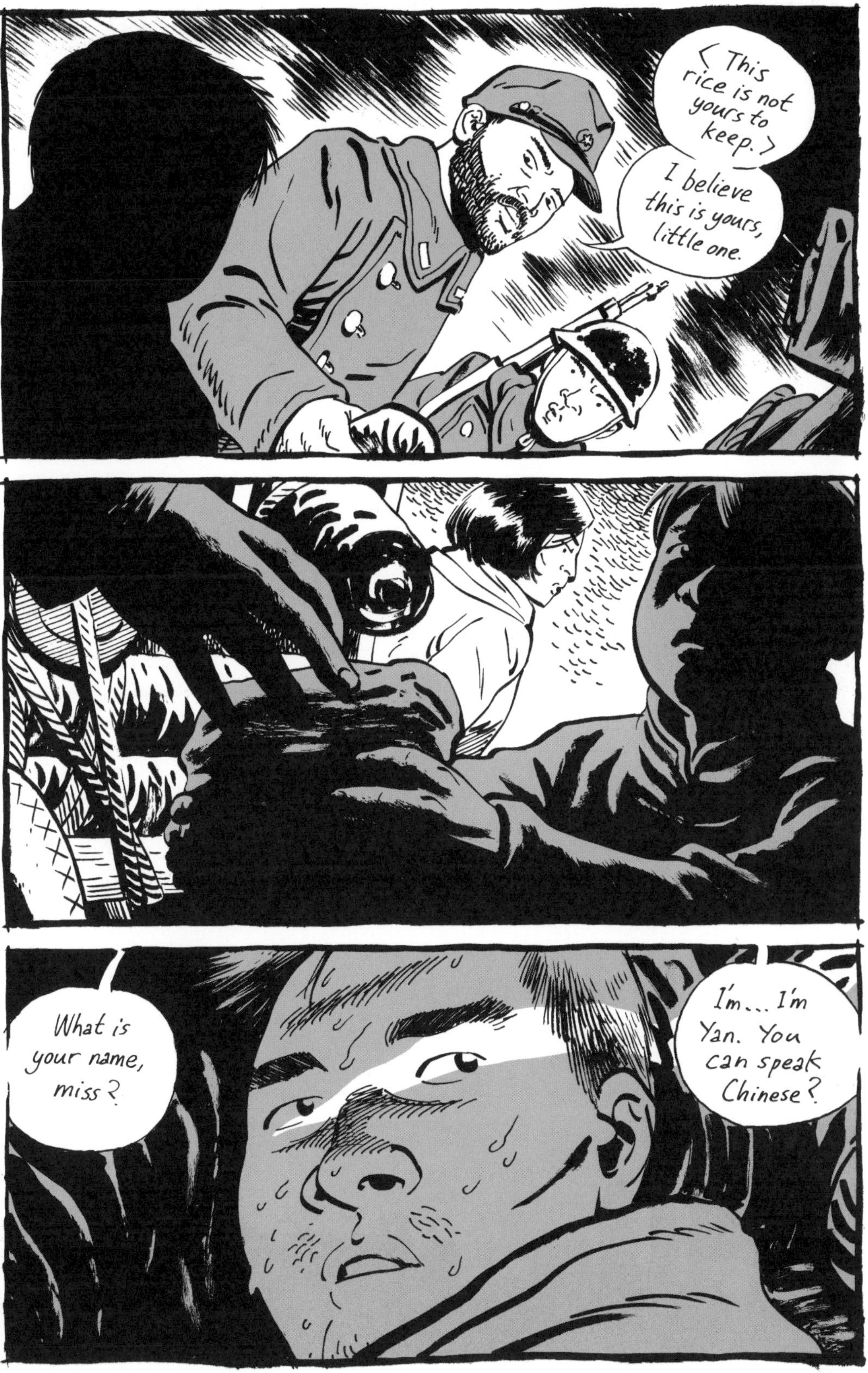
<This rice is not yours to keep.>
I believe this is yours, little one.
What is your name, miss?
I'm... I'm Yan. You can speak Chinese?

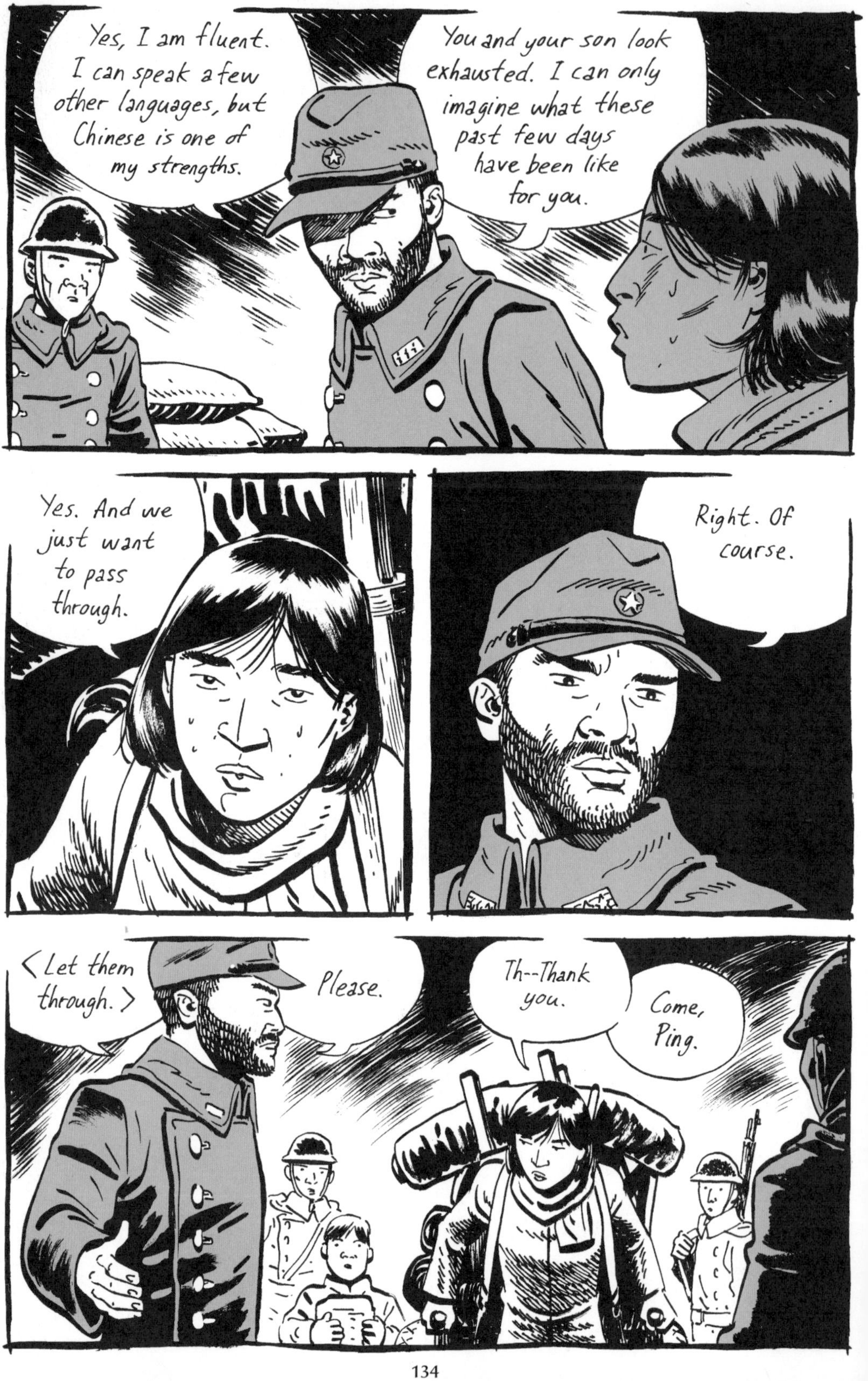
Yes, I am fluent. I can speak a few other languages, but Chinese is one of my strengths.
You and your son look exhausted. I can only imagine what these past few days have been like for you.
Yes. And we just want to pass through.
Right. Of course.
<Let them through.>
Please.
Th--Thank you.
Come, Ping.

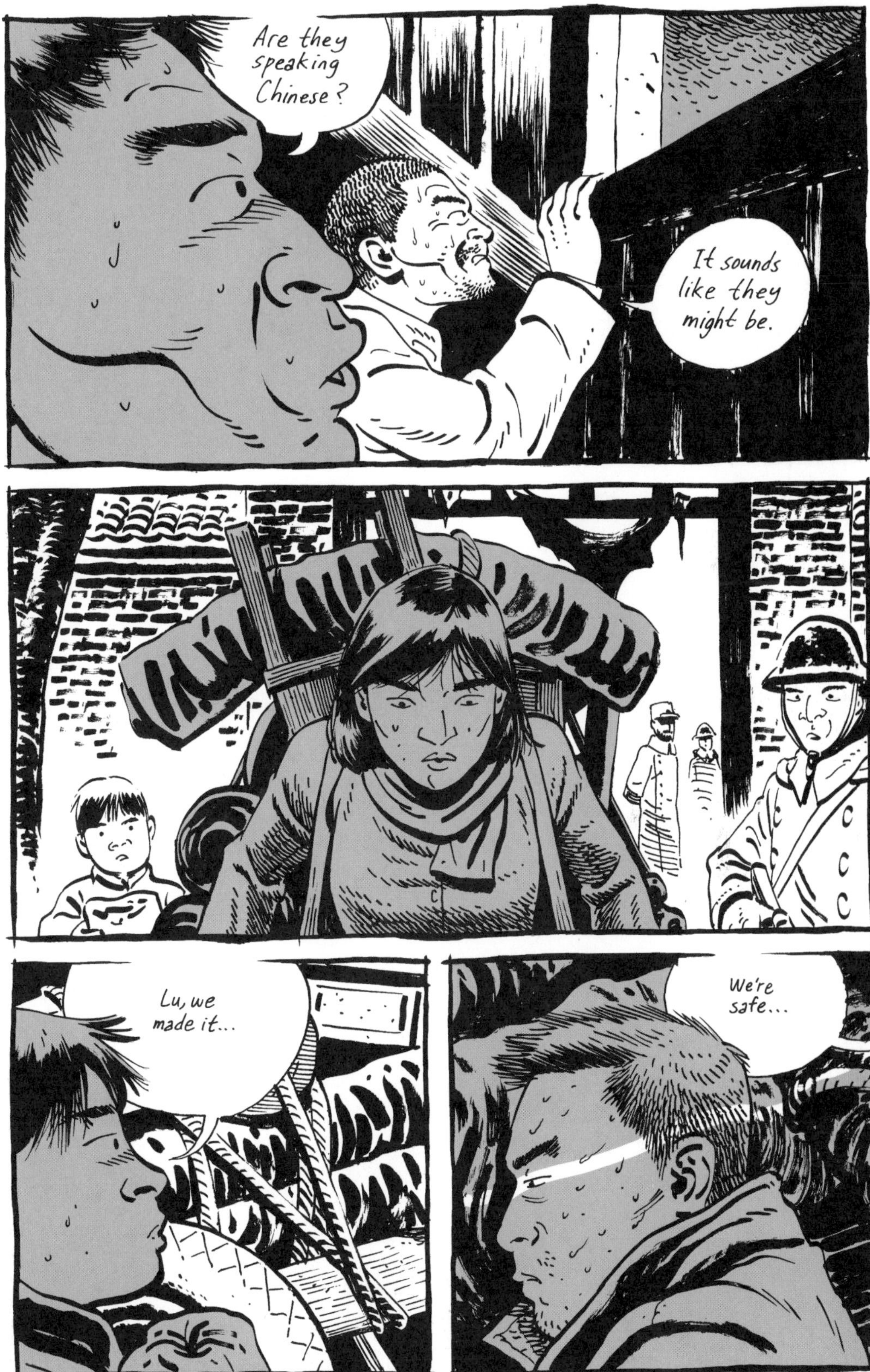
Are they speaking Chinese?
It sounds like they might be.
Lu, we made it...
We're safe...

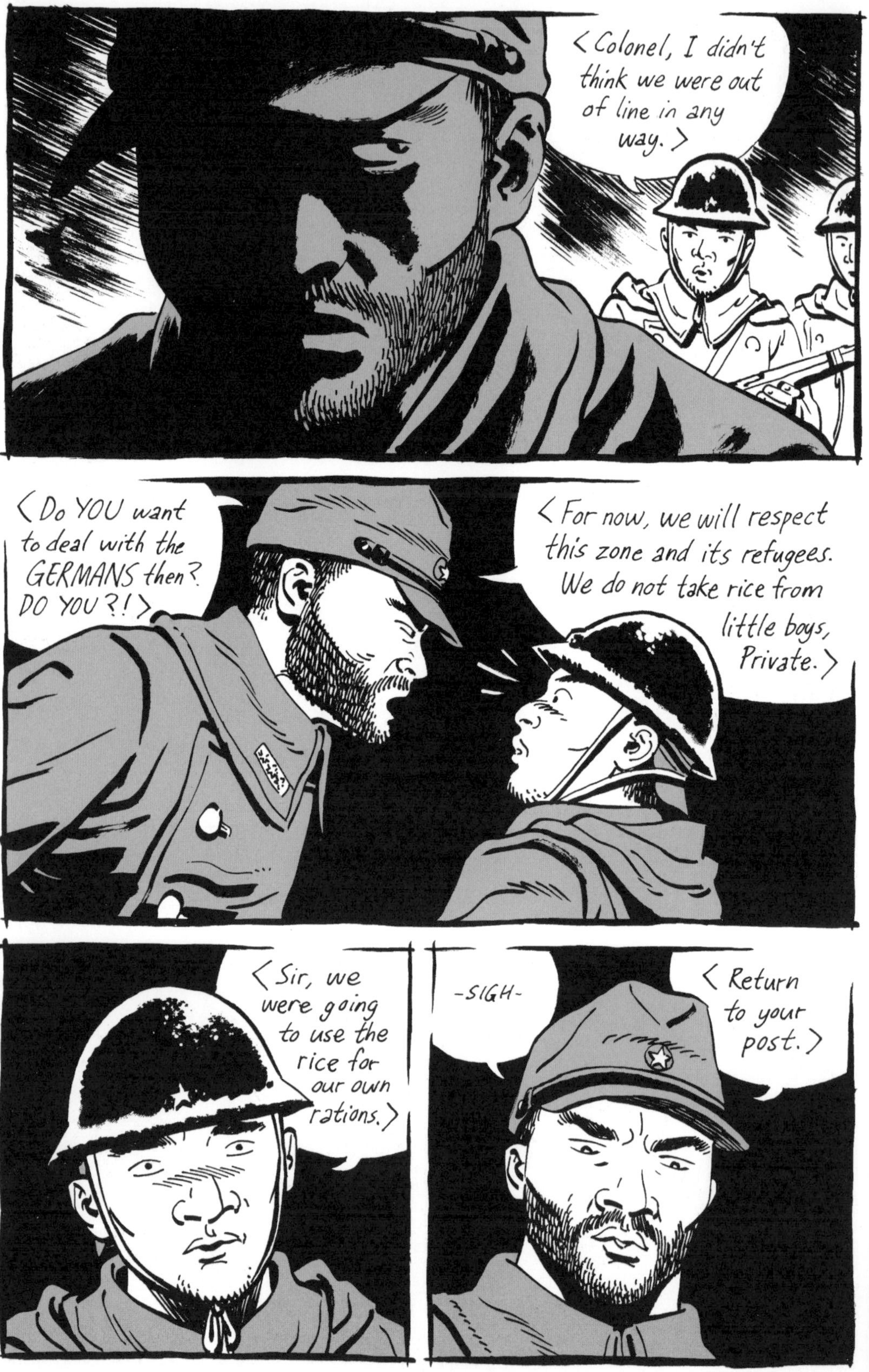

< Colonel, I didn't think we were out of line in any way. >
< Do YOU want to deal with the GERMANS then? DO YOU?! >
< For now, we will respect this zone and its refugees. We do not take rice from little boys, Private. >
< Sir, we were going to use the rice for our own rations. >
-SIGH-
< Return to your post. >

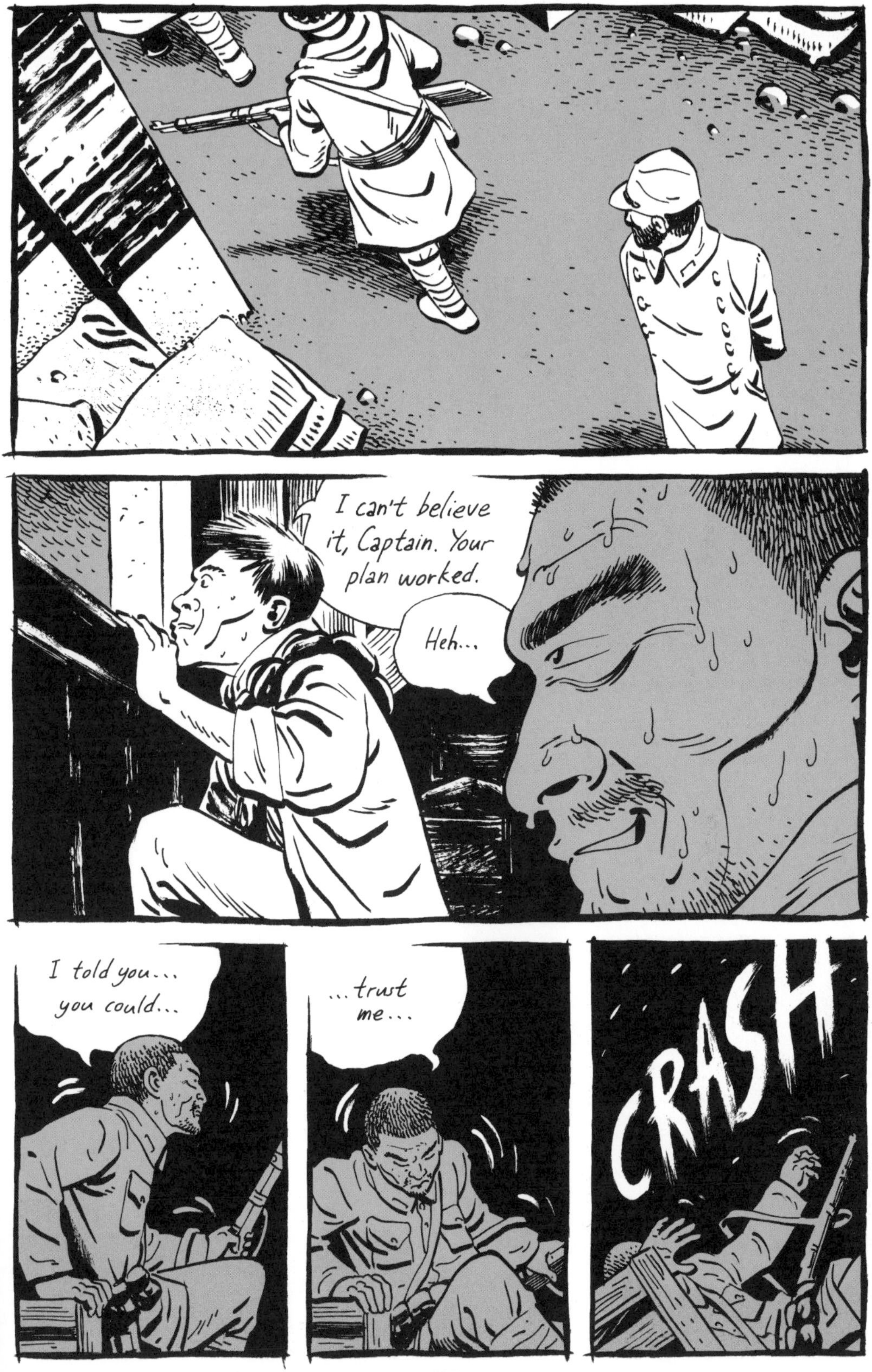
I can't believe it, Captain. Your plan worked.
Heh...
I told you... you could...
...trust me...
CRASH

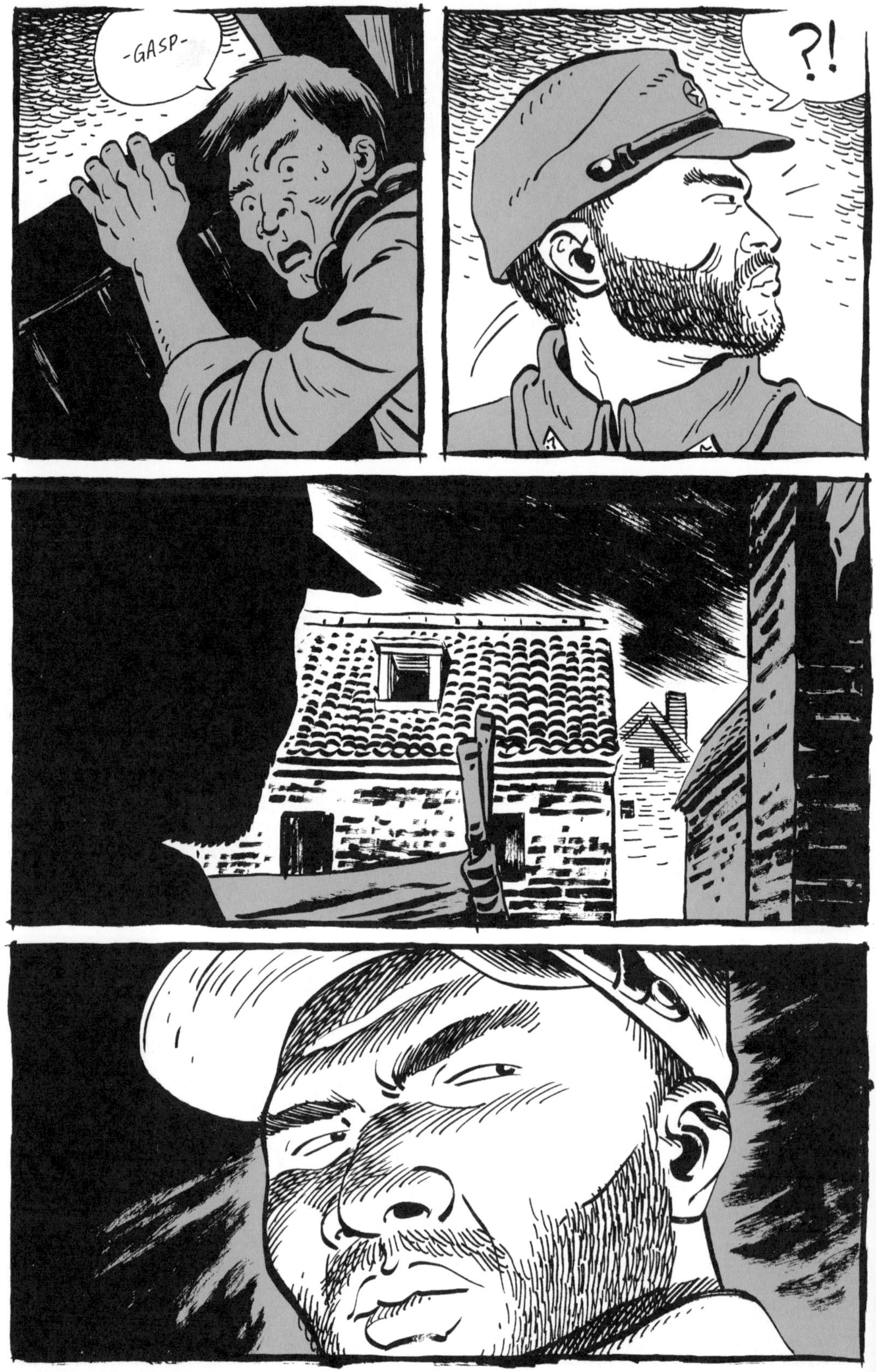
-GASP-
?!

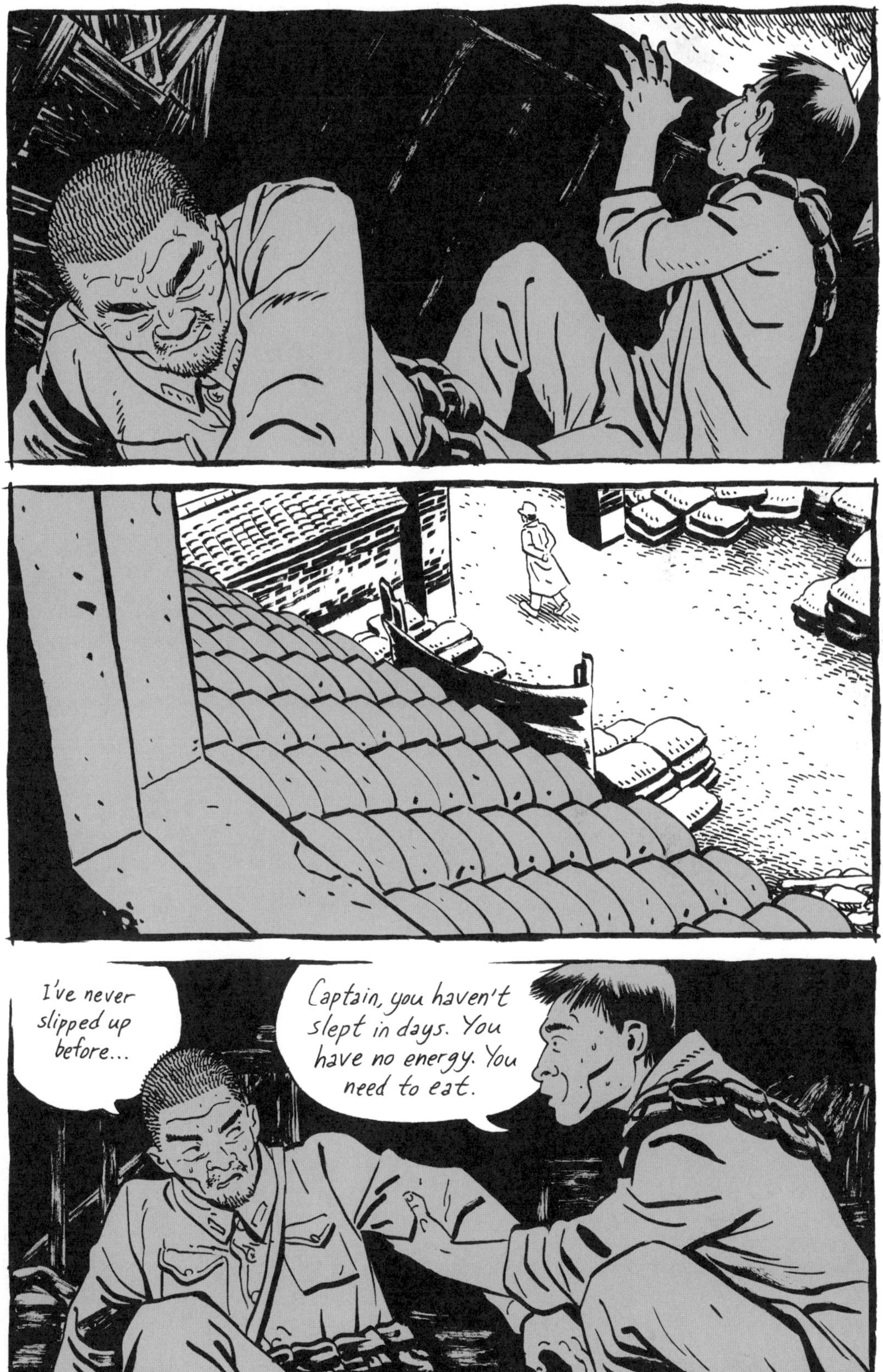
I've never slipped up before...
Captain, you haven't slept in days. You have no energy. You need to eat.

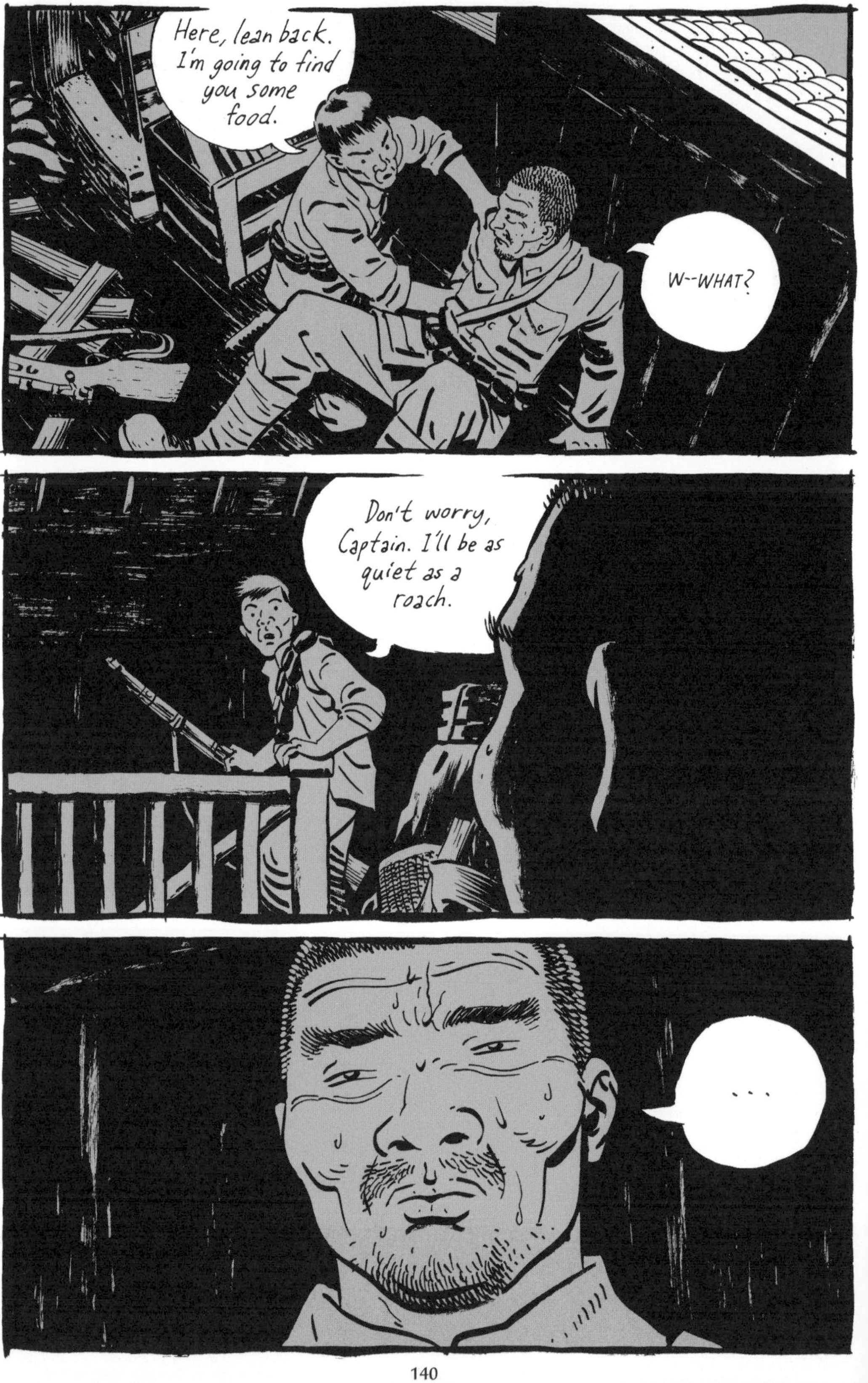
Here, lean back. I'm going to find you some food.
W--WHAT?
Don't worry, Captain. I'll be as quiet as a roach.
. . .

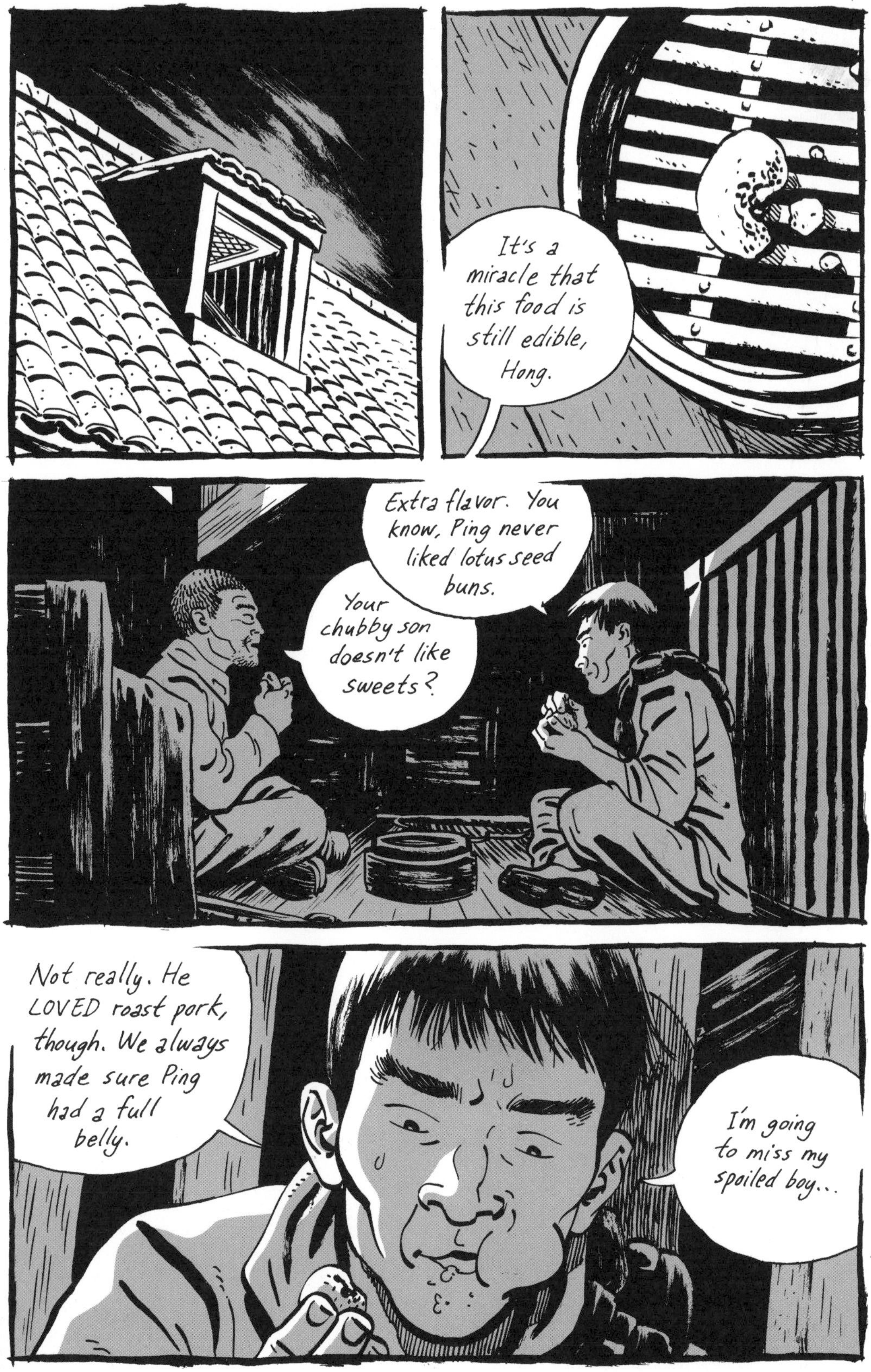

It's a miracle that this food is still edible, Hong.
Extra flavor. You know, Ping never liked lotus seed buns.
Your chubby son doesn't like sweets?
Not really. He LOVED roast pork, though. We always made sure Ping had a full belly.
I'm going to miss my spoiled boy...

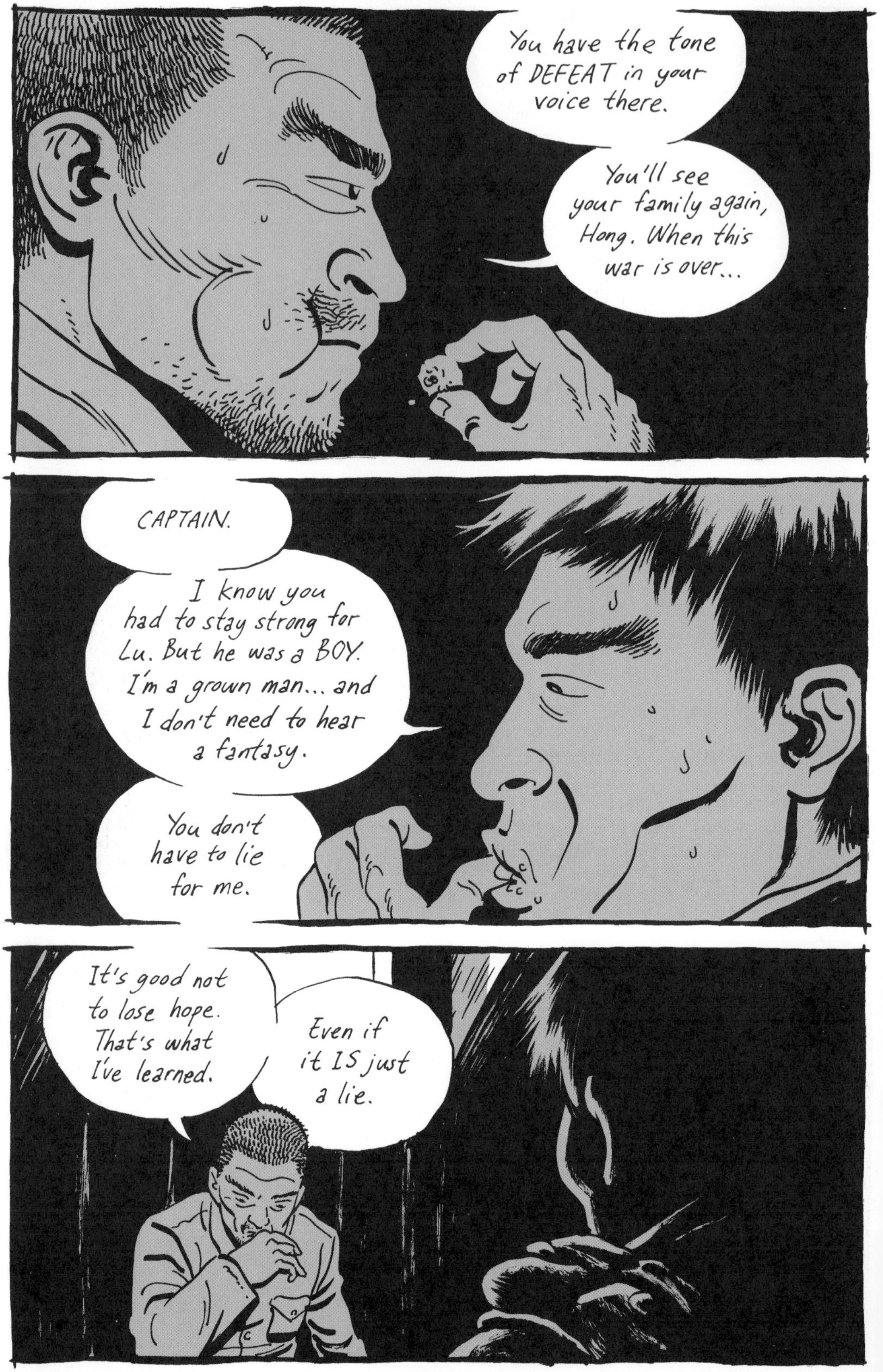
You have the tone of DEFEAT in your voice there.
You'll see your family again, Hong. When this war is over...
CAPTAIN.
I know you had to stay strong for Lu. But he was a BOY. I'm a grown man... and I don't need to hear a fantasy.
You don't have to lie for me.
It's good not to lose hope. That's what I've learned.
Even if it IS just a lie.

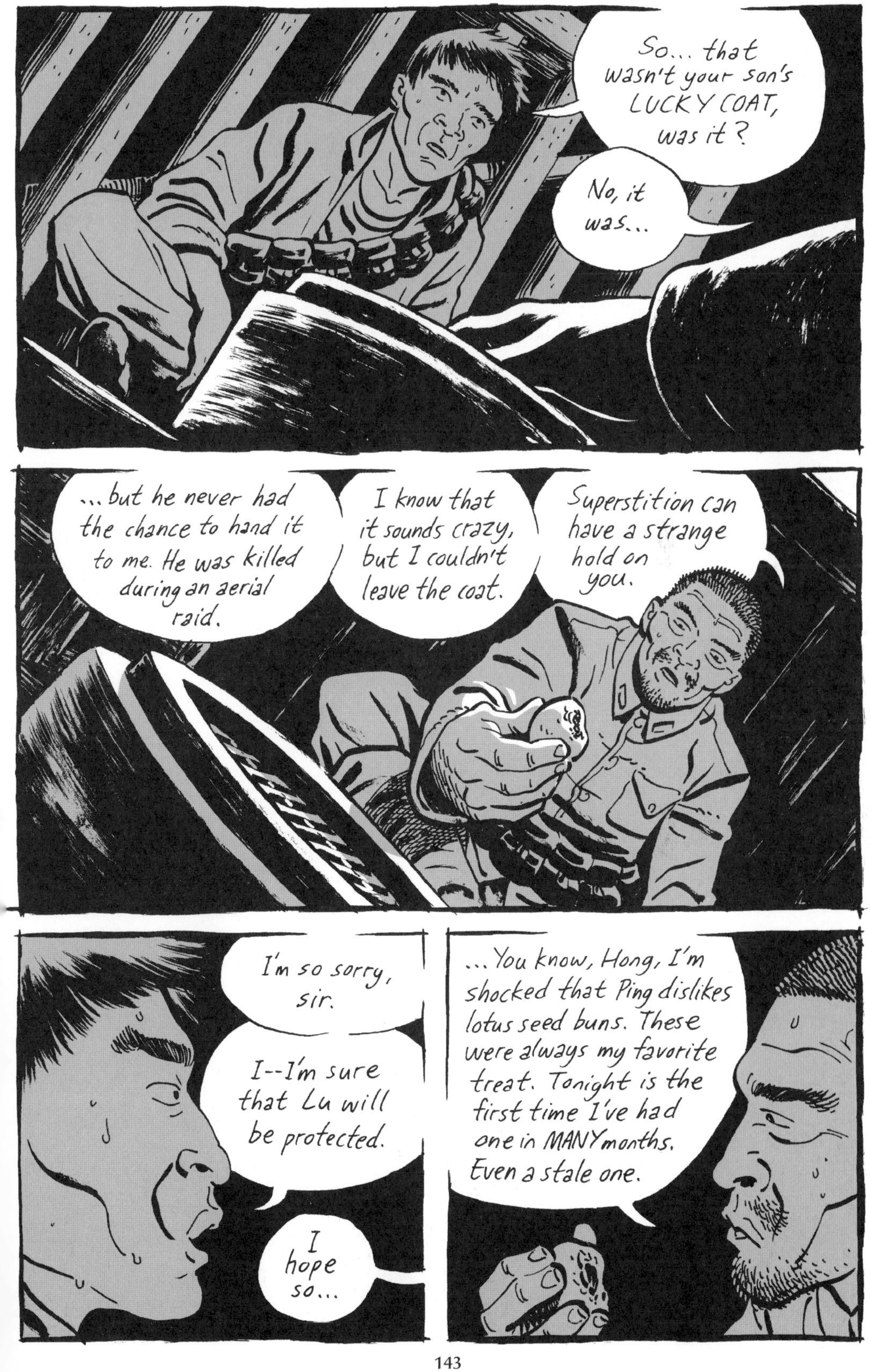
So... that wasn't your son's LUCKY COAT, was it?
No, it was...
...but he never had the chance to hand it to me. He was killed during an aerial raid.
I know that it sounds crazy, but I couldn't leave the coat.
Superstition can have a strange hold on you.
I'm so sorry, sir.
I--I'm sure that Lu will be protected.
I hope so...
...You know, Hong, I'm shocked that Ping dislikes lotus seed buns. These were always my favorite treat. Tonight is the first time I've had one in MANY months. Even a stale one.

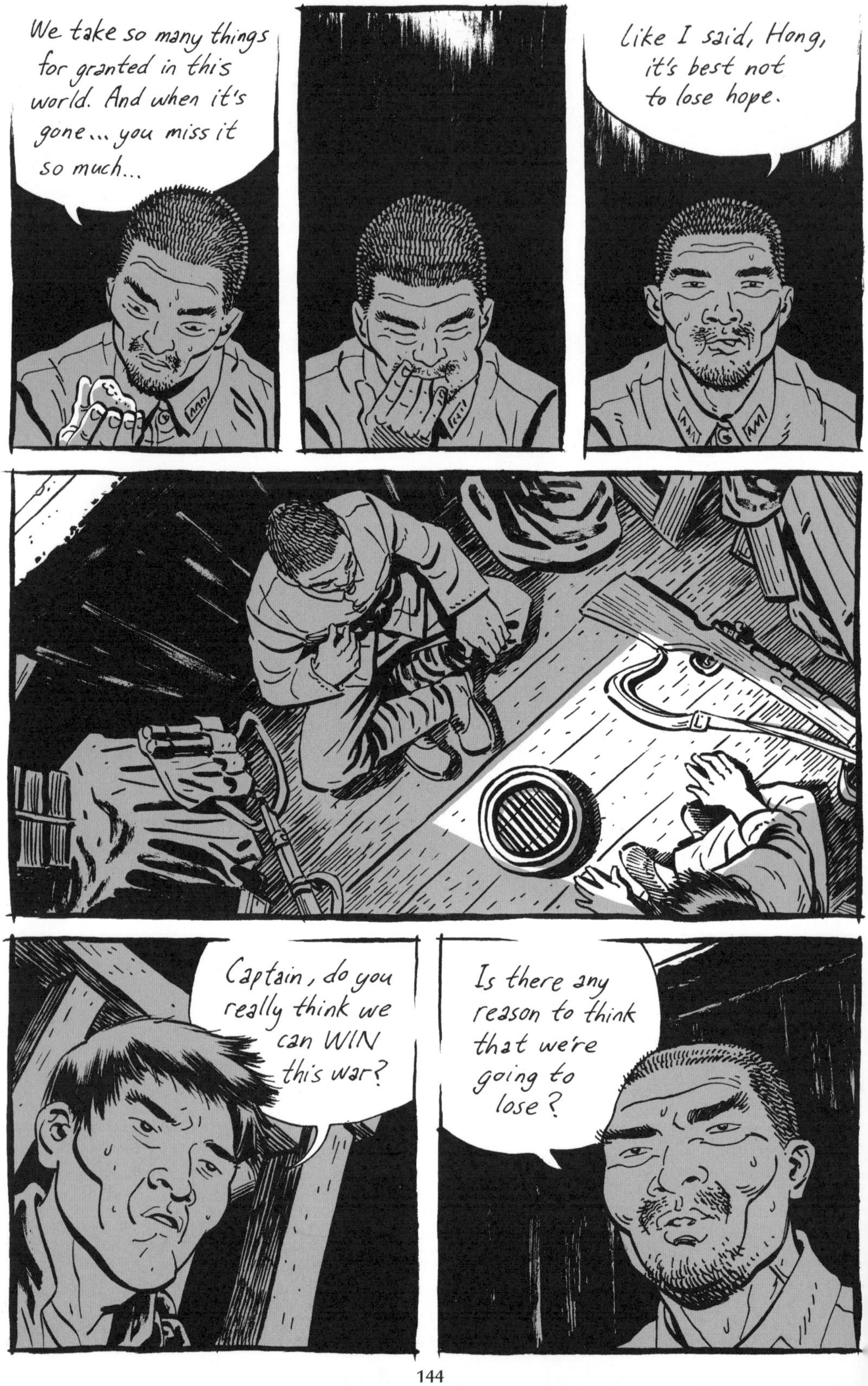
We take so many things for granted in this world. And when it's gone... you miss it so much...
Like I said, Hong, it's best not to lose hope.
Captain, do you really think we can WIN this war?
Is there any reason to think that we're going to lose?

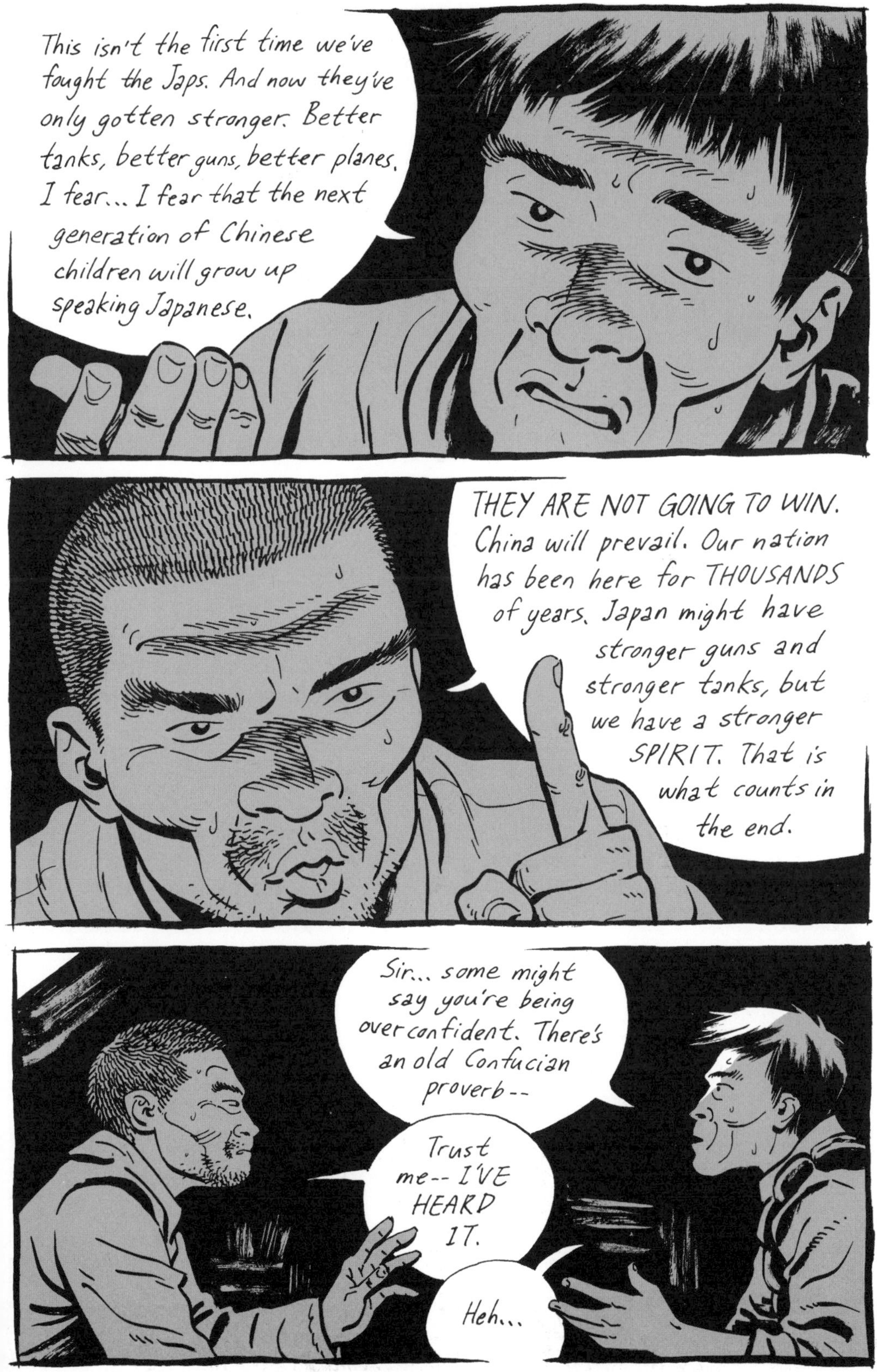
This isn't the first time we've fought the Japs. And now they've only gotten stronger. Better tanks, better guns, better planes. I fear... I fear that the next generation of Chinese children will grow up speaking Japanese.
THEY ARE NOT GOING TO WIN. China will prevail. Our nation has been here for THOUSANDS of years. Japan might have stronger guns and stronger tanks, but we have a stronger SPIRIT. That is what counts in the end.
Sir... some might say you're being over confident. There's an old Confucian proverb--
Trust me-- I'VE HEARD IT.
Heh...

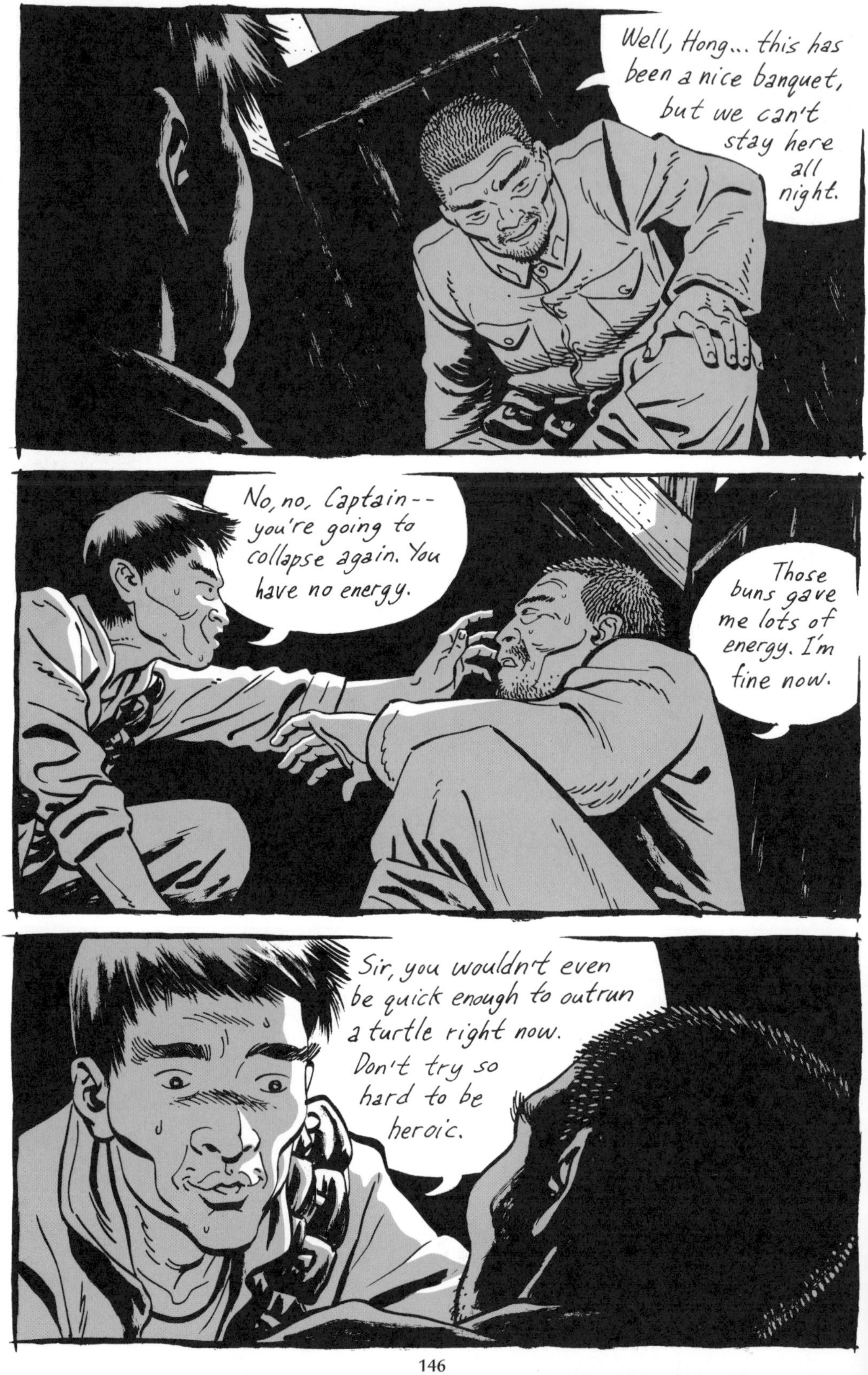
Well, Hong... this has been a nice banquet, but we can't stay here all night.
No, no, Captain-- you're going to collapse again. You have no energy.
Those buns gave me lots of energy. I'm fine now.
Sir, you wouldn't even be quick enough to outrun a turtle right now. Don't try so hard to be heroic.

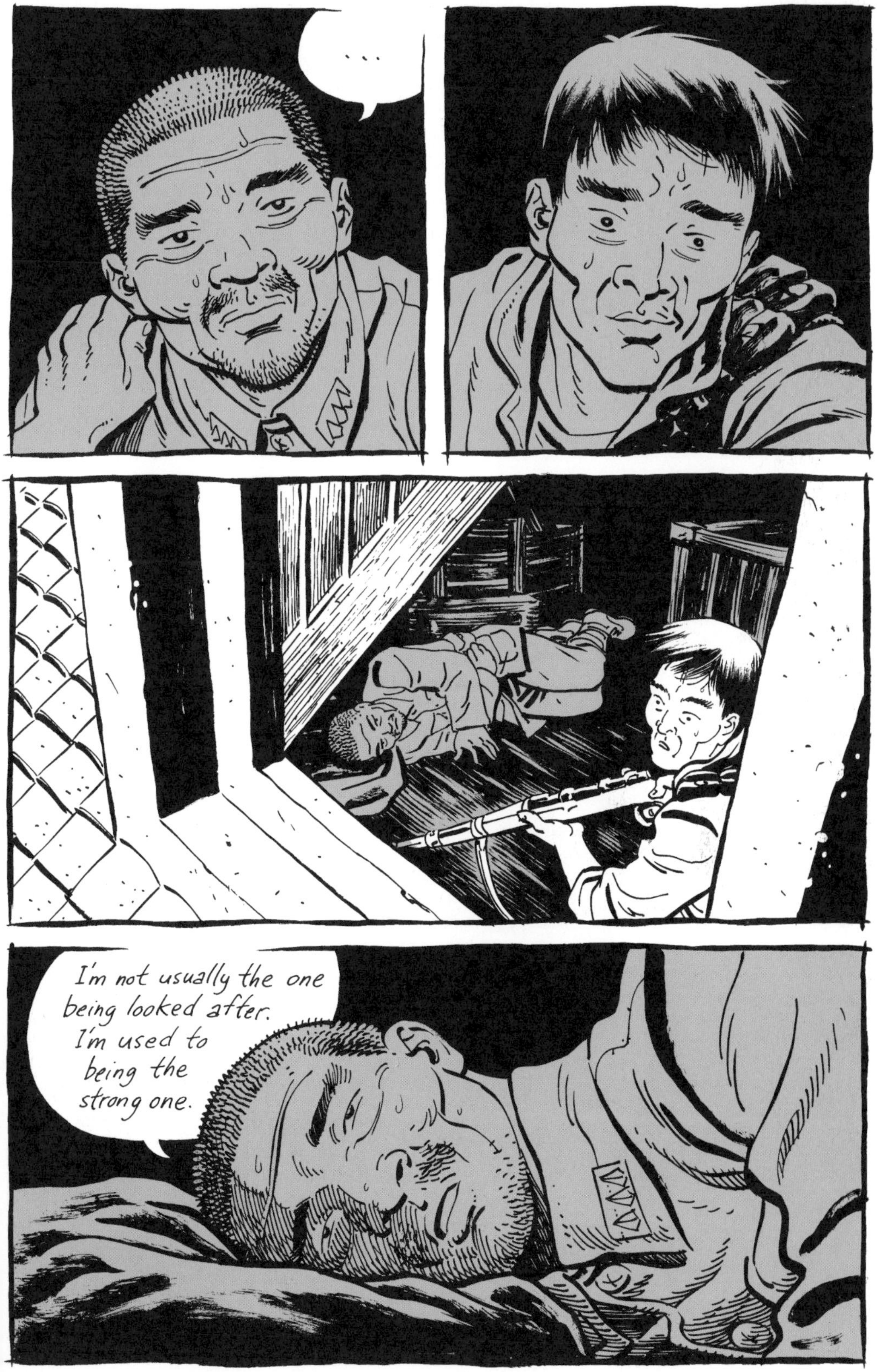
...
I'm not usually the one being looked after. I'm used to being the strong one.

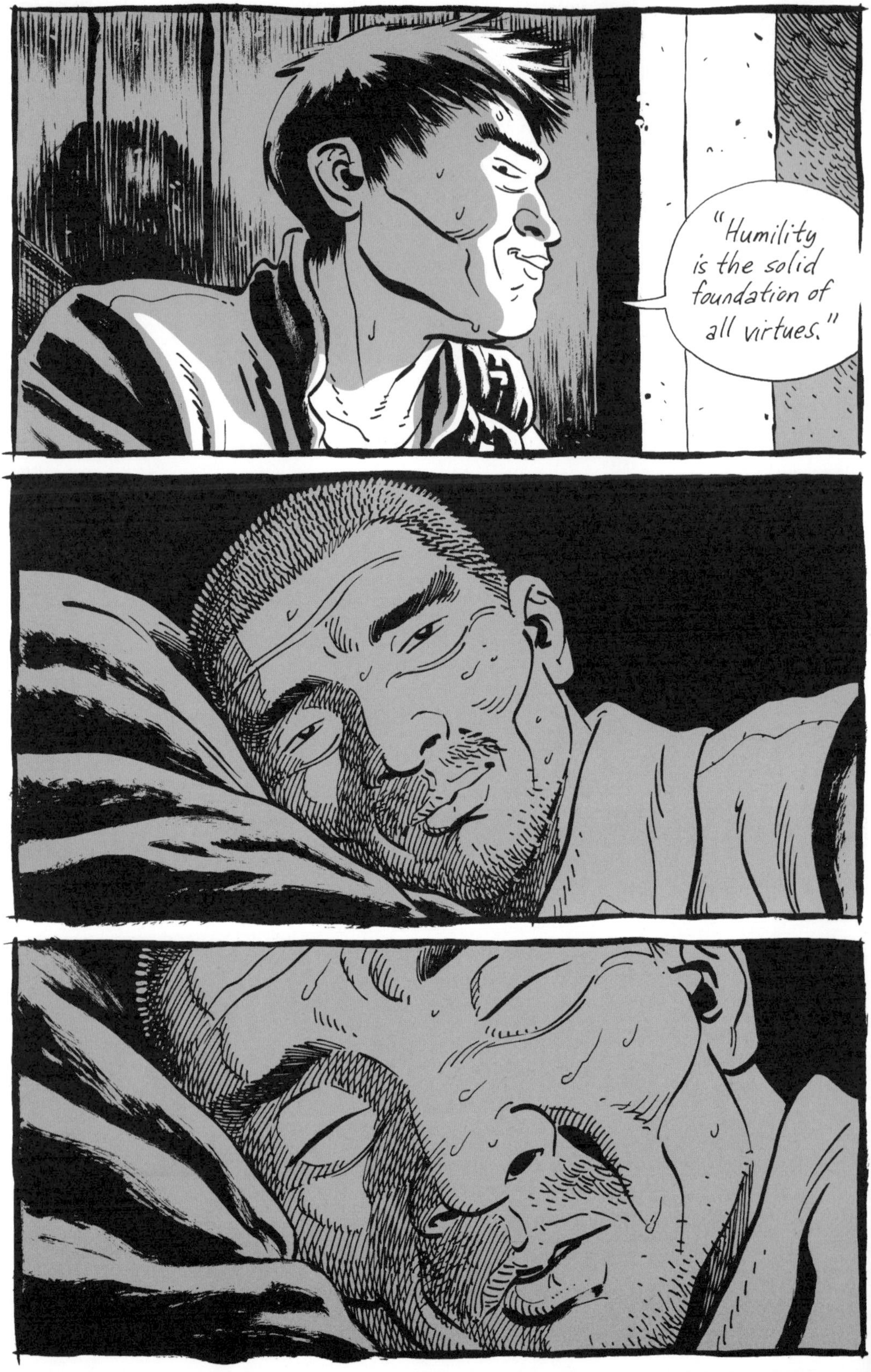
"Humility is the solid foundation of all virtues."

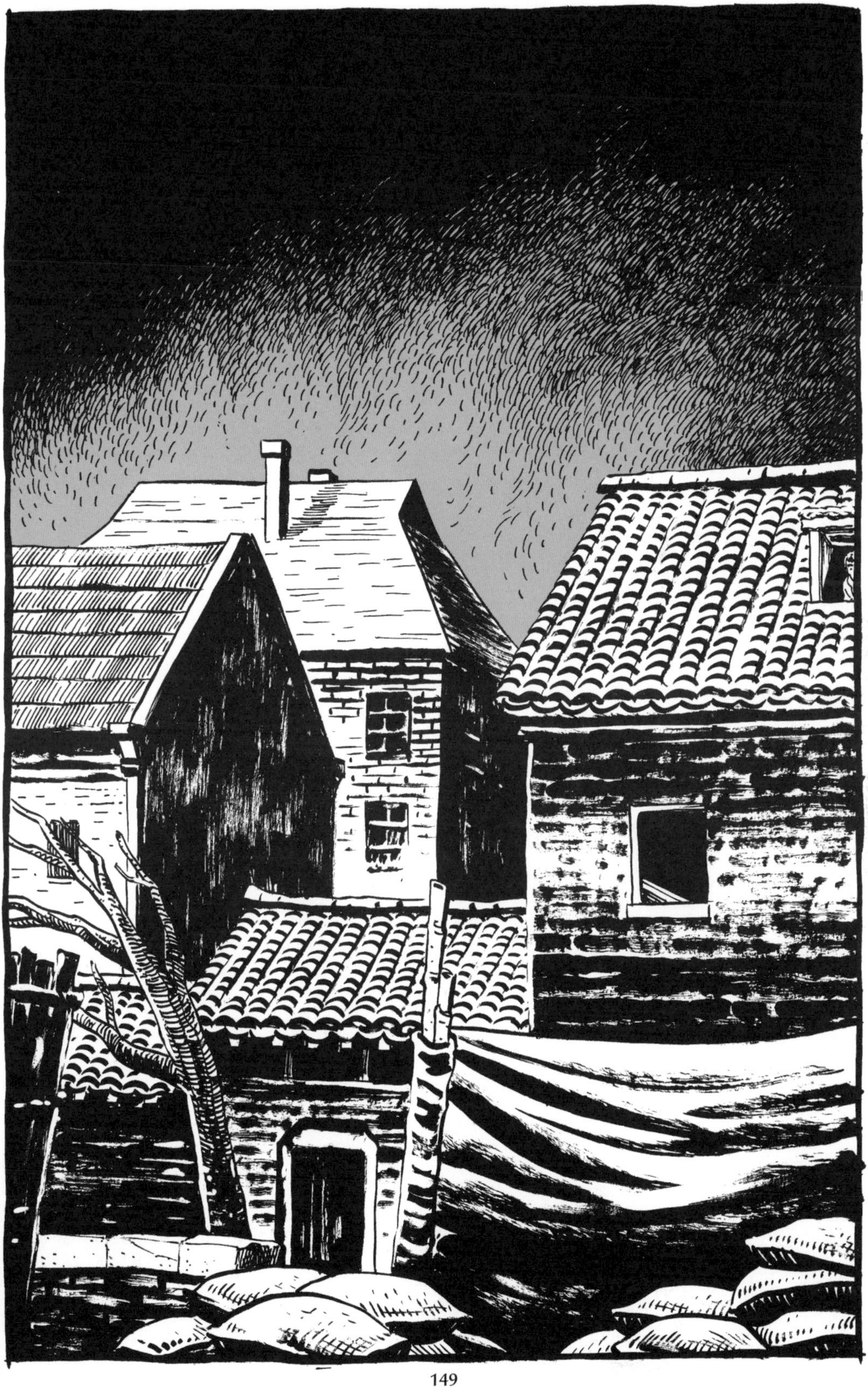

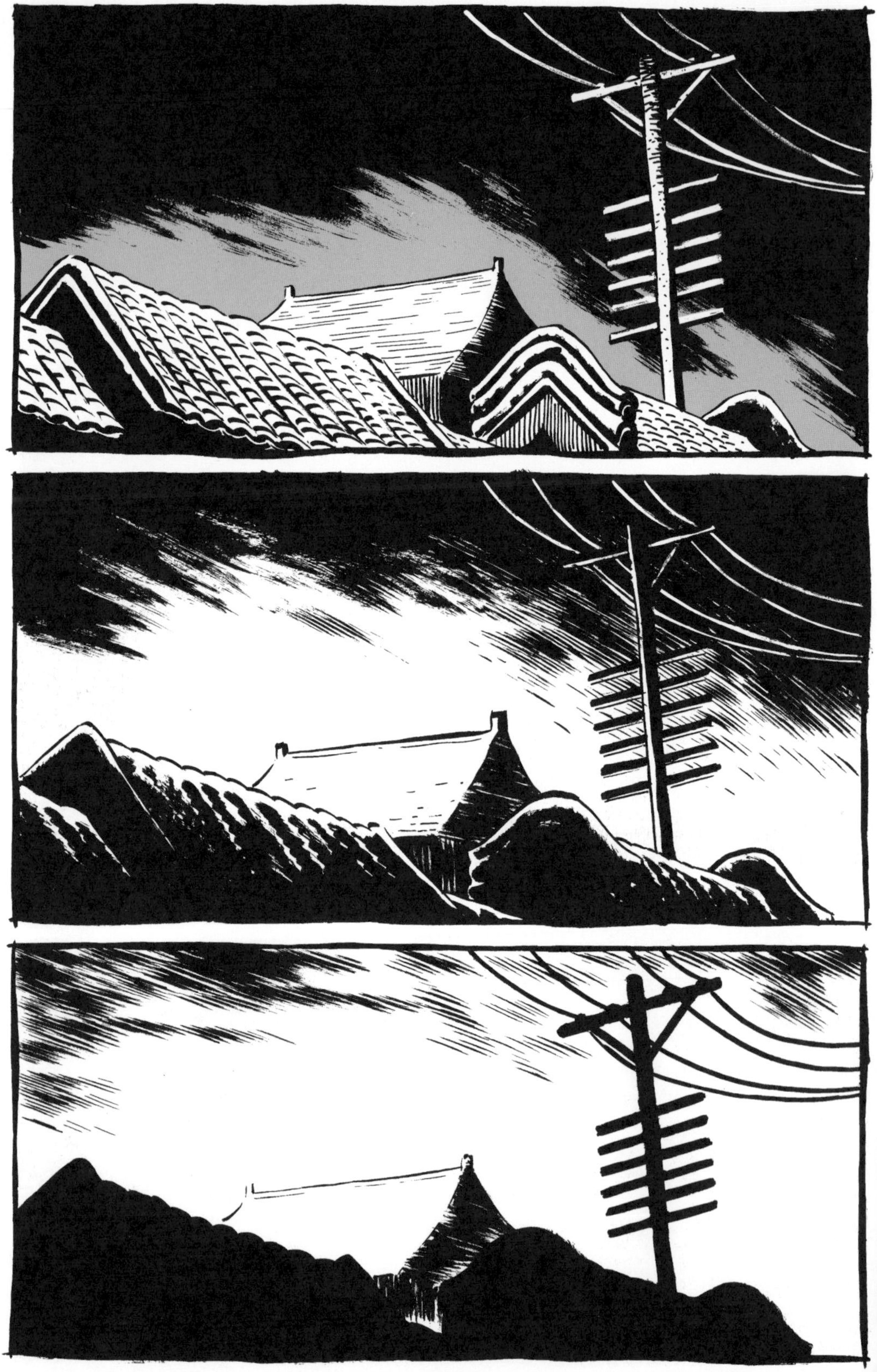

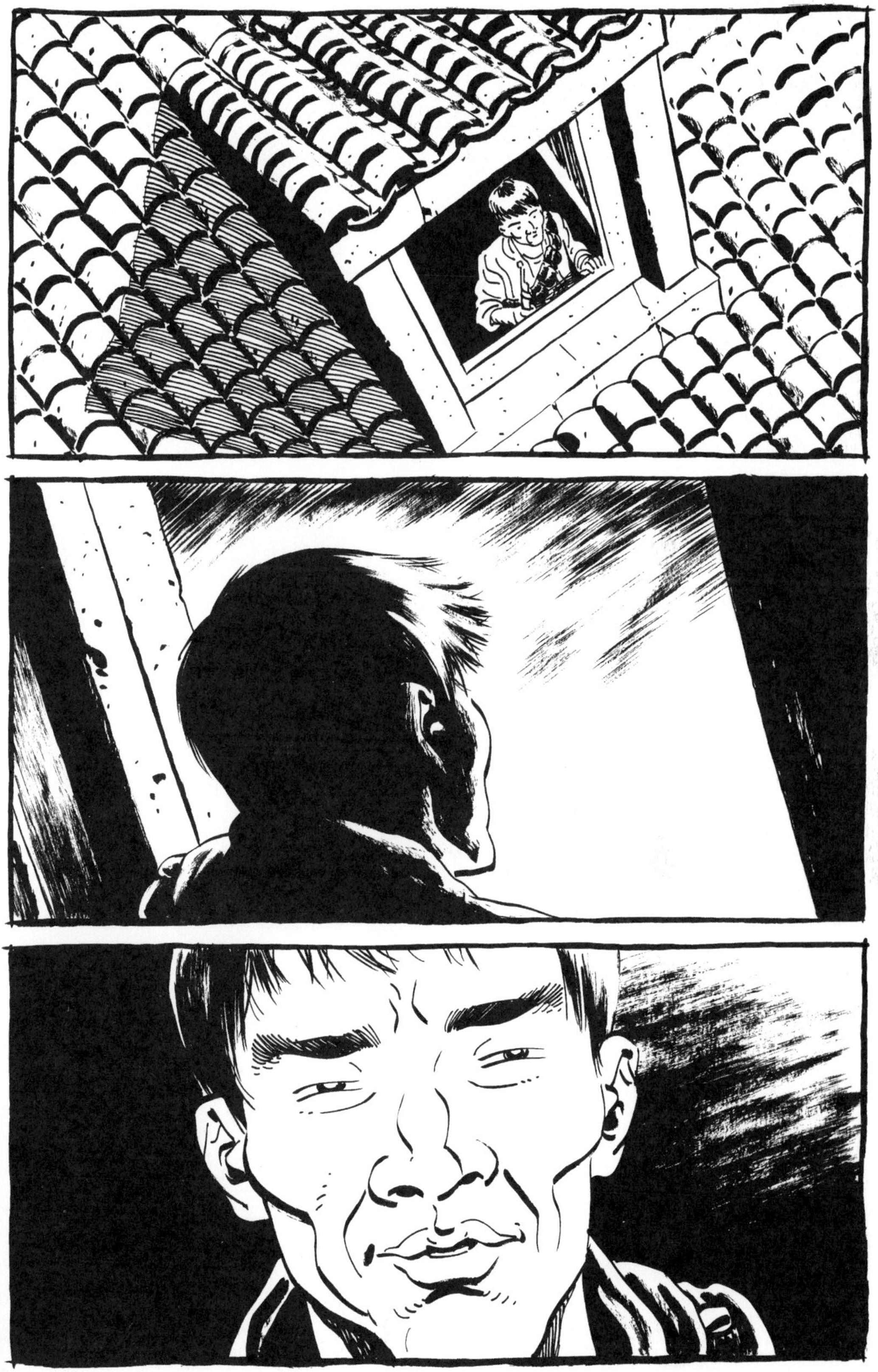

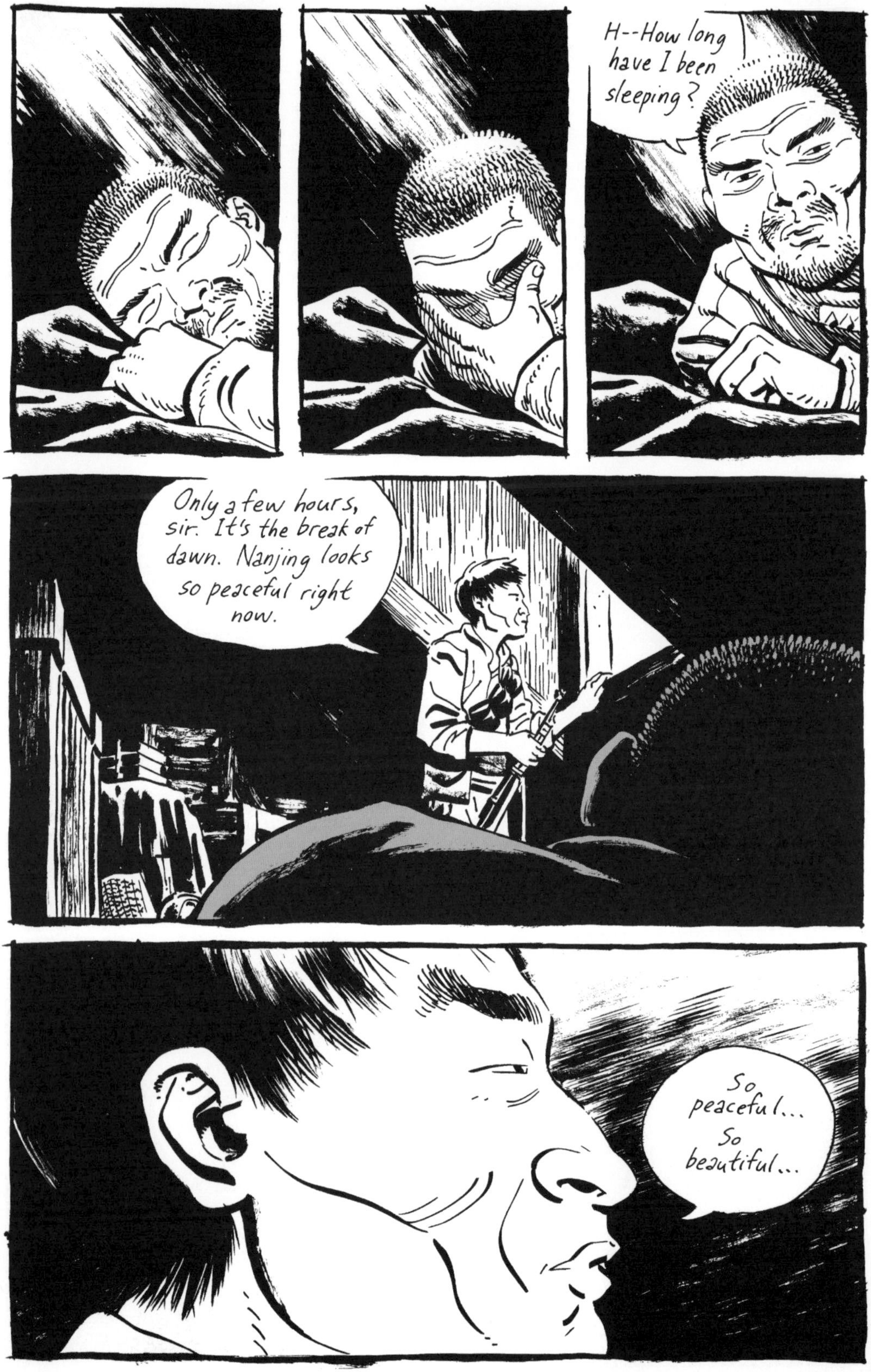
H--How long have I been sleeping?
Only a few hours, sir. It's the break of dawn. Nanjing looks so peaceful right now.
So peaceful... So beautiful...

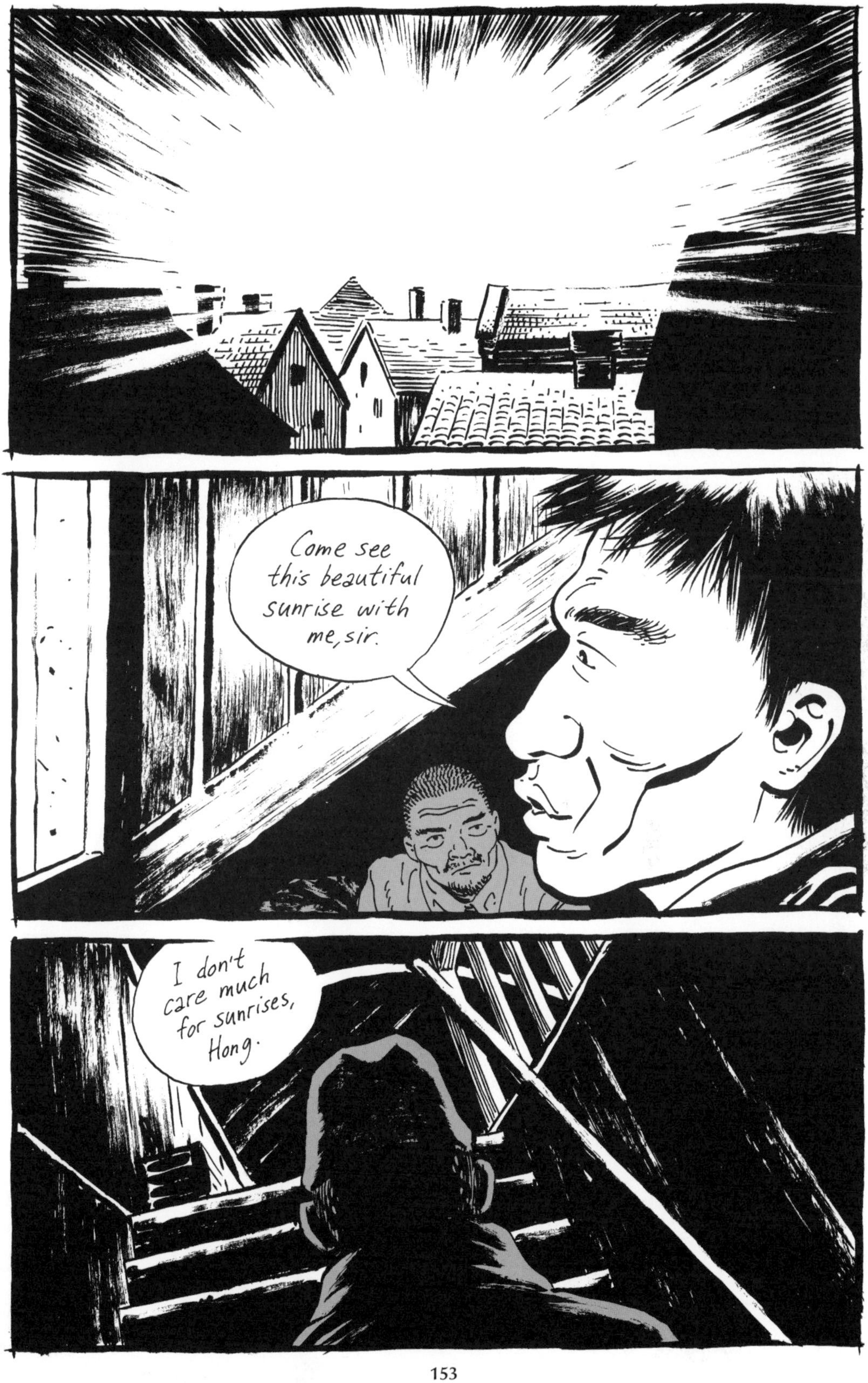
Come see this beautiful sunrise with me, sir.
I don't care much for sunrises, Hong.

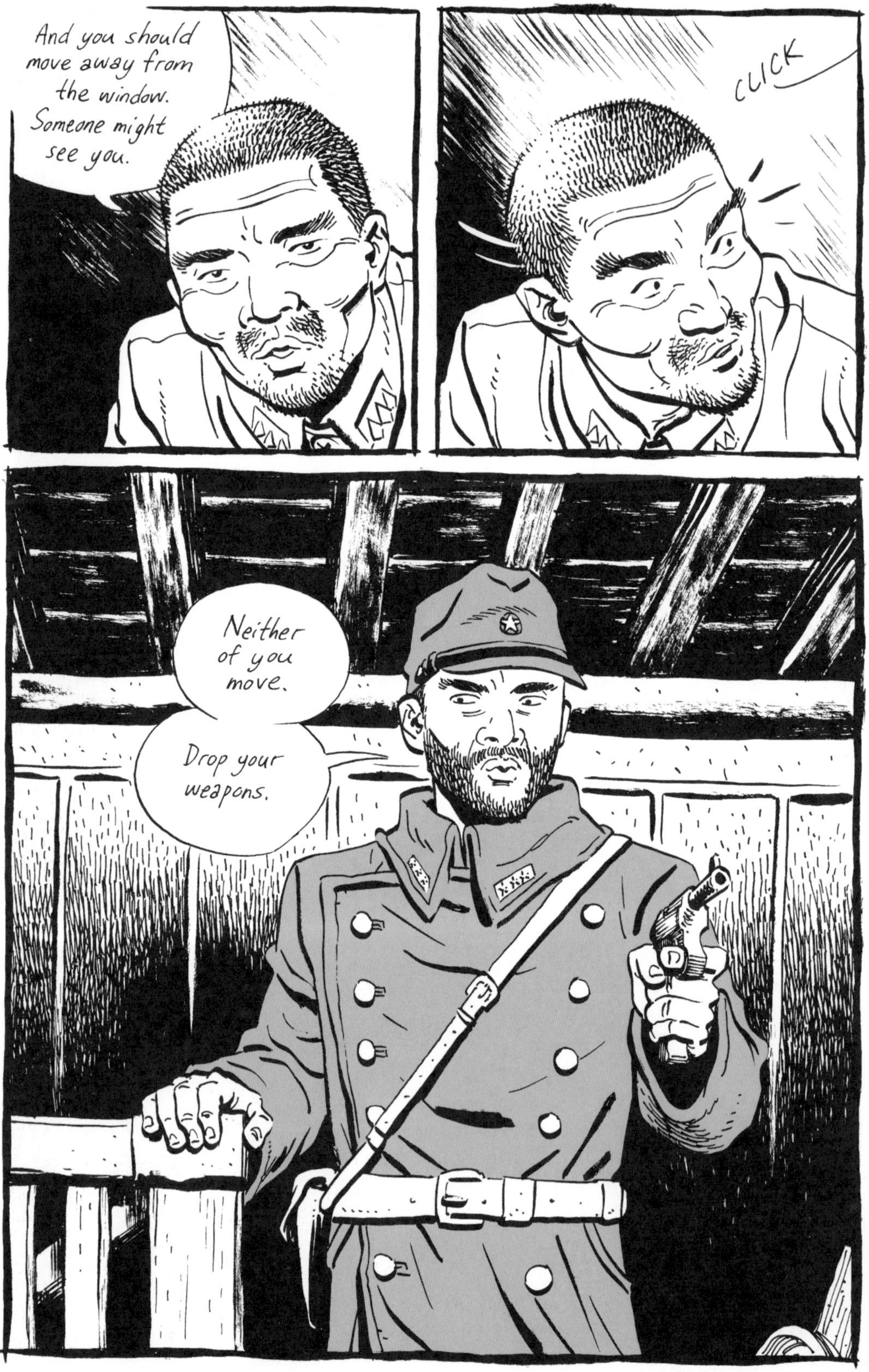
And you should move away from the window. Someone might see you.
CLICK
Neither of you move.
Drop your weapons.

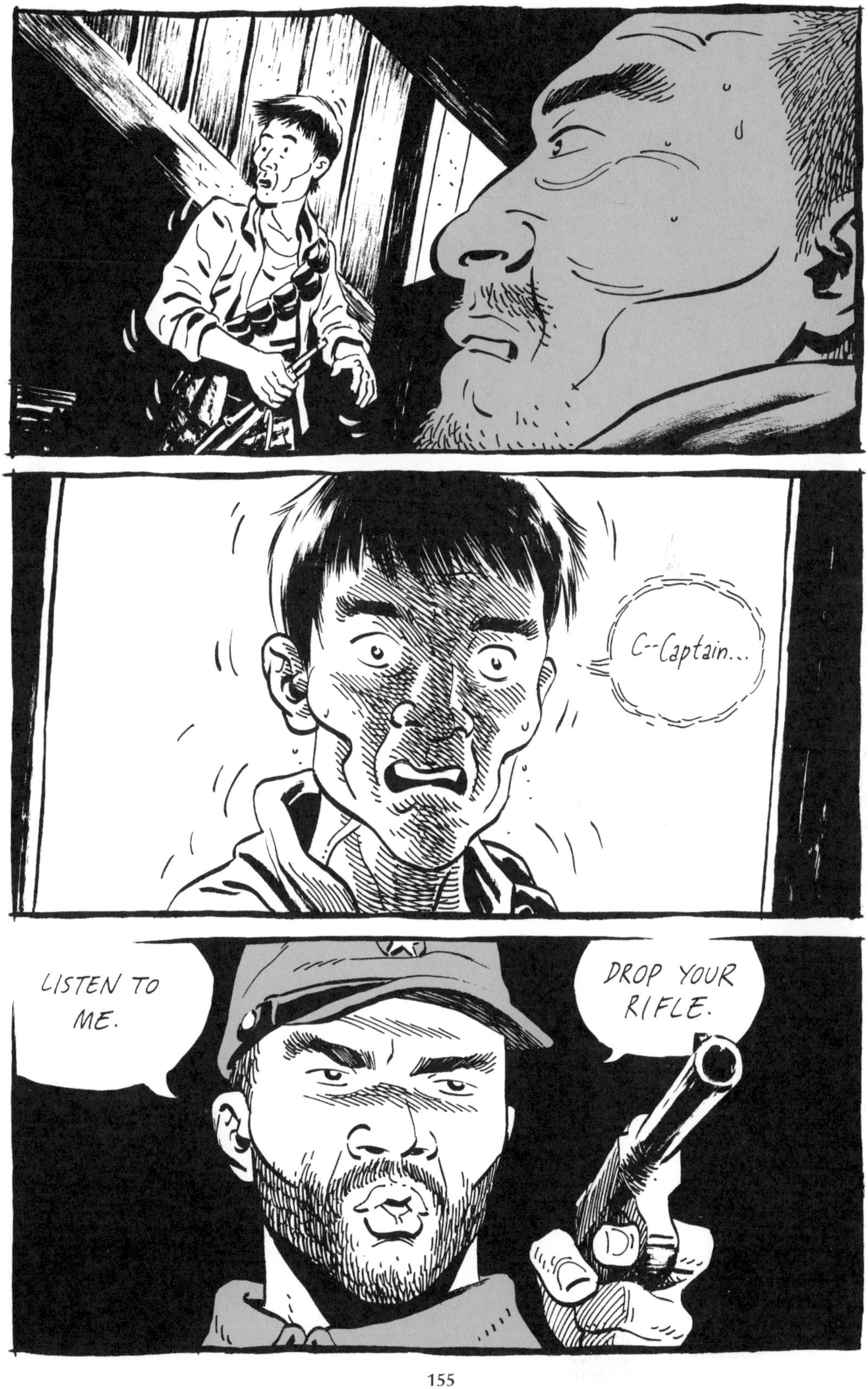
C--Captain...
LISTEN TO ME.
DROP YOUR RIFLE.

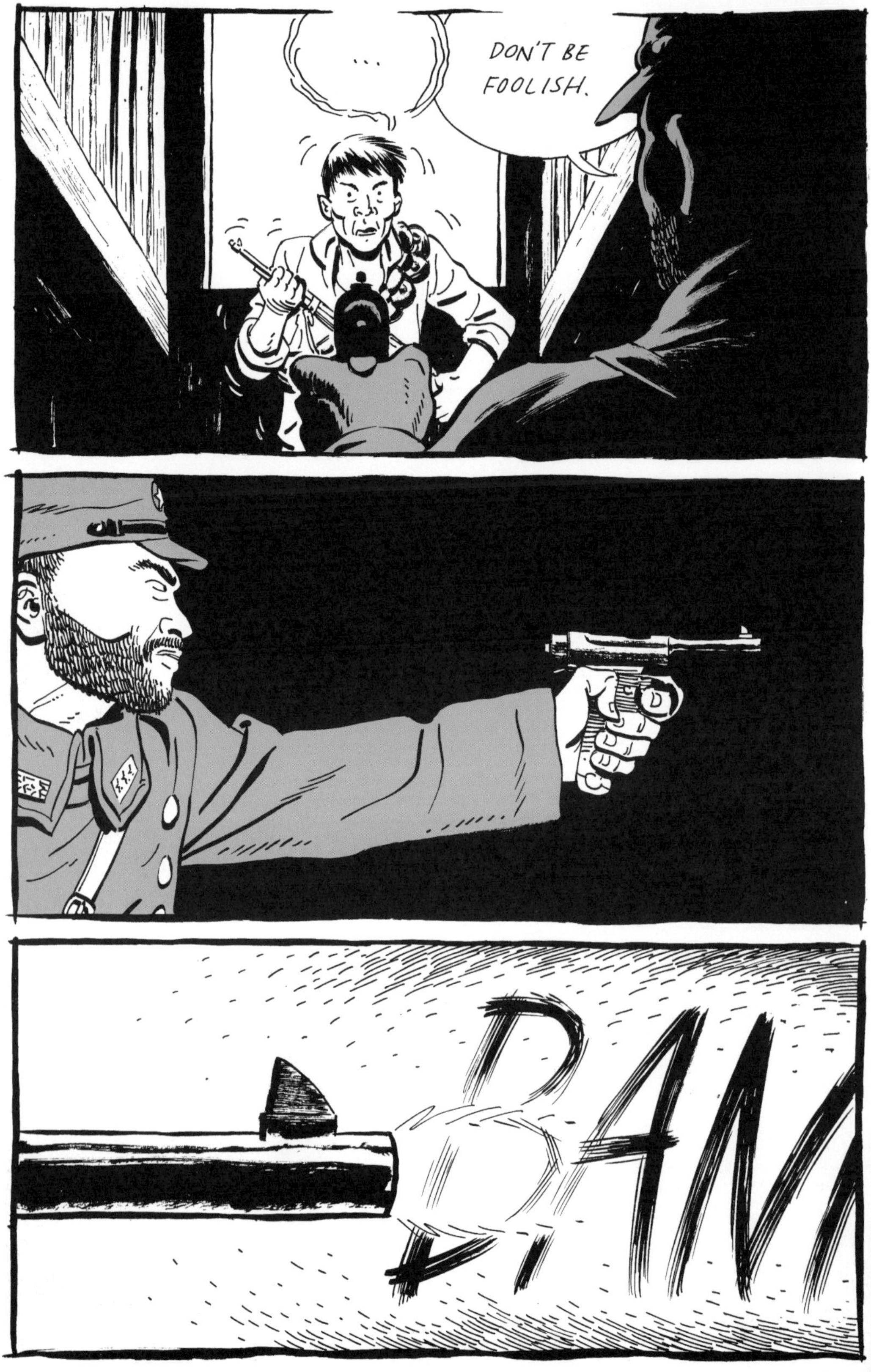
...
DON'T BE FOOLISH.
BAM

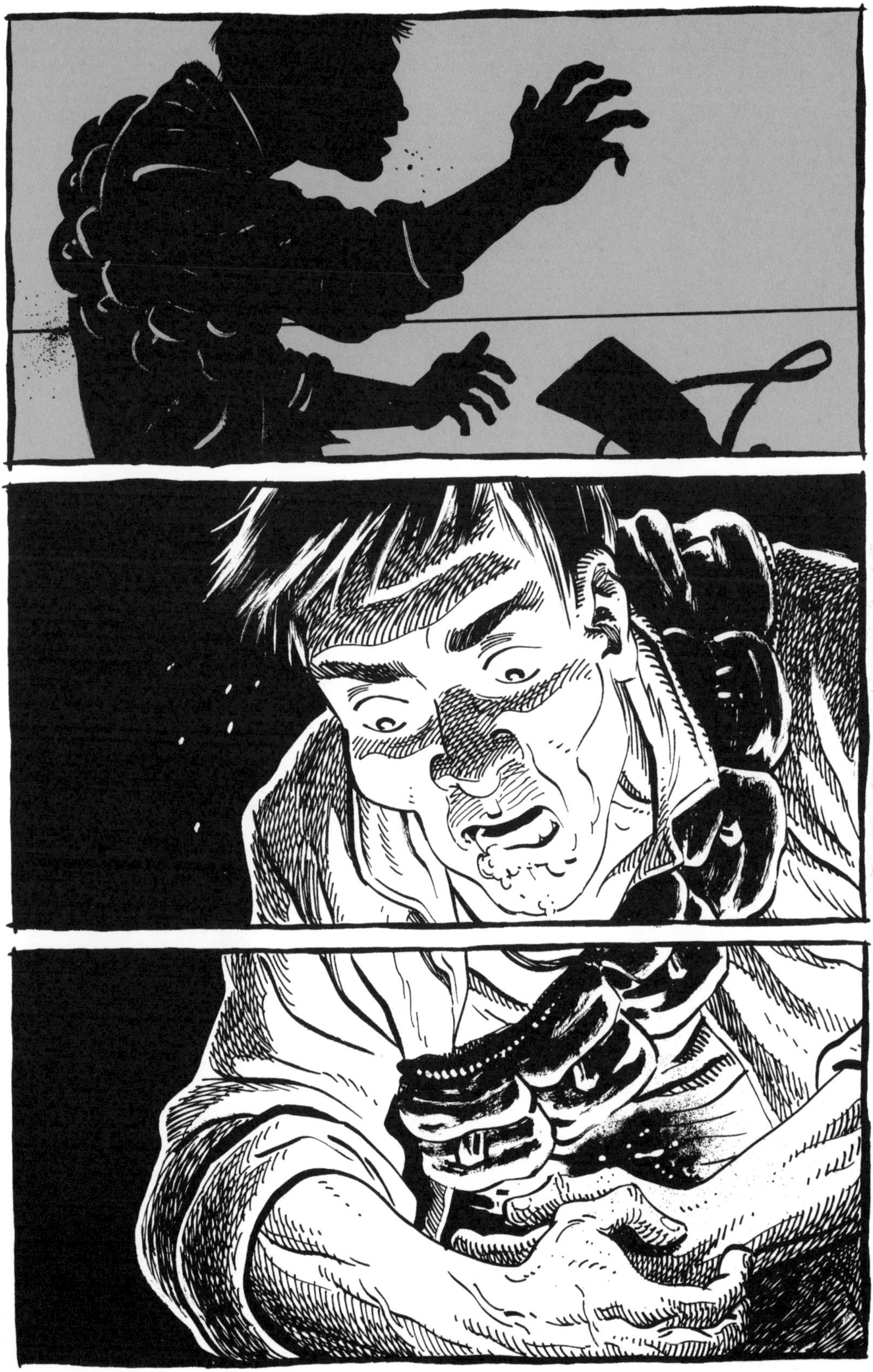

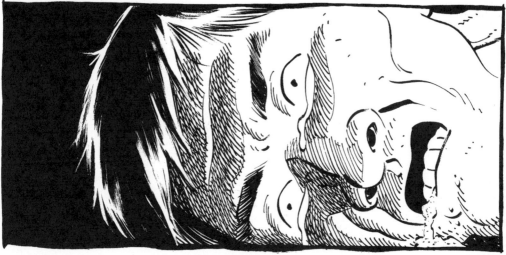

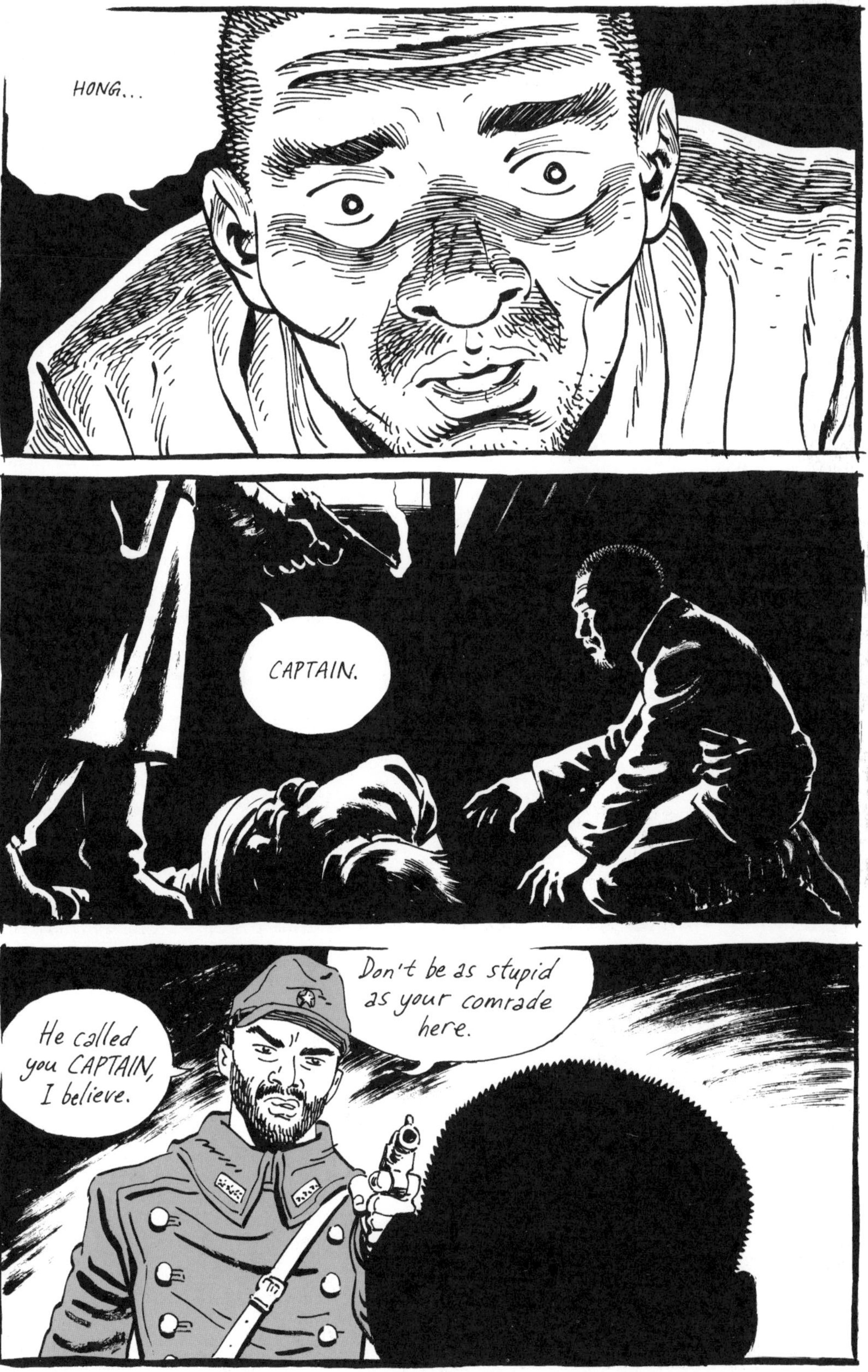
HONG...
CAPTAIN.
Don't be as stupid as your comrade here.
He called you CAPTAIN, I believe.

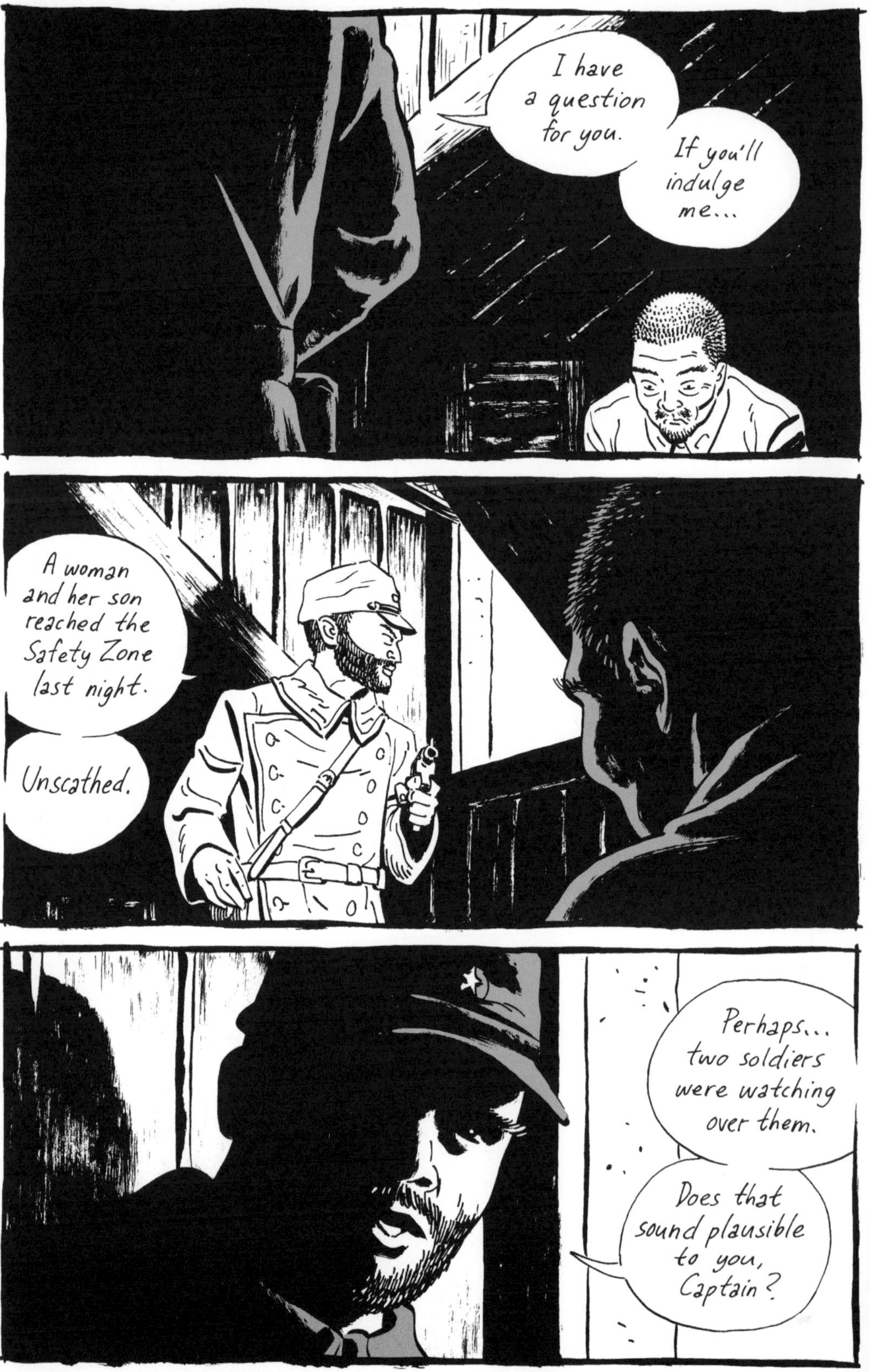
I have a question for you.
If you'll indulge me...
A woman and her son reached the Safety Zone last night.
Unscathed.
Perhaps... two soldiers were watching over them.
Does that sound plausible to you, Captain?

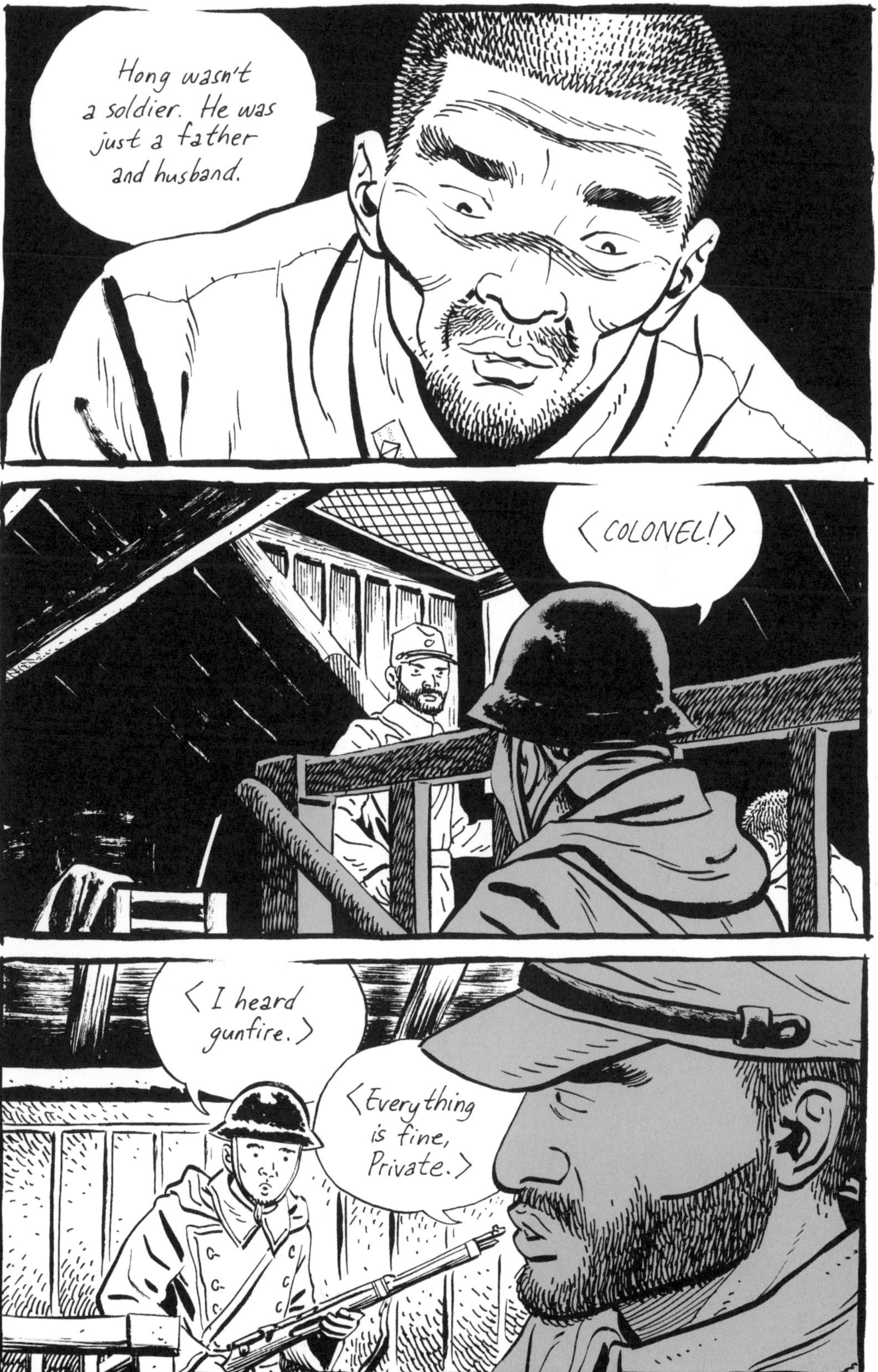
Hong wasn't a soldier. He was just a father and husband.
⟨COLONEL!⟩
⟨I heard gunfire.⟩
⟨Everything is fine, Private.⟩

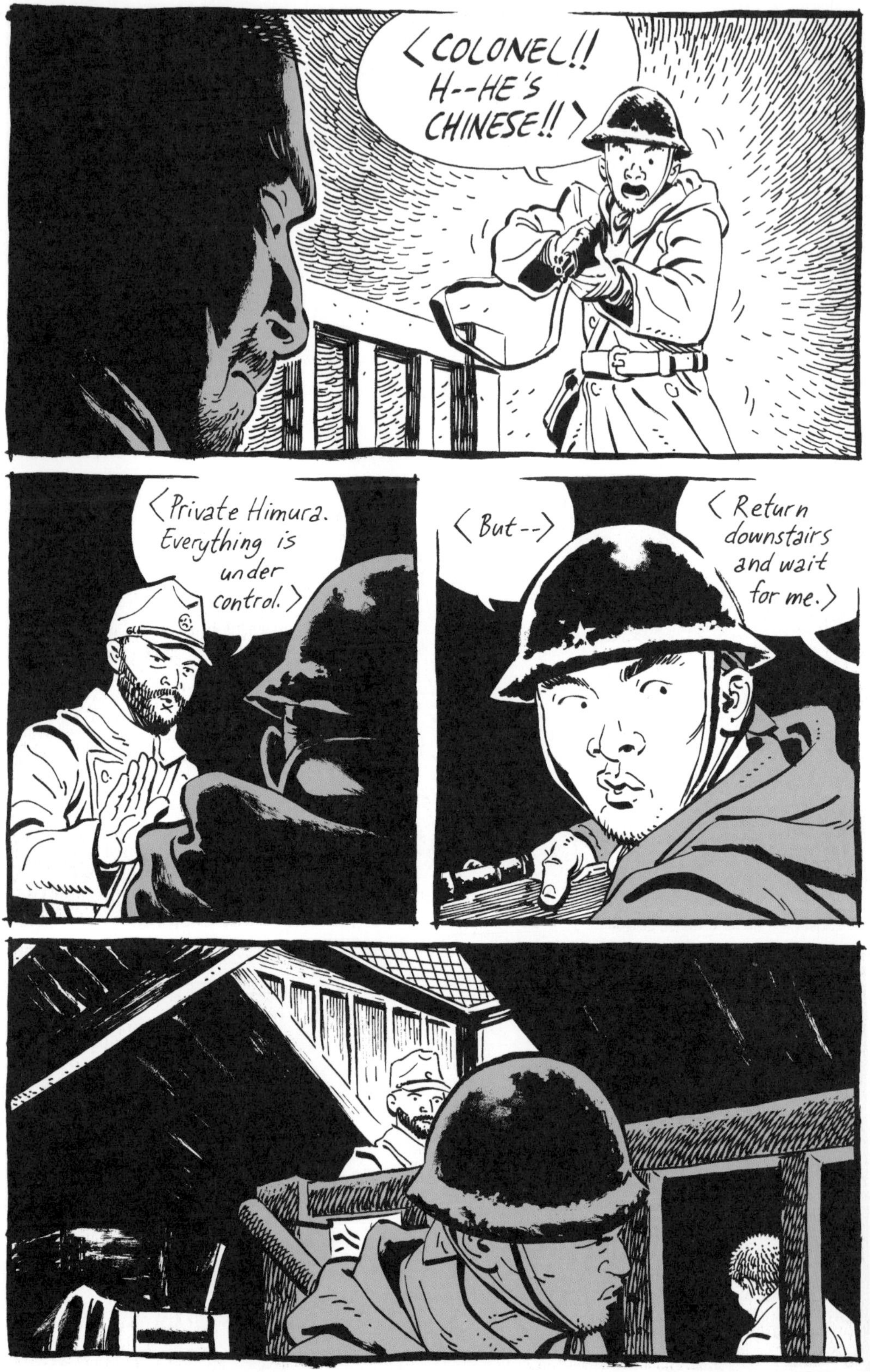
<COLONEL!! H--HE'S CHINESE!!>
<Private Himura. Everything is under control.>
<But-->
<Return downstairs and wait for me.>

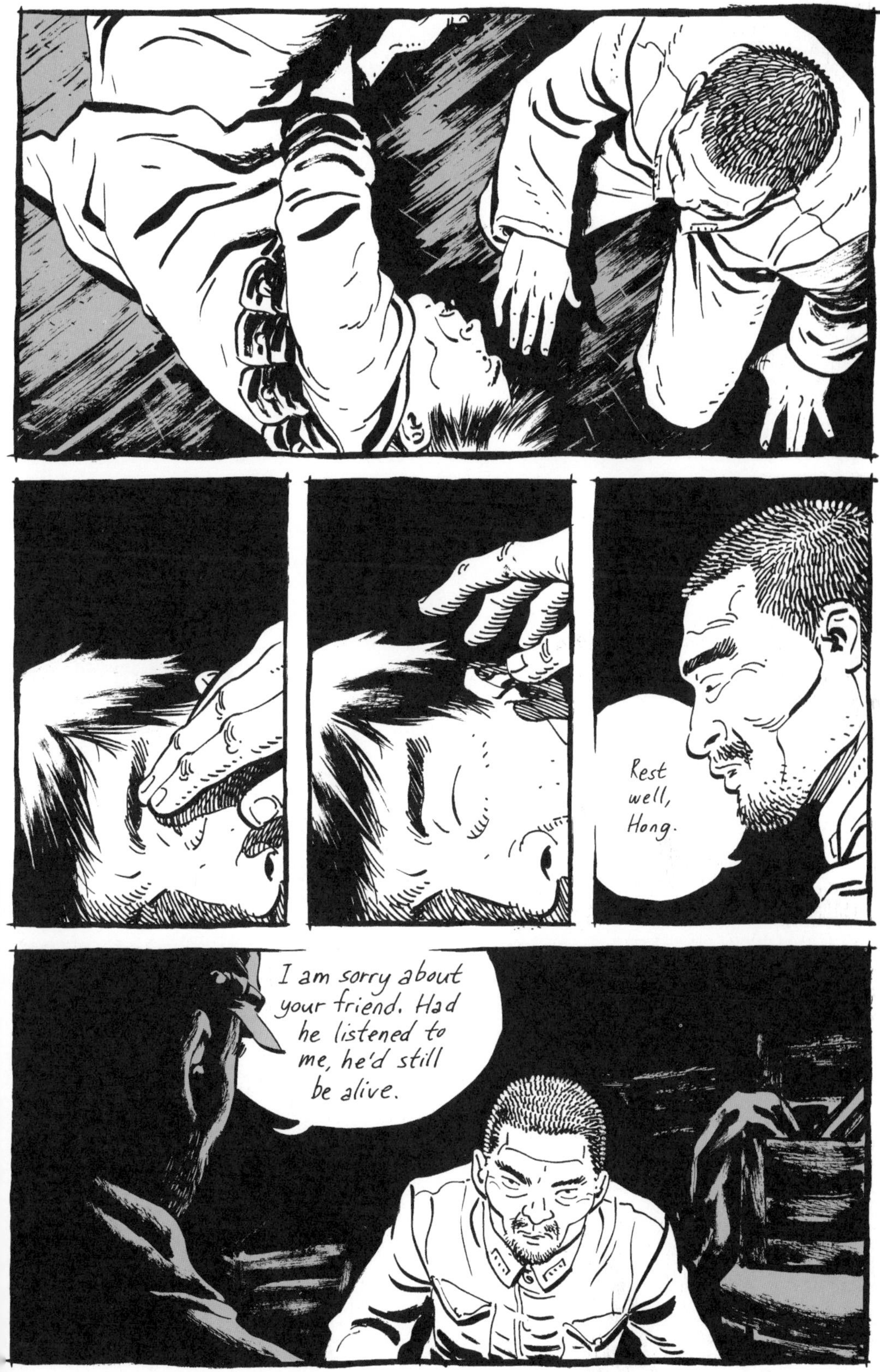
Rest well, Hong.
I am sorry about your friend. Had he listened to me, he'd still be alive.

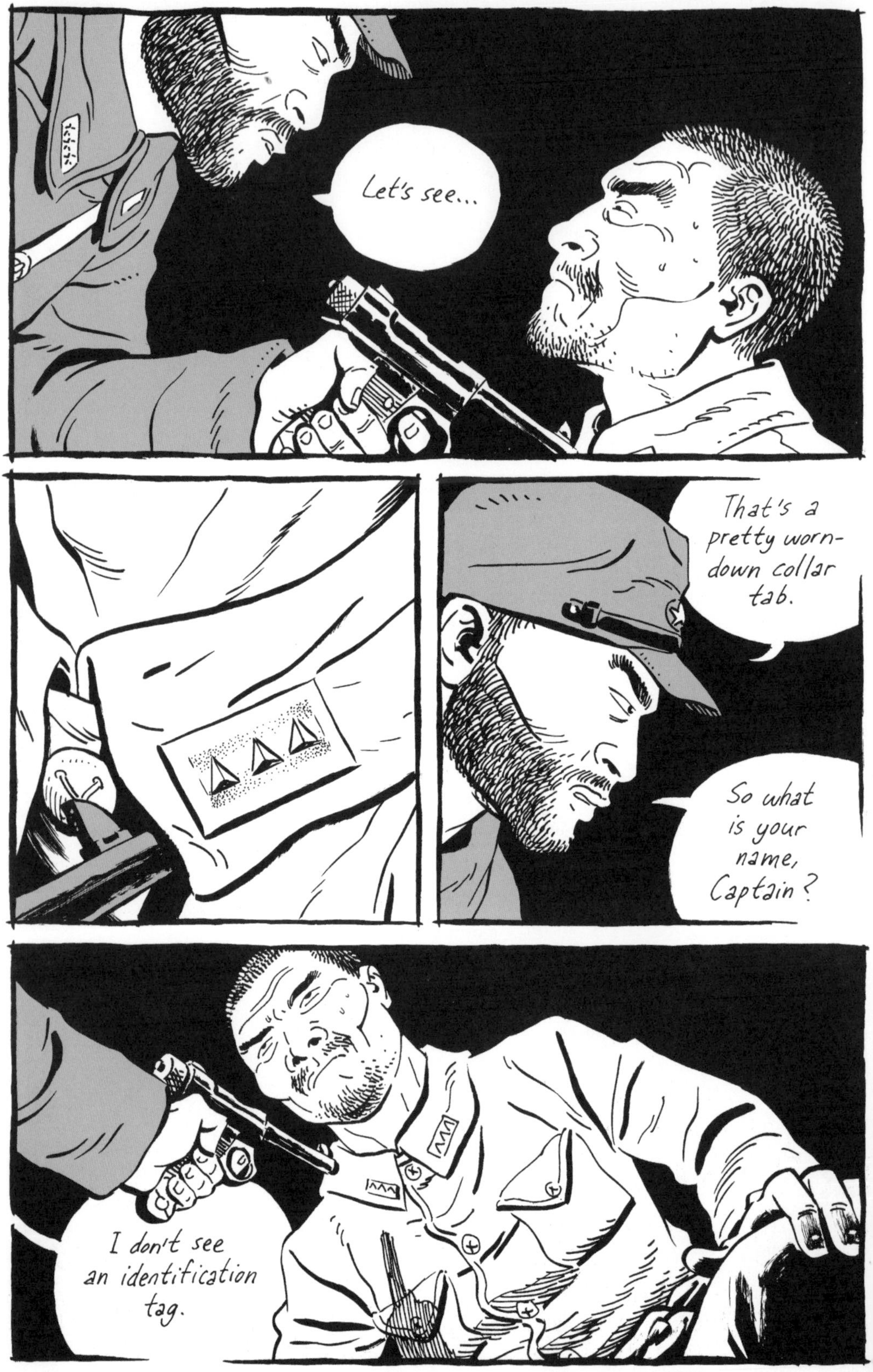
Let's see...
That's a pretty worn-down collar tab.
So what is your name, Captain?
I don't see an identification tag.

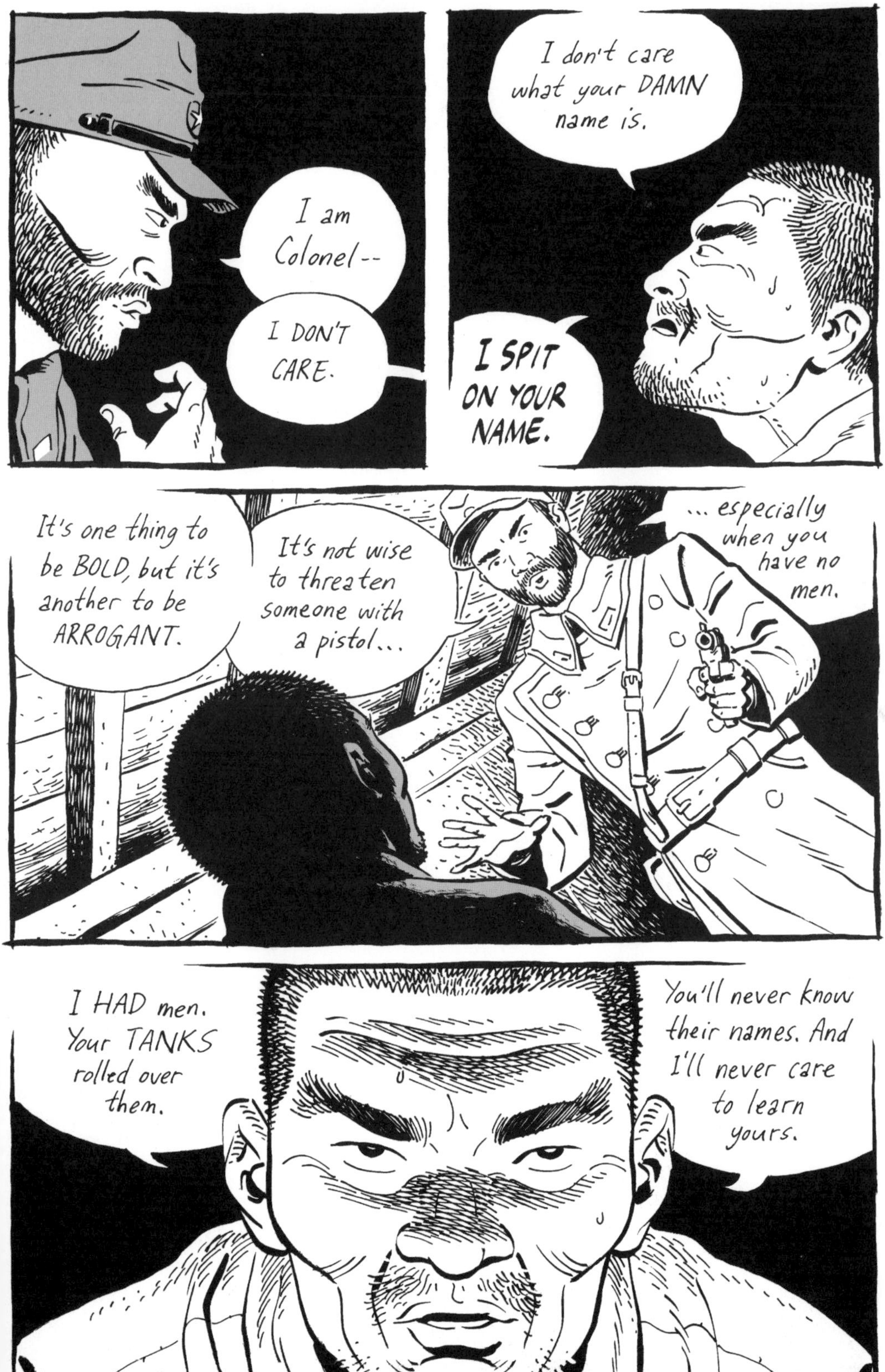
I am Colonel--
I DON'T CARE.
I don't care what your DAMN name is.
I SPIT ON YOUR NAME.
It's one thing to be BOLD, but it's another to be ARROGANT.
It's not wise to threaten someone with a pistol...
...especially when you have no men.
I HAD men. Your TANKS rolled over them.
You'll never know their names. And I'll never care to learn yours.

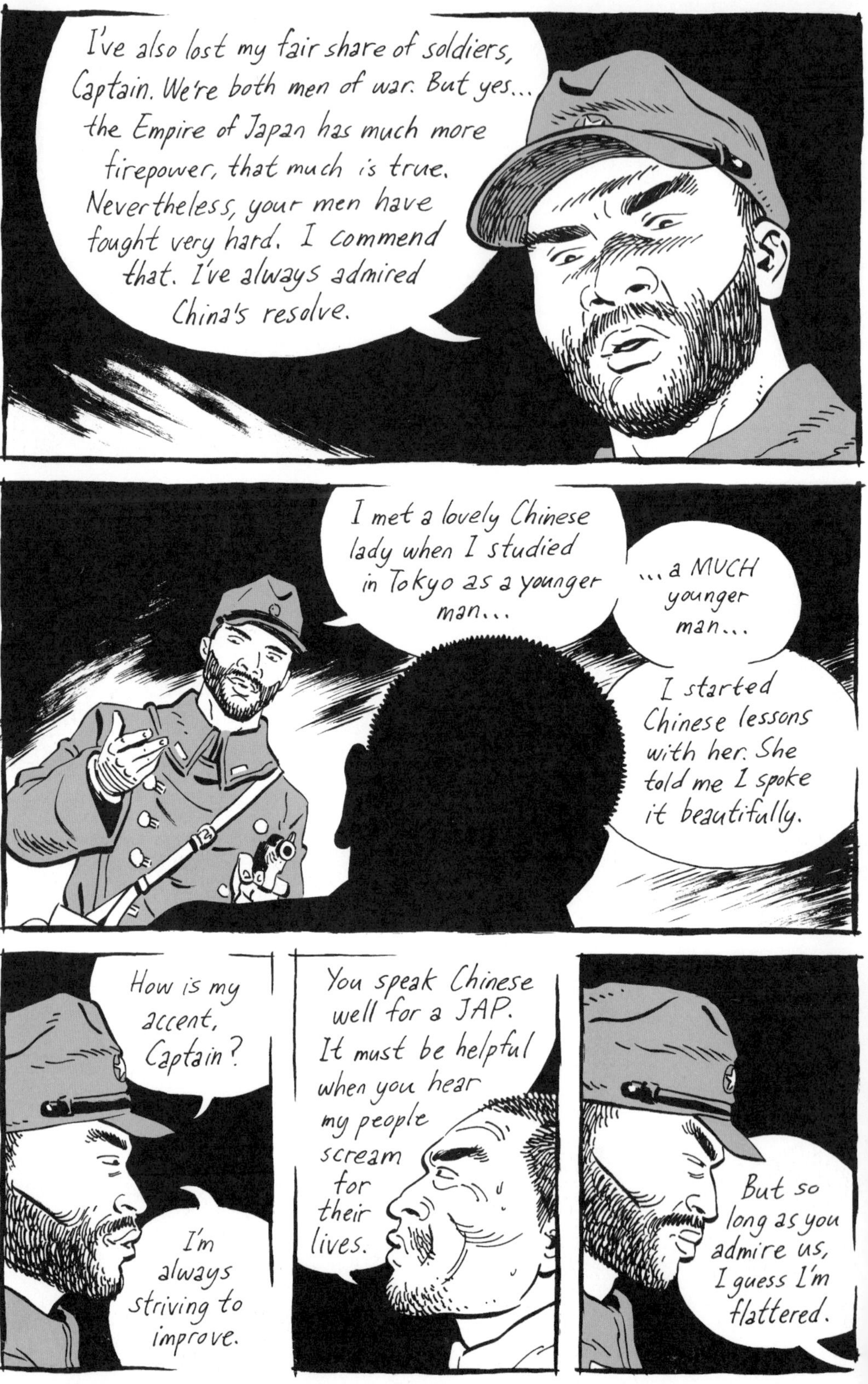
I've also lost my fair share of soldiers, Captain. We're both men of war. But yes... the Empire of Japan has much more firepower, that much is true. Nevertheless, your men have fought very hard. I commend that. I've always admired China's resolve.
I met a lovely Chinese lady when I studied in Tokyo as a younger man...
...a MUCH younger man...
I started Chinese lessons with her. She told me I spoke it beautifully.
How is my accent, Captain?
I'm always striving to improve.
You speak Chinese well for a JAP. It must be helpful when you hear my people scream for their lives.
But so long as you admire us, I guess I'm flattered.

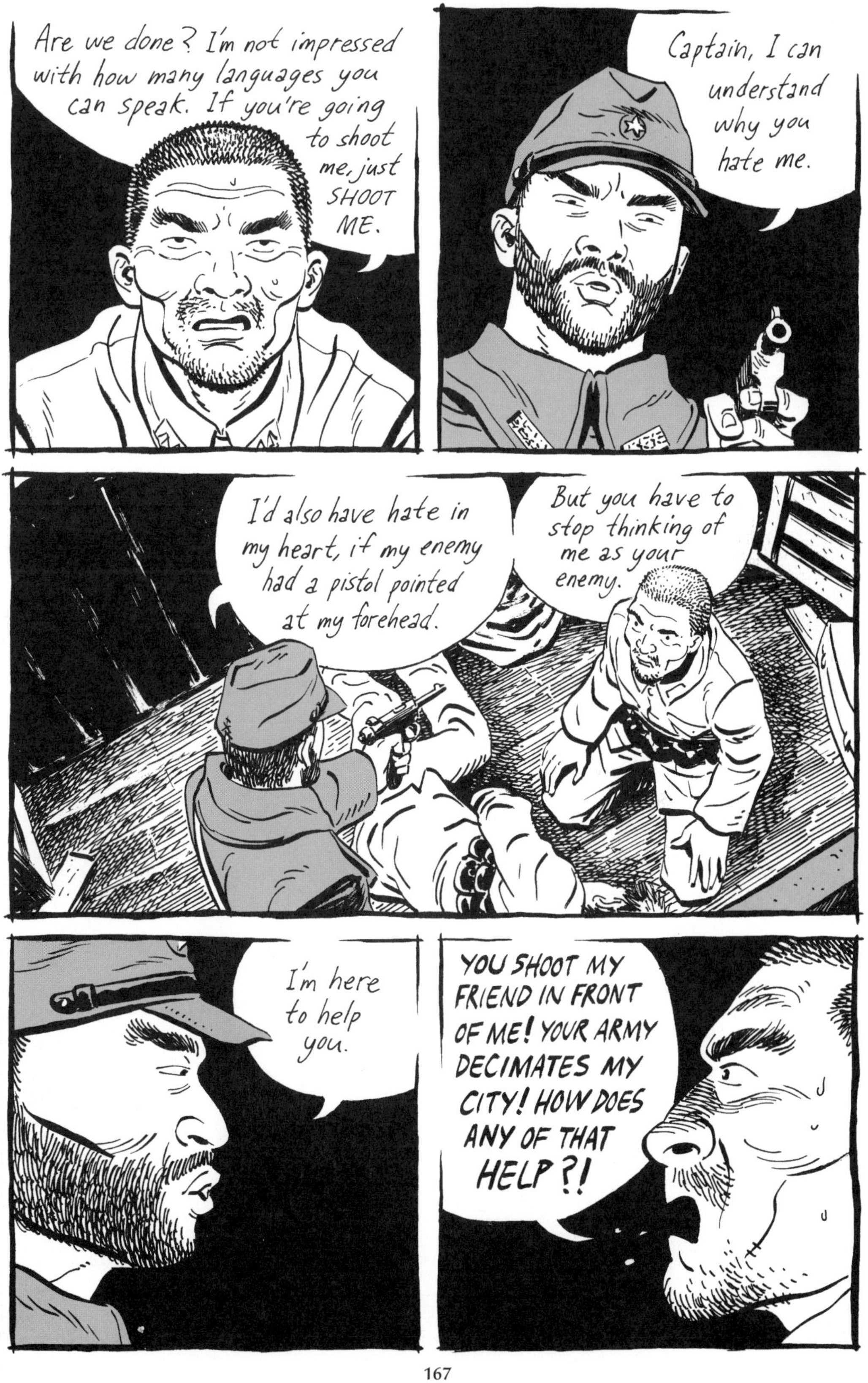
Are we done? I'm not impressed with how many languages you can speak. If you're going to shoot me, just SHOOT ME.
Captain, I can understand why you hate me.
I'd also have hate in my heart, if my enemy had a pistol pointed at my forehead.
But you have to stop thinking of me as your enemy.
I'm here to help you.
YOU SHOOT MY FRIEND IN FRONT OF ME! YOUR ARMY DECIMATES MY CITY! HOW DOES ANY OF THAT HELP?!

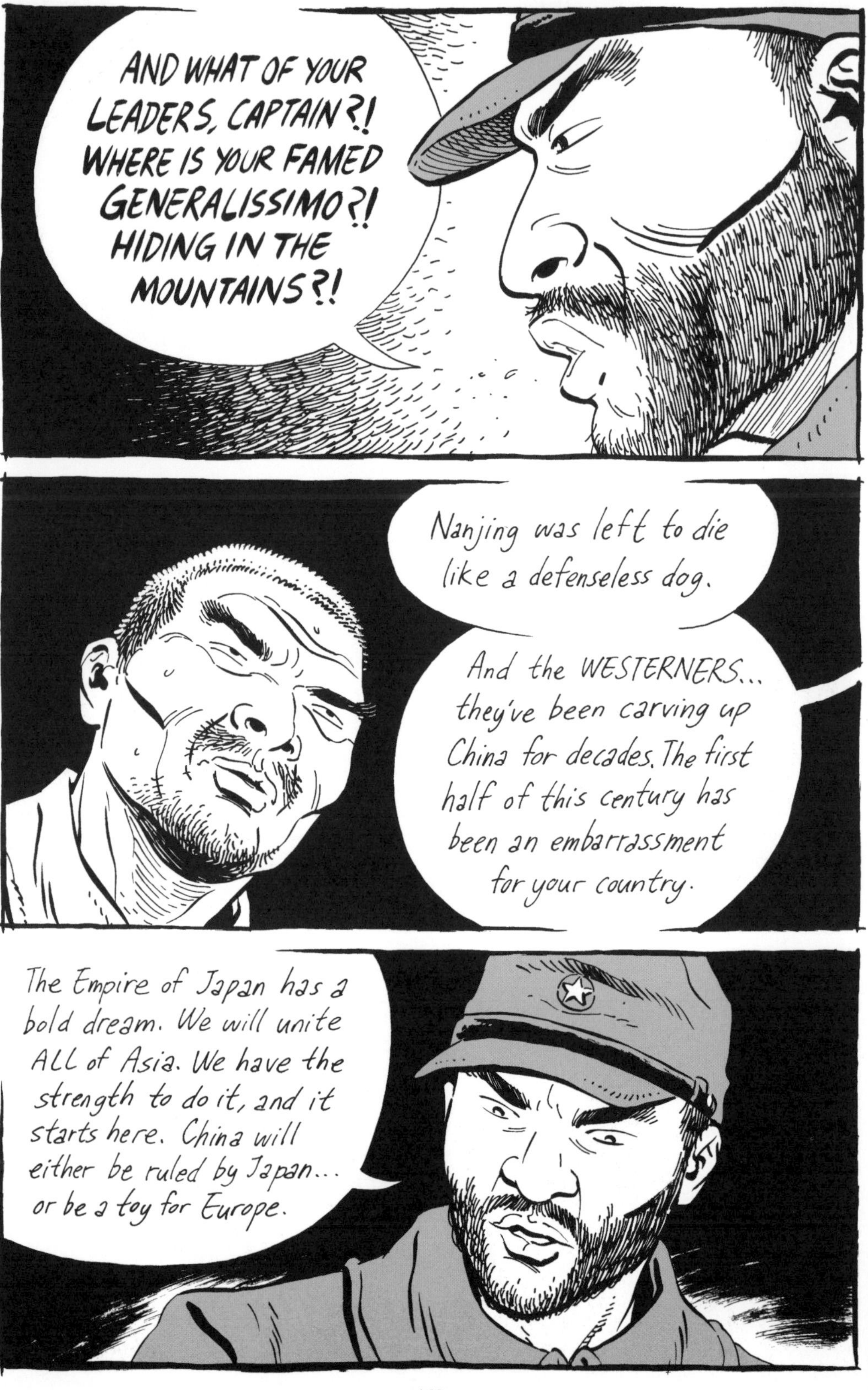
AND WHAT OF YOUR LEADERS, CAPTAIN?! WHERE IS YOUR FAMED GENERALISSIMO?! HIDING IN THE MOUNTAINS?!
Nanjing was left to die like a defenseless dog.
And the WESTERNERS... they've been carving up China for decades. The first half of this century has been an embarrassment for your country.
The Empire of Japan has a bold dream. We will unite ALL of Asia. We have the strength to do it, and it starts here. China will either be ruled by Japan... or be a toy for Europe.

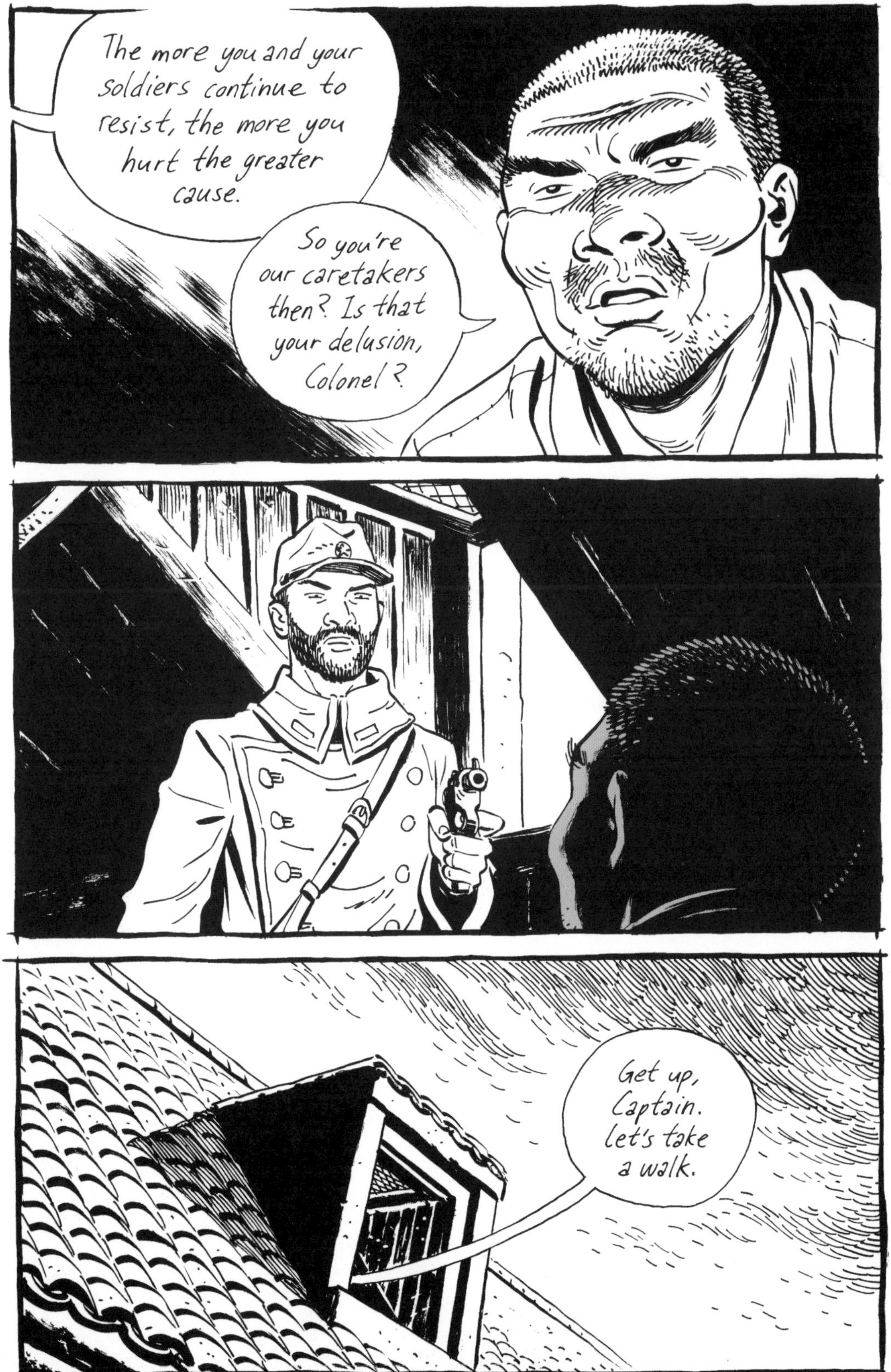
The more you and your soldiers continue to resist, the more you hurt the greater cause.
So you're our caretakers then? Is that your delusion, Colonel?
Get up, Captain. let's take a walk.

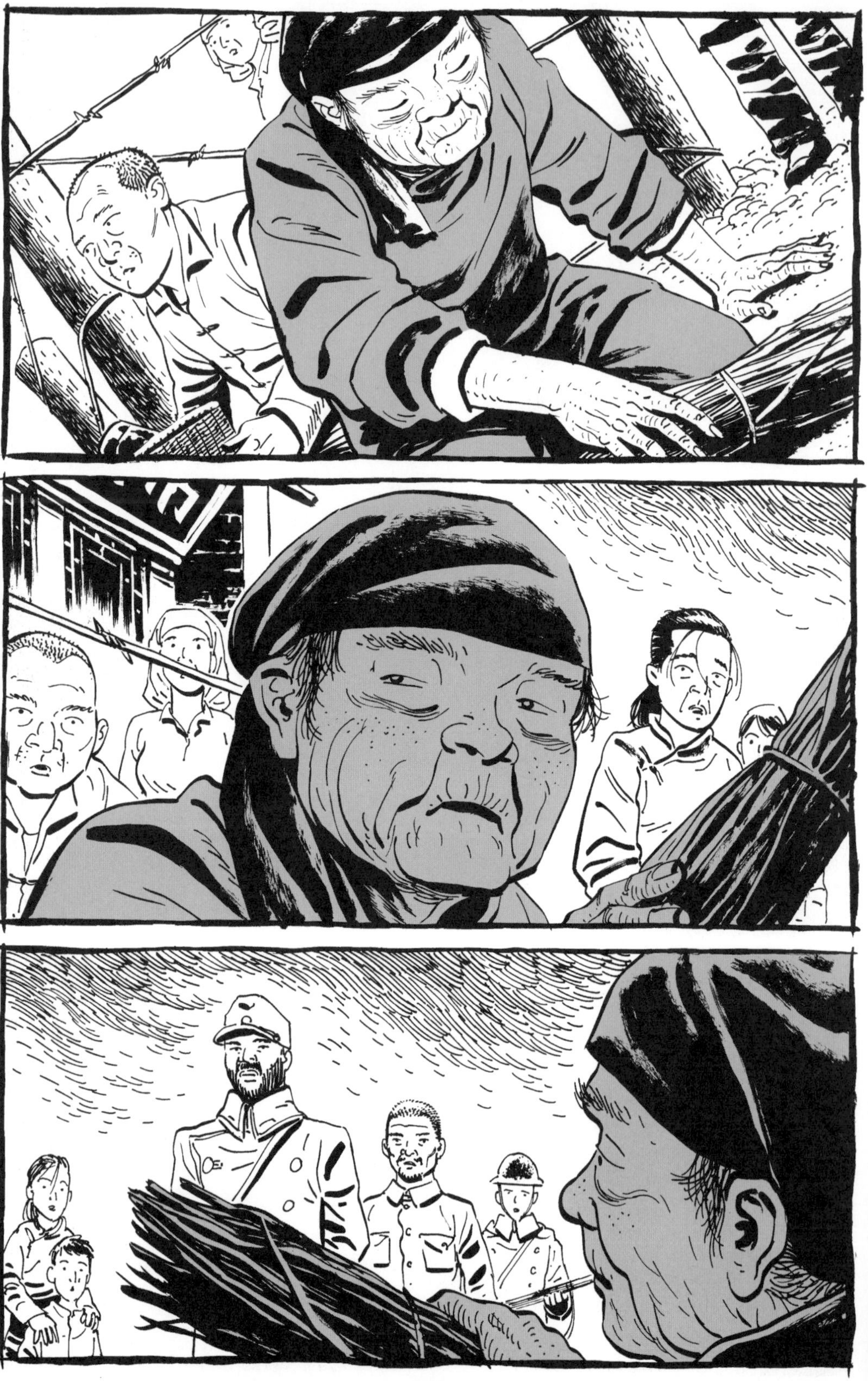

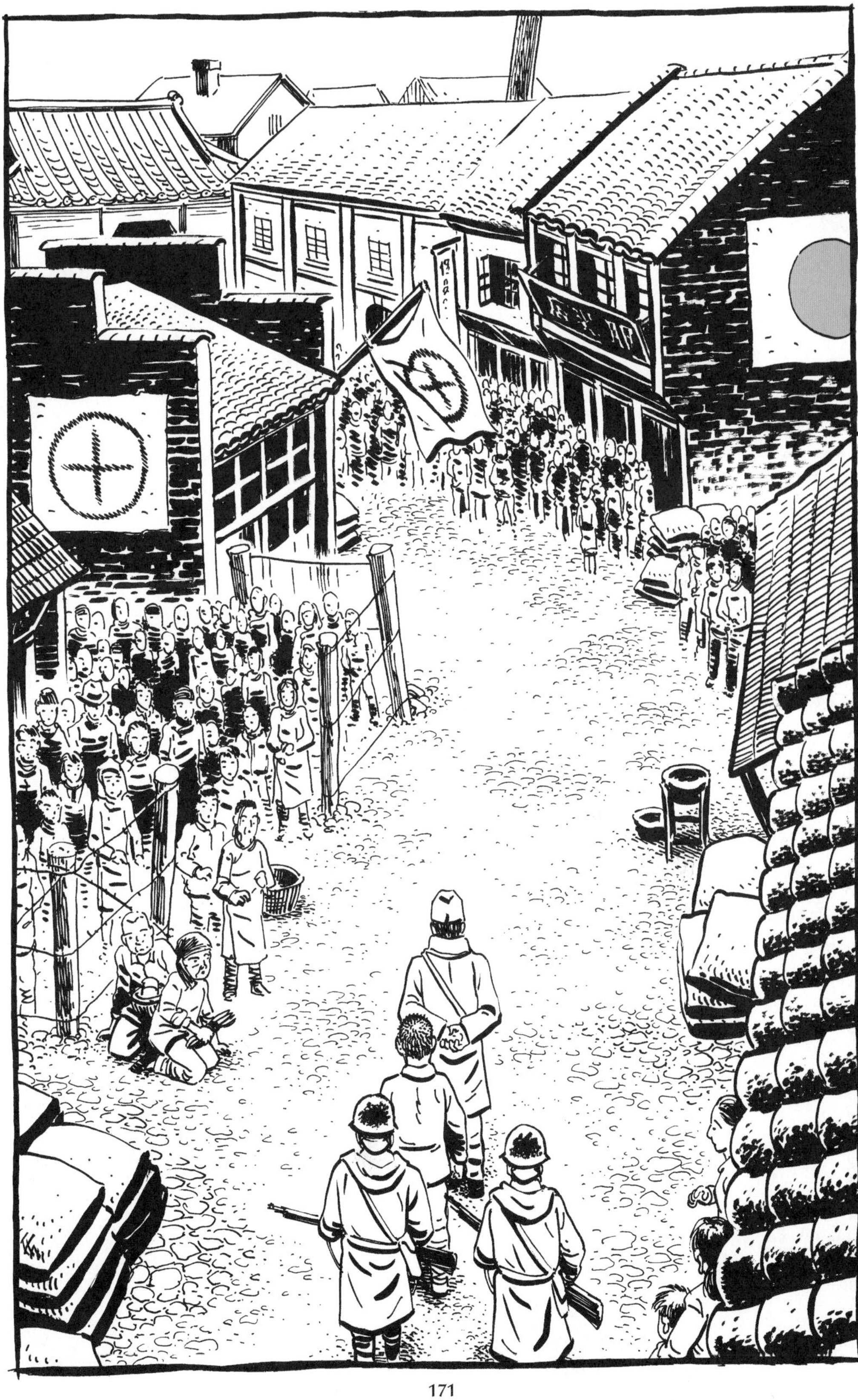

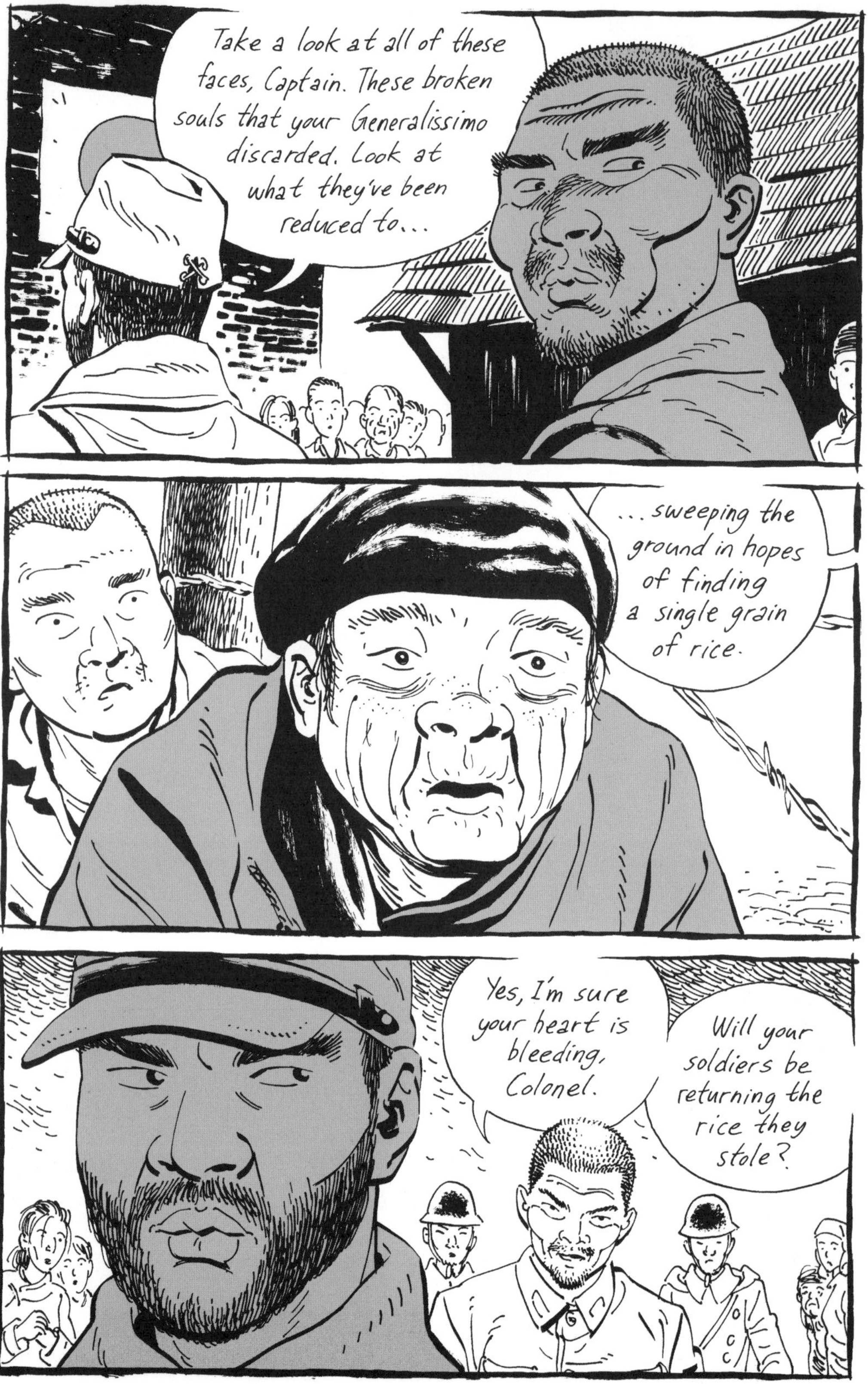
Take a look at all of these faces, Captain. These broken souls that your Generalissimo discarded. Look at what they've been reduced to...
...sweeping the ground in hopes of finding a single grain of rice.
Yes, I'm sure your heart is bleeding, Colonel.
Will your soldiers be returning the rice they stole?

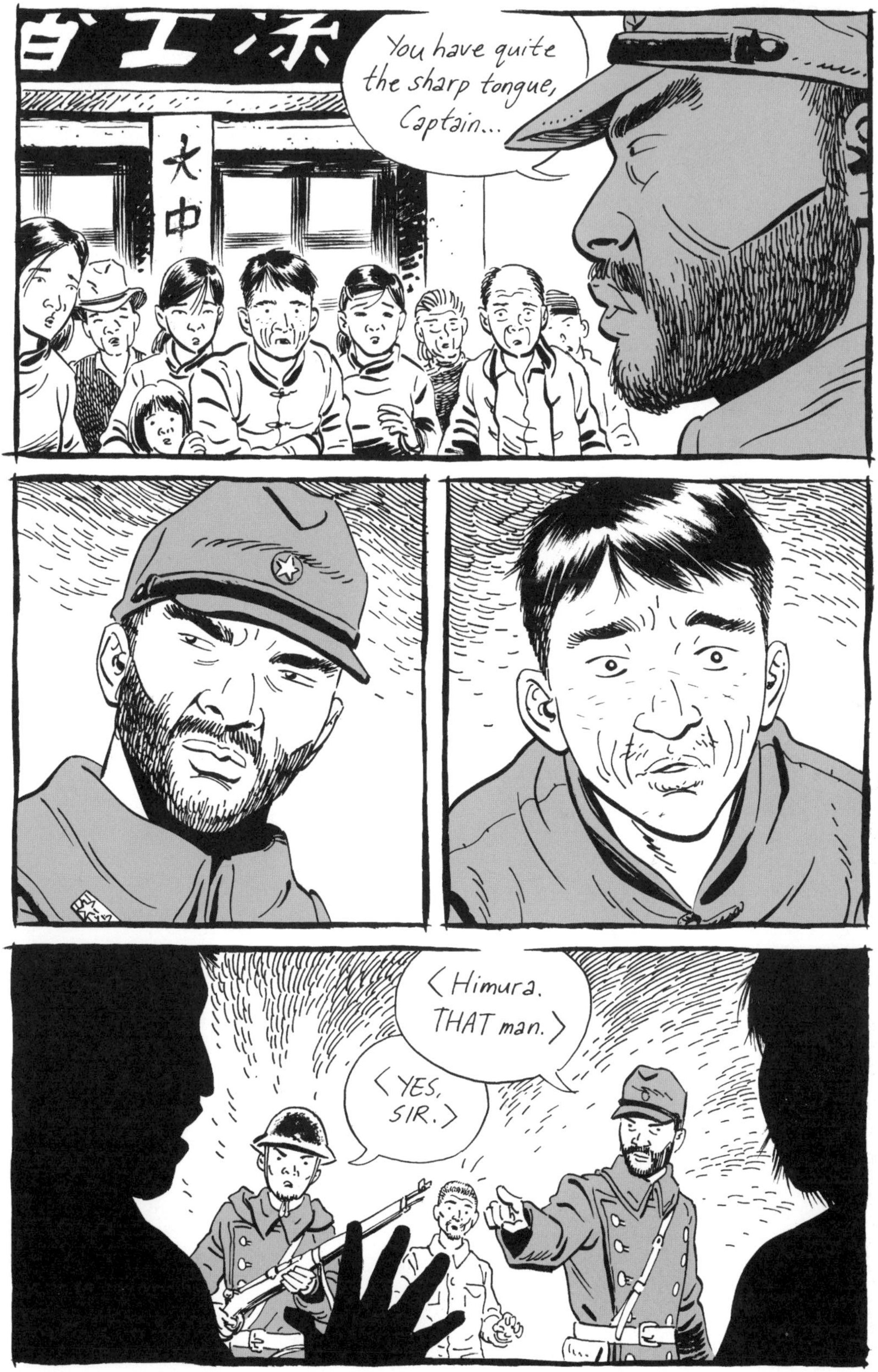
大中
You have quite the sharp tongue, Captain...
〈Himura. THAT man.〉
〈YES, SIR.〉

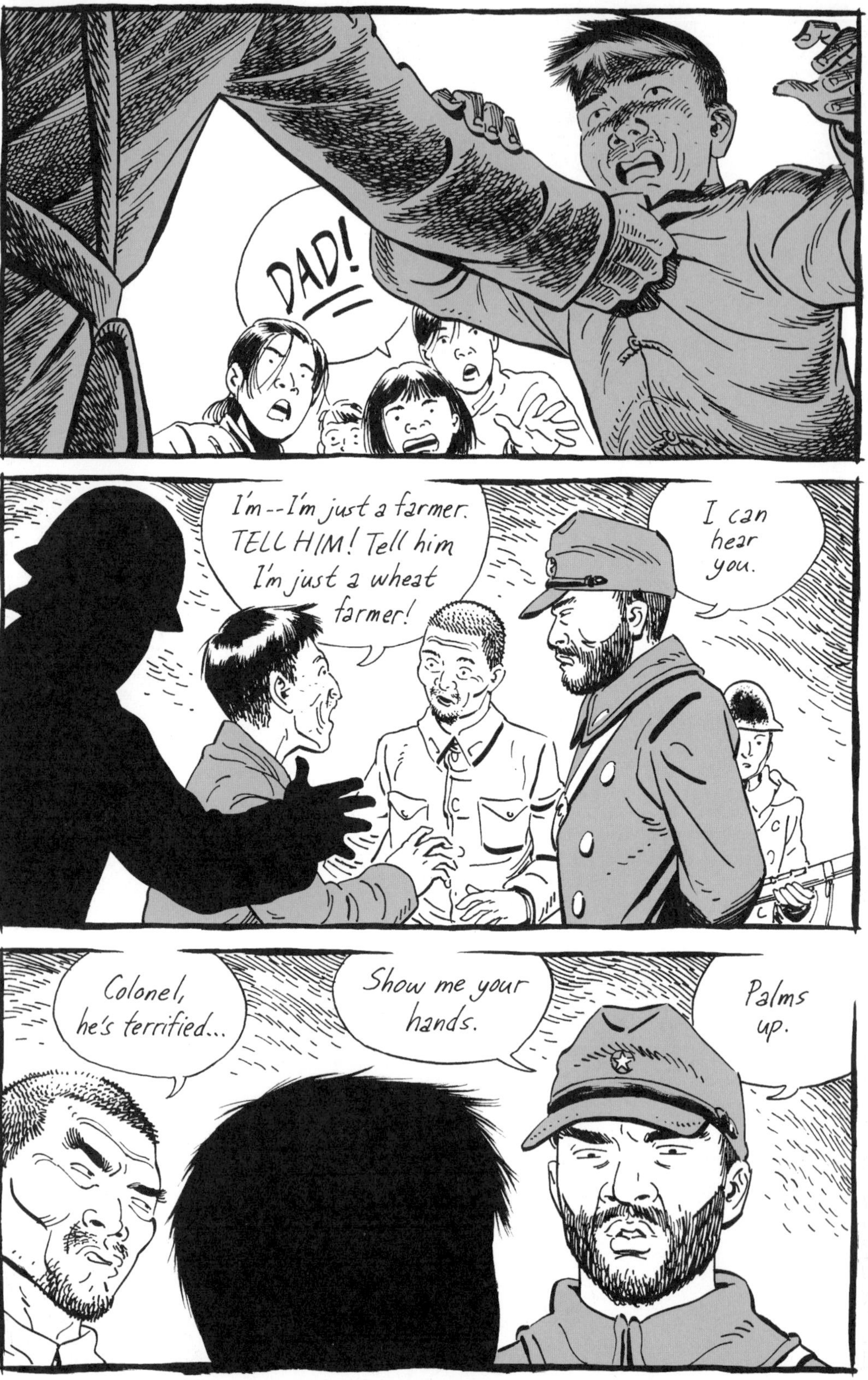
DAD!
I'm--I'm just a farmer. TELL HIM! Tell him I'm just a wheat farmer!
I can hear you.
Colonel, he's terrified...
Show me your hands.
Palms up.

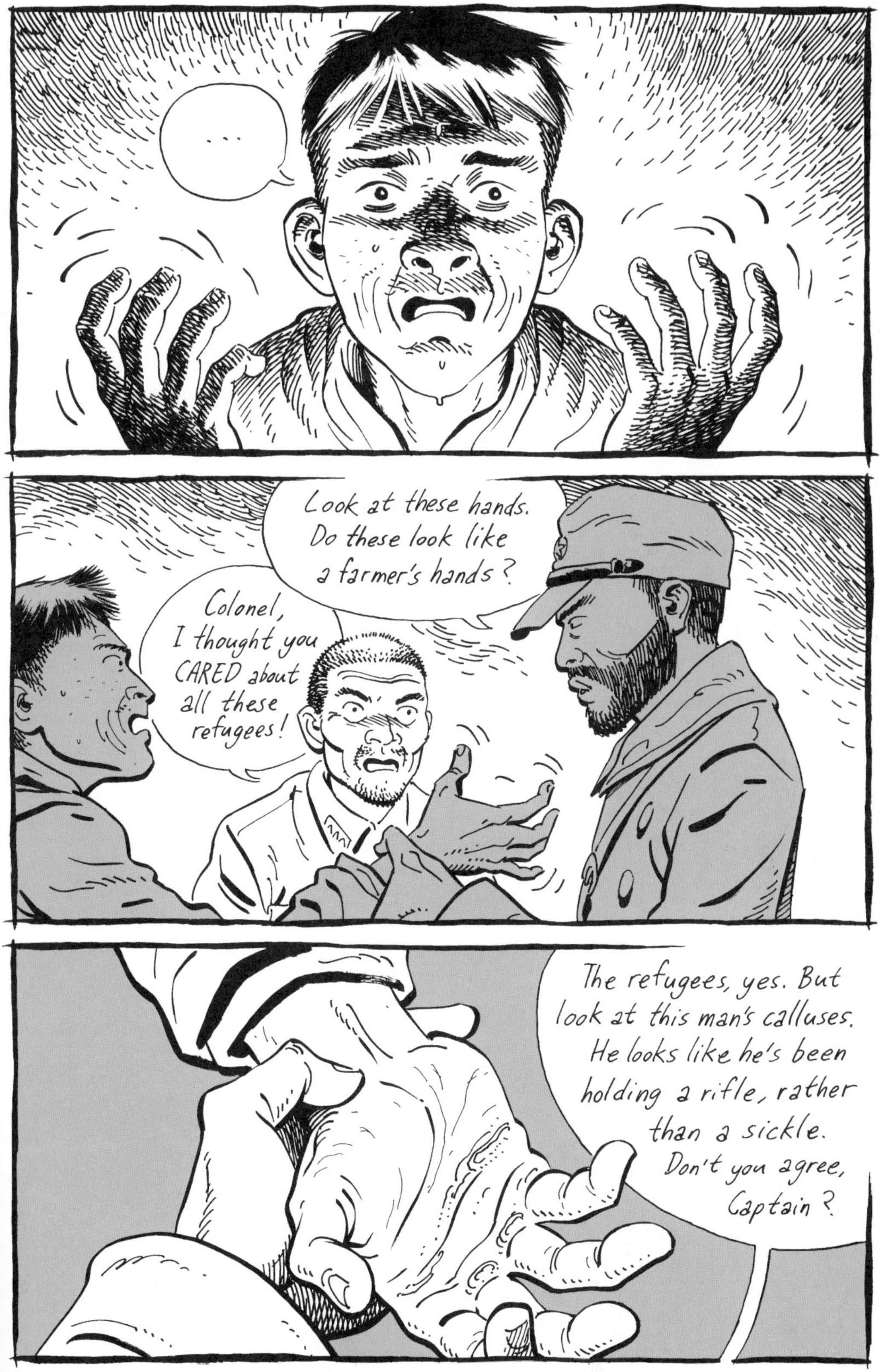
...
Look at these hands. Do these look like a farmer's hands?
Colonel, I thought you CARED about all these refugees!
The refugees, yes. But look at this man's calluses. He looks like he's been holding a rifle, rather than a sickle. Don't you agree, Captain?

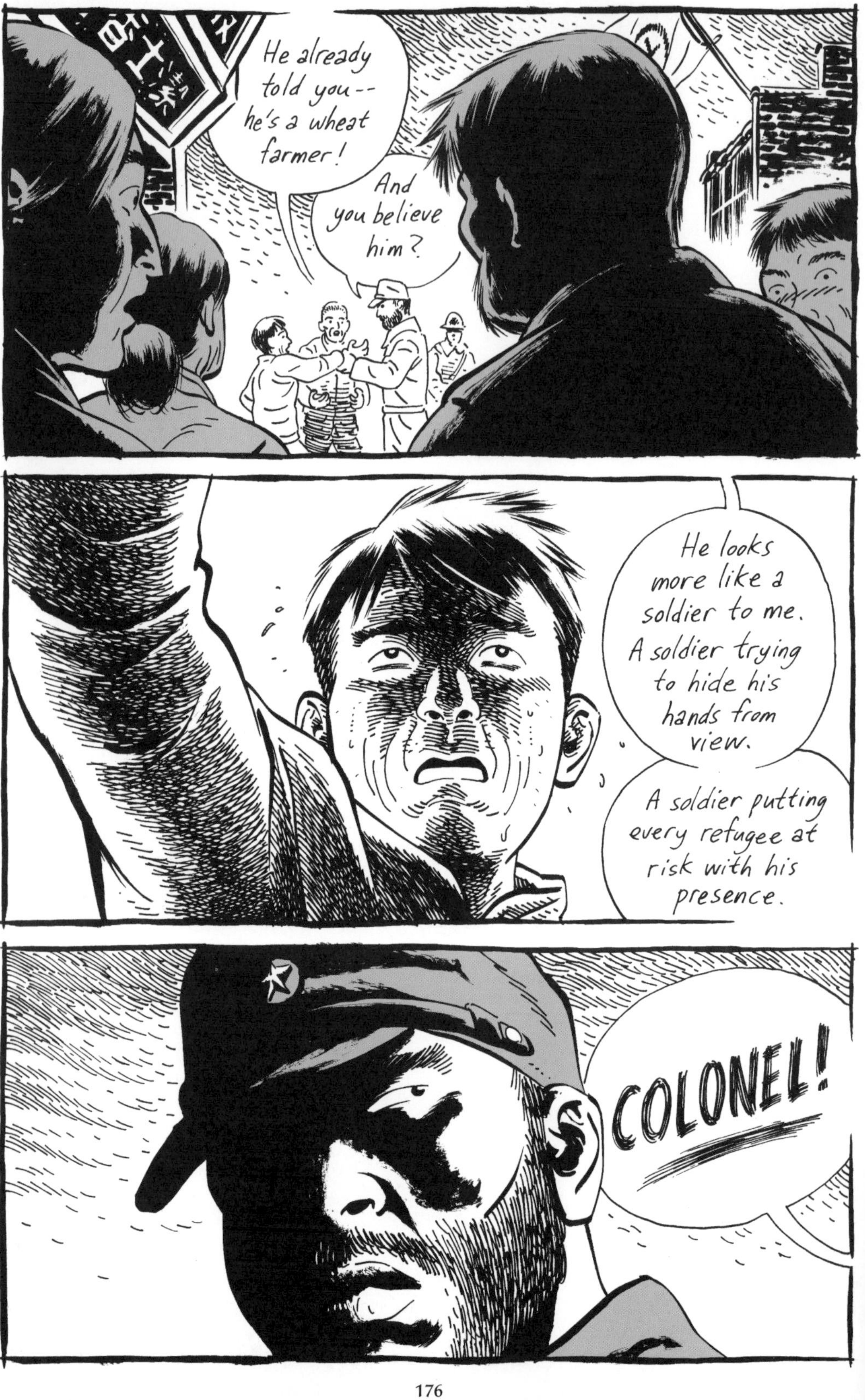
He already told you-- he's a wheat farmer!
And you believe him?
He looks more like a soldier to me. A soldier trying to hide his hands from view.
A soldier putting every refugee at risk with his presence.
COLONEL!

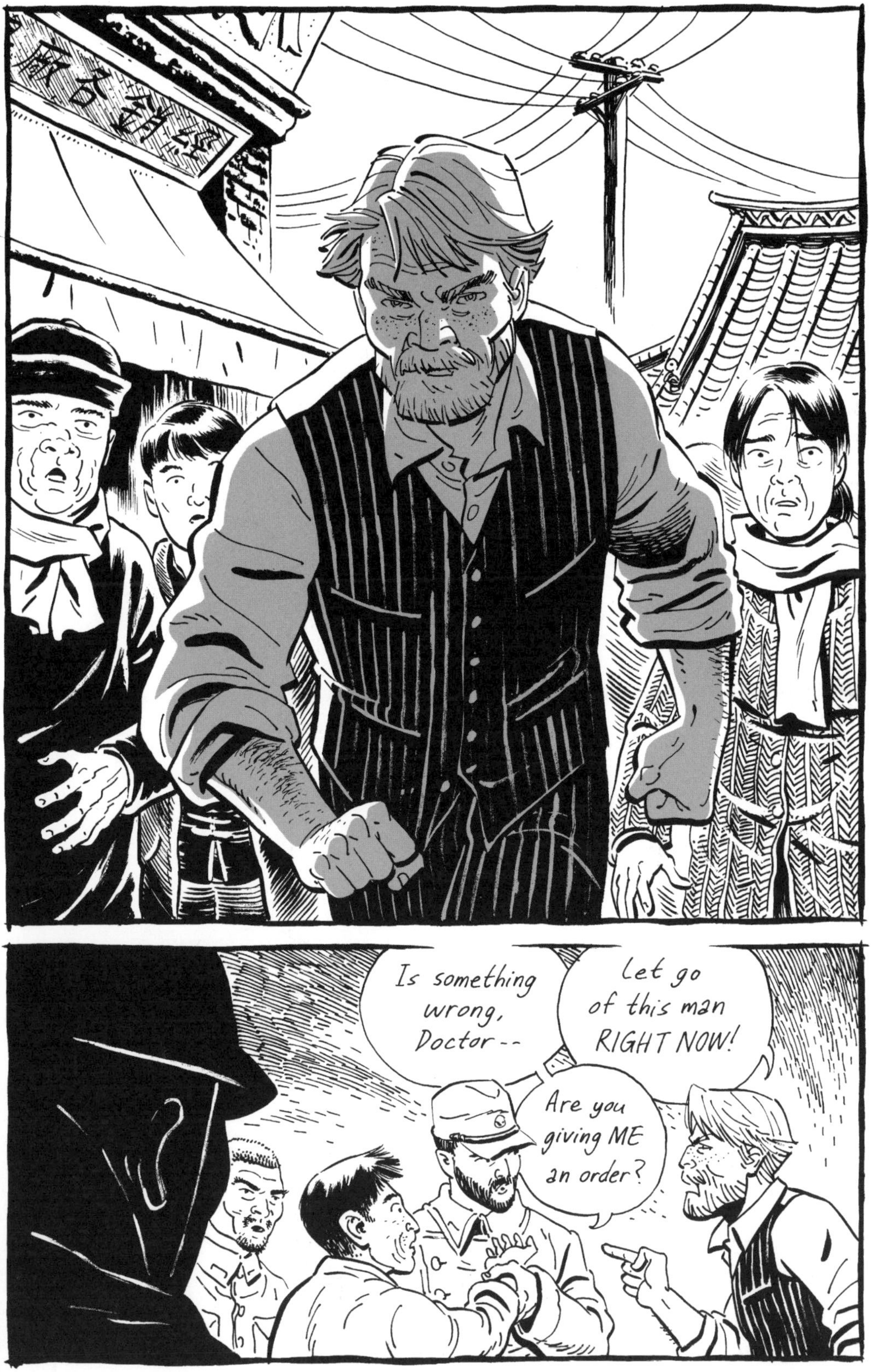
Is something wrong, Doctor--
Let go of this man RIGHT NOW!
Are you giving ME an order?

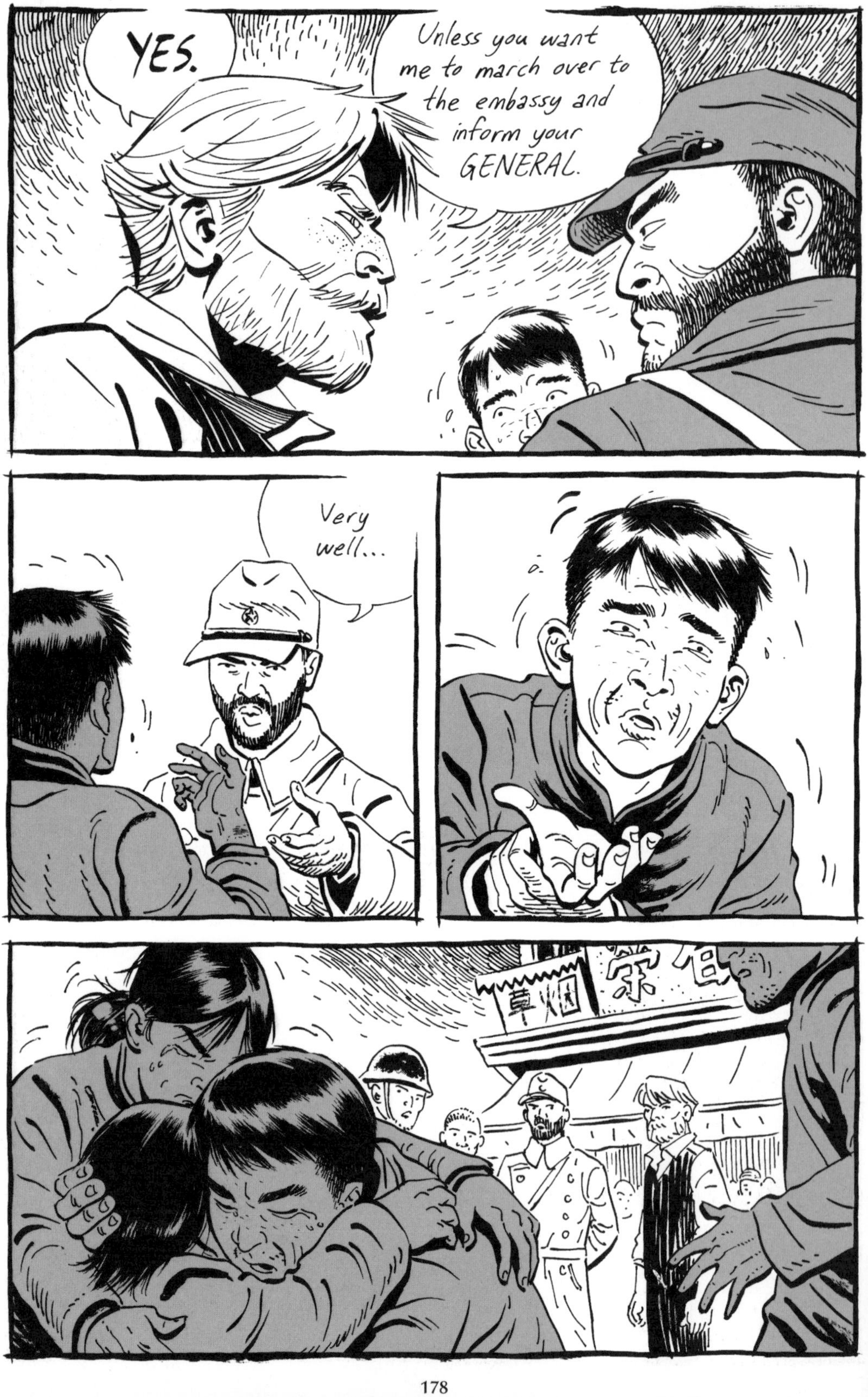
YES.
Unless you want me to march over to the embassy and inform your GENERAL.
Very well...

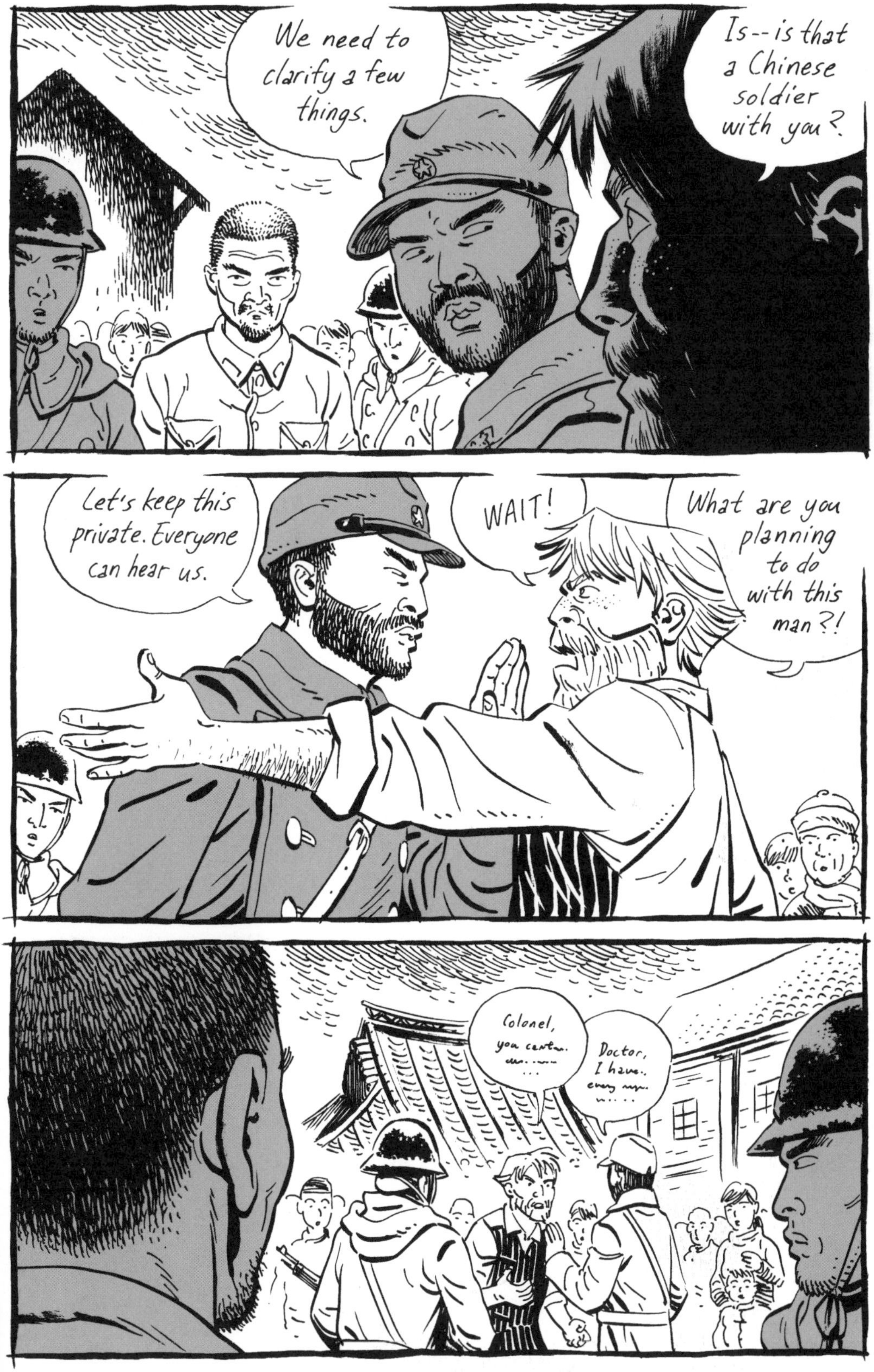
We need to clarify a few things.
Is--is that a Chinese soldier with you?
Let's keep this private. Everyone can hear us.
WAIT!
What are you planning to do with this man?!
Colonel,
Doctor, I have..

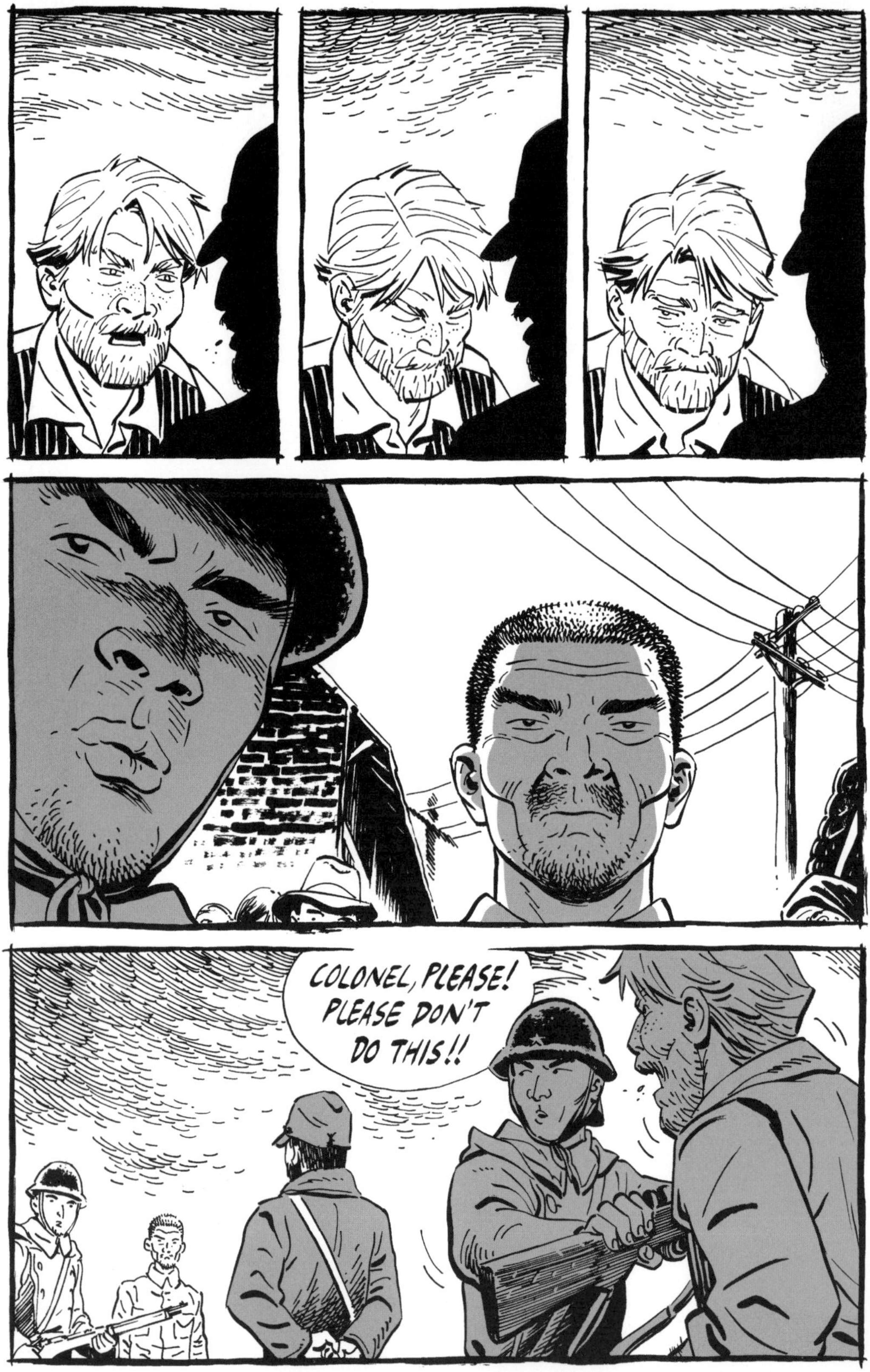
COLONEL, PLEASE! PLEASE DON'T DO THIS!!

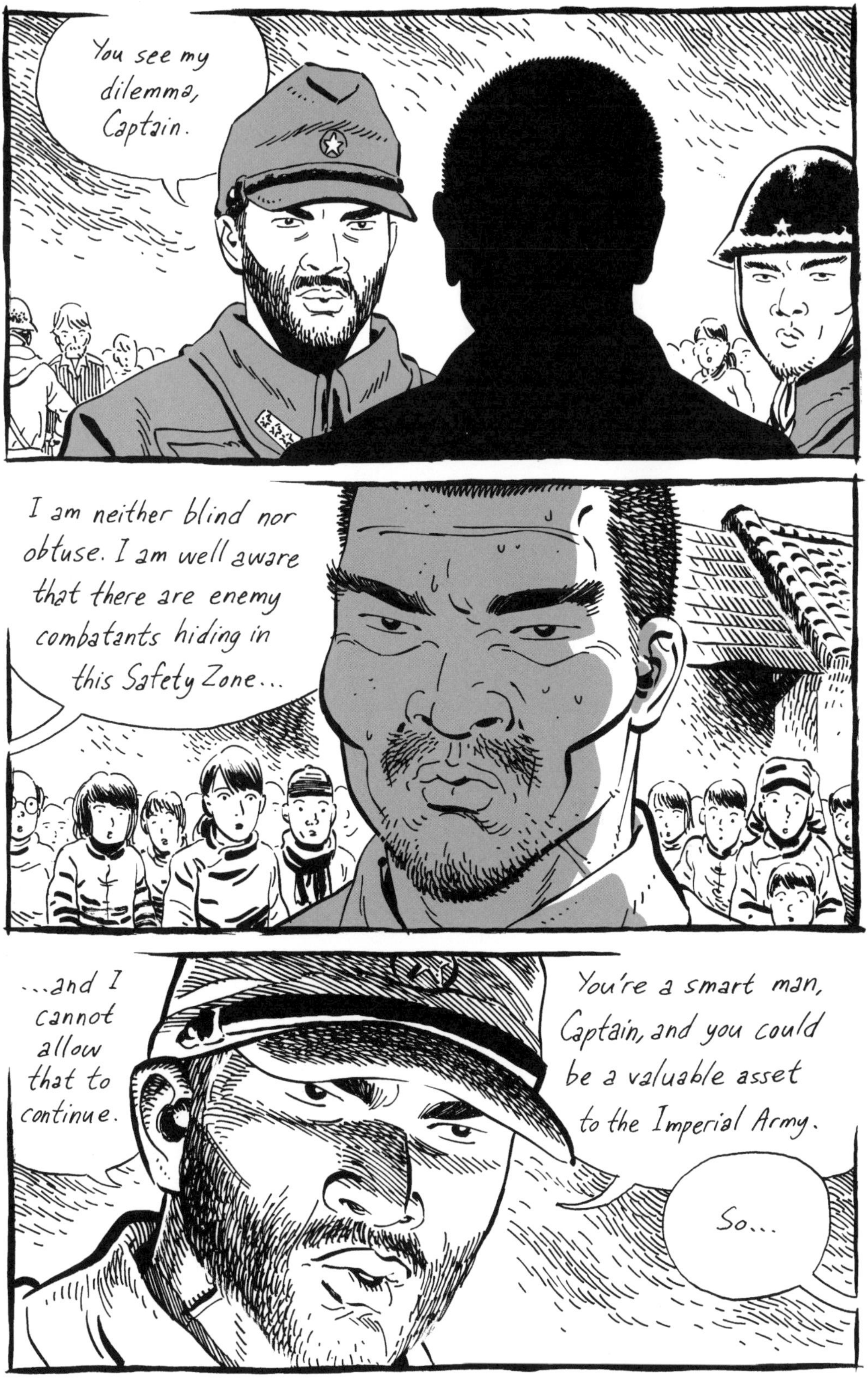
You see my dilemma, Captain.
I am neither blind nor obtuse. I am well aware that there are enemy combatants hiding in this Safety Zone...
...and I cannot allow that to continue.
You're a smart man, Captain, and you could be a valuable asset to the Imperial Army.
So...

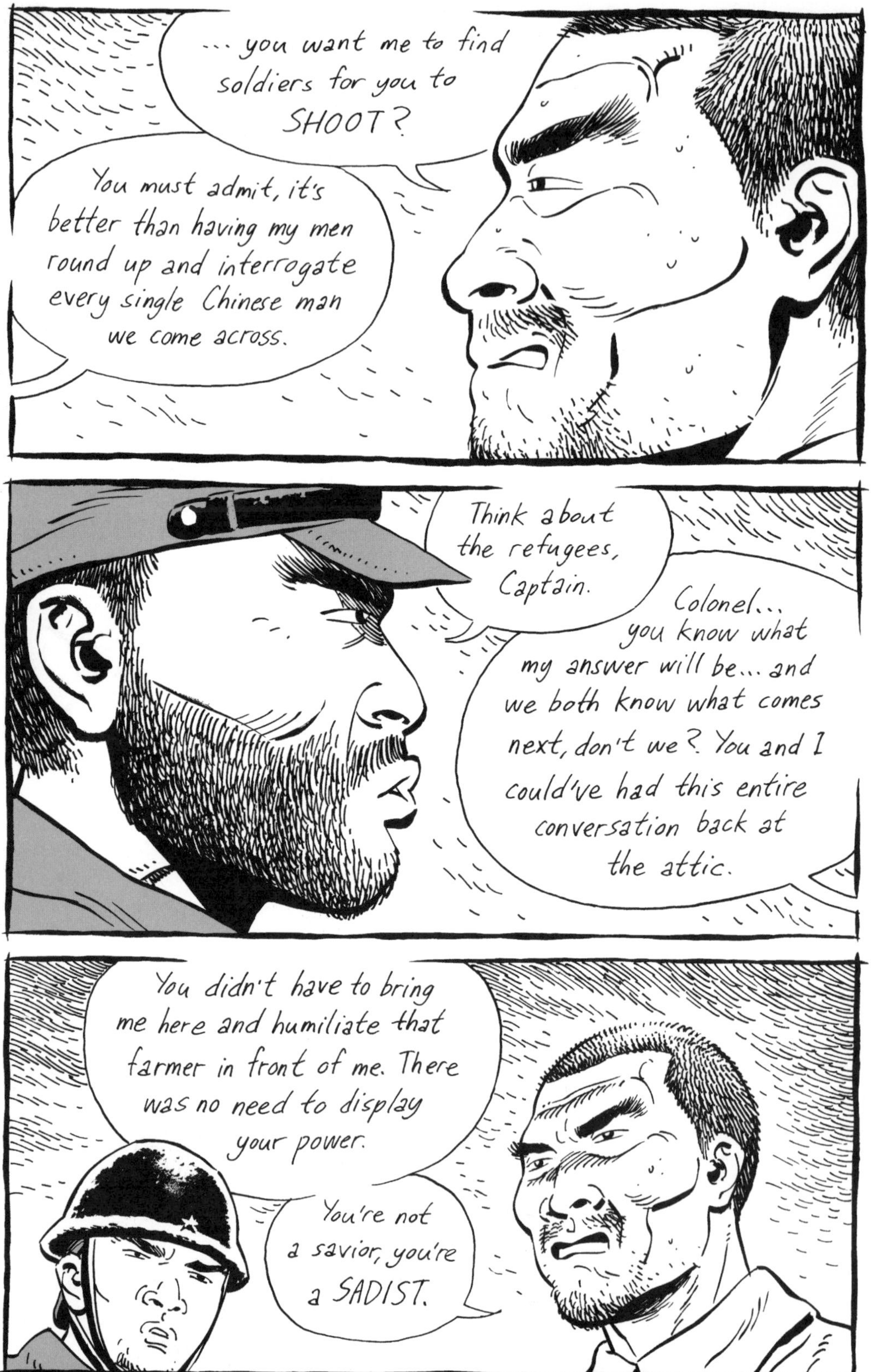
...you want me to find soldiers for you to SHOOT?
You must admit, it's better than having my men round up and interrogate every single Chinese man we come across.
Think about the refugees, Captain.
Colonel... you know what my answer will be... and we both know what comes next, don't we? You and I could've had this entire conversation back at the attic.
You didn't have to bring me here and humiliate that farmer in front of me. There was no need to display your power.
You're not a savior, you're a SADIST.

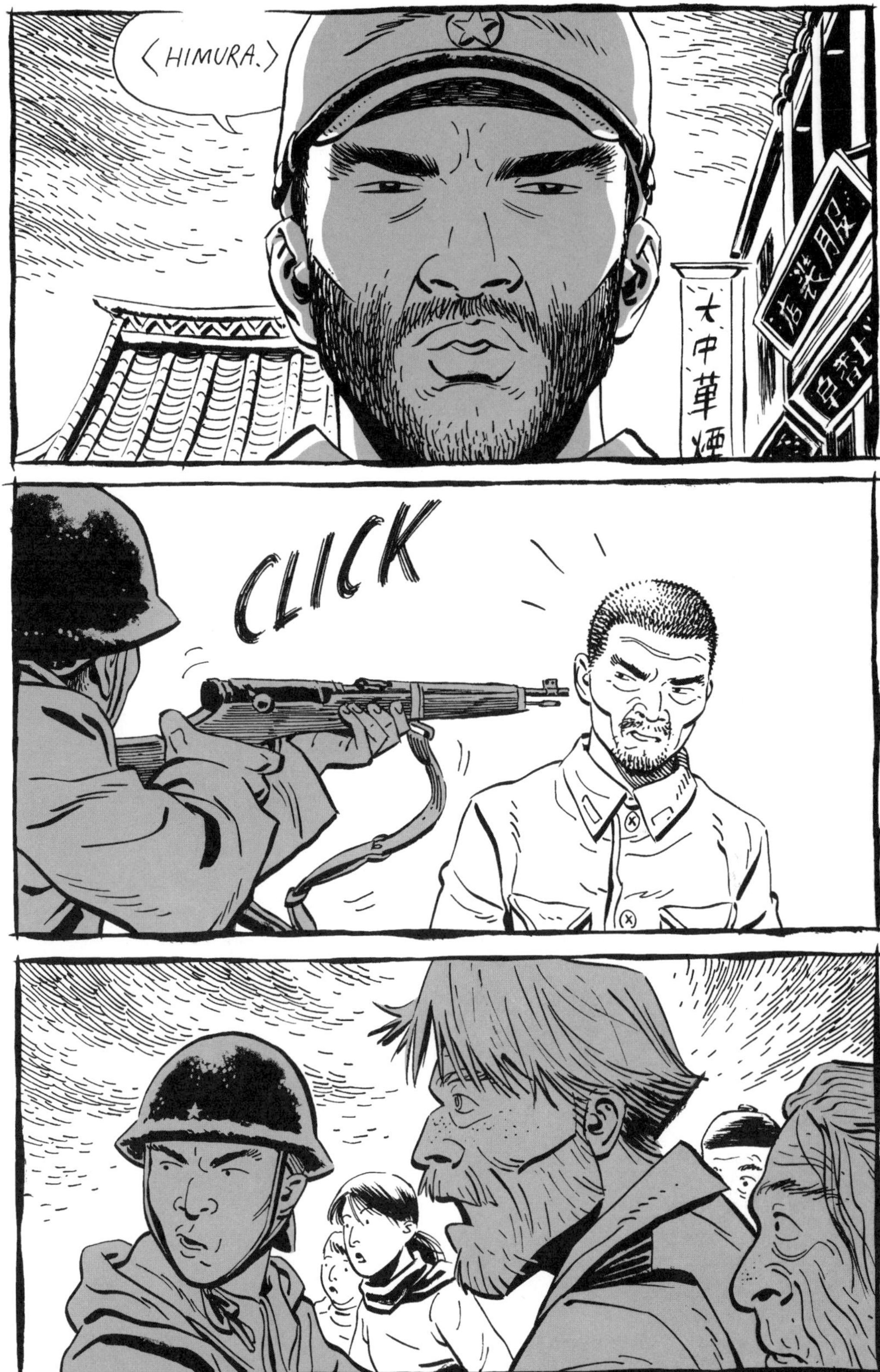
〈HIMURA.〉
大中華煙
CLICK

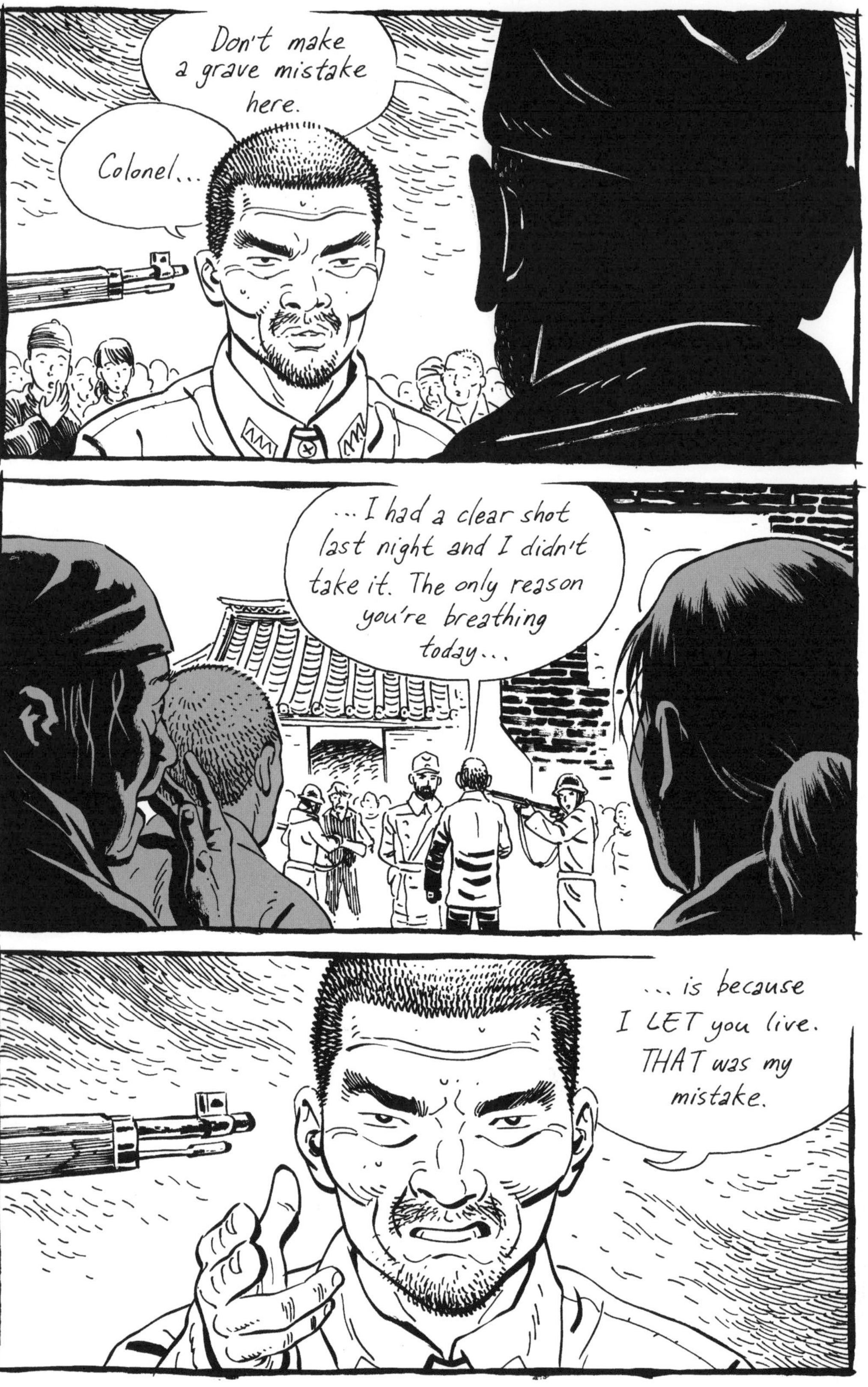
Colonel...
Don't make a grave mistake here.
...I had a clear shot last night and I didn't take it. The only reason you're breathing today...
...is because I LET you live. THAT was my mistake.

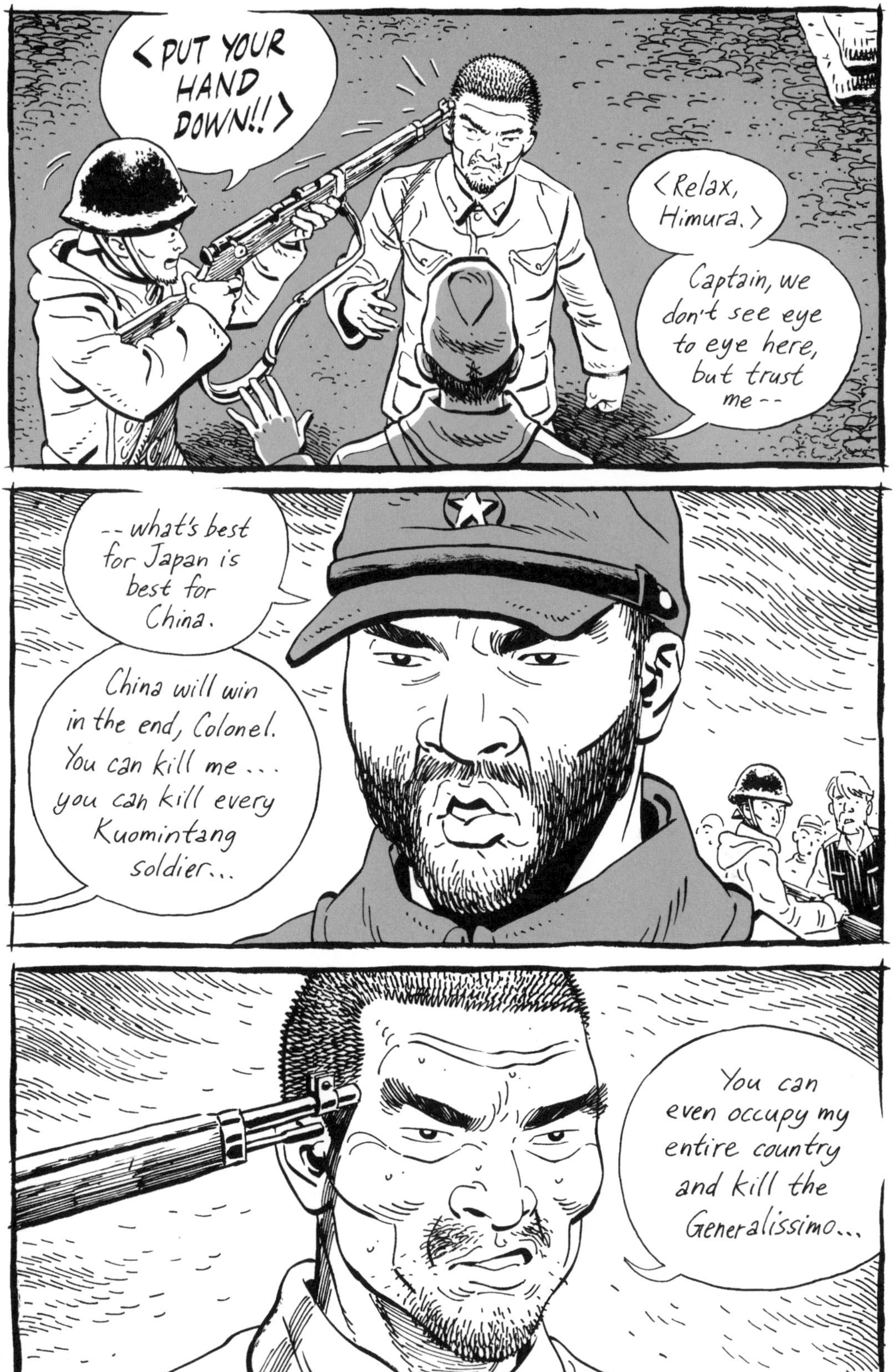
<PUT YOUR HAND DOWN!!>
<Relax, Himura.>
Captain, we don't see eye to eye here, but trust me--
--what's best for Japan is best for China.
China will win in the end, Colonel. You can kill me... you can kill every Kuomintang soldier...
You can even occupy my entire country and kill the Generalissimo...

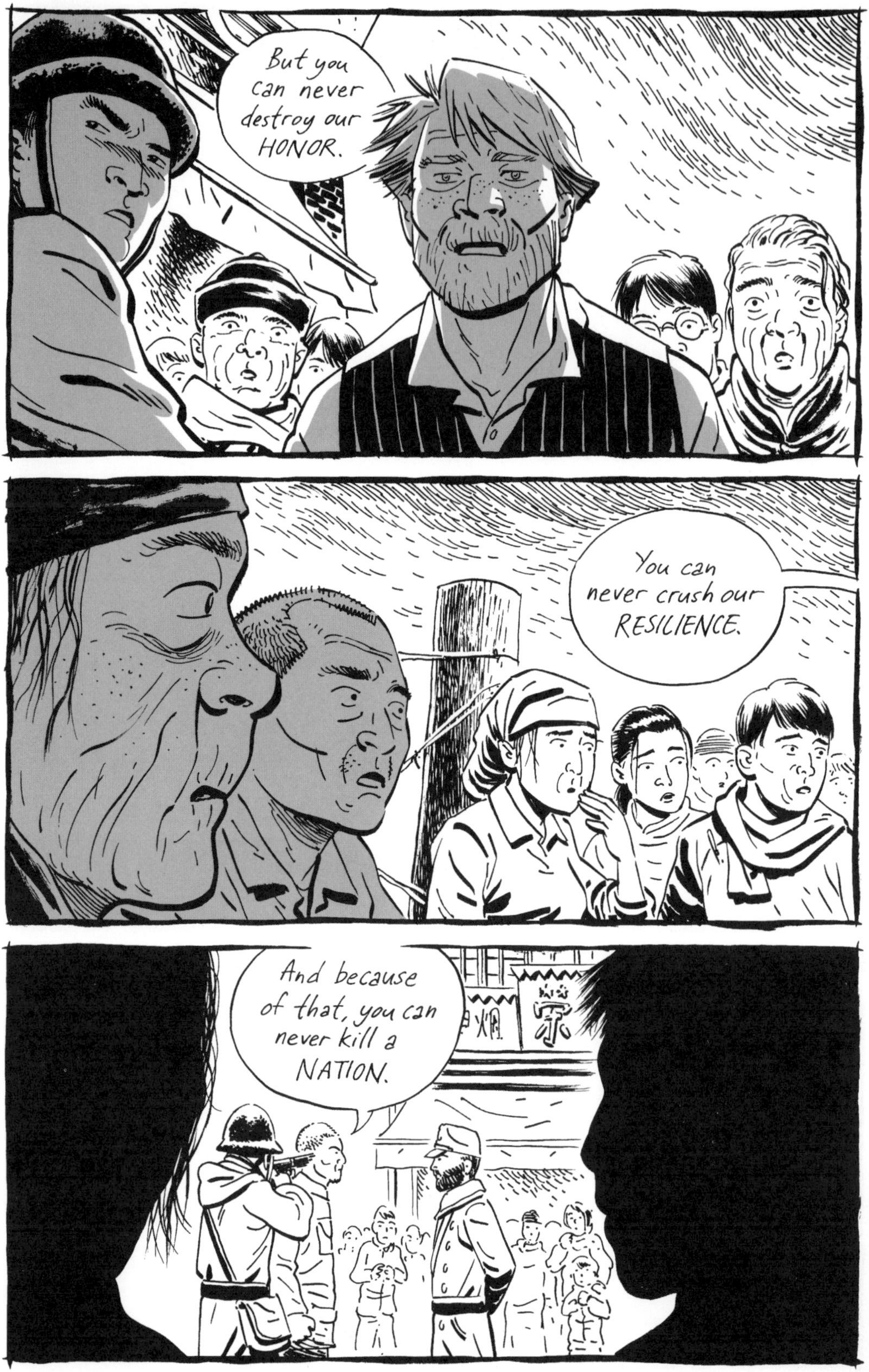
But you can never destroy our HONOR.
You can never crush our RESILIENCE.
And because of that, you can never kill a NATION.

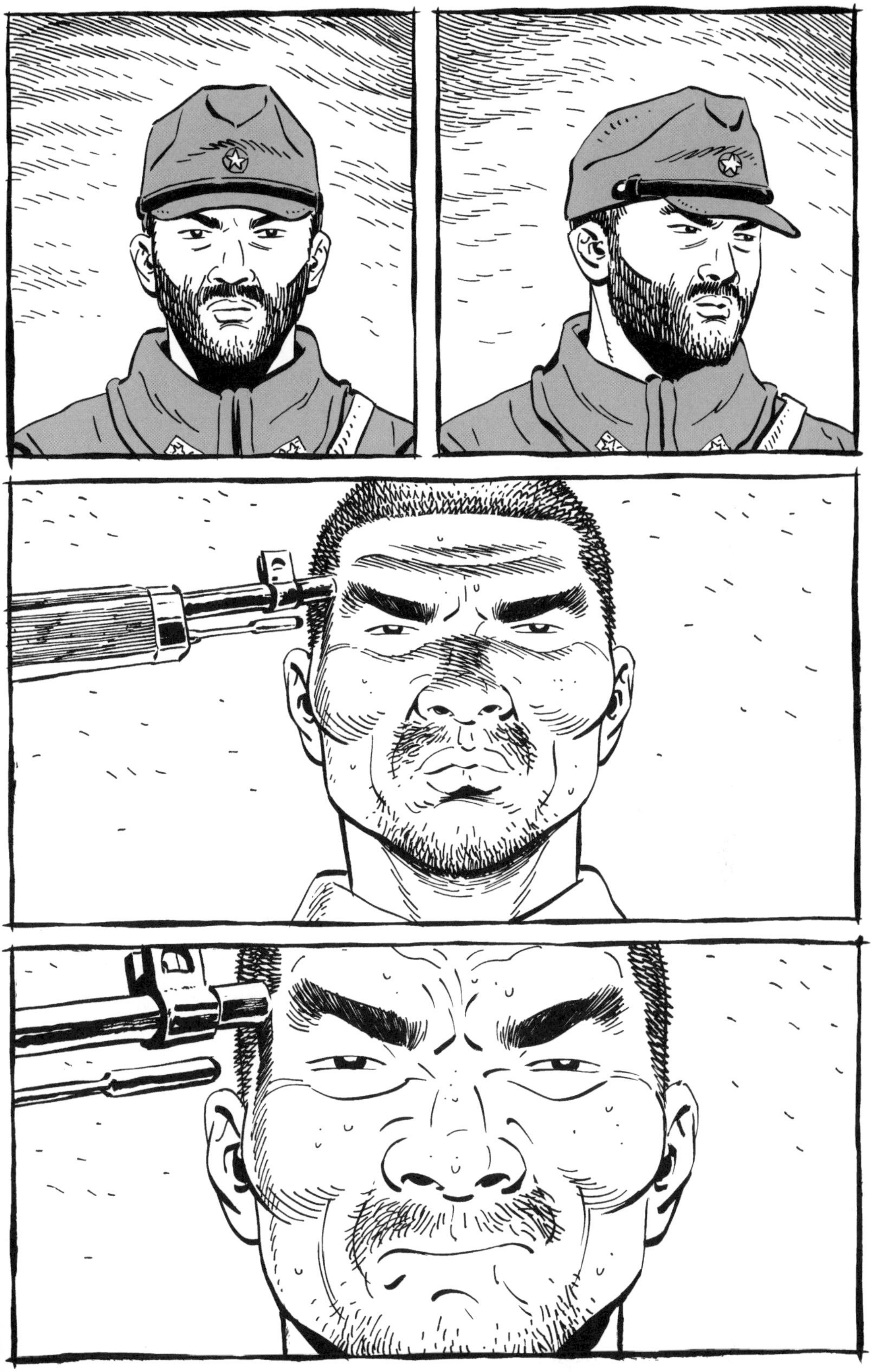

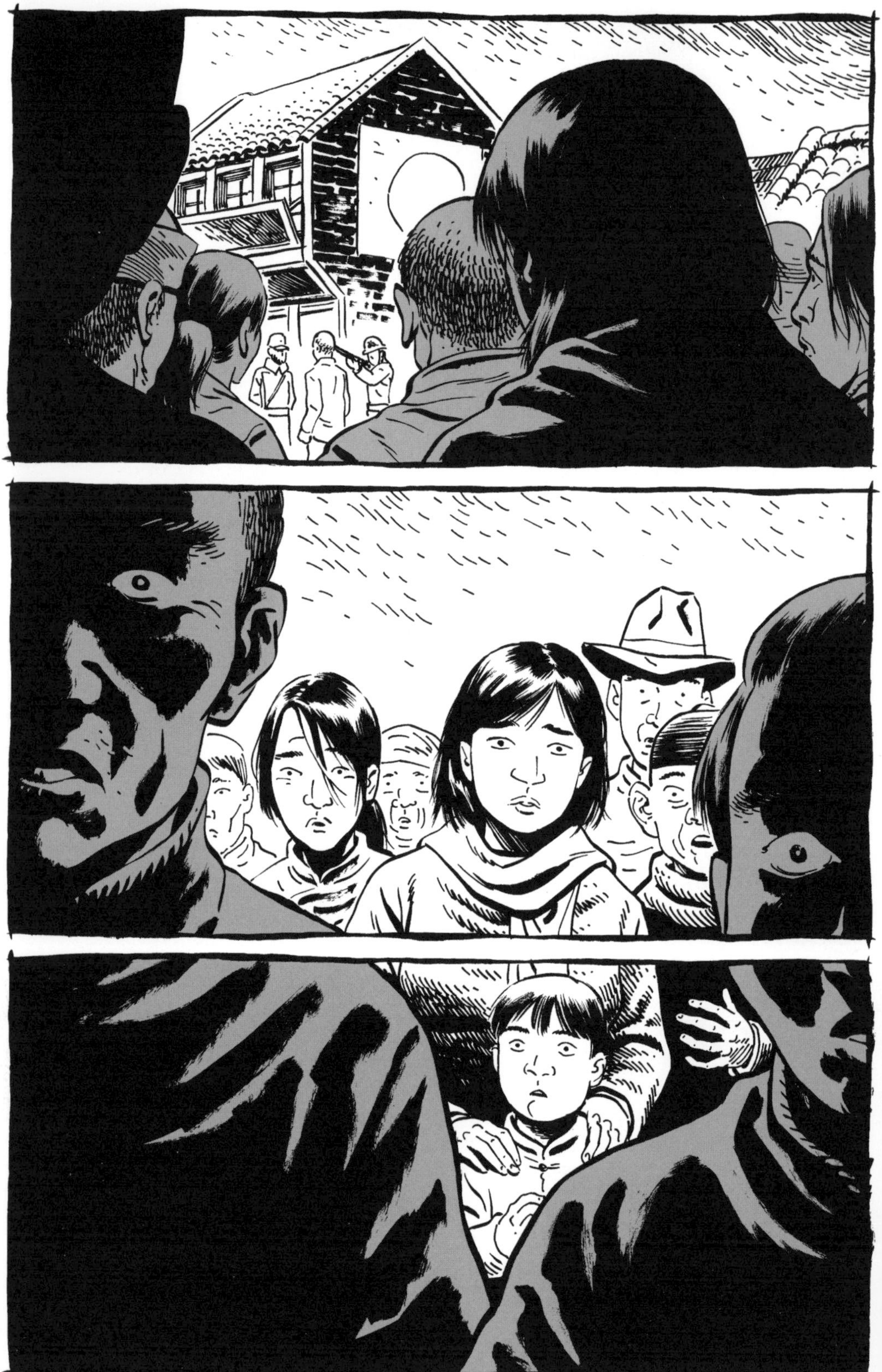

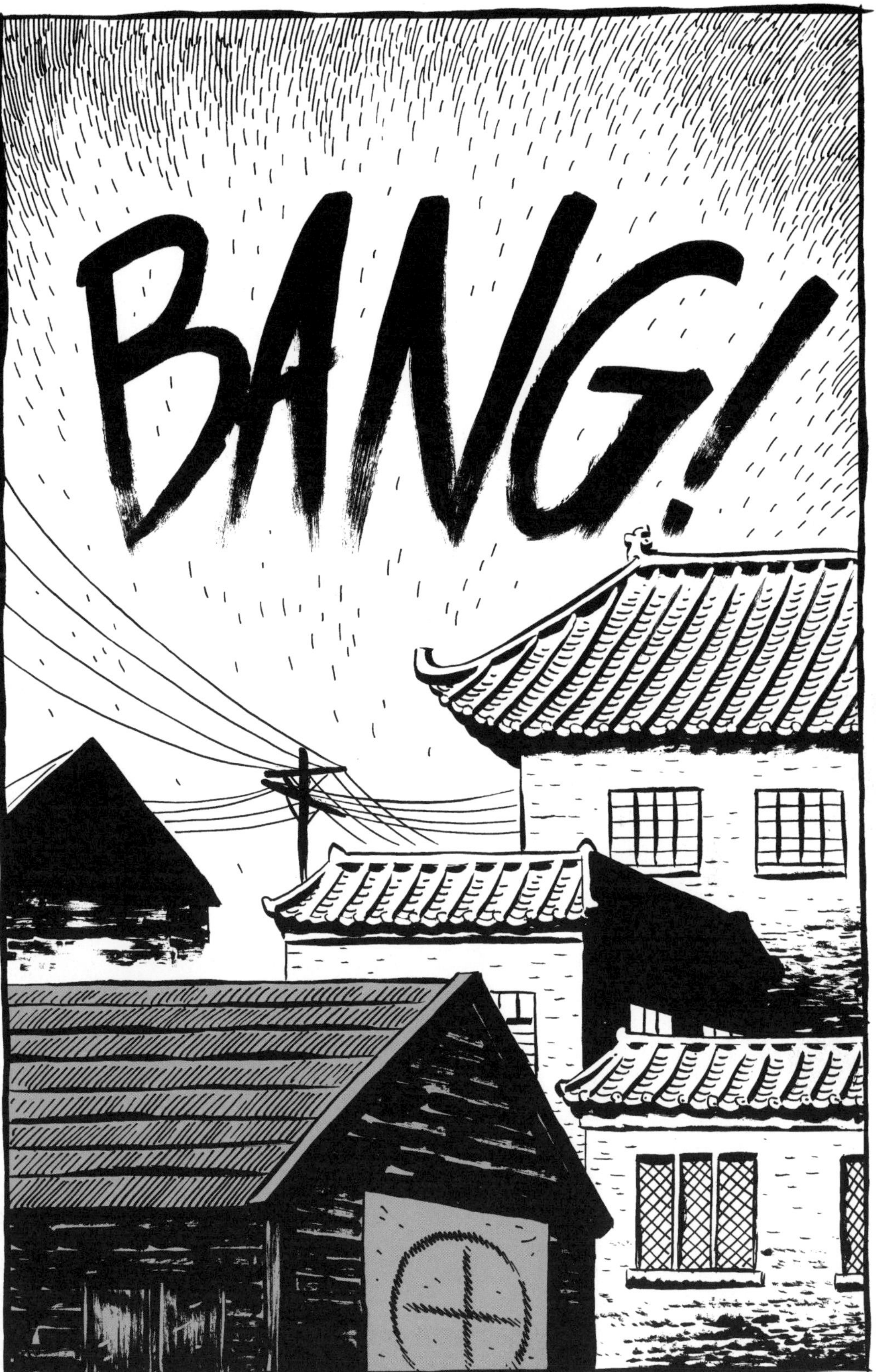
BANG!

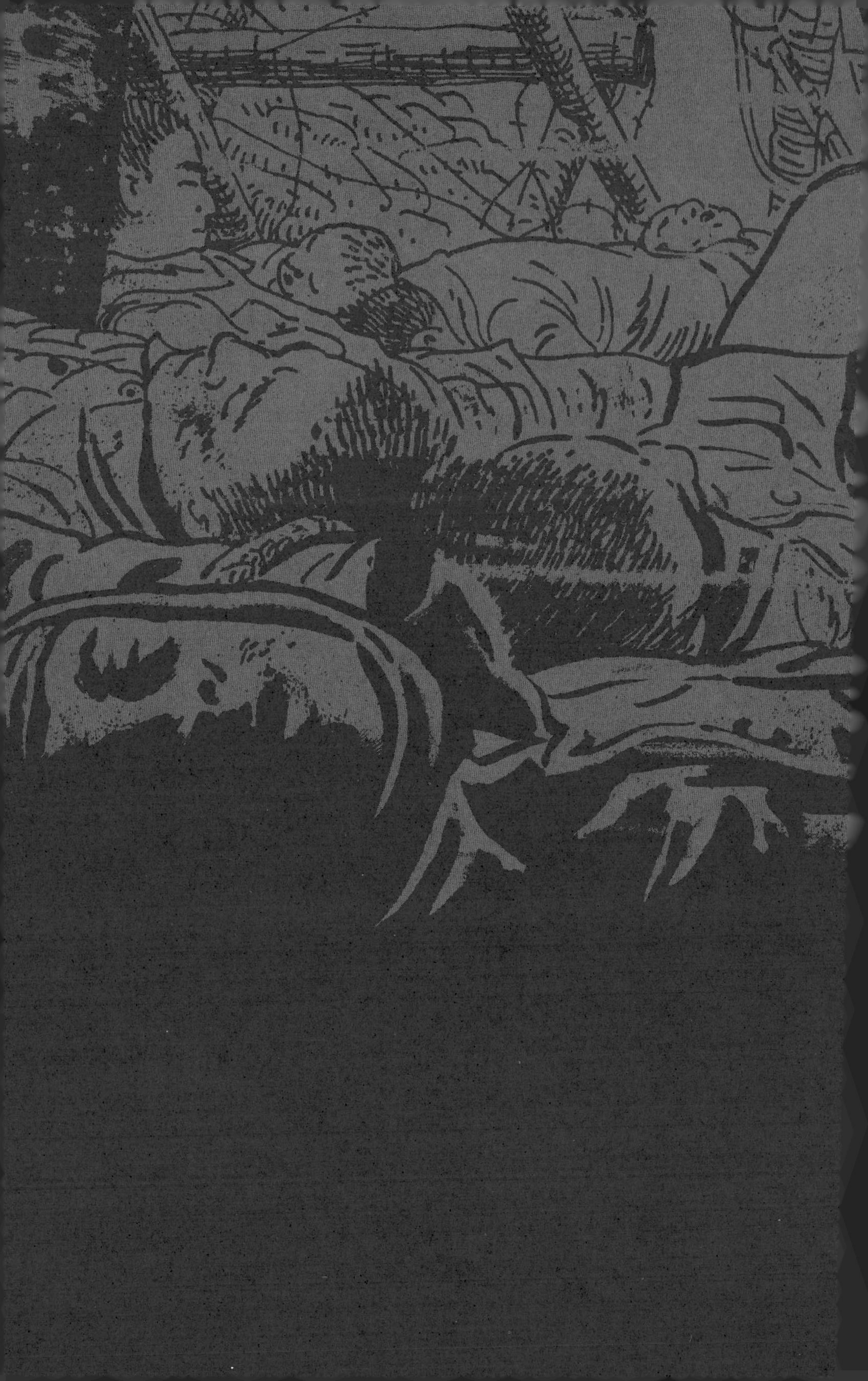

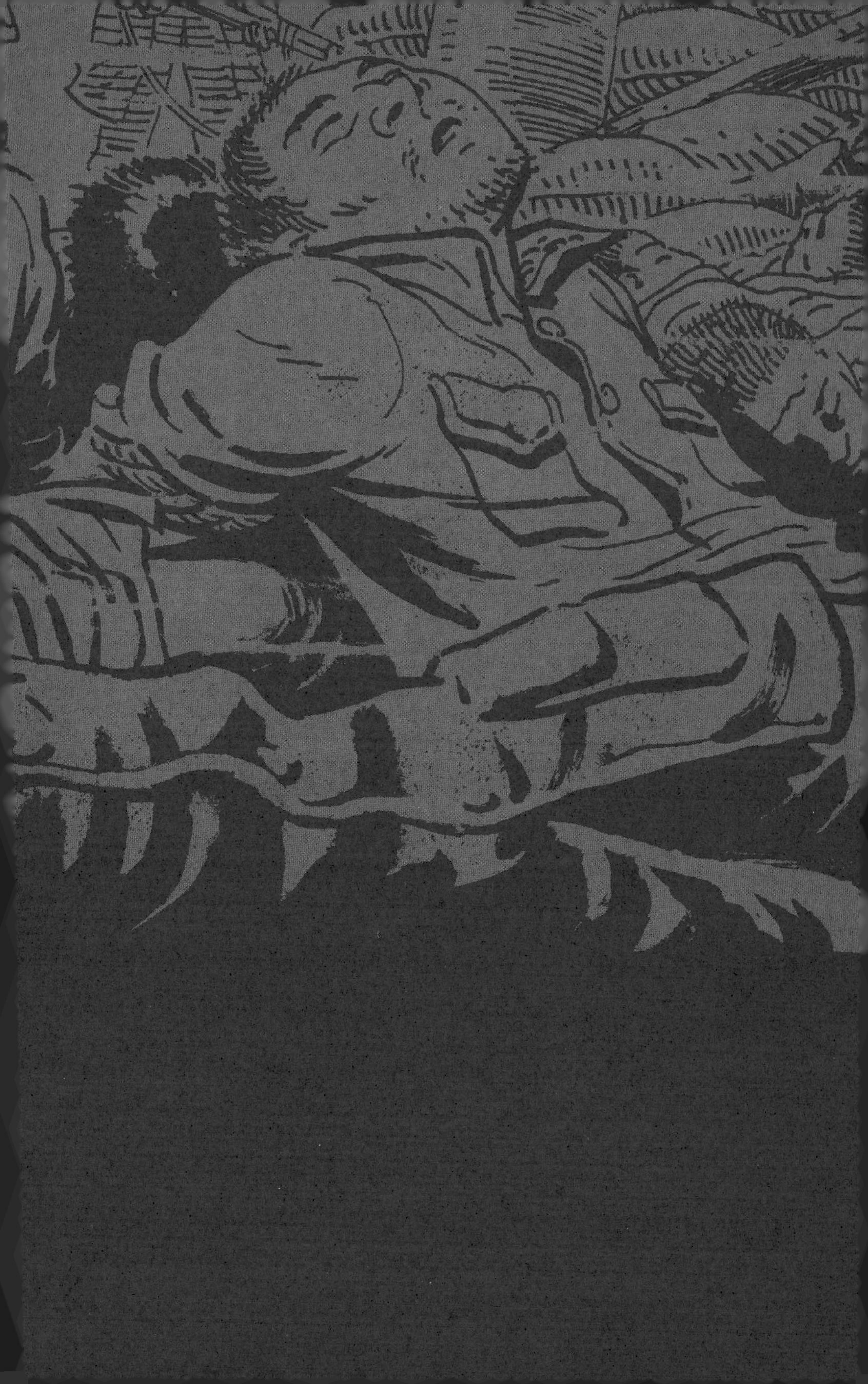

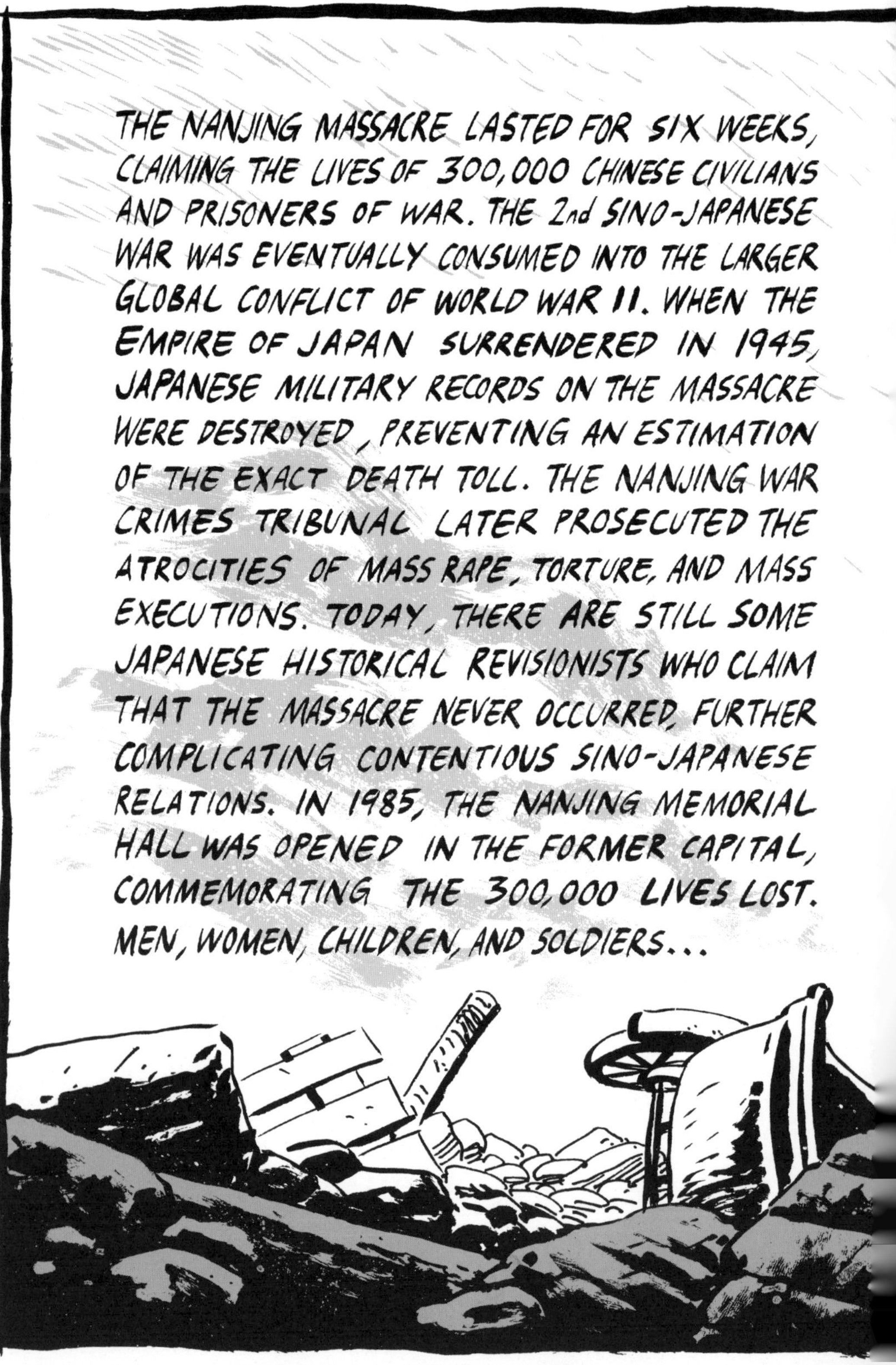
THE NANJING MASSACRE LASTED FOR SIX WEEKS, CLAIMING THE LIVES OF 300,000 CHINESE CIVILIANS AND PRISONERS OF WAR. THE 2nd SINO-JAPANESE WAR WAS EVENTUALLY CONSUMED INTO THE LARGER GLOBAL CONFLICT OF WORLD WAR II. WHEN THE EMPIRE OF JAPAN SURRENDERED IN 1945, JAPANESE MILITARY RECORDS ON THE MASSACRE WERE DESTROYED, PREVENTING AN ESTIMATION OF THE EXACT DEATH TOLL. THE NANJING WAR CRIMES TRIBUNAL LATER PROSECUTED THE ATROCITIES OF MASS RAPE, TORTURE, AND MASS EXECUTIONS. TODAY, THERE ARE STILL SOME JAPANESE HISTORICAL REVISIONISTS WHO CLAIM THAT THE MASSACRE NEVER OCCURRED, FURTHER COMPLICATING CONTENTIOUS SINO-JAPANESE RELATIONS. IN 1985, THE NANJING MEMORIAL HALL WAS OPENED IN THE FORMER CAPITAL, COMMEMORATING THE 300,000 LIVES LOST. MEN, WOMEN, CHILDREN, AND SOLDIERS...

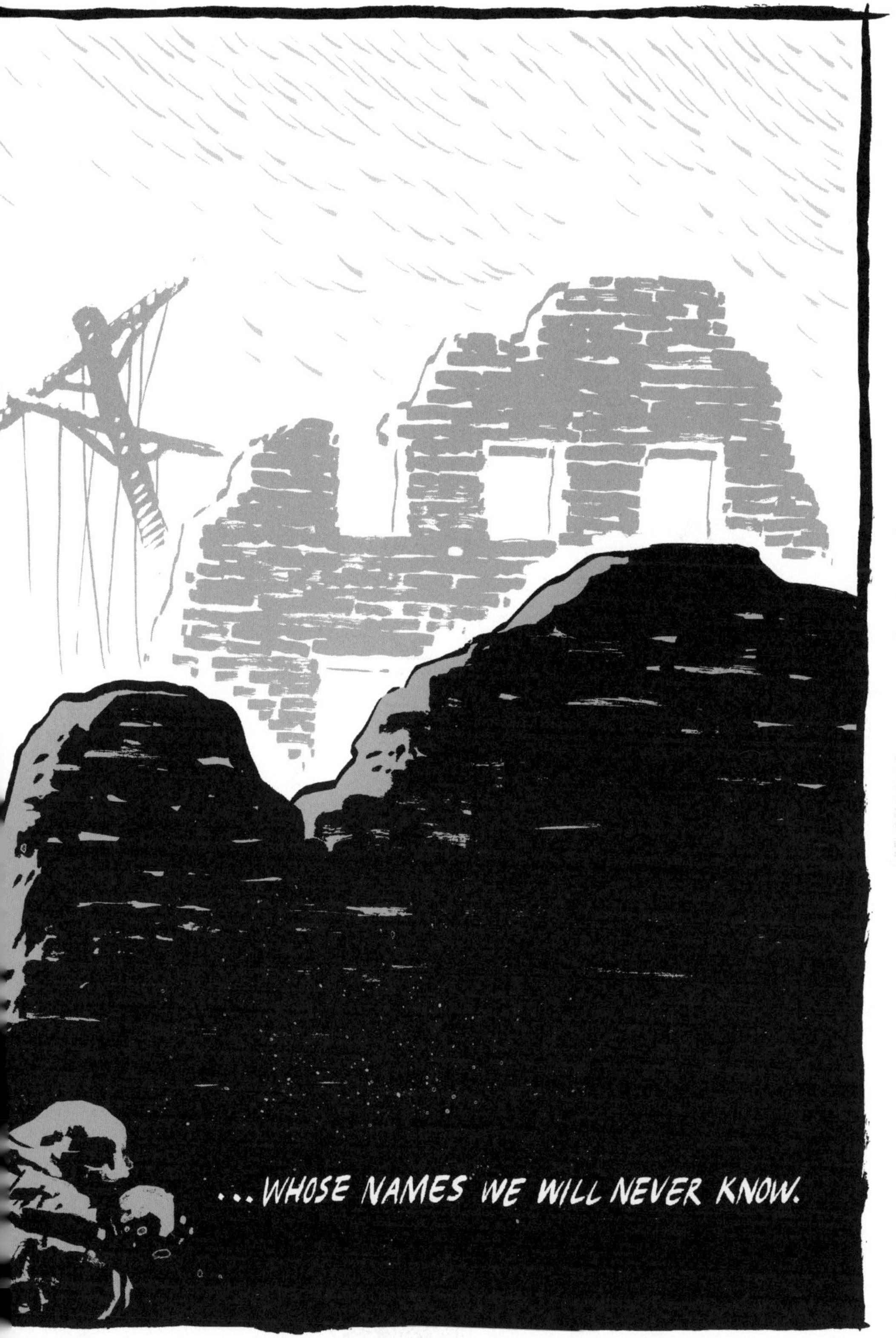
...WHOSE NAMES WE WILL NEVER KNOW.

NANJING

THE BURNING CITY
SKETCHBOOK

COMMENTARY BY
ETHAN YOUNG

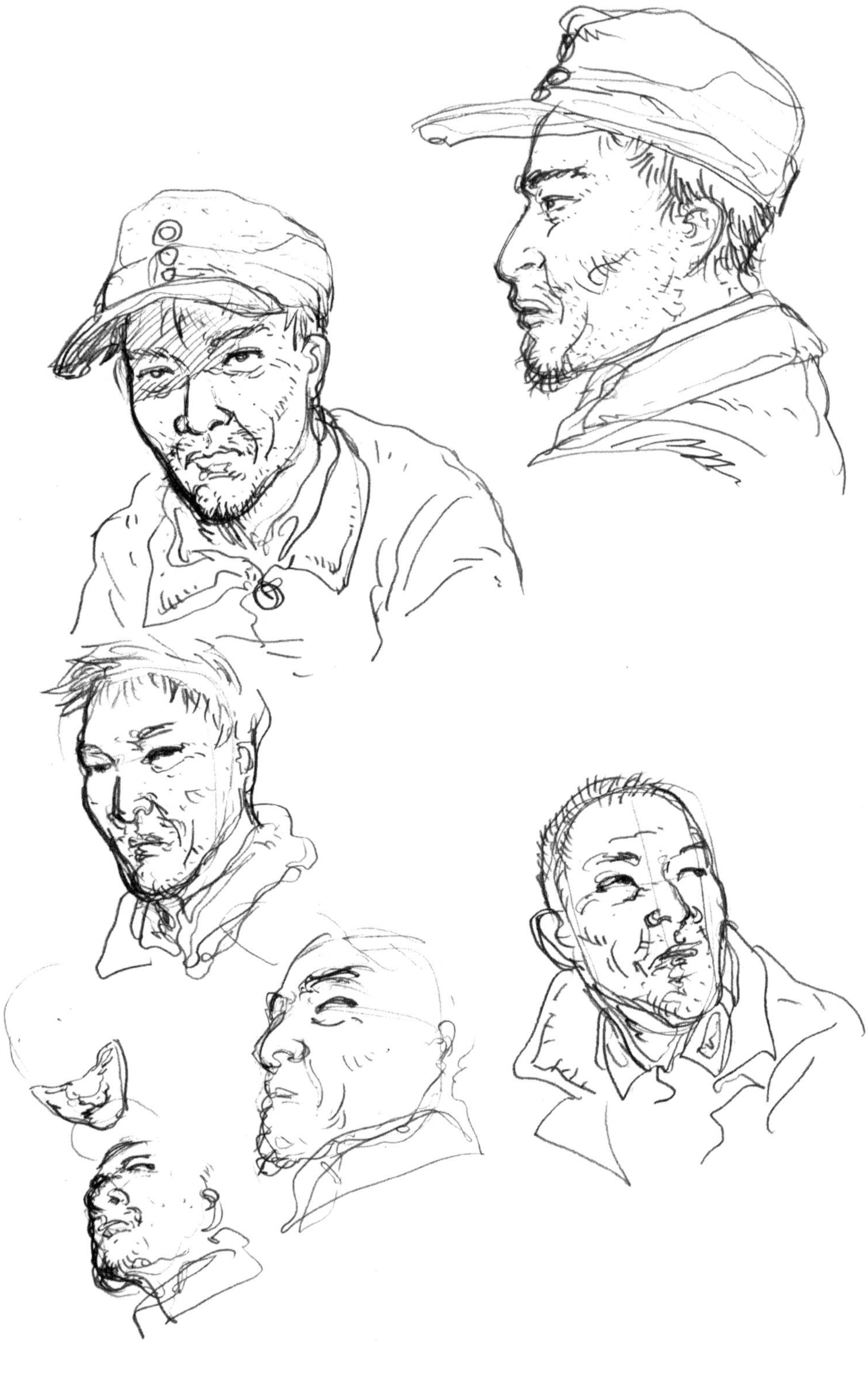

I was originally leaning towards a more down-to-earth approach to the Captain's design, using his weathered face to distinguish him, but he looked too similar to Lu.

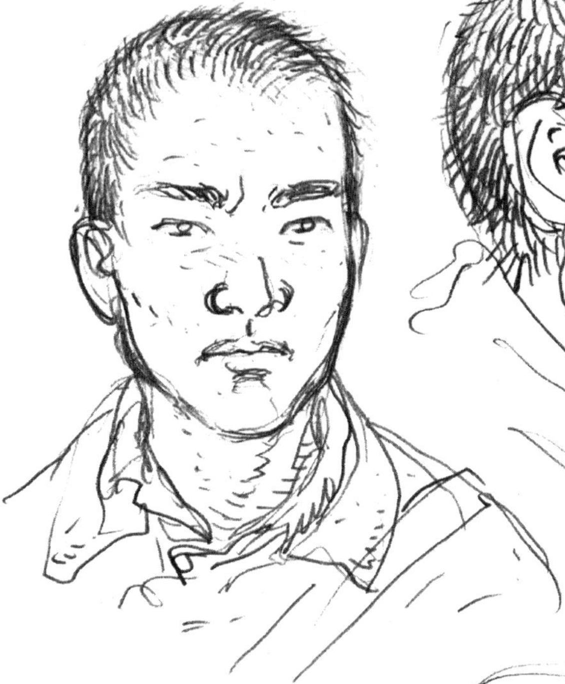
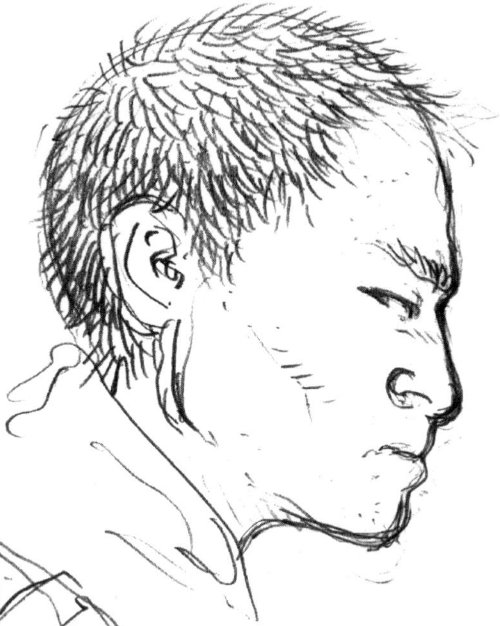
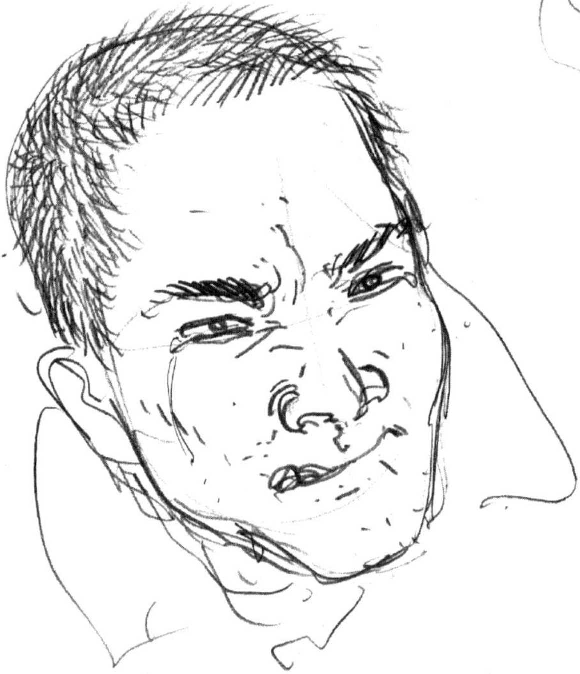
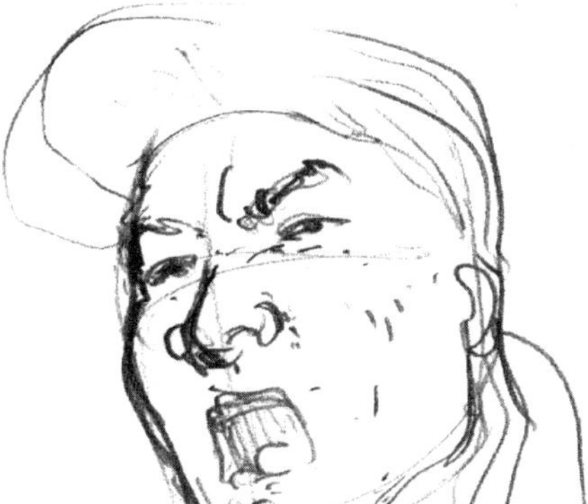

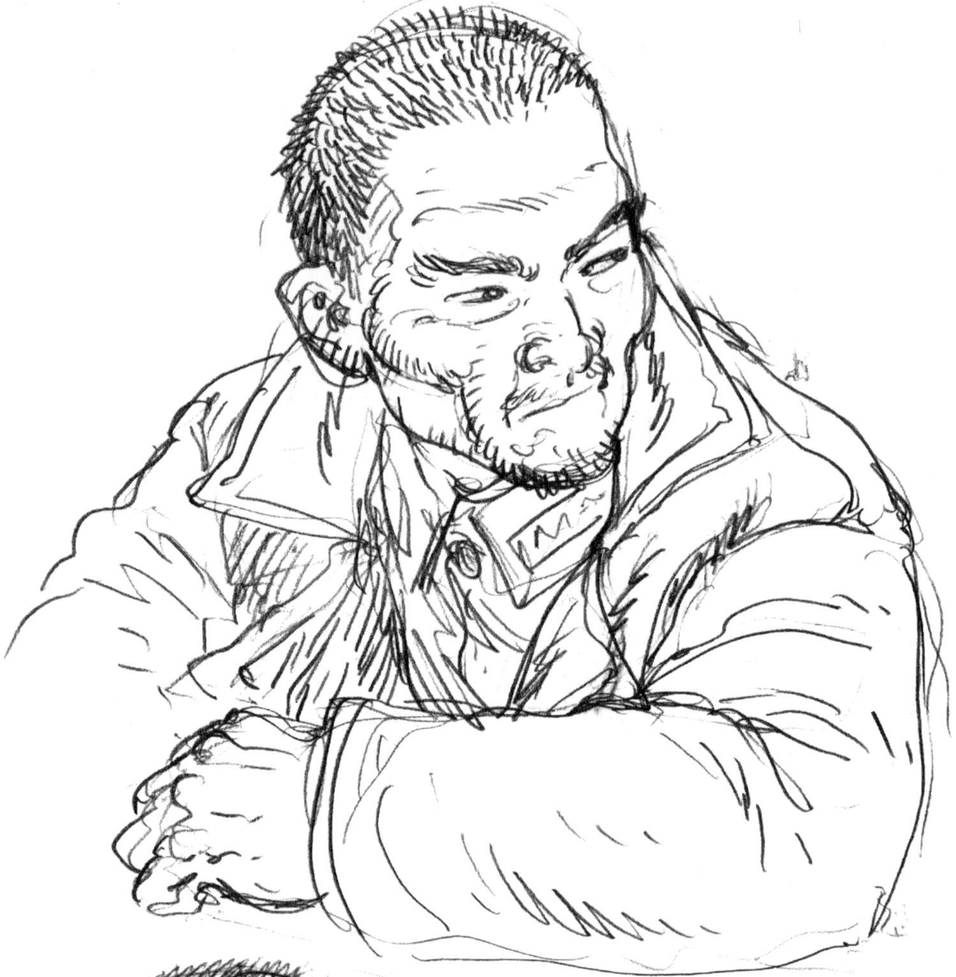

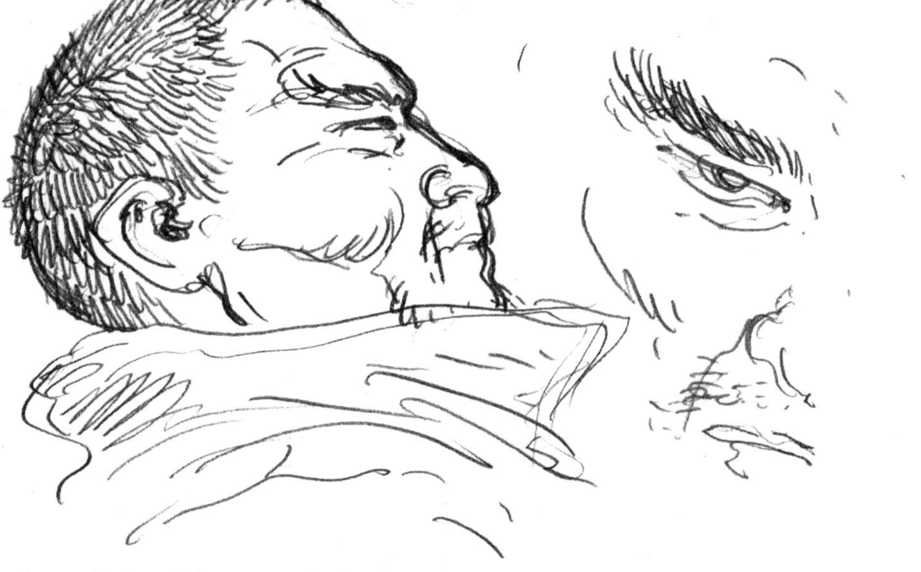

Eventually, I settled on giving the Captain a more striking presence. I removed his Kuomintang cap and draped him in an overcoat. His silhouette needed to be striking.

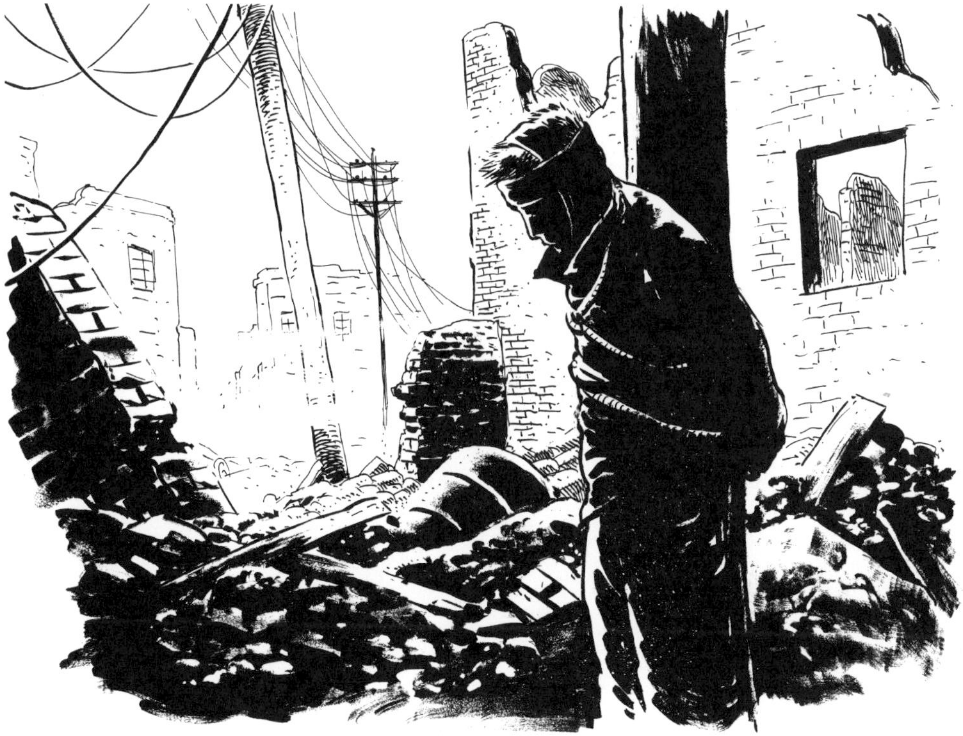

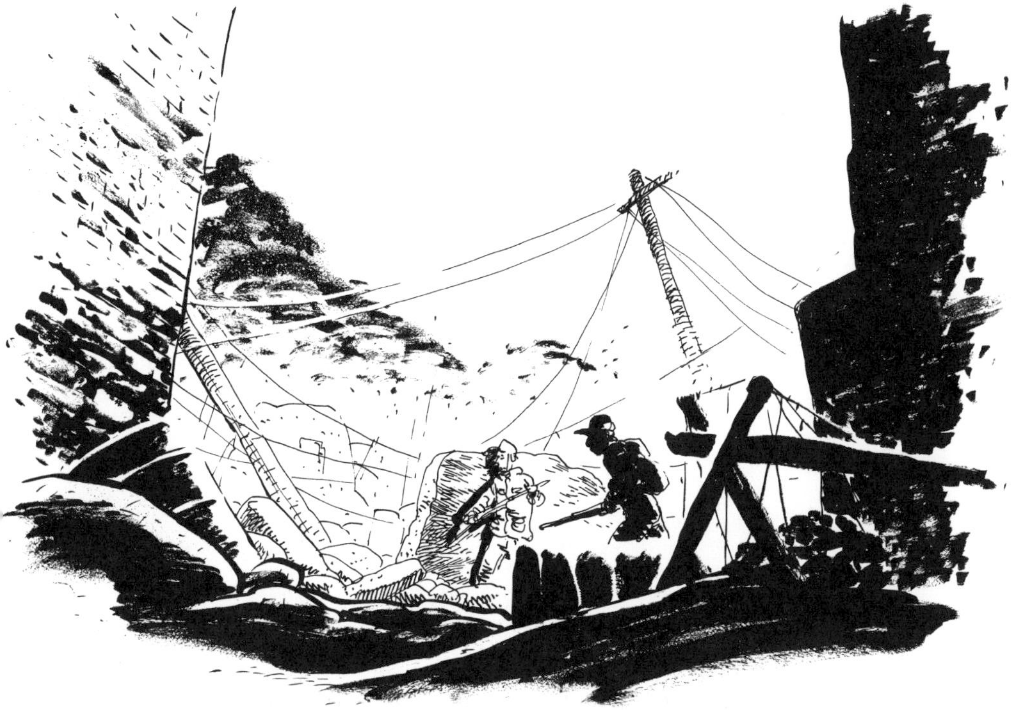

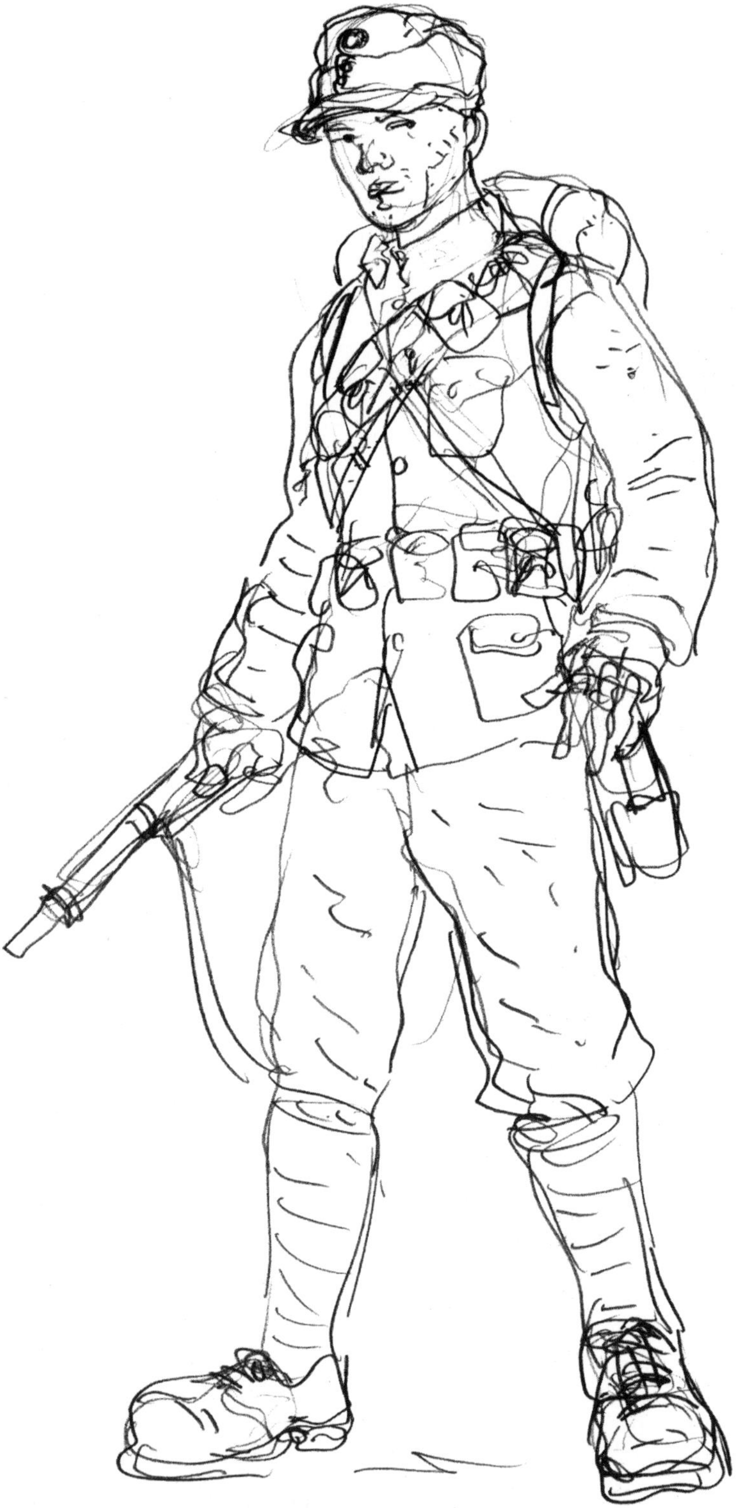

Lu was designed to be a very prototypical Kuomintang (Chinese Nationalist Party) soldier.

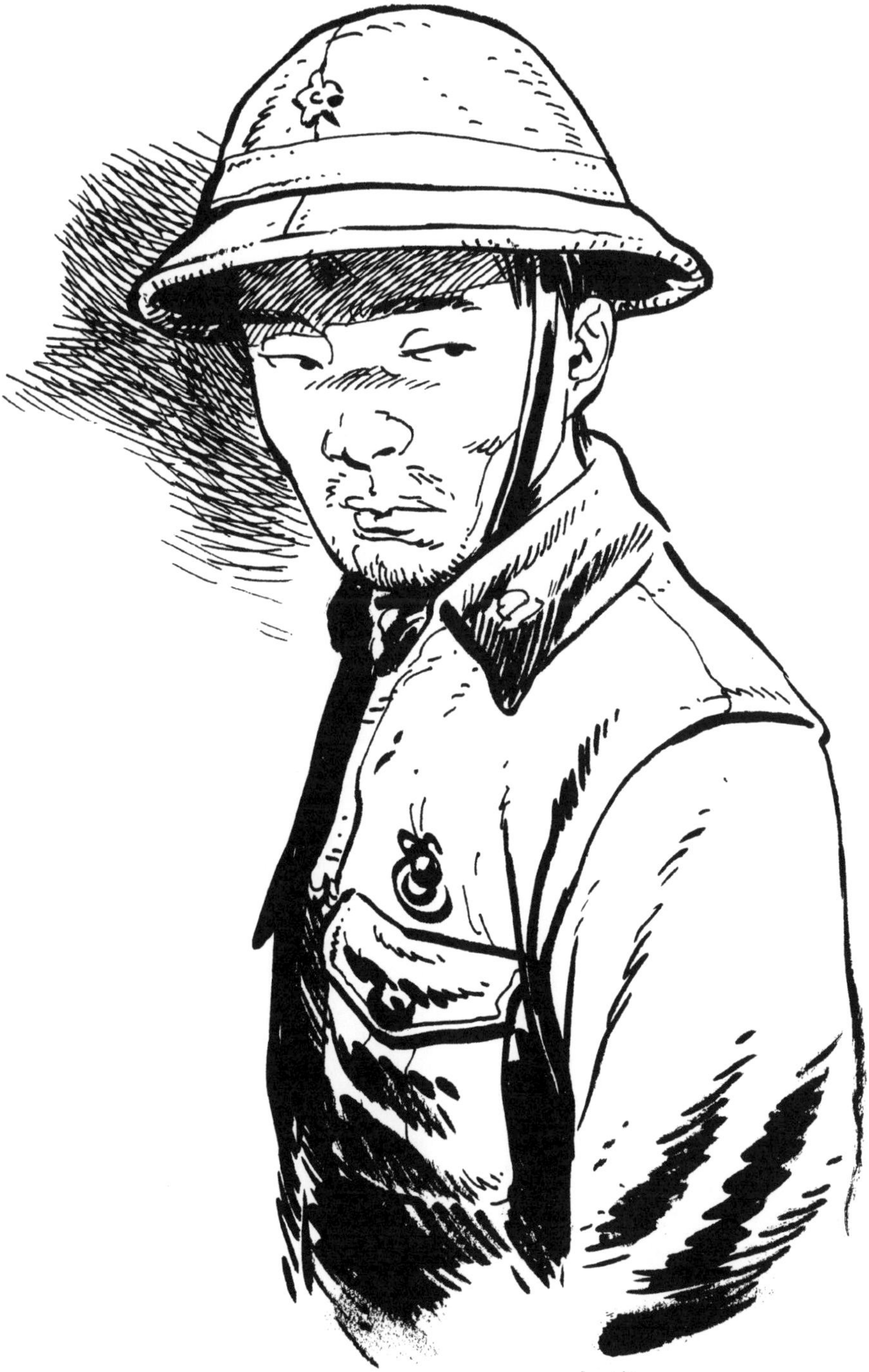

My first concept sketch of a Japanese soldier, using reference photos of the Kempeitai, the military police arm of the Imperial Japanese Army.

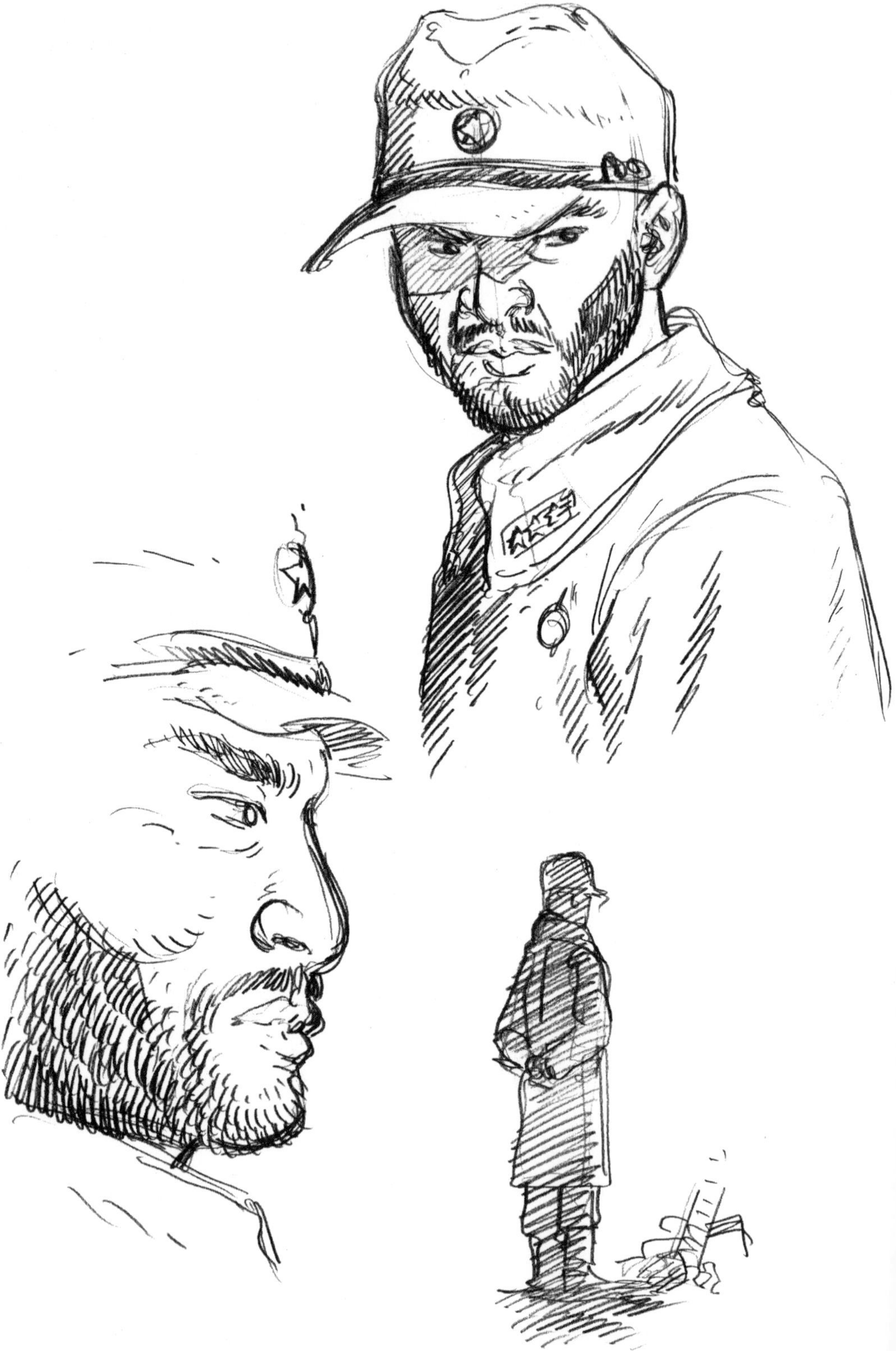

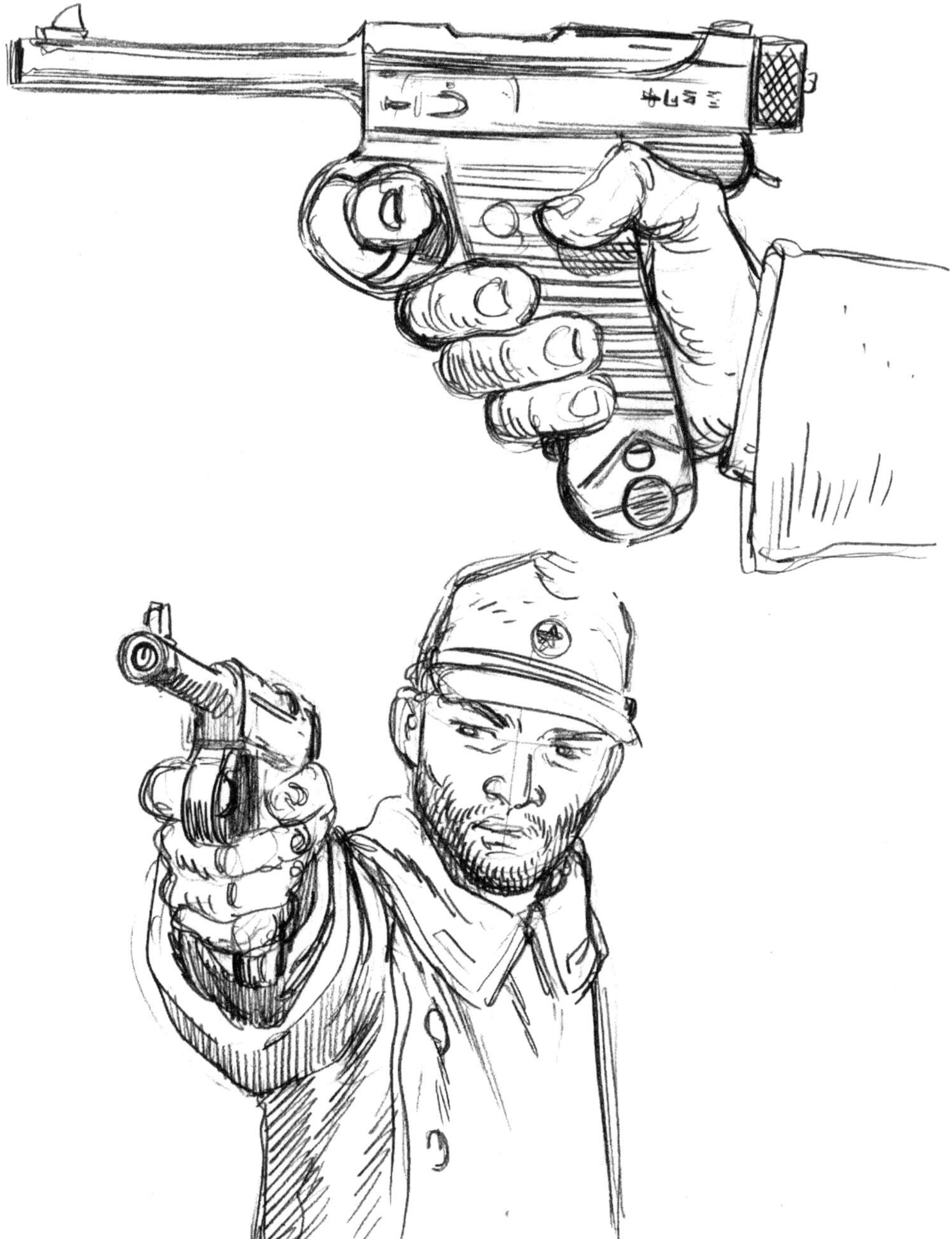

I wanted the Colonel to be equal parts authoritative, handsome, and intimidating.
I wanted him to be a Japanese version of Idris Elba.

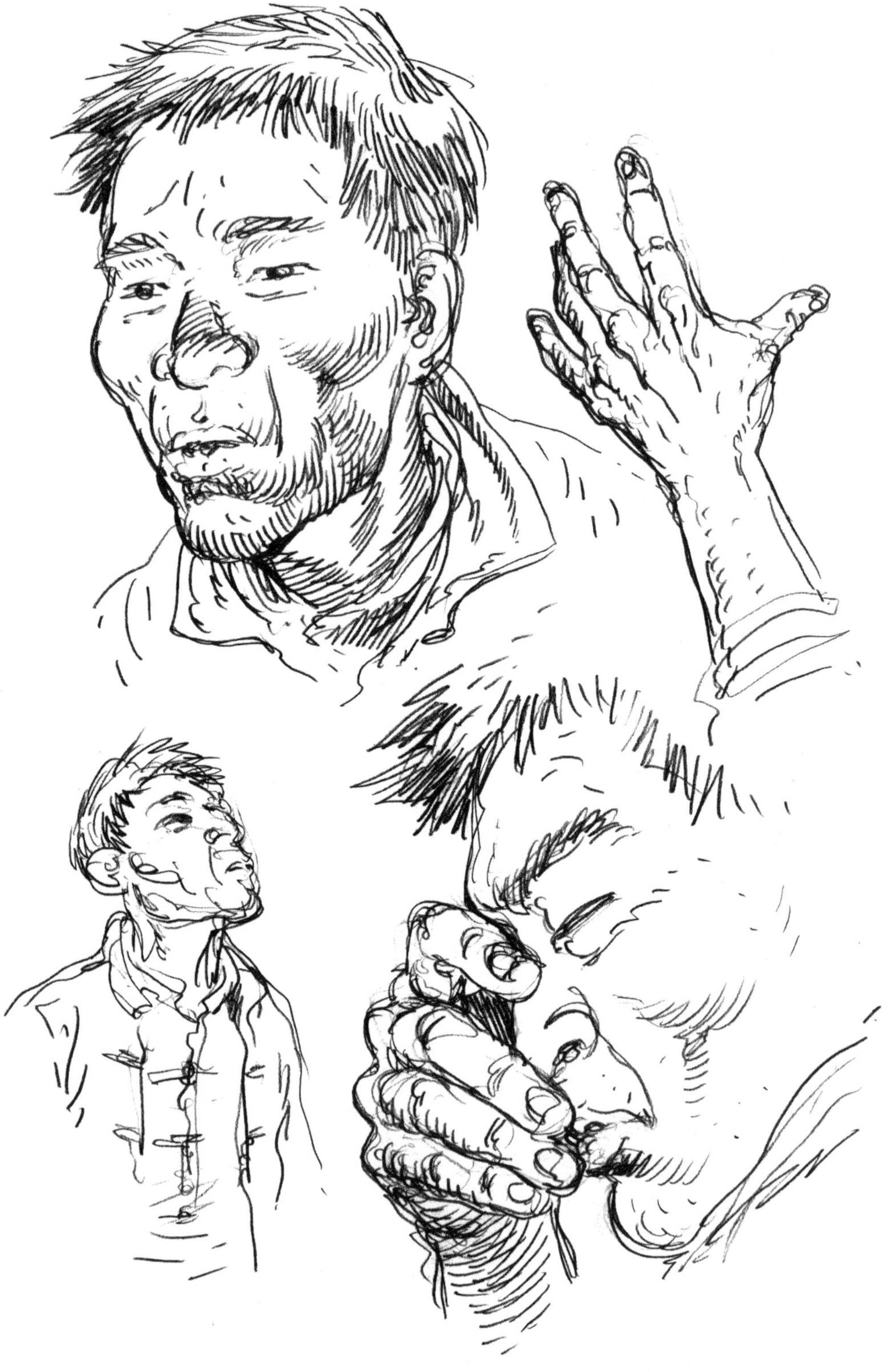

Miscellaneous sketches of Chinese civilians that eventually inspired the characters of Hong and Yan.

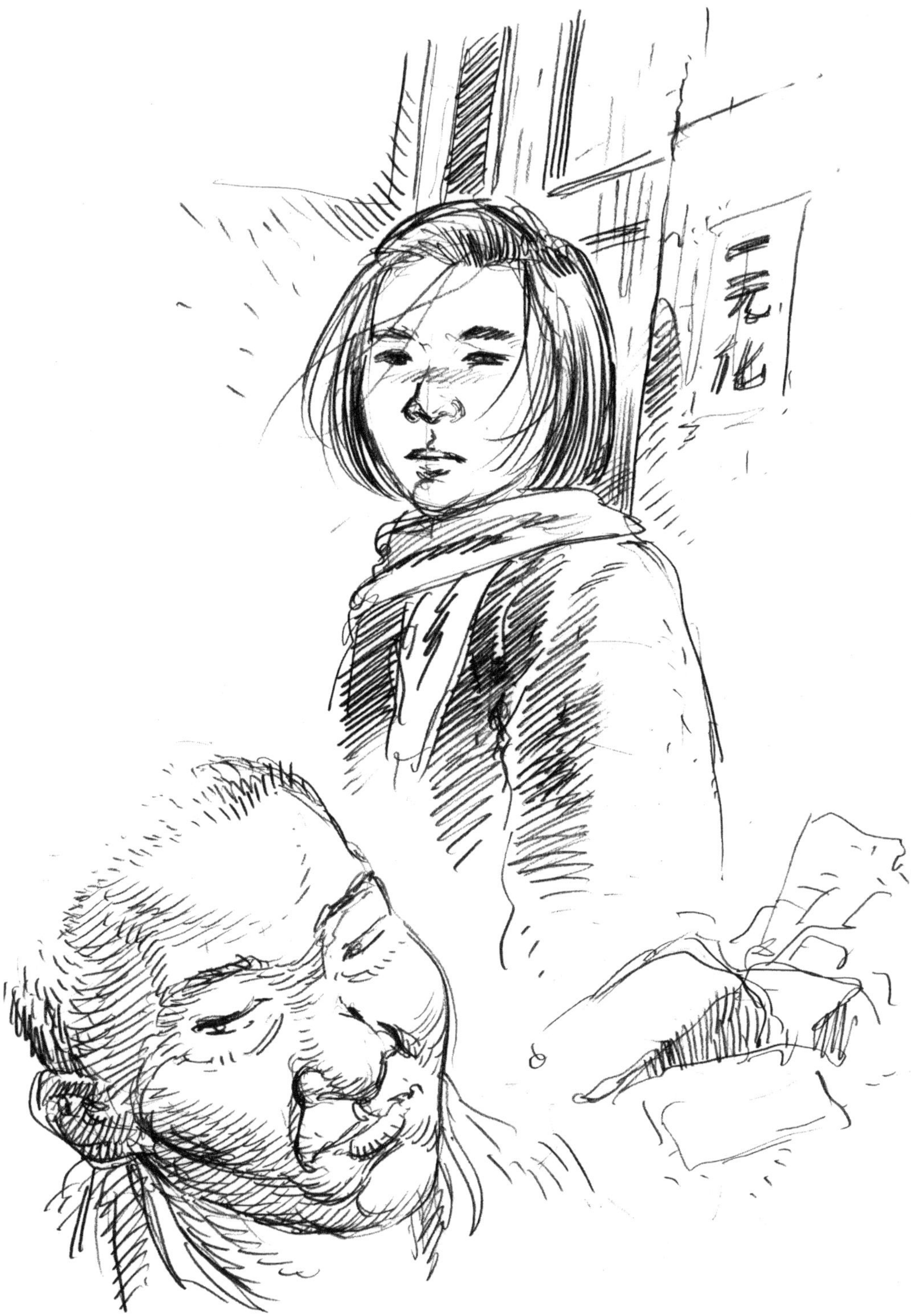

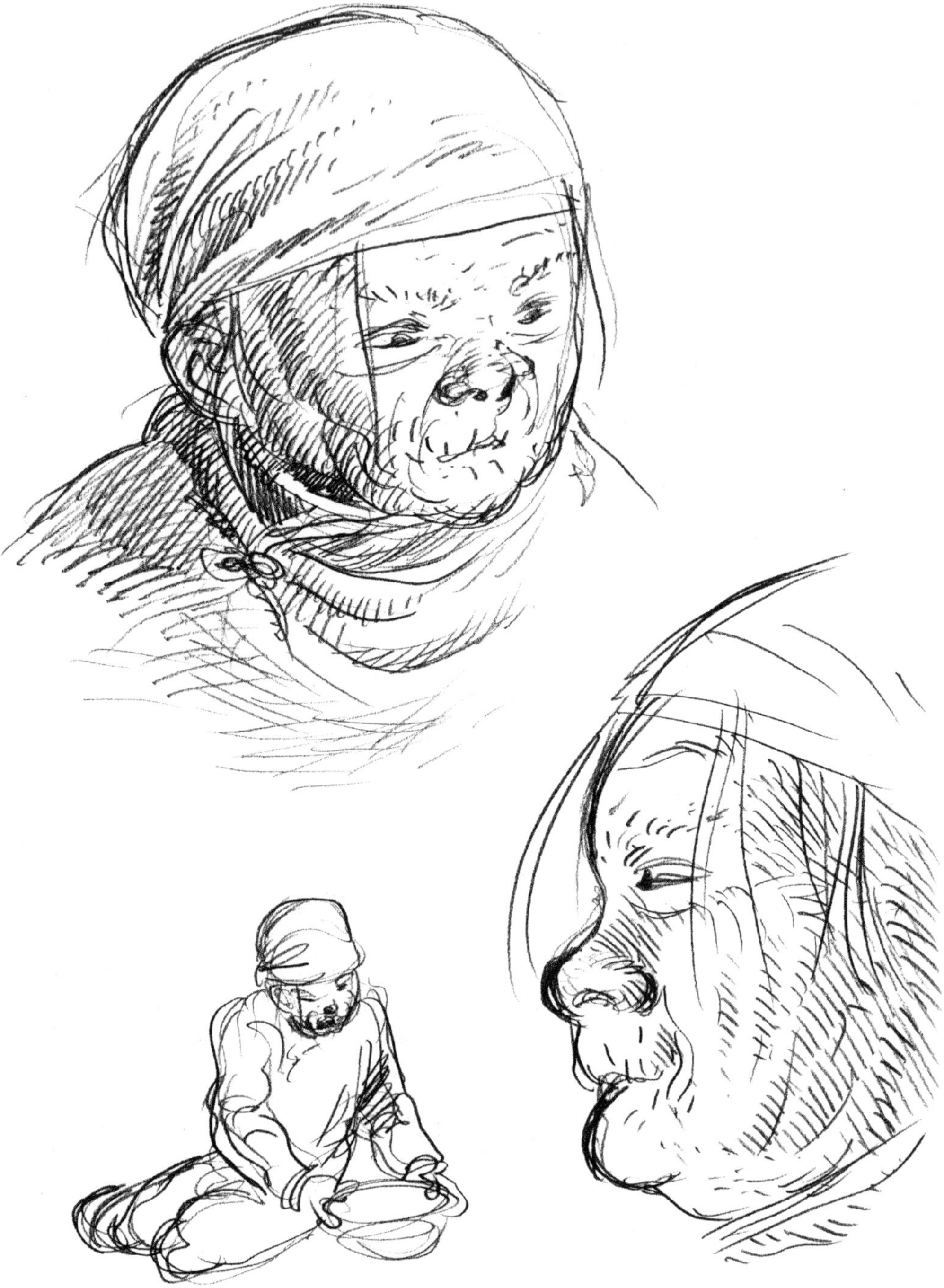

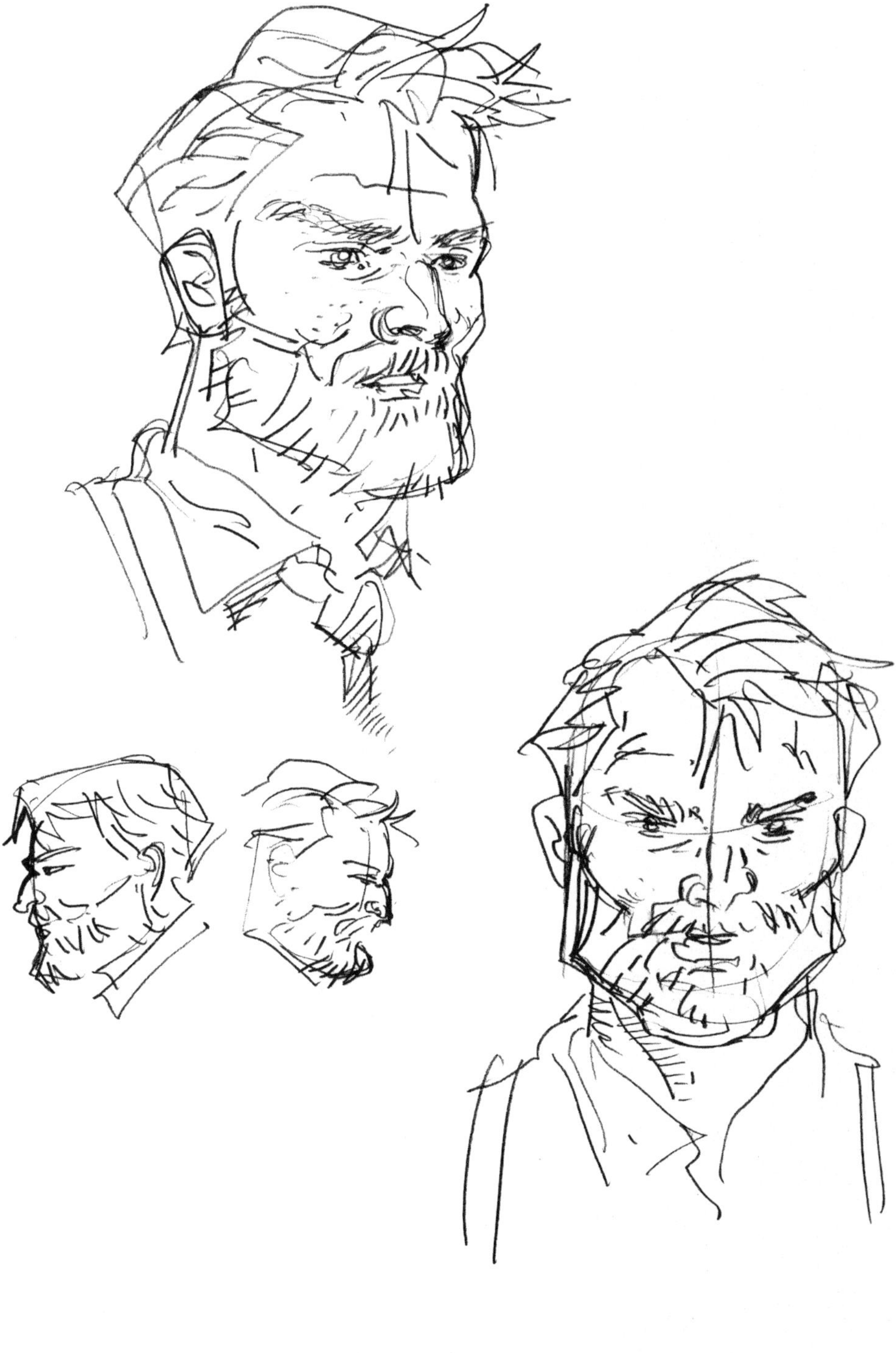

The Doctor, although he appears only briefly, plays an important role in the third act. I wanted him to look as if he stepped straight out of a David Lean movie. A man who could posture with the Colonel.

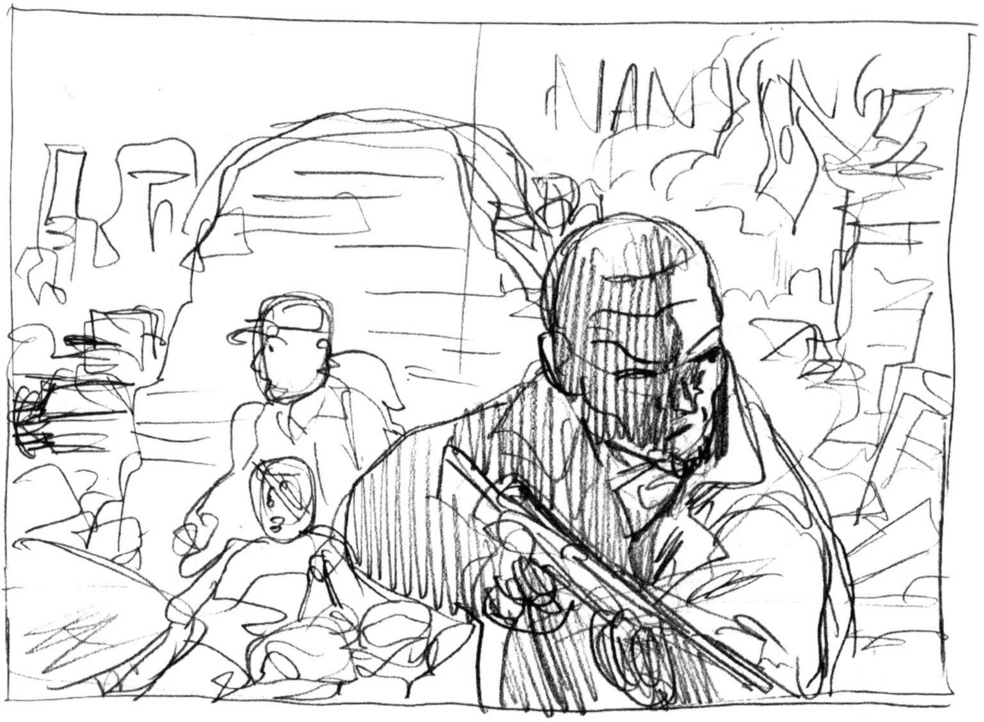
NANJING

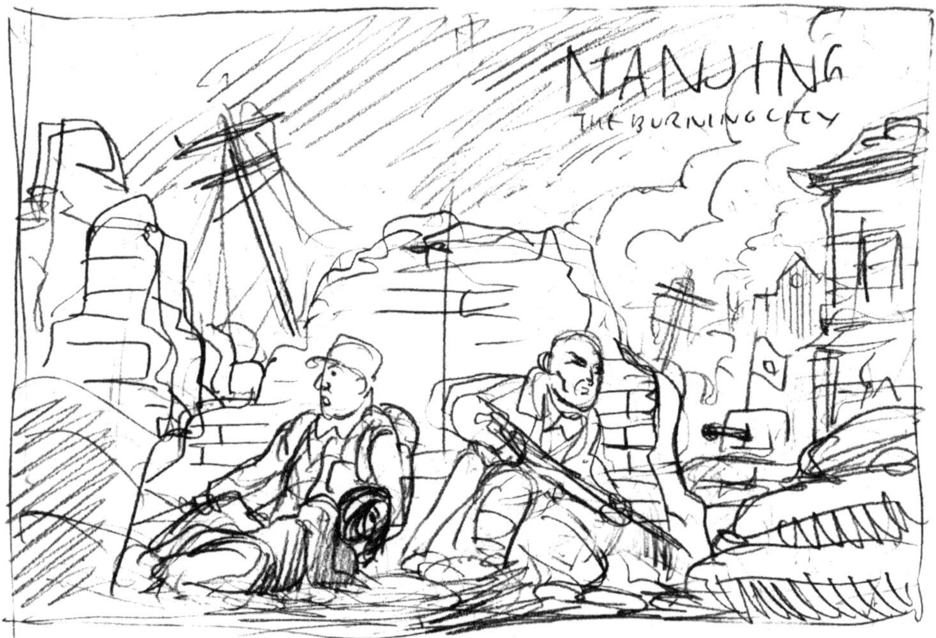
NANJING
THE BURNING CITY

Some cover ideas that were thrown around. I wanted a more understated, voyeuristic approach, but my editor rightfully changed my mind. Giving the readers a better look at the main characters on the cover creates a more immediate response.

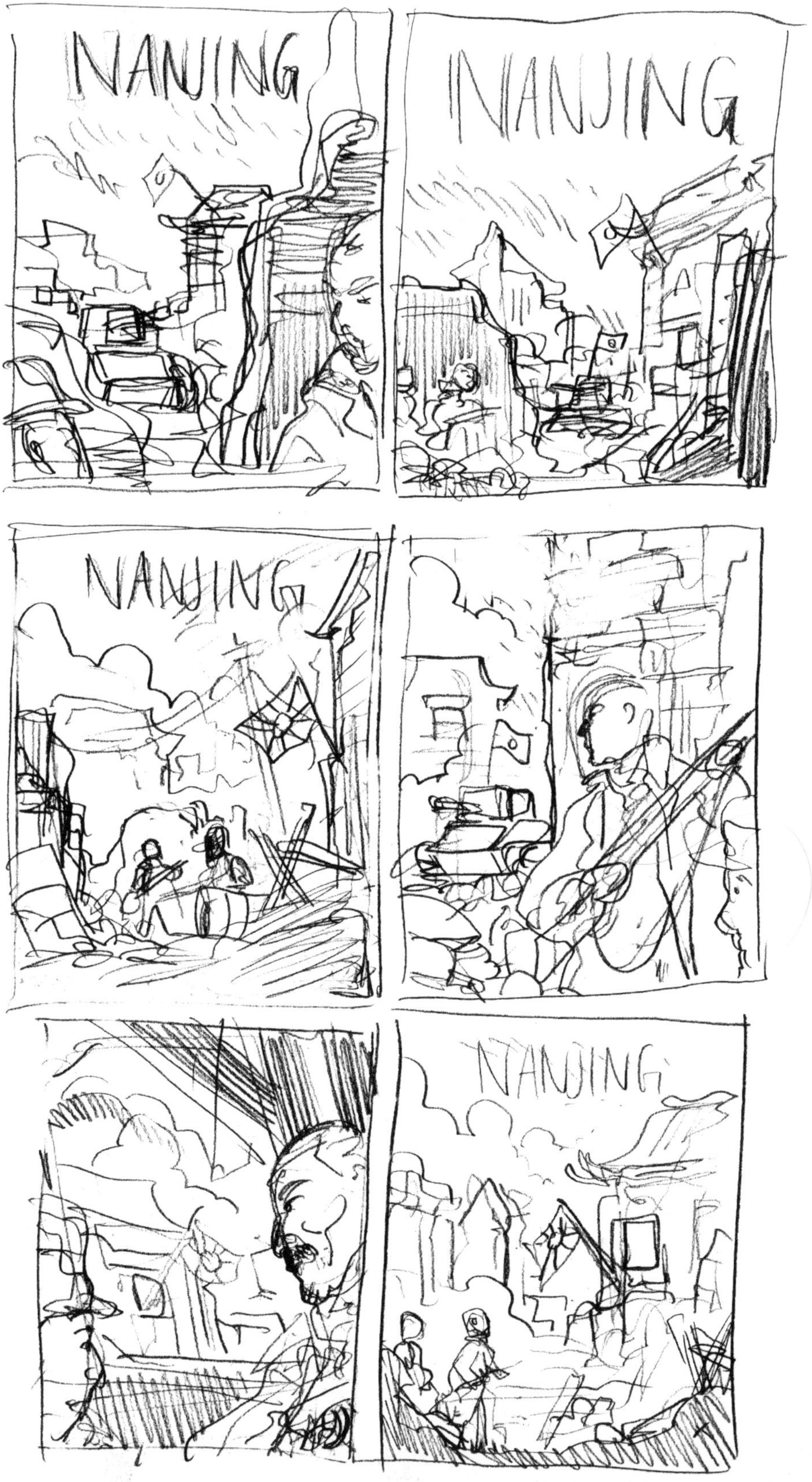
NANJING
NANJING
NANJING
NANJING

BIBLIOGRAPHY

Barber, Stephen. *Annihilation Zones: Far East Atrocities of the 20th Century*. Creation Books, 2002.

Chang, Iris. *The Rape of Nanking: The Forgotten Holocaust of World War II*. New York: Basic Books, 1997.

Chant, Christopher. *World War II*. New York: Chartwell Books, 2010.

Hu, Hua-ling. *American Goddess at the Rape of Nanking: The Courage of Minnie Vautrin*. Carbondale, IL: Southern Illinois University Press, 2000.

Miller, David. *Fighting Men of World War II Axis Forces: Uniforms, Equipment, and Weapons*. New York: Chartwell Books, 2011.

Mitter, Rana. *Forgotten Ally: China's World War II, 1937–1945*. New York: Houghton Mifflin Harcourt, 2013.

Mizuki, Shigeru. *Showa 1926–1939: A History of Japan*. Montreal: Drawn & Quarterly, 2013.

Rabe, John. *The Good Man of Nanking: The Diaries of John Rabe*. Trans. John E. Woods. New York: Alfred E. Knopf, 1998.

Spence, Jonathan D. *The Search for Modern China*. New York: W. W. Norton & Company, 1991.

Ethan Young was born in 1983 in New York City to Chinese immigrant parents. The youngest of three sons, he took to drawing at the age of three. After attending the School of Visual Arts for one semester, Young left to pursue an illustration career. His first graphic novel, *Tails: Life in Progress*, was named best graphic novel at the 2007 Independent Publisher Book Awards. His works include *Tails*, *Comic Book Tattoo*, *A Piggy's Tale*, and *Nanjing: The Burning City*. In addition to comic book work, Young is also a prolific freelance illustrator. He lives in Ithaca with his family and a lot of cats.

ALSO FROM

darkhorseoriginals | great creators original visions

2 sisters
by Matt Kindt

MIND MGMT
matt kindt
volume one:
THE MANAGER
"Best comic I have read in many, many, MANY months. Exquisitely dense in all the right ways. Bravo."
—DAMON LINDELOF, COCREATOR OF LOST

"Terrific. It's got the scariest opening sequence I've read in years, and the novel as a whole makes compelling stay-up-late reading. Great, creepy stuff."
—STEPHEN KING
GREEN RIVER KILLER
A TRUE DETECTIVE STORY
JEFF JENSEN | JONATHAN CASE

BRIAN WOOD
CHANNEL ZERO
THE COMPLETE COLLECTION
WITH BECKY CLOONAN
INTRODUCTION BY WARREN ELLIS

THE AWARD-WINNING INTERNATIONAL BESTSELLER
DARK HORSE BOOKS presents
BLACKSAD
Juan DÍAZ CANALES Juanjo GUARNIDO
"As good as it gets!"
—Stan Lee

SPEAK OF THE DEVIL
GILBERT HERNANDEZ

2 SISTERS
Matt Kindt
ISBN 978-1-61655-721-8 | $27.99

MIND MGMT VOLUME 1
Matt Kindt
ISBN 978-1-59582-797-5 | $19.99

CITIZEN REX
Gilbert Hernandez, Mario Hernandez
ISBN 978-1-59582-556-8 | $19.99

SPEAK OF THE DEVIL
Gilbert Hernandez
ISBN 978-1-59582-193-5 | $19.99

BLACKSAD
Juan Díaz Canales, Juanjo Guarnido
ISBN 978-1-59582-393-9 | $29.99

BLACKSAD: A SILENT HELL
Juan Díaz Canales, Juanjo Guarnido
ISBN 978-1-59582-931-3 | $19.99

BLACKSAD: AMARILLO
Juan Díaz Canales, Juanjo Guarnido
ISBN 978-1-61655-525-2 | $17.99

CHANNEL ZERO
Brian Wood, Becky Cloonan
ISBN 978-1-59582-936-8 | $19.99

GREEN RIVER KILLER
Jeff Jensen, Jonathan Case
ISBN 978-1-59582-560-5 | $24.99

DE:TALES
Gabriel Bá, Fábio Moon
ISBN 978-1-59307-485-2 | $14.95

JAYBIRD
Jaakko and Lauri Ahonen
ISBN 978-1-61655-469-9 | $19.99

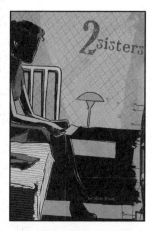

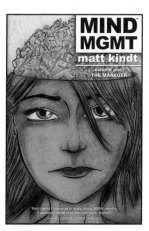

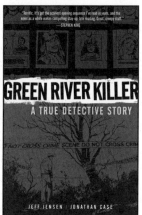

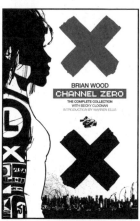

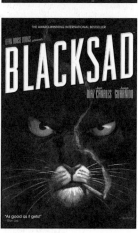

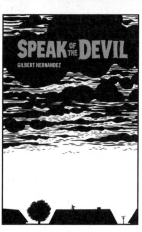

ALSO FROM

darkhorse**originals** | great creators original visions

TWO BROTHERS
Fábio Moon
Gabriel Bá

JONATHAN CASE
THE NEW DEAL

THE COMPLETE
MATT KINDT
JASON HALL
PISTOL WHIP

BAD HOUSES
SARA RYAN
CARLA SPEED MCNEIL

APOCALYPTIGIRL
AN ARIA FOR THE END TIMES

Sabertooth
Swordsman
GENTRY
CONLEY

TWO BROTHERS
Gabriel Bá, Fábio Moon
ISBN 978-1-61655-856-7 | $24.99

THE NEW DEAL
Jonathan Case
ISBN 978-1-61655-731-7 | $16.99

THE COMPLETE PISTOLWHIP
Jason Hall, Matt Kindt
ISBN 978-1-61655-720-1 | $27.99

BAD HOUSES
Sara Ryan, Carla Speed McNeil
ISBN 978-1-59582-993-1 | $19.99

APOCALYPTIGIRL: AN ARIA FOR THE END TIMES
Andrew MacLean
ISBN 978-1-61655-566-5 | $9.99

SABERTOOTH SWORDSMAN
Damon Gentry, Aaron Conley
ISBN 978-1-61655-176-6 | $17.99

SIN TITULO
Cameron Stewart
ISBN 978-1-61655-248-0 | $19.99

THE TRUE LIVES OF THE FABULOUS KILLJOYS
Gerard Way, Shaun Simon, Becky Cloonan
ISBN 978-1-59582-462-2 | $19.99

DEMO
Brian Wood, Becky Cloonan
ISBN 978-1-61655-682-2 | $24.99

MOTEL ART IMPROVEMENT SERVICE
Jason Little
ISBN 978-1-59582-550-6 | $19.99

AVAILABLE AT YOUR LOCAL COMICS SHOP OR BOOKSTORE! • To find a comics shop in your area, call 1-888-266-4226.
For more information or to order direct visit DarkHorse.com or call 1-800-862-0052 Mon.–Fri. 9 AM to 5 PM Pacific Time. Prices and availability subject to change without notice.

DarkHorse.com

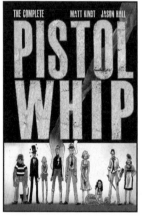

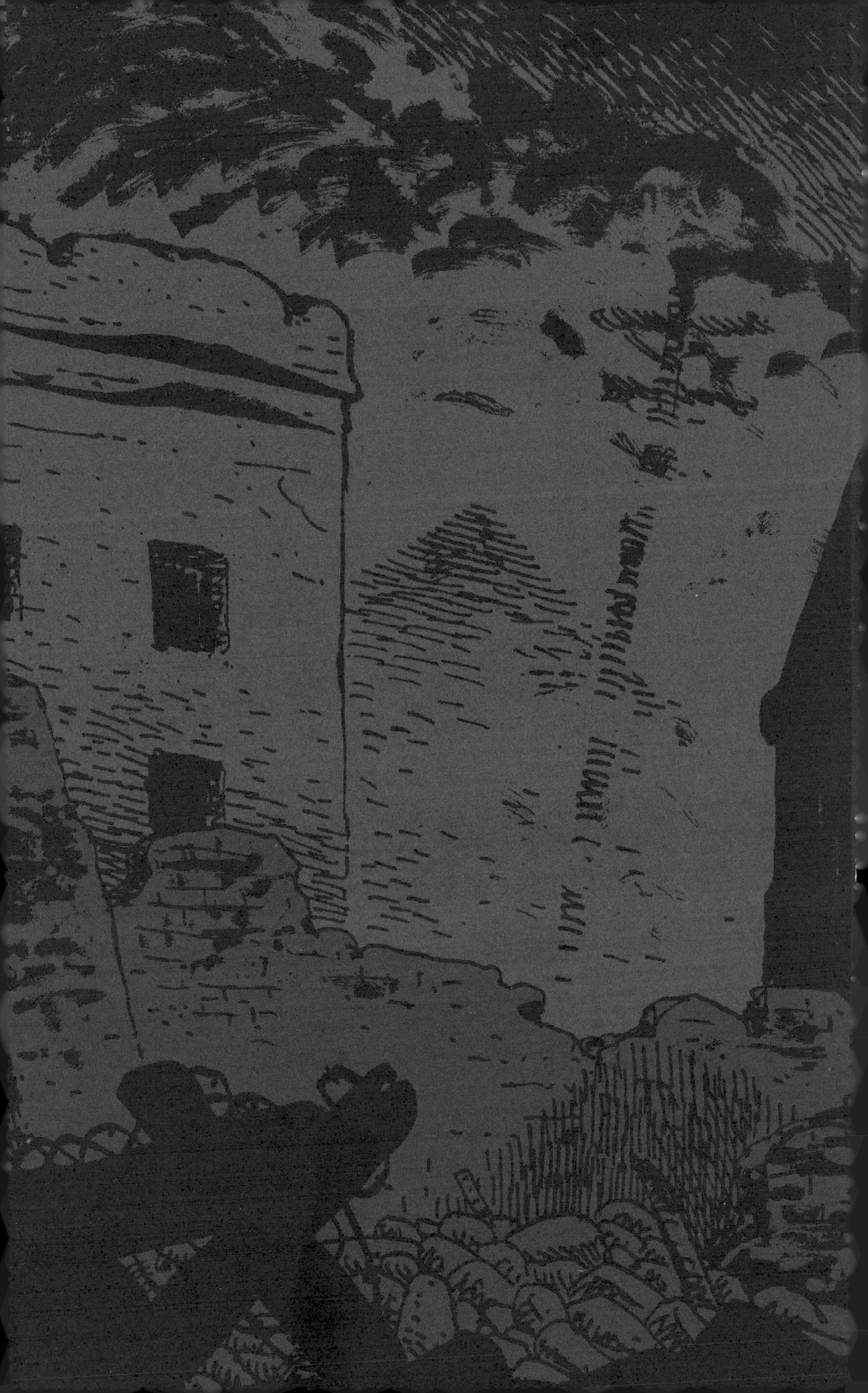